Lecture Notes in Computer Science 8699

Commenced Publication in 1973
Founding and Former Series Editors:
Gerhard Goos, Juris Hartmanis, and Jan van Leeuwen

Yiwei Cao · Terje Väljataga
Jeff K.T. Tang · Howard Leung
Mart Laanpere (Eds.)

New Horizons in Web Based Learning

ICWL 2014 International Workshops
SPeL, PRASAE, IWMPL, OBIE,
and KMEL, FET
Tallinn, Estonia, August 14–17, 2014
Revised Selected Papers

 Springer

Editors

Yiwei Cao
IMC AG
Saarbrücken
Germany

Terje Väljataga
Institute of Informatics
Tallinn University
Tallinn
Estonia

Jeff K.T. Tang
Department of Computer Science
Caritas Institute of Higher Education
Tseung Kwan
Hong Kong SAR

Howard Leung
Department of Computer Science
City University of Hong Kong
Kowloon
Hong Kong SAR

Mart Laanpere
Institute of Informatics, Centre
    for Educational Technology
Tallinn University
Tallinn
Estonia

ISSN 0302-9743   ISSN 1611-3349   (electronic)
Lecture Notes in Computer Science
ISBN 978-3-319-13295-2   ISBN 978-3-319-13296-9   (eBook)
DOI 10.1007/978-3-319-13296-9

Library of Congress Control Number: 2014956244

Springer Cham Heidelberg New York Dordrecht London
© Springer International Publishing Switzerland 2014

Printed on acid-free paper

Springer International Publishing AG Switzerland is part of Springer Science+Business Media
(www.springer.com)

Preface to ICWL 2014 Workshops

It is our pleasure to welcome you to ICWL 2014 workshops associated with ICWL 2014 in Tallinn, Estonia during August 14–17, 2014. ICWL is an annual international conference series on Web-based learning that has so far been held in Asia, Europe, and Australia. It has been a tradition to host workshops together with the ICWL main conferences since years. The goal of ICWL workshops was to give researchers and participants a forum to discuss cutting-edge research in Web-based learning and to discuss about work-in-progress research, in order to explore the new trends in Web-based learning. The workshops provided a networking forum for exchanging innovative ideas and research of work-in-progress.

This year, we are glad that some ICWL workshops from previous years were held again with ICWL. We are also delighted to host some new workshops. Finally, we have selected SPeL, PRASAE, IWMPL, OBIE, KMEL, and FeT competitively. The topics of the ICWL workshops range from social learning, mobile learning, and knowledge management, to peer assessment, open badges, and ebooks.

We would like to thank the Workshop Chairs David Lamas, Dickson K.W. Chiu, Elvira Popescu, Jelena Jovanovic, Martin Homola, and Ray Yueh-Min Huang, etc. as well as their Program Committees for their organization of the workshops and for selecting the papers in this volume. We would also like to thank the main ICWL 2014 Conference Committees, particularly the Conference Co-chairs, Howard Leung and Mart Laanpere, the conference Program Co-chairs Elvira Popescu, Rynson Lau, and Kai Papa, as well as the other ICWL Organization Committees for their support in putting the program and proceedings together.

We also appreciate the support from Springer. Since 2010, we have published ICWL workshop proceedings as a post-workshop proceedings band besides ICWL conference proceedings in cooperation with Springer.

August 2014

Yiwei Cao
Terje Väljataga
Jeff K.T. Tang

Workshop Editors

SPeL 2014

Elvira Popescu
Computers and Information Technology Department
University of Craiova
A.I. Cuza 13, 200585 Craiova, Romania
E-mail: opescu_elvira@software.ucv.ro

Sabine Graf
Athabasca University
School of Computing and Information Systems 1100
10011-109 Street Edmonton, AB T5J-3S8, Canada
Email: sabineg@athabascau.ca

PRASAE 2014

Martin Homola
Faculty of Mathematics, Physics and Informatics
Comenius University
Mlynská dolina, 84248 Bratislava, Slovakia
E-mail: homola@fmph.uniba.sk

Zuzana Kubincová
Faculty of Mathematics, Physics and Informatics
Comenius University
Mlynská dolina, 84248 Bratislava, Slovakia
E-mail: kubincova@fmph.uniba.sk

IWMPL 2014

Ray Yueh-Min Huang
Department of Engineering Science
National Cheng Kung University
41503R, ES Department Building 5F, NCKU, Tainan 701-01, Taiwan,
Republic of China
E-mail: huang@mail.ncku.edu.tw

OBIE 2014

Jelena Jovanovic
Department of Software Engineering
University of Belgrade
Jove Ilica 154, 11000 Belgrade, Serbia
E-mail: jeljov@gmail.com, jeljov@fon.rs

Vladan Devedzic
Department of Software Engineering
University of Belgrade
Jove Ilica 154, 11000 Belgrade, Serbia
E-mail: devedzic@gmail.com, devedzic@fon.rs

Weiqin Chen
Faculty of Social Science
University of Bergen
Fosswinckels gate 6, P.O. Box 7802, 5020 Bergen, Norway
E-mail: weiqin.chen@infomedia.uib.no

Dragan Gasevic
School of Computing and Information Systems
Athabasca University
1 University Drive, Athabasca, AB T9S 3A3, Canada
E-mail: dgasevic@acm.org

KMEL 2014

Dickson K.W. Chiu
Faculty of Education, University of Hong Kong
Pokfulam Road, Hong Kong
E-mail: dicksonchiu@ieee.org

Maggie M. Wang
Faculty of Education, University of Hong Kong
Pokfulam Road, Hong Kong
Email: magwang@hku.hk

FeT 2014

Mart Laanpere
Tallinn University, Institute of Informatics, Centre for Educational Technology
Narva mnt. 29, 10120 Tallinn, Estonia
E-Mail: mart.laanpere@tlu.ee

David Lamas
Tallinn University, Institute of Informatics, Centre for Educational Technology
Narva mnt. 29, 10120 Tallinn, Estonia
E-Mail: david.lamas@tlu.ee

ICWL 2014 Workshops Organization

General Co-chairs

Yiwei Cao   IMC AG, Germany
Terje Väljataga   Tallinn University, Estonia
Jeff K.T. Tang   Caritas Institute of Higher Education, Hong Kong

SPeL 2014 Workshop Chairs

Elvira Popescu   University of Craiova, Romania
Sabine Graf   Athabasca University, Canada

SPeL 2014 Program Committee

Ting-Wen Chang   Athabasca University, Canada
Stavros Demetriadis   Aristotle University of Thessaloniki, Greece
Michael Derntl   RWTH Aachen University, Germany
Giuliana Dettori   Institute for Educational Technology (ITD-CNR),
                           Italy
Gabriel Gorghiu   Valahia University of Târgovişte, Romania
Gabriela Grosseck   West University of Timişoara, Romania
Franka Grünewald   University of Potsdam, Germany
Hazra Imran   Athabasca University, Canada
Malinka Ivanova   TU Sofia, Bulgaria
Mirjana Ivanovic   University of Novi Sad, Serbia
Milos Kravcik   RWTH Aachen University, Germany
David Lamas   Tallinn University, Estonia
Chung Hsien Lan   Nanya Institute of Technology, Taiwan
Elise Lavoué   Université Jean Moulin Lyon 3, France
Frederick Li   University of Durham, UK
Alke Martens   PH Schwäbisch Gmünd University of Education,
                           Germany
Alexandros Paramythis   Johannes Kepler University of Linz, Austria
Philippos Pouyioutas   University of Nicosia, Cyprus
Demetrios Sampson   University of Piraeus and CERTH, Greece
Olga Santos   Spanish National University for Distance
                           Education, Spain
Marcus Specht   Open University of the Netherlands,
                           The Netherlands

| Marco Temperini | Sapienza University of Rome, Italy |
| Stefan Trausan-Matu | Politehnica University of Bucharest, Romania |

PRASAE 2014 Workshop Chairs

| Martin Homola | Comenius University in Bratislava, Slovakia |
| Zuzana Kubincová | Comenius University in Bratislava, Slovakia |

PRASAE 2014 Program Committee

Veronika Bejdová	Comenius University in Bratislava, Slovakia
Yiwei Cao	IMC AG, Germany
Fu-Yuan Chiu	National Hsinchu University of Education, Taiwan
Raquel M. Crespo García	Charles III University of Madrid, Spain
Ed Gehringer	North Carolina State University, USA
Samuel Greiff	University of Luxembourg, Luxembourg
Christopher Hundhausen	Washington State University, USA
María José Hernández Serrano	University of Salamanca, Spain
Mike Keppell	University of Southern Queensland, Australia
Miloš Kravčík	RWTH Aachen University, Germany
Irena Nančovska Šerbec	University of Ljubljana, Slovenia
Eugenia Ng	Hong Kong Institute of Education, Hong Kong
Elvira Popescu	University of Craiova, Romania
Lakshmi Ramachandran	North Carolina State University, USA
Marco Temperini	Sapienza University of Rome, Italy
Keith Topping	University of Dundee, UK
Tzu-Hua Wang	National Hsinchu University of Education, Taiwan
Bebo White	Stanford University, USA

IWMPL 2014 Workshop Chair

| Ray Yueh-Min Huang | National Cheng Kung University, Taiwan |

IWMPL 2014 Program Committee

Chia-Ju Liu	National Kaohsiung Normal University, Taiwan
Daniel Spikol	Malmö University, Sweden
Frode Eika Sandnes	Oslo and Akershus University College of Applied Sciences, Norway
Kinshuk	Athabasca University, Canada
Kuo-en Chang	National Taiwan Normal University, Taiwan
Neil Y. Yen	University of Aizu, Japan
Sumalee Chaijaroen	Khon Kaen University, Tailand

Ting-Ting Wu	Chia Nan University of Pharmacy and Science, Taiwan
Tzu-Chien Liu	National Central University, Taiwan
Yao-Ting Sung	National Taiwan Normal University, Taiwan

OBIE 2014 Workshop Chairs

Weiqin Chen	University of Bergen, Norway
Vladan Devedzic	University of Belgrade, Serbia
Dragan Gasevic	Athabasca University, Canada
Jelena Jovanovic	University of Belgrade, Serbia

OBIE 2014 Program Committee

Samuel Abramovich	University at Buffalo – SUNY, USA
Simon Cross	The Open University, UK
Elizabeth Dalton	University of New Hampshire, USA
Rebecca Galley	The Open University, UK
Sheryl Grant	Duke University, USA
Richard Kimbell	Goldsmiths, University of London, UK
Rudy McDaniel	University of Central Florida, USA
Ivana Mijatovic	University of Belgrade, Serbia
Michael R. Olneck	University of Wisconsin-Madison, USA
Razvan Rughinis	Politehnica University of Bucharest, Romania
Jose Luis Santos Odriozola	KU Leuven, Belgium
Julian Sefton-Green	London School of Economics and Political Science, UK
Felicia M. Sullivan	Tufts University, USA
Dennis Viehland	Massey University, New Zealand

KMEL 2014 Workshop Chairs

| Dickson K.W. Chiu | Dickson Computer Systems, Hong Kong |
| Maggie M. Wang | University of Hong Kong, Hong Kong |

KMEL 2014 Program Committee

Patricia A. Abbott	Johns Hopkins University, USA
Elizabeth Borycki	University of Victoria, Canada
Michael Chau	University of Hong Kong, Hong Kong
Irene Y.L. Chen	National Changhua University of Education, Taiwan
Lei Chen	Hong Kong University of Science and Technology, Hong Kong
Kuan-Chung Chen	National University of Tainan, Taiwan
Xiaochun Cheng	Middlesex University, UK

Chi-hung Chi	Tsinghua University, China
Alexandra I. Cristea	University of Warwick, UK
Liya Ding	Macau University of Science and Technology, China
Xun Ge	University of Oklahoma, USA
Sabine Graf	Athabasca University, Canada
David Guralnick	Kaleidoscope Learning, USA
Heinz Ulrich Hoppe	University of Duisburg-Essen, Germany
Haiyang Hu	Zhejiang Gongshang University, China
Wendy W.Y. Hui	University of Nottingham at Ningbo, China
Patrick C.K. Hung	University of Ontario Institute of Technology, Canada
Hiroshi Igaki	Kobe University, Japan
Tsukasa Ishigaki	National Institute of Advanced Industrial Science and Technology, Japan
Jiyou Jia	Peking University, China
Eleanna Kafeza	Athens University of Economics and Business, Greece
Kengo Katayama	Okayama University of Science, Japan
David M. Kennedy	Lingnan University, Hong Kong
Rajiv Khosla	La Trobe University, Australia
Ichiro Kobayashi	Ochanomizu University, Japan
Mario Koeppen	Kyushu Institute of Technology, Japan
Siu Cheung Kong	Hong Kong Institute of Education, Hong Kong
P. Radha Krishna	SET Labs – Infosys Technologies Ltd., India
Andre W. Kushniruk	University of Victoria, Canada
Carmen Ka Man Lam	Hong Kong Baptist University, Hong Kong
Jean H.Y. Lai	City University of Hong Kong, Hong Kong
Raymond Y.K. Lau	City University of Hong Kong, Hong Kong
Chien-Sing Lee	Multimedia University, Malaysia
Chei Sian Lee	Nanyang Technological University, Singapore
Ho-fung Leung	Chinese University of Hong Kong, Hong Kong
Xiaojing Liu	Indiana University, USA
Pierre Levy	University of Ottawa, Canada
Tieyan Li	Institute for Infocomm Research (I2R), Singapore
Fu-ren Lin	National Tsing Hua University, Taiwan
Wenyin Liu	City University of Hong Kong, Hong Kong
Edwin Lughofer	Fuzzy Logic Laboratorium Linz-Hagenberg, Austria
Zongwei Luo	University of Hong Kong, Hong Kong
Yinghua Ma	Shanghai JiaoTong University, China
Huiye Ma	Eindhoven University of Technology, The Netherlands
Akira Maeda	Ritsumeikan University, Japan
Mitsunori Matsushita	Kansai University, Japan
Farid Meziane	University of Salford, UK

Marcelo Milrad	Linnaeus University, Sweden
Atsuyuki Morishima	University of Tsukuba, Japan
Anders Morch	University of Oslo, Norway
Jürgen Moormann	Frankfurt School of Finance & Management, Germany
Koichi Moriyama	Osaka University, Japan
Sanaz Mostaghim	University of Karlsruhe, Germany
Yoichi Motomura	National Institute of Advanced Industrial Science and Technology, Japan
Kiyoshi Nakabayashi	Chiba Institute of Technology, Japan
Eugenia M.W. Ng	Hong Kong Institute of Education, Hong Kong
Mark E. Nissen	Naval Postgraduate School, USA
Murali Raman	Multimedia University, Malaysia
Waltraut Ritter	Knowledge Enterprises, Hong Kong
Qiyun Wang	Nanyang Technological University, Singapore
Mudasser F. Wyne	National University, USA
Ming-Hsiung Ying	Chung Hua University, Taiwan
Jianwei Zhang	State University of New York at Albany, USA
Xiaohui Zhao	Unitec Institute of Technology, New Zealand

FeT 2014 Workshop Chairs

Mart Laanpere	Tallinn University, Estonia
David Lamas	Tallinn University, Estonia

FeT 2014 Program Committee

Andri Ioannou	Cyprus University of Technology, Cyprus
Effie Lai-Chong Law	University of Leicester, UK
Elvira Popescu	University of Craiova, Romania
Jelena Jovanovic	University of Belgrade, Serbia
Panayiotis Zaphiris	Cyprus University of Technology, Cyprus
Paulo Dias	Universidade Aberta, Portugal
Sebastian Fiedler	Tallinn University, Estonia
Sónia Sousa	Tallinn University, Estonia
Terje Väljataga	Tallinn University, Estonia
Tobias Ley	Tallinn University, Estonia

The Seventh International Workshop on Social and Personal Computing for Web-Supported Learning Communities (SPeL 2014) Chairs' Message

The workshop followed the previous SPeL 2008, SPeL 2009, SPeL 2010, SPeL 2011, DULP & SPeL 2012, and SPeL 2013 workshops, held in conjunction with SAINT 2008, WI/IAT 2009, DEXA 2010, ICWL 2011, ICALT 2012, and ICSTCC 2013 conferences, respectively. The general topic of the workshop is the social and personal computing for web-supported learning communities, focusing on emergent technologies for applied computing in education.

Web-based learning is moving from centralized, institution-based systems to a decentralized and informal creation and sharing of knowledge. Social software (e.g., blogs, wikis, social bookmarking systems, media sharing services) is increasingly being used for e-learning purposes, helping to create novel learning experiences and knowledge. In the world of pervasive Internet, learners are also evolving: the so-called *digital natives* want to be in constant communication with their peers, they expect an individualized instruction and a personalized learning environment, which automatically adapt to their individual needs. The challenge in this context is to provide intelligent and adaptive support for collaborative learning, taking into consideration the individual differences between learners.

This workshop dealt with current research on collaboration and personalization issues in Web-supported learning communities. Its aim was to provide a forum for discussing new trends and initiatives in this area, including research on the planning, development, application, and evaluation of intelligent e-learning systems, where people can learn together in a personalized way through social interaction with other learners.

The event was targeted at academic researchers, developers, educationists, and practitioners alike. The proposed field is interdisciplinary and very dynamic, taking into account the recent advent of Web 2.0 and ubiquitous personalization, and it attracted a large audience. After a thorough review process (each paper being reviewed by at least three PC members), five high-quality papers were selected for presentation and included in these proceedings.

We would like to take this opportunity to thank all authors who contributed to this workshop, the Program Committee members for their valuable and timely reviews, as well as the ICWL 2014 Workshop Chairs and Organizing Committee for their support and cooperation.

August 2014

Elvira Popescu
Sabine Graf

The First International Workshop on Peer-Review, Peer-Assessment, and Self-Assessment in Education (PRASAE 2014) Chairs' Message

Learner-driven assessment methodologies, such as peer-review, peer-assessment, and self-assessment, have recently gained increased interest, especially as education is shifting toward a less formal and more learner-centered process. The International Workshop on Peer-Review, Peer-Assessment, and Self-Assessment (PRASAE) is a new workshop dedicated to these topics. Its main aim is to bring together the research community in learner-driven assessment, communicate current research trends, and exchange experience.

The first edition, PRASAE 2014, was collocated with the 13th International Conference on Web-based Learning (ICWL 2014), Tallinn, Estonia, during August 14–17, 2014. PRASAE 2014 gained significant interest in the community: it received six submissions, which were all reviewed by at least three members of the Program Committee and out of which five were accepted. The authors of the submitted papers came from Austria, Denmark, Germany, Italy, Slovakia, UK, and USA, which marks a truly international spirit of the workshop.

We would like to thank all members of the Program Committee, and to ICWL 2014 for excellent organization and for hosting the workshop. We hope that PRASAE 2014 will start a tradition, and that it will further reinforce in the coming years.

August 2014

Martin Homola
Zuzana Kubincová

International Workshop on Mobile and Personalized Learning (IWMPL 2014) Chairs' Message

It is a great honor for us to welcome all authors who have contributed their manuscripts to the 2014 International Workshop on Mobile and Personalized Learning (IWMPL 2014) in Tallinn, Estonia. The IWMPL 2014 aims at bringing together professionals and researchers who are interested in recent trends of mobile and personalized learning.

In recent years, m-learning has been widely applied to various fields and has become a popular issue in educational research. M-learning can be simply defined as the application of hand-held devices, such as smart phones, laptops, palmtop computers, and electronic readers (e-readers), in order to enable learners to proceed with electronic learning (e-learning) anywhere and anytime, rather than limiting them to the confines of a classroom. On the other hand, those hand-held devices are basically for personal use, which can combine with some sensor technologies, such as screen touching track and GPS, to record the learning context and learning behavior along with the mobility. Nowadays, cloud computing is a prevailing technology which can help the teacher timely realize learning status to enhance personalized learning. Thus, fueled by the technology, e-learning is entering the era of mobile and personalized learning, where those web-based paradigms or its extension remains applicable with this trend. Thus, we believe those concepts from web-based learning can still benefit the development of mobile and personalized learning. Finally, we appreciate those who are doing the related research to share their works or demonstrate their implementations with all ICWL2014 participants. We truly hope that all of you will enjoy the conference program and activities in Tallinn.

August 2014   Ray Yueh-Min Huang

The First International Workshop on Open Badges in Education (OBIE 2014) Chairs' Message

The concept and technology of Open Badges (OBs) have emerged from a collaborative effort of MacArthur Foundation[1], HASTAC[2] and Mozilla Learning team[3], and have continued to progress as a community effort aimed at introducing novel means and practices for knowledge/skill assessment, recognition, and credentialing. Along the way, OBs are also promoting values such as openness and learners' agency, as well as participatory learning practices and peer-learning communities.

Although digital badges are not a new phenomenon, their use prior to the emergence of the OBs initiative was largely associated with isolated efforts of individual organizations, and there was no systematic approach to issuing and using badges. Likewise, OBs should not be equated with digital badges that are used solely as a part of gamification efforts aimed at motivating users for different kinds of tasks. OBs differ in at least two significant ways. First, they allow learners to gather badges that originate from different sources (i.e., organizations acting as badge issuers), and to select and combine the earned badges into custom profiles suitable for the given occasion (e.g., job application). Second, OBs are self-sufficient in the sense that they carry all the information one would need to understand and value the achievement/ status they refer to.

These novel and distinctive features have positioned OBs as suitable candidates for addressing some of the pressing challenges in the context of lifelong and Web-based learning, including the recognition of learning in multiple and diverse locations and environments that go beyond traditional classrooms, as well as recognition of diverse kinds of skills and knowledge, including soft and general skills. Furthermore, they are perceived as suitable candidates for supporting new and alternative forms of assessment, as well as for assuring transparent and easily verifiable digital credentials. Finally, OBs open new avenues for personalizing learning paths and representing one's learning achievements in a highly personalized way.

OBs are rapidly gaining traction among educational practitioners as well as education-oriented companies and nonprofit organizations. Accordingly, public discourse on OBs and related topics, is mainly taking place on the open Web, i.e., on blogs, project websites and wikis, and other informal venues. There have been only a few research studies aimed at validating the propositions related to OBs. Therefore, the primary objective of this workshop is to raise awareness about OBs in academic

---

[1] http://www.macfound.org/
[2] http://www.hastac.org/
[3] https://wiki.mozilla.org/Learning

circles, and contribute to the establishment and development of a research community dedicated to a deeper understanding of not only OBs and their potential roles, but also the larger educational ecosystem within which they operate and evolve.

August 2014

Jelena Jovanovic
Vladan Devedzic
Weiqin Chen
Dragan Gasevic

The Fourth International Symposium on Knowledge Management & E-Learning (KMEL 2014) Chairs' Message

Fierce competition, globalization, and dynamic economy have forced organizations to search for new ways to improve competitive advantage. In pursuance of this, knowledge is seen as the core resource and learning is viewed as the important process. It is crucial for organizations to enhance the capabilities for effective learning and knowledge management (KM), especially via using information and communication technologies in the digital economy.

The creation, operation, and evolution of such research and practice raise concerns that vary from high-level requirements and policy modeling through to the deployment of specific implementation technologies and paradigms, and involve a wide and ever-growing range of methods, tools, and technologies. They also cover a broad spectrum of vertical domains, industry segments, and even government sectors. We intentionally seeks educators, researchers, scientists, engineers, industry people, policy makers, decision makers, and others who have insight, vision, and understanding of the big challenges in knowledge management and e-learning (KM&EL). After review, we selected three quality papers in this Symposium, for presentation covering various aspects of KM&EL.

We appreciate the interest and support of all attendees. In particular, we thank the ICWL organizers, the International Journal of Systems and Service-Oriented Engineering (IJSSOE), and the Knowledge Management & E-Learning: An International Journal (KM&EL) for their generous support. The great success of the symposium is indebted to the hard work of all Program Committee members. We also thank all the authors for their contributions.

August 2014

Dickson K.W. Chiu
Maggie M.H. Wang

The Future of e-Textbooks Workshop (FeT 2014) Chairs' Message

Digitizing textbooks is becoming an increasingly important practice in formal education. While higher education has been the main focus of research on e-textbooks so far, the topic is also gaining attention in K-12 education.

In recent years, academic and educational publishers have started to follow the phenomenon of extensive digitization by converting printed textbooks into digital formats that can be read on a computer screen, a special e-book reader, a personal digital assistant (PDA), or even a mobile phone. Unfortunately, the first generation of electronic textbooks cannot be considered successful as, although digital, they are but downloadable versions of traditional textbooks or digitally generated static e-book files (epub, pdf), usually monolithic and not at all interactive. Further, most of today's students do not read textbooks regularly (most fit into the description of the YouTube Generation) and they prefer short pieces of content, preferably in different media (videos, texts, pictures) and actively follow peer recommendations, on top their teachers' suggestions.

The goal of the FeT workshop was to re-think the e-Textbook, moving away from the replication of traditional practices and models, laying the foundations for its next generation.

The Program Committee accepted eight contributions to FeT 2014 workshop, six of these came from Estonia. While all papers address the future of e-textbooks, they have taken quite different perspectives on the topic. Kristo Käo and Margus Niitsoo introduce a prototype of automatic feedback for online multimedia textbook on guitar playing. Kai Pata and her colleagues envisage an upcoming turn in e-textbook industry from the perspective of socio-technical transitions theory. Mario Mäeots et al. summarize a case study on designing and implementing an e-textbook on programming in Scratch. António Pedro Costa and his colleagues introduce an innovative user-centered methodology for developing e-textbooks as software applications. Andrej Flogie et al report on the results of Slovenian national e-textbook project "E-schoolbag". Eradze and her colleagues have studied methods for bridging online and offline learning analytics in researching e-textbook use in classroom settings. Terje Väljataga and Sebastian Fiedler provide a roadmap toward a new conceptual model for e-textbook research and development, based on LEARNMIX project results. And finally, Arman Arakelyan and his colleagues explore the value-driven approach to e-textbook design within LEARNMIX project.

August 2014

David Lamas
Mart Laanpere

Contents

2014 International Workshop on Mobile and Personalized Learning

2014 International Workshop on Open Badges in Education

2014 International Symposium on Knowledge Management & E-Learning

2014 International Workshop on Social and Personal Computing for Web-Supported Learning Communities

Social Network Analysis and Evaluation of Communities of Practice of Teachers: A Case Study

Maria De Marsico[2], Carla Limongelli[1], Filippo Sciarrone[3(✉)],
Andrea Sterbini[2], and Marco Temperini[3]

[1] Faculty of Engineering, Roma Tre University,
Via della Vasca Navale, 79, 00146 Rome, Italy
`limongel@dia.uniroma3.it`
[2] Department of Computer Science, Sapienza University of Rome,
Via Salaria 146, 00134 Rome, Italy
`{demarsico,sterbini}@di.uniroma1.it`
[3] Department of Computer, Systems and Management Engineering,
Sapienza University of Rome, Via Ariosto 25, 00185 Rome, Italy
`sciarro@dia.uniroma3.it, marte@dis.uniroma1.it`

Abstract. *Communities of Practice* (CoPs) may be interpreted as kinds of a vertical evolution of social networks, where members share common interests in a particular domain or area, and exchange practical experiences to increase their knowledge and skills with respect to that specific field. In this paper we present some evaluation aspects of an experiment conducted within the framework of the European project *Understan-dIT*. The experiment involved the use of a CoP providing an educational program on *Web2.0 Technologies for education* for Vocational Education and Training teachers. The CoP was designed on the basis of the foundational Wenger's concepts of *domain, community* and *practice*. In particular, we present a study of some social aspects of the CoP dynamics, basing our study on some evaluation metrics coming from the Social Network Analysis research area, i.e., using metrics such as *betweenness, centrality,* and *closeness,* in order to elicit useful relationships information. The experimental results confirm the goodness of the use of such approach for the elicitation of hidden information in the communicative network processes.

1 Introduction

Communities of Practice (CoPs) may be interpreted as kinds of a vertical evolution of social networks, where members share a common interest in a particular domain or area, and exchange practical experiences to increase knowledge and skills related to that specific field [24]. CoPs are in fact based on a very flexible model of organization and interaction, which in principle does not necessarily prescribe the use of the Internet; yet the applicability of CoPs is significantly boosted by the use of network technology and communication tools based on

© Springer International Publishing Switzerland 2014
Y. Cao et al. (Eds.): ICWL 2014 Workshops, LNCS 8699, pp. 3–12, 2014.
DOI: 10.1007/978-3-319-13296-9_1

the web. In this way CoPs can widely extend their usefulness to the field of professional education and lifelong learning through the use of a social web-based environment. Focusing on the topic of education, it is generally agreed that a significant part of knowledge, protocols, strategies and rules of a professional activity, may remain only partially covered in educational activities, or even reach the extreme of being implicit and hidden. In other words, traditional training may fail to provide a ready-to-exploit expertise, which is effective in real situations. CoPs can provide a good approach to that problem, as their model can be easily adapted to support career education. In this paper we present some evaluation aspects of an experiment conducted within the framework of the european project *UnderstandIT*[1]. The experiment involved the use of a CoP (*UnderstandIT*[2]) providing an educational program on *Web2.0 Technologies for education* dedicated to Italian *Vocational Education and Training* (VET) teachers. Technical information and best practices were presented to use some Web 2.0 tools and systems for the development and administering of educational activities pertaining everyday teaching activity.

The UnderstandIT project arose from the need to bridge the gap between the use of Web 2.0 by teachers, compared to that by pupils, and to make digital immigrants (the former) and digital natives (the latter) encounter on a common ground [19] and share a common suite of languages and tools. In fact, the underlying hypothesis is that the use of these tools has great potentialities to make teaching more effective. The UnderstandIT CoP was designed based on the concepts of *domain, community* and *practice* [23]. The domain of shared competence addressed here is the teaching activity for VET education; the community members are VET teachers while the practice is the use of the Web 2.0 instruments and tools in the teaching activities. We used the open source ELGG social network engine[3] as the technological platform. It is one of the most used frameworks delivering the building blocks that enable companies, schools, universities and associations to create their own fully-featured social networks and applications. This web engine runs as a web application, providing a social environment with a wide range of Web 2.0 services such as forum, chat, wiki and so on: members are free to create wiki activities and to participate to all the social activities put on line by the platform. As introduced above, the main aim of this paper is to present an evaluation of the social activities carried on by its members. An early research question of our work was to test whether the approach to learning and teaching allowed by the UnderstandIT community was beneficial for the learners and fostered a social interaction among them, aimed at sharing and learning. In [4] we presented the UnderstandIT CoP at its early stage of development, discussing an early research question, related to learners participation in the network social activities (e.g.: blogs, wiki, forum,...). Then the research question has been expanded and we have investigated other aspects of the CoP dynamics. Here we present an evaluation of the UnderstandIT CoP,

---

[1] http://aitel.hist.no/understandit/

[2] http://understandit.di.uniroma1.it/

[3] http://elgg.org

based on the techniques coming from Social Network Analysis: we base the analysis on metrics such as *betweeness*, *centrality*, and *closeness*, in order to gather more information about the network dynamics, that would be not directly available by means of the simple descriptive statistics we used earlier. The rest of the paper presents in Sect. 2 some related work in the area of CoP. In Sect. 3 a brief description of the Social Network Analysis is given while in Sect. 4 the experimental results are reported. Finally, in Sect. 5 conclusions are drawn.

2 CoPs: Literature Review and Related Work

In the past, learning and training were almost always based on the role of "imitation" and on the predecessor of the modern "learning by doing". The artisan workshops were the privileged places for transmitting and preserving arts and crafts, looking at the "master" or "maestro" and at more expert companions. Common practice and storytelling were the vehicles of knowledge/skill transmission. Even if this was mostly true for "concrete" skills more than for knowledge, it is true that in a wider perspective even abstract knowledge was enforced through continuous debates and sharing with other scholars. Therefore, it sounds strange that the industrial age, with the triumph of materialism and practical intelligence, also stated the prevalence of "abstract knowledge" over actual concrete practice, whose details were considered as contingent, easily derived after the relevant abstractions, and therefore less essential. This soon established a separation between learning and working, and most of all between learners and workers. This separation had as a consequence that a large part of experiential knowledge, the so-called implicit knowledge acquired while performing concrete tasks in an ecologically significant context, was left out from training. This may cause confusion and difficulties in the following application of training to real working situations. We are all aware that people often work according to patterns and rules which are quite different from manuals guidelines and from the "theoretical" descriptions of job tasks. It often happens that complementary or even completely alternative strategies and rules drive the actual practice, except for very basic and "gross" activities. Experience suggests a number of workarounds and shortcuts that support a more effective activity, and are the most precious achievement given by a long experience. Nonetheless, organizations tend(ed) to rely on a "static" form of training to transmit work practice. However the success of the term and the spreading of its concrete practices were finally spurred by the works of Lave and Wenger [10,11]. They built on a theory of learning based on practice. Its core concept is the *Legitimate Peripheral Participation* in CoPs [11]. In a CoP external observers may be allowed to watch, though without actively participating. The novices firstly access the community from the periphery. They acquire experience though the support of more experienced members, and gain reputation also a consequence of the support that they in turn are able to provide to companions. In this way, they finally achieve full participation and membership. In general, the structure of a CoP is characterized by: (1) a group of core experts, who achieved high reputation and trustworthiness, as assessed by their peers, (2) the major group of active participants, who fully participate to the exchange of information and experiences, and (3) the peripheral participants, who start as observers and can gradually level-up. At the same time, the community itself develops through different levels of interaction among the members. Self-development originates by active participation to the community, and the community develops together with its members. Two central elements of the CoP approach are situated learning [8] and community reflection on practice. Knowledge is acquired from and applied back to everyday real settings, while discussing it with peers and experts in a rich social system [23]. Starting from the earliest forms of forums, till to the modern Social Networks (SN), supported by Web2.0 technologies, it is the most powerful vehicle of participatory growth. According to the above described perspective, we can consider learning as the main activity but even as the core topic of the CoP strategies. In [2] the authors underline "the growing need to integrate educational research and practice" in order to connect what we know with what we do. The back of the coin is in that shared lists of recommended practices often fail to promote the personal responsibility and exploration ability. This not only affects educational researchers and teachers, but also students and their parents. On the contrary, the main achievement of a CoP should be to encourage and motivate every member of the educational community to personally analyze, constructively criticize, and effectively complement each other's experiences. Teachers should be encouraged in taking active part in research activities. The authors consider CoPs a very promising tool, able to allow reaching these goals, even compared with other strategies to join research and practice, e.g., action research [3], or professional development schools. The common goal is breaking "the linear relationship through which information is handed down from those who discover professional knowledge to those who provide and receive educational services" [2]. Other approaches that can find a joint implementation with CoPs tools in a comprehensive educational framework are: (i) a personalized learning, through a didactic able to adapt its patterns to the learners' specific real needs (see for example [7,13,14,16,20]) (ii) an approach related to ontology-based systems helping teachers to search for suitable educational material in the Internet (see [12]). Technology enhanced learning can further take advantage from research lines (e.g. [5,6]) aiming at integrating more traditional individualized e-learning and social-collaborative e-learning [15]. Finally, a project very similar to our proposal is the SEDA project [18]. This project supports members working in higher education institutions. The proposed CoP is an environment where educational developers can highlight their needs and fruitfully share their experiences. The spirit of the SEDA project is the mutual support provided by the members of the community.

3   Social Network Analysis

A Social Network is a group of collaborating and/or competing individuals or entities that are related to each other and is formally defined as a set of social actors, or nodes, that are connected by one or more types of relations [22].

Social Network Analysis (SNA) deals with the analysis of social networks in order to trace the relationships, learn their meanings and apply the information inferred among the members of the network. SNA borrows many concepts and tools from the graph theory because a Social Network can be represented as a graph where the actors are represented by the nodes and the relationships among them by the edges of the graph and where weights can be assigned to the edges between nodes to designate different interactions strengths [17, 22, 25]. Consequently, graph theory is used to describe Social Networks together with their dynamics among individuals or groups. To this aim many graph tools have been developed to help researchers to visualize Social Networks. For our goals we used the *Gephi* graph tool, an open source tool useful for Social Network analysis. In this Section we show the metrics we based our study on. In the literature there are a lot of metrics proposed to discover the characteristics of a Social Networks, like *Size* and *Density*, all type of centralities like *Degree, Betweenness, Closeness* and *Eigenvector*, clustering coefficient, path analysis (reachability, reciprocity, transitivity and distance), flow, cohesion and influence, and other useful information obtained by various types of analysis [21]. In particular, our analysis was carried out starting from the log files generated during the Social Network life. We used the following metrics [9, 25]:

- *Degree Centrality.* This metric aims to detect the most *important nodes* in the network. The *degree* of a node is defined as the number of direct connections a node has with other actors or nodes. A node with a high degree centrality acts as a hub in the network having it a lot of edges coming in and a lot of edges coming out. It signifies activity or popularity;
- *Betweenness Centrality.* This metrics measures how the position of a node is important, and is defined as the number of times a node connects pairs of other nodes, who otherwise would not be able to reach one another or to what extent a node can play the role of intermediary in the interaction between the other nodes. A node can have fewer connections than another node, but its position could be more relevant with respect to the network flows;
- *Closeness Centrality.* This metric is based on the notion of the geodesic distance (i.e., shortest path) among the nodes of the graph and measures the independence of a node. It is defined as the mean geodesic distance between a node and all other nodes reachable from it. Closeness can be regarded as a measure of how long it will take information to spread from a given node to other nodes in the network;
- *Density.* This metric describes the general level of linkage among the nodes of a graph. A *complete* graph is a graph having all its nodes directly connected, i.e., each node is connected to each other by e direct link. This metric aims to measure how far from this state of completion the graph is. Given a direct graph, $G \equiv (V, E)$, Density is defined as: $Density = \frac{|E|}{|V|*(|V|-1)}$, being $|V|$ the total number of vertices and $|E|$ the total number of the edges of the graph.
- *Clique.* A clique is a sub-set of nodes where all possible pairs of nodes are directly connected. Detecting cliques in a graph is important in order to elicit sub-communities.

4   A Social Analysis of the UnderstandIT CoP

In this Section we present a first study of the UnderstandIT CoP with the aim to elicit some useful information by means of the use of SNA and in particular of the metrics shown in Sect. 3. There are a lot of tools for graph management and SNA like NodeXL[4], NetMiner[5], Pajek[6], Gephi[7] and many others. As already mentioned in Sect. 3, we used the *Gephi* graph tool. *Gephi* is an open source software for graph and network analysis. It uses a 3D render engine to display large networks in real-time and to speed up the network exploration. Moreover, it provides easy and broad access to network data and allows for filtering, navigating, manipulating and clustering [1]. In a recent paper [4] we introduced the UnderstandIT CoP, together with a brief description and evaluation of the main activities carried out by its members. We used some popular CoP descriptive metrics such as the number of visits, the number of blog posts and so on and, after having shown the participation, we evaluated the feeling of the CoP teachers with respect to the Web 2.0 instruments and tools by means of a pre-test and post-test questionnaire. Here we propose the study of the CoP from a social point of view, with the goal of elicit information from the dynamics of the relationships among the members of the network. To this aim we used a subset of the metrics of Sect. 3. In particular, we present some preliminary studies about the following relationships: Participation to groups activities, Friendship relationships and Exchange of messages for knowledge sharing, starting from the log files generated by the ELGG platform.

4.1   Friendship Relationships

In Fig. 1 is shown the graph of the CoP, having 292 edges and 77 nodes, based on the *Friendship* Relationships. The system discovered four sub-communities among members. This graph presents 2313 shortest paths with $Density = 0,05$ and $AveragePathLenght = 4$.

4.2   Members Participation to Group Activities

In Fig. 2 the network representing the participation of the community members to web 2.0 social activities is shown. The social activities were: forum, blog, file and so on. The graph was formed by 50 nodes and 80 edges with a $density = 0.03$, with 5 sub-communities, with 80 shortest paths.

4.3   Knowledge Exchanges

In Fig. 3 is shown the graph representing the exchange of knowledge among members, after a brief period of the online activities. The Gephi tool revealed 4

---

[4] www.nodexl.org

[5] www.netminer.com

[6] vlado.fmf.uni-lj.si/pub/networks/pajek/

[7] www.gephi.org

Fig. 1. The Friendship relationships. It is easy to individuate four sub-communities.

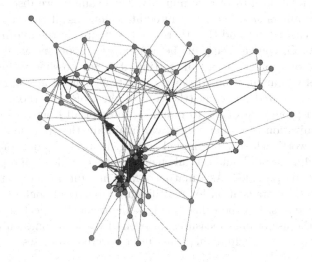

Fig. 2. Members participation to social activities.

sub-communities, *density* = 0.096, number of shortest paths: 186, *AveragePath Lenght* = 2.62 and 7 edges equally distributed from 10 to 40.

4.4 Lesson Learned

The application of the SNA methods and techniques to our case study, i.e., the UnderstandIT CoP, allowed us to perform a structural analysis of the network

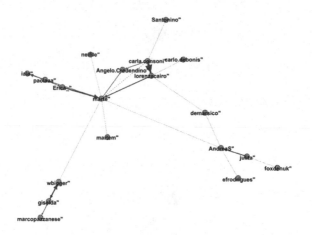

Fig. 3. Knowledge exchange among members.

from the point of view of the relationships among all the members involved in
the learning process in a more deeper way and focussed on the dynamics of
the members relationships of a community. For example, we discovered different sub-communities showing a few integration among all the members in all
the activities carried out and that there are key figures in the information flows
between them. Of course, being in the context of a spontaneous flow of information as the one spurred in a CoP setting, it is not possible to force changes
in the pace of communication. However, it is true that an appropriate feeding
by the most estimated members (the core of the CoP, i.e., those with higher
reputation), a prompt feedback to inquiries, most of all from novice members,
and the organization of online events, can maintain the community alive and
healthy. In a worth while multi-lingual setting, it would be quite natural that
the language dimension should prevail on other aspects, unless appropriate translation services are provided. As a matter of fact, in a future perspective we plan
to include keyword translation for multilingual labeling of contents and online
translation of pages. On the other hand, a hierarchical inspection of detected
clusters and the use of finer measures, or even of the same ones on a restricted
set of participants, can help highlighting more covered processes.

5   Conclusions and Future Work

In this paper we presented the study of the UnderstandIT Community of Practice from a social point of view. In a previous work we proposed an evaluation
of the same CoP from a *degree of satisfaction* point of view, i.e., by submitting
a pre-test and a post-test questionnaires and finally a happy sheet to the community members. Here we focussed on the members relationships to elicit useful
information about the CoP dynamic from a social point of view. To this aim
we used one of the graph visualization and analysis tools proposed in the literature and studied some social activities, using some classical centrality metrics.

By this approach we discovered some unknown social structures in the network such as sub-communities and other important weighed relationships, strengthening the validity of this approach. As a future work we plan to investigate the relationships between these metrics and the learning process behind the network dynamics.

References

1. Bastian, M., Heymann, S., Jacomy, M.: Gephi: An open source software for exploring and manipulating networks. In: Proceedings of the International AAAI Conference on Weblogs and Social Media (2009)
2. Buysse, V., Sparkman, K.L., Wesley, P.W.: Communities of practice: connecting what we know with what we do. Except. Child. **69**(3), 263–278 (2003)
3. Calhoun, E.F.: How to Use Action Research in the Self-Renewing School. Association for Supervision and Curriculum Development, Alexandria (1994)
4. De Marsico, M., Limongelli, C., Sciarrone, F., Sterbini, A., Temperini, M.: Understandit: A community of practice of teachers for vet education. In: Proceedings of Webist 2014: 10th International Conference on Web Information Systems and Technologies, pp. 338–345 (2014)
5. De Marsico, M., Sterbini, A., Temperini, M.: The definition of a tunneling strategy between adaptive learning and reputation-based group activities. In: Proceedings of 11th IEEE International Conference on Advanced Learning Technologies, ICALT, pp. 498–500 (2011)
6. De Marsico, M., Sterbini, A., Temperini, M.: A strategy to join adaptive and reputation-based social-collaborative e-learning, through the zone of proximal development. Int. J. Distance Educ. Technol. **19**(2), 105–121 (2012)
7. De Marsico, M., Temperini, M.: Average effort and average mastery in the identification of the zone of proximal development. In: Proceedings of 17th IEEE International Conference on System Theory, Control and Computing, ICSTCC 2013 (2013)
8. Hummel, H.G.K.: Distance education and situated learning: paradox or partnership? Educ. Technol. **33**(12), 11–22 (1993)
9. Hussain, D.M.A.: Investigation of key-player problem in terrorist networks using bayes conditional probability. In: Furht, B. (ed.) Handbook of Social Network Technologies, pp. 523–547. Springer, New York (2010)
10. Lave, J.: Situating learning in communities of practice. In: Resnick, L.B., Levine, J.M., Teasley, S.D. (eds.) Perspectives on Socially Shared Cognition, Chap. 4, pp. 63–82. American Psychological Association, Washington, DC (1991)
11. Lave, J., Wenger, E.: Situated Learning: Legitimate Peripheral Participation. Cambridge University Press, Cambridge (1991)
12. Limongelli, C., Mosiello, G., Panzieri, S., Sciarrone, F.: Virtual industrial training: Joining innovative interfaces with plant modeling. In: Proceedings of ITHET 2012, pp. 1–6. IEEE (2012)
13. Limongelli, C., Sciarrone, F., Temperini, M., Vaste, G.: Lecomps5: A web-based learning system for course personalization and adaptation. In: Proceedings of IADIS 2008, Amsterdam, The Netherlands, July 22–25, 2008, pp. 325–332 (2008)
14. Limongelli, C., Sciarrone, F., Temperini, M., Vaste, G.: The lecomps5 framework for personalized web-based learning: a teacher's satisfaction perspective. Comput. Hum. Behav. **27**(4), 1310–1320 (2011)

15. Limongelli, C., Sciarrone, F., Vaste, G.: LS-PLAN: an effective combination of dynamic courseware generation and learning styles in web-based education. In: Nejdl, W., Kay, J., Pu, P., Herder, E. (eds.) AH 2008. LNCS, vol. 5149, pp. 133–142. Springer, Heidelberg (2008)
16. Limongelli, C., Sciarrone, F., Vaste, G.: Personalized e-learning in moodle: the moodle-ls system. J. E-Learning Knowl. Soc. 7(1), 49–58 (2011)
17. Marin, A., Wellman, B.: Social network analysis: an introduction. In: Carrington, P., Scott, J. (eds.) Handbook of Social Network Analysis. Sage, Thousand Oaks (2010)
18. Nixon, S., Brown, S.: A community of practice in action: Seda as a learning community for educational developers in higher education. Innov. Educ. Teach. Int. 50(4), 357–365 (2013)
19. Prensky, M.: Digital natives, digital immigrants part 1. Horiz. 9(5), 1–6 (2001)
20. Sciarrone, F.: An extension of the q diversity metric for information processing in multiple classifier systems: a field evaluation. Int. J. Wavelets Multiresolut. Inf. Process. 11(6) (2013)
21. Slaninova, K., Martinovic, J., Drazdilova, P., Obadi, G., Snasel, V.: Analysis of social networks extracted from log files. In: Furht, B. (ed.) Handbook of Social Network Technologies, pp. 115–146. Springer, New York (2010)
22. Wasserman, S., Faust, K.: Social Network Analysis: Methods and Applications. Cambridge University Press, Cambridge (1994)
23. Wenger, E.: Communities of practice: learning as a social system. Syst. think. 9(5), 2–3 (1998)
24. Wenger, E.: Communities of practice and social learning systems: the career of a concept. In: Blackmore, C. (ed.) Social Learning Systems and Communities of Practice, Chap. 11, pp. 179–198. The Open University, London (2010)
25. Zhang, M.: Social network analysis: History, concepts, and research. In: Furht, B. (ed.) Handbook of Social Network Technologies, pp. 3–21. Springer, New York (2010)

Utilization of Exercise Difficulty Rating by Students for Recommendation

Martin Labaj[(✉)] and Mária Bieliková

Faculty of Informatics and Information Technologies,
Slovak University of Technology in Bratislava,
Ilkovičova 2, 842 16 Bratislava, Slovakia
{martin.labaj,maria.bielikova}@stuba.sk

Abstract. Recommendation plays a vital role in adaptive educational systems. Learners often face large body of educational materials including not only texts (explanations), but also interactive content such as exercises and questions. These require various knowledge levels of multiple topics. For effective learning, personalized recommendation of the most appropriate items according to the learner's current knowledge level and preferences is an essential feature. In this paper, we describe a learning object recommendation method based on students' explicit difficulty ratings during and after exercise/question solving. It is based on comparing the learner's state when the recommendation is to be made against his peers with similar knowledge in the moment when they rated the difficulty. To deal with sparsity of ratings that are even further filtered, we also propose two solutions to either adaptively elicit ratings in appropriate moments during learners work, or to predict ratings from implicit user actions. We evaluate the method in ALEF – adaptive web-based educational system.

Keywords: Learning object difficulty · Exercise difficulty rating · Personalized recommendation · Rating prediction · Learning network

1 Introduction and Related Work

Nowadays educational systems contain large body of content including both objects geared towards passive consumption (e.g. texts explaining various topics) and interactive objects such as exercises. Courses presented in educational systems are sometimes organized in a narrow sequential way explaining one topic after another, but this is not always feasible, since various objects can depend on multiple other topics and different learners progress differently. Learners are then often faced with vast number of choices where to look, especially when choosing an exercise to try next.

Recommender systems are deployed in the domain of technology enhanced learning (TEL) to help learners in such situations [1]. In commonly employed recommendation techniques, content attributes stemming from domain model, user features derived from the user feedback (e.g. ratings), and the user model (e.g. concept knowledge) are used in combination. Among tasks supported by current TEL recommender systems [1], *finding good items* – i.e. receiving list of learning resources – is an important task helping learners not to become lost in the content offered by a large personalized educational system.

© Springer International Publishing Switzerland 2014
Y. Cao et al. (Eds.): ICWL 2014 Workshops, LNCS 8699, pp. 13–22, 2014.
DOI: 10.1007/978-3-319-13296-9_2

Both collaborative filtering and content based recommendation techniques are used in the TEL domain [2]. Difficulty of items to be recommended is sometimes considered in utility function (e.g., in time limited learning recommendation [3]). Item difficulty became an important part of computerized adaptive testing (CAT) [4], stemming from Item response theory (IRT) [5], where tested subject response to an initial medium difficulty item determines following items. An optimal item for the learner is the item with difficulty appropriate to the learner knowledge, difficult enough to keep them occupied to solve it, but easy enough not to dissuade. With optimal difficulty level, both the learner and adaptation mechanisms gain the most information.

When the learner is solving exercises, or choosing an exercise to solve, an exercise too easy for their current knowledge provides little value to them in terms of checking current knowledge and grasping new concepts. It also provides little feedback to the user knowledge model. When the exercise is too difficult, the learner can be dissuaded by not being able to solve it in reasonable time. In this paper, we focus on recommendation considering learning object difficulty. The difficulty of an object for the learner is not a static property of the item, but rather a combination of prerequisite knowledge required for the item, and of learner state. Therefore, while a domain expert (teacher, course author, etc.) can estimate learning object difficulty, the difficulty for the learner with his current knowledge can be different.

We propose a method for recommendation based on difficulty determined by learners themselves during and after solving exercises and questions, matching them with their peers with similar knowledge. However, users' difficulty ratings, as a form of explicit user feedback, is burdened with problems typical for collecting explicit feedback – sparsity, noise, and reluctance to provide ratings. We propose to use adaptive explicit feedback questions to obtain difficulty and usefulness ratings from users after they finished working with a learning object (either successfully or leaving).

Our method is realized and evaluated within Adaptive Learning Framework (ALEF). ALEF [6] is a framework for web-based adaptive educational systems developed at the Faculty of Informatics and Information Technologies, Slovak University of Technology in Bratislava and used therein in several courses. ALEF presents content in three types of learning objects (LOs): explanations, exercises and questions. Whereas explanations are mostly passive learning objects, where learners could gather new information in a manner similar to book chapters or sub-chapters, exercises and questions are interactive. Both self-assessment exercises ("my solution is correct/ wrong, same/different as the sample one", e.g., for software design course) and exercises tested through solution-evaluator (for programming tasks) are offered.

Being a personalized adaptive solution, ALEF models both the users, tracking their knowledge based on their interaction with the exercises and questions [7], and the domain, allowing both for human-authoring and automated generation of course metadata [8]. Among other attributes, the domain model captures relevant domain terms (RDTs) related to each learning object, with their relevance weight. This serves as a basis for overlay-type user model, where learner knowledge of RDTs is tracked.

The rest of this paper is organized as follows. In Sect. 2, we describe expert estimated and learner rated learning object difficulty. The next Sect. (3) focuses on the proposed recommendation method, which we evaluate in the following Sect. (4).

In Sect. 5, we also elaborate on the quantity of ratings and user motivations to provide them. The paper closes with conclusions outlining future work on the approach.

2   Student Explicit Expression of Difficulty

We consider two sources of learning object difficulty:

- *Expert estimated static difficulty.* When a domain expert authors exercises and questions for the educational system, and creates a domain model of relevant domain terms, prerequisite relations, learning objects properties, etc., they also estimate learning object difficulty. This can be a numeral rating for the object, for example 0.1 for trivial exercise, to 1.0 for advanced material, or expressed as a weighted relation to various relevant domain terms. In our case, we consider difficulty as a single scalar value, but combined with weighted *related-to* relations between learning objects and relevant domain terms. This difficulty estimation is considered "static", it depends only on the content in the educational system.
- *Dynamic student determined difficulty.* When learner interacts with a learning object (exercise or question), they have opportunity to provide explicit expression of its difficulty for them. After the learner submits a solution, they can use interface under the object, shown in Fig. 1, to express their opinion on its difficulty. Note that the scale does not have a neutral value and we mapped the response to values $<0, 1>$ such that the *Relatively difficult* option is the optimal (middle) difficulty. We consider this expression of difficulty "dynamic". The learner rates according to their experience with the learning object and their current state.

The ALEF is currently being used for its fifth year, having served over 1200 students in courses on Functional Programming, Logic Programming, Procedural Programming and Principles of Software Engineering. We started collecting the difficulty ratings halfway through. Perhaps the most relevant ratings are for exercises in programming courses. We observed 3,540 user expressed difficulty ratings for these learning objects, the distribution is shown in Fig. 2. Let the student determined difficulty ratings *for a learning object* be denoted as x_u and expert estimated difficulty as x_e. We found that students see the difficulty similarly to the domain expert with $\bar{x}_u = 0.56$, $\bar{x}_e = 0.54$; $\tilde{x}_u = 0.55$, $\hat{x}_e = 0.5$; and $corr(x_u, x_e) = 0.62$.

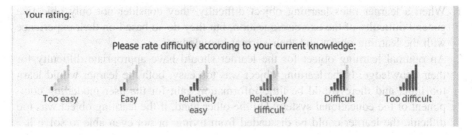

Fig. 1. Student rating estimation interface shown after interaction with exercise-type or question-type learning object.

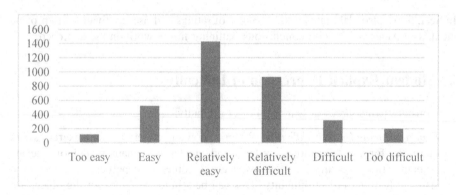

Fig. 2. Observed student difficulty estimations for programming exercises over long term usage of ALEF.

This can be explained by the fact that "in the wild", when students freely choose learning objects without recommendation, they will choose learning objects both currently too easy and too difficult for them. This comparison is made per learning object and users randomly choosing a given learning object when it is too difficult and too easy will cancel out each other and the final rating for the object would mimic the general difficulty estimation of the expert (e.g. an object is more often too easy). This observation could be useful for crowdsourcing the static difficulty from learners.

We can, however, not only observe the ratings as aggregated per object averaging out ratings outside the "real" difficulty, but consider these individual ratings with the context of the user – specifically user knowledge during the rating – creating the dynamic difficulty estimation. We could then predict for a learner with similar knowledge that the given learning object is currently going to be too easy or too difficult for them and create recommendation list by selecting appropriate objects.

3   Recommendation with Dynamic Student Determined Difficulty

We propose a method for learning object recommendation based on the following assumptions from related work and observed user behaviour in ALEF:

1. When a learner rates learning object difficulty, they consider not only objective general difficulty of the exercise/question, but they do so based on their experience with the learning object and their current knowledge.
2. An optimal learning object for the learner should have appropriate difficulty for their knowledge. If the learning object was too easy, both the learner would learn too little, and there would be little information gain for the user modelling component of the educational system. On the other hand, if the learning object was too difficult, the learner could be dissuaded from trying, or not even able to solve it.

3. Therefore, appropriate objects for a given learner are those, which they would, given their current knowledge, rate in the middle of the scale.

The recommendation method looks for difficulty ratings of candidate learning objects (LOs) to be recommended. Only those ratings are considered, which are made by users who had the same or similar level of knowledge for relevant domain terms related to the given learning object during interaction with it and when expressing the difficulty rating afterwards. The method works as follows:

```
function get_recommendations(user)
    var unsolved = find_unsolved_LOs(user, FADE_TIME)
    var lo_candidates = []

    foreach lo in unsolved
        difficulty = predicted_difficulty(user, lo)
        lo_candidates.add(lo, abs(difficulty - OPTIMAL_DIFF))
    end

    return lo_candidates.sort_by_difficulty.pick(TOP_N)
end
```

We set optimal difficulty (OPTIMAL_DIFF) to 0.5 from the range $\langle 0, 1 \rangle$. Note that while we are looking for difficulty appropriate for the learner knowledge, which is not necessarily a difficulty 0.5 of the learning object, we are predicting difficulty from peer users considering their knowledge in the moment of rating, therefore this aspect is carried over in the predicted difficulty, not in the optimal difficulty. FADE_TIME represents time function for which is the learning object considered solved and not to be recommended again. Its shape depends on how is the recommendation deployed, e.g., in long term use as a course support, a value related to (a multiple of) time distance between subsequent lessons should be used; in short term "crash-courses", the fade time can be in hours, or even infinite in order to not to repeat any learning objects at all. Here, we recommended top 4 items (TOP_N = 4).

The difficulty predicted from similar peers is calculated as a weighted arithmetic mean of difficulty ratings from knowledge-similar users weighted by their similarity to target user (denoted U):

$$predicted\_difficulty(U, LO)$$
$$= \frac{\sum_i rating(U_i, LO) * sim(U, U_i, LO, time(rating(U_i, LO)))}{\sum_i sim(U, U_i, LO)}$$

The learner similarity for a given learning object considers only knowledge (understanding), $underst(user, relevant\_term, time)$, of those relevant domain terms, $prereq(LO)$, that are required to understand and solve the given learning object, LO. For a target user, we consider their current knowledge in the time of recommendation, and for peers, we consider their knowledge at the time when they produced rating for the object. The similarity is based on Euclidean distance of learners' knowledge:

$$sim(U, U_x, LO, time) =$$

$$1 - \frac{\sqrt{\sum_{RDT_i \in prereq(LO)} (underst(U, RDT_i, now) - underst(U_x, RDT_i, time))^2}}{\sqrt{|prereq(LO)|}}$$

When the learner follows one of the shown recommendations and provides difficulty rating after the interaction, they form a feedback loop, both evaluating the recommendation and further contributing to the rating matrix for recommendation to other peers.

4   Evaluation

We evaluated the proposed method with students evenly distributed into two groups. One group was shown recommendations derived from learning object difficulty determined by peer students (the *proposed method*, see Sect. 3) and the other group was shown recommendations using static learning object difficulty estimated by a domain expert responsible for course authoring (a *control method*).

The *control method* gathers list of learning objects that could be possibly recommended (i.e., user has not solved them recently) and compares user's knowledge of all relevant domain terms that need to be understood to solve the exercise/question with its difficulty. For example, we are considering a learning object LO_1 to be recommended to user U and in order to solve the LO_1, the user must have understood relevant domain terms $prereq(LO_1) = \{RDT_1 \ldots RDT_N\}$, e.g., in order to solve exercise LO_1= "Number division" (C programming language), relevant domain terms RDT_1 = "Operator /" and RDT_2 = "double" must be understood (multiple other terms are required, but omitted here for simplicity). If $underst(U, RDT_1) = 0.5$ and $underst(U, RDT_2) = 0.7$ and:

$$required\_knowledge(U, LO_1) = \frac{\sum_{RDT_i \in prereq(LO_1)} underst(U, RDT_i)}{|prereq(LO_1)|}$$

then the required knowledge is in this case 0.6. This is compared with $difficulty(LO_1)$ and the closer is the user's knowledge to the difficulty, the more likely is LO_1 to be recommended. In other words, if the student knows very little from the prerequisites for a given learning object, the easier it must be in order to be appropriate to them, and vice versa, when the student knows almost everything needed for the learning object, it is only recommended when it is difficult, so it would still pose at least a little challenge to the student.

Results. We evaluated the proposed method in a controlled experiment with 30 students from various technical universities learning in the course on procedural programming using C language. The students have had some previous knowledge of procedural programming, some had experience specifically with the C language, therefore after a brief familiarization with the course by reading through some explanation-type learning objects, they were able to almost immediately start with both introductory and more advanced exercises and questions. Because the user input – difficulty rating after following a recommendation – is crucial for the proposed method to offer recommendation to other students, all students participated in the experiment at the same time in one three hour session.

Our hypotheses for the experiment were as follows:

- H_1. *Learning objects recommended based on difficulty are more appropriate than those selected freely by students themselves.*
- H_2. *Learning objects recommended based on dynamic student determined difficulty (proposed method) are more appropriate than those recommended based on expert estimated static difficulty (control method).*
- H_3. *Students using appropriate learning objects recommended based on dynamic student determined difficulty do progress better during the learning session than control group.*

Originally, we expected to see differing levels of knowledge gained during the learning session (the strongest hypothesis H_3). However, the average knowledge achieved by students in the group G_T with the proposed method was only slightly higher than the knowledge achieved in the control group G_C (overall term knowledge of 13.6 % as compared to 12.6 %).

On the other hand, we evaluated the appropriateness of the recommended learning objects (hypotheses H_1 and H_2) by observing the difficulty ratings provided by the users after interacting with recommended items. To compare the recommendations based on difficulty (either made with the proposed method or the control method) against freely chosen learning objects (H_1), e.g., selected by browsing the menu, we looked at the properties of ratings observed in the experiment. The arithmetic mean of ratings was again 0.56 (the same as in long term usage without recommendation, see 3.1), however, the average expert estimated difficulty of the items was now 0.73. This suggest that while we recommended more difficult learning objects (speaking in terms of their static difficulty), they were appropriate for the learners given their knowledge, since they still rated them as medium difficulty (dynamic difficulty). The correlation with expert estimated static difficulty was also lower: $corr(x_u, x_e) = 0.53$.

To compare the proposed and control method (H_2), we found the distance of individual difficulty ratings in the two groups from the target medium difficulty. In the proposed method, the distance was 20.0 %, while in the control group, it was 31.6 %. Using the dynamic student determined difficulty, we can make personalized recommendations of learning objects close to the optimal difficulty for the given learner.

5 Rating Quantity, Rating Elicitation and Estimation

In our experiment, participants were encouraged to rate learning object difficulty after interacting with an object. They actually provided these ratings very often, out of 796 visits to learning objects where difficulty is tracked (exercises and questions, but not explanations), there were 583 visits where the participant could rate difficulty (they attempted a solution, regardless of its correctness). Out of these, there were 532 ratings provided. 91.3 % of the time when the participant was able to rate, they did.

In standard educational system usage this is, however, not the case. Out of 147,364 visits to exercises and questions in the ALEF system instance that is used in normal coursework, students have had the opportunity to rate difficulty in 48,820 cases, which is 33.1 % of the visits. This ratio is sound due to the fact that when browsing for an exercise or question to try next, the student does not start interacting with all visited learning objects. Then, out of these, the rating was provided in 16,373 cases (34.3 % times). The controlled recommendation experiment described in this paper was carried outside of this ALEF instance; visits and ratings during experiment do not contribute to these observations.

Approximately one in three times is still a relatively high visited-to-rated ratio compared to other domains, e.g. online stores, where items are browsed and/or bought many thousand times, but rated perhaps in hundreds of the cases. This can be explained from various reasons. A possible cause is the fact that students are informed by the ALEF that it personalizes their experience according to their inputs – and the ratings can be attributed to the following human motivations [9]: when they perceive that they get better experience themselves – "When I rate, I will get better recommendations.", or when they perceive that they help others who might reciprocate – "When I rate, I will inform others about too difficult or too easy exercises."

The feedback quantity described above, when collected from many users, possibly over multiple iterations of the course in succeeding academic terms, can be enough for item recommendation. However, remind that our method performs filtering on the ratings by considering only ratings made by learners in the moment of their knowledge being similar to the target user. Therefore our target is to not only obtain as many ratings for learning objects as possible (have abundance of feedback), but to also cover various learner knowledge states, i.e. obtain difficulty ratings from as heterogeneous learners as possible and as often as possible. Ideally, each interaction with the learning object, regardless of its successfulness (learner has solved the exercise/question correctly, incorrectly or even left it untouched), would end with learner rating its difficulty. We propose two approaches to either achieve or mimic this effect.

Adaptive explicit rating elicitation. To further motivate the learners to provide ratings and also to collect the ratings in other key moments of interaction with the learning object, we can use an approach for adaptive explicit feedback elicitation, like the one we proposed for conversational evaluation of personalized approaches in [10]. We conducted preliminary experiments, where we displayed modal (on top of the content) adaptive questions asking the user to rate learning object difficulty not only after the interaction is over, but while the learner is still solving the exercise or question.

When predicting whether a given item would be too difficult for a user, it is important to avoid so-called *survivorship bias*, i.e. consider not only ratings of those who "survived" to the successful or unsuccessful end of interaction (providing correct or incorrect solution, or choosing that they do not know the solution), but also those, who may have left before. We asked users for their estimation of difficulty when they looked like they were leaving the exercise (e.g., started browsing the menu with the mouse cursor), or when they were partway through the interaction (e.g., they chose to see a hint for the exercise). While we may not be able to always exactly predict that the user is leaving, we can still obtain a difficulty rating. In the case when the learner persists afterwards, we can obtain another, final, rating for the given learning object. In the case when they leave, we have a rating from partial interaction, together with the information that the user did not finish or succeeded with such learning object and these can be valuable for more precise prediction of difficulty to others.

Estimating user perceived difficulty from implicit interactions. Another option is to directly use information about user interaction with the learning object. Even when we do not obtain explicit rating from the user, in the future, we can consider implicit feedback suggesting that the item is too easy or too difficult, e.g., when the user starts solving, asks for hint, and then leaves, refusing or turning off adaptive questions. The time which it took for the learner to find the solution (normalized to personal speed of the learner), or number of retries in the programming exercises tested through solution-evaluator, are other possible candidates for difficulty estimation indicators.

6 Conclusions

In this paper, we centred on two approaches to learning object difficulty in adaptive educational systems: dynamic student determined difficulty and expert estimated static difficulty. The properties of these difficulty ratings were evaluated from the long term usage of ALEF adaptive educational system in multiple courses.

We proposed a recommendation method considering difficulty predicted for a given target user from difficulty ratings expressed by their peers while having similar knowledge to the target user. We also described a control recommendation method that picks learning object based only on knowledge of the target user and domain expert estimated difficulty. These two methods were compared in a controlled experiment with two groups of students using the proposed and the control method respectively. The group with proposed recommendation approach outperformed the control group only negligibly in the knowledge gained throughout the experiment, possibly due to the short scope of the experiment. However, the difficulty ratings expressed after using self-chosen learning objects and after using learning objects suggested by proposed and control methods suggest that the user learning experience is better using the difficulty-based recommendation method, since users receive learning objects with appropriate difficulty for them.

The control method which considered only user's knowledge with static difficulty was afterwards deployed as a fall-back in *cold-start* scenarios, when the learner has not yet made enough actions to estimate their knowledge and find similar users, or when there are insufficient peer difficulty ratings to recommend learning objects.

In future work, the recommendation can be further personalized for preferences of each learner. We have assumed that the optimal exercises/questions are those with medium difficulty for the learner's current knowledge, which is actually best to progress further without dissuading the learner and to model user's knowledge. However one learner can welcome the challenge and prefer more difficult learning objects, or on the other hand can be easily dissuaded by even moderately difficult ones. This could be detected, for example, by comparing learner ratings after using recommendations to their peer ratings, by observing successfulness of solving recommended items, or even by observing whether the learner has left the learning object without attempting a solution. Conserving the same rating prediction mechanisms described here, one learner could receive recommendations computed for different (personalized) target difficulty than another.

Acknowledgement. This work was partially supported by grants. No. VG1/0971/11, KEGA 009STU-4/2014, and APVV-0233-10. We thank Matej Noga for recommender method implementation in ALEF system.

References

1. Manouselis, N., Drachsler, H., Vuorikari, R., Hummel, H., Koper, R.: Recommender Systems in technology enhanced learning. In: Ricci, F., Rokach, L., Shapira, B., Kantor, P.B. (eds.) Recommender Systems Handbook, pp. 387–415. Springer, Boston (2011)
2. Drachsler, H., Hummel, H.G.K., Koper, R.: Personal recommender systems for learners in lifelong learning networks: the requirements, techniques and model. Int. J. Learn. Technol. **3**, 404–423 (2008)
3. Michlík, P., Bieliková, M.: Exercises recommending for limited time learning. Procedia Comput. Sci. **1**, 2821–2828 (2010)
4. Linacre, J.M.: Computer-adaptive testing: a methodology whose time has come. In: Chae, S., Kang, U., Jeon, E., Linacre, J.M. (eds.) Development of Computerised Middle School Achievement Tests, MESA Research Memorandum 69 (2000)
5. Embretson, S.E., Reise, S.P.: Item Response Theory for Psychologists. Psychology Press, New York (2000)
6. Bieliková, M., Šimko, M., Barla, M., Tvarožek, J., Labaj, M., Móro, R., Srba, I., Ševcech, J.: ALEF: from application to platform for adaptive collaborative learning. In: Manouselis, N., Drachsler, H., Verbert, K., Santos, O.C. (eds.) Recommender Systems for Technology Enhanced Learning. Springer, New York (2014)
7. Šimko, M., Barla, M., Bieliková, M.: ALEF: a framework for adaptive web-based learning 2.0. In: Reynolds, N., Turcsányi-Szabó, M. (eds.) IFIP Advances in Information and Communication Technology, vol. 324, pp. 367–378. Springer, Heidelberg (2010)
8. Šimko, M., Bieliková, M.: Automated educational course metadata generation based on semantics discovery. In: Cress, U., Dimitrova, V., Specht, M. (eds.) EC-TEL 2009. LNCS, vol. 5794, pp. 99–105. Springer, Heidelberg (2009)
9. Carenini, G., Smith, J., Poole, D.: Towards more conversational and collaborative recommender systems. In: Proceedings of the 8th International Conference on Intelligent User Interfaces - IUI '03, pp. 12–18. ACM Press, New York, (2003)
10. Labaj, M., Bieliková, M.: Conversational evaluation of personalized solutions for adaptive educational systems. In: 3rd Workshop on Personalization Approaches for Learning Environments (PALE 2013), pp. 13–18. CEUR-WS (2013)

The Organization of Large-Scale Repositories of Learning Objects with Directed Hypergraphs

Luigi Laura[1,2]([✉]), Umberto Nanni[1,2], and Marco Temperini[1]

[1] Department of Computer, Control, and Management Engineering Antonio Ruberti,
Sapienza University, Via Ariosto 25, 00185 Roma, Italy
{laura,nanni,marte}@dis.uniroma1.it
[2] Research Centre for Transport and Logistics (CTL),
Sapienza University, Roma, Italy

Abstract. In this paper we focus on the problem of finding personalized learning paths in presence of a large number of available learning components. In particular, we model the relationships holding between learning activities and the related (needed/achieved) competence, by adopting directed hypergraph. We show as the complexity of optimizing learning paths depends dramatically on the adopted metrics; in particular, we prove that finding a learning path with minimum *timespan* can be done in quasi-linear time, whilst finding one with minimum *total effort* (apparently, a very similar problem) is NP-hard. Therefore in some cases, it is possible to use simple and fast algorithms for computing personalized e-learning paths, while in other cases the developers must rely on approximated heuristics, or adequate computational resources. We are implementing this modeling and the related algorithms in the framework provided by the LECOMPS system for personalized e-learning. The final aim is to apply the modeling in large repositories, or in wider web-based e-learning environments.

1 Introduction

The personalization of learning experience is widely recognized as a main success factor in (e-)education. Taking care of personal traits of the learner, and making the learning activities compliant with them is a main issue, in particular, in web-based e-learning. The model of competence-based learning is widely used to render personal learning accomplishments and needs: roughly summarizing, given a target for a study course, basing on the present "state of knowledge" (amount of possessed competence) of the individual learner, a set of learning activities (LAs) can be stated for the learner to undertake, so that only the lacking competences are addressed and the target can be reached with less effort and study time. Provided that assessment means are usable to test the state of knowledge during the course, the set of LAs can also be continuously adapted to the changing learner's model.

In this paper we base on the LMS architecture provided by an existing system for personalized e-learning (LECOMPS). In that system, as in many others,

© Springer International Publishing Switzerland 2014
Y. Cao et al. (Eds.): ICWL 2014 Workshops, LNCS 8699, pp. 23–33, 2014.
DOI: 10.1007/978-3-319-13296-9_3

the basic factors defining the personal student model are competence-based: the knowledge that the individual student possesses, before of the course or at any stated moment during course taking, is used to define and maintain the course structure. Accordingly, competence is also appearing in the definition of the learning objects. In the system numerous learning objects repositories have to be managed, each one possibly amounting to a huge number of items. Moreover learning objects in such repositories are connected by a possibly large quantity of relations (such as the dependency linking one object enabling the taking of another). The repositories can be depicted as graphs, where the amount of nodes (learning objects) and arcs (dependencies) presents the e-learning system with possibly very challenging computational requirements, when automatic construction and continuous adaptation of personalized courses is to be supported.

Directed hypergraph (see, e.g., [10]) can be used to model in a very natural way the relationships holding among learning activities. Several works propose hypergraphs in order to model processes, Petri-nets, or workflow nets (see, e.g. [1,7,14,16]). Interestingly, Sun and Lu [15] propose directed hypergraphs to describe personalized learning processes, together with the relationships among the process itself, the learning component and the learner. They show the effectiveness of using the directed hypergraphs as a robust model for learning processes. Compared to this work, we use directed hypergraphs in a different (somehow, dual) way. Li et al. [12] address analogous problems in the more unstructured context of self-directed and community-based learning, in particular, they consider the difficulty for the learners to locate suitable learning resources.

As observed in [7], in most of today's learning support systems, the structuring of learning activities *is hard-wired and tied to a specific learning domain and system, especially when tightly integrated with the graphical user interface of the system.* Thus, re-usability in different learning systems is restricted.

We focus on the problem of finding learning paths in large repositories (or in a context of web based education) where each learning component is characterized by means of needed and achieved knowledge. In this context we show how directed hypergraph can be used to model the relationships holding among learning activities and skills, and characterize the complexity of finding learning paths according quite natural optimization criteria, showing that finding a learning paths with minimum *timespan* can be done in quasi-linear time, and finding one with minimum *total effort* (apparently, a very similar problem) is NP-hard. These results show as, at least in some cases, it is possible to use fast time algorithms for computing personalized e-learning paths, thus allowing to support large scale e-learning frameworks. In other cases the computational load suggests the adoption of approximated heuristics, or adequate computational resources. In particular, we have started an implementation on the framework provided by the LECOMPS system [9,13] for personalized e-learning.

2   The Lecomps System and the Adopted Learning Model

LECOMPS is a web-based Learning Management System: the functional architecture is shown in Fig. 1. Here we recall the few aspects of LECOMPS that are related to our proposed directed hypergraph approach, and refer the interested reader to [9,13] for a complete description of the LECOMPS system. The LECOMPS system provides functionalities to support the usual management of learner and teacher users in courses, the authoring activities in repositories of *Learning Components*[1] (*LC*), and the automated definition of personalized courses, that are then adaptively delivered to learners. Referring to Fig. 1, the set of *LC*s defined for a given subject matter, collected in a *LC Pool*, is the *Learning Domain* (*LD*) for the courses on that matter. Each $lc \in LC$ describes a learning activity, in terms of the *effort* needed to take the associated learning material, the *questions* that can be used to test the competence that can be acquired through the learning activity, and the competence denoted in the *lc*. The competence in a learning component *lc* is defined by two sets of *Required Knowledge* (*lc*.RK) and *Acquired Knowledge* (*lc.AK*). The semantics of *RK* and *AK* in a *lc* is of straightforward interpretation: "you need *RK* to take the *lc*, and by that you could gain the competence denoted by *AK*". The knowledge (skills, competence) denoted in the above ways throughout a *LC* pool, is called the *Knowledge Domain* (*KD*) of the repositories. In particular, *RK* and *AK* in a *lc* (both subsets of *KD*) are defined as sets of *Learning Objectives* (*LO*s). A *LO* is a predicate *LO(level, keyword, concepts, context)* where:

- *level* and *keyword* are cognitive features that label the concepts; they are based on the taxonomy of cognitive levels of Bloom [8];
- each *concept* is a designation (identifier) for an ability or skill or knowledge, on which the above mentioned cognitive traits are significant;
- the *context* identifies the learning context of the concept(s).

The labeling of concepts allows to state some derivation rules among *LO*s: in particular, a competence *cpt* possessed at a certain cognitive level in a given context *ctx* implies the possession of *cpt* at lower levels in *ctx*:

$$LO(3, apply, cpt, cxt) \implies LO(2, describe, cpt, cxt)$$

LECOMPS builds personalized courses by synthesizing a set of Learning Components, $\mathcal{C} = \{lc_1, \ldots, lc_n\} \subseteq LD$ (linearizable in a sequence) basing on a statement for the *Target Knowledge* (*TK*) and an evaluation of the initial state of knowledge of the individual learner (cfr. *CS* below). The aim of the course is to bridge the gap between the present state of learner's *CS* and *TK*:

$$CS^{init}|_{KD}, \bigcup_{i \in [1...n]} lc_i.AK \vdash TK$$

(meaning that the set of *LO* comprised in the initial state of *CS*, together with the *LO* acquired through the course, entails the target knowledge).

---

[1] A Learning Component is a SCORM compliant Learning Object, where an instructional content is enriched with specification elements, to make it usable in an automated process of selection [13].

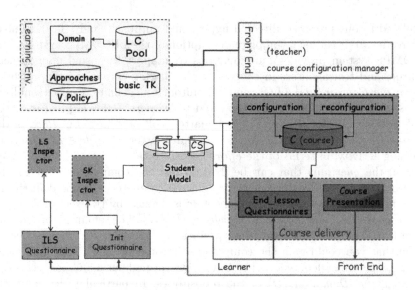

Fig. 1. LECOMPS [13] functional architecture.

3   Modeling Repositories with Directed Hypergraphs

Following the model provided in the previous section, let us suppose to have a set of LOs in a given subject matter. Here we will use a simplified version of the LO model given in Sect. 2, where we regard a learning objective lo as a pair $\langle c, l \rangle$, i.e., a concept c, and a level/degree of competence l; we will denote this as c_l. Moreover we will define a *Repository* $\mathcal{R}$ of Learning Components as a collection $\mathcal{R} = \{lc_1, lc_2, \ldots, lc_m\}$, while each learning component is a 4-tuple $lc_i = \langle C_i, RK_i, AK_i, E_i \rangle$, where (cfr. previous section),

- C_i is the *Learning Content* of the component;
- $RK_i \subseteq KD$ is the *Required Knowledge* in lc_i;
- $AK_i \subseteq KD$ is the *Acquired Knowledge* through lc_i;
- E_i is the *Effort* (quantitative measure of global effort endured to take C_i).

We will denote as $LO(\mathcal{R})$ and $\mathcal{C}(\mathcal{R}) = \mathcal{C}(LO(\mathcal{R}))$, resp., the set of learning objectives used in $\mathcal{R}$ and the collection of concepts used to define the learning objectives in $LO(\mathcal{R})$.

Directed Hypergraphs and Hyperpaths. Directed hypergraphs are a generalization of directed graphs which have been used to model properties of structures in a variety of contexts (see, e.g., [2,6,10]). A *directed hypergraph* $\mathcal{H}$ is a pair $\langle N, H \rangle$, where N is a set of *nodes* and $H \subseteq \mathcal{P}^+(N) \times \mathcal{P}^+(N)$ is a set of *hyperarcs*, where $\mathcal{P}^+(N)$ is the collection of nonempty subsets of N. Each hyperarc is an ordered pair $h = (S, T)$, where both the *source set* S (or *head*), and the *target set* T (or *tail*) are arbitrary nonempty sets of nodes: $S, T \subseteq N$.

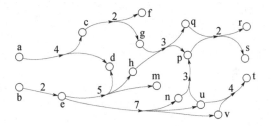

Fig. 2. An example of weighted directed hypergraph.

A *weighted directed hypergraph* $\mathcal{H}_W$ is a triple $\langle N, H; w \rangle$, where $\langle N, H \rangle$ is a directed hypergraph and each hyperarc $\langle S, T \rangle \in H$ is associated to a real value $w_{\langle S, T \rangle} \in \Re$ called the *weight* of the hyperarc. An example of weighted directed hypergraph is given in Fig. 2.

The hyperpaths that we are interested to will never use twice the same hyperarc. Based on this observation, for the purposes of this paper, we can define hyperpaths as follows. Let $\mathcal{H} = \langle N, H \rangle$ be a directed hypergraph, $X \subseteq N$ be a non-empty subset of nodes, and y be a node in N. A *hyperpath* from X to y in $\mathcal{H}$ is a minimal set of hyperarcs such that one of the following conditions holds:

(a) $y \in X$ (*extended reflexivity*); in this case, the hyperpath $h(X, y)$ is the empty set;

(b) there is a hyperarc $(Z, y) \in H$ and hyperpaths from X to each node $z_i \in Z$ (*extended transitivity*); in this case, the hyperpath $h(X, y)$ includes the hyperarc (Z, y) and all the hyperpaths $h(X, z_i)$.

If there exists a hyperpath from X to y, then we say that vertex y is *reachable* from X, or $X \rightsquigarrow \{y\}$. We can generalize this definition to a hyperpath from a source set $X \subseteq N$ to a target *set* $Y \subseteq N$ as a union of hyperpaths $h(X, Y) = \bigcup_{y_i \in Y} h(X, y_i)$. If there exists a hyperpath from X to Y we say that the vertices in Y are all *reachable* from X, or $X \rightsquigarrow Y$.

In Fig. 2, we can see that $\{bg\} \rightsquigarrow \{q\}$, in fact there is the hyperpath $h(bg, q) = \{(b, e), (e, dhm), (gh, pq)\}$, but $\{b\} \not\rightsquigarrow \{q\}$, since the only hyperarc entering node q is (gh, pq), but there is no way to reach g from b. On the other side, $\{ab\} \rightsquigarrow N$, that is, from the source set $\{a, b\}$ we can reach any node in the hypergraph.

Hyperpaths metrics. There are many possible ways to measure a directed hyperpath. A quite natural metric is to measure the **size** of the hyperpath, which can be defined as the sum of the weights of all the hyperarcs, that is:

$$\texttt{size}(h(X, y)) = \sum_{(S, t) \in h(X, y)} w(S, t)$$

In particular, the **size** of the empty hyperpath is zero.

Another possible metrics consist in the **rank** of the hyperpath, defined as the maximum consecutive chaining of the weights. In particular, the **rank** of an

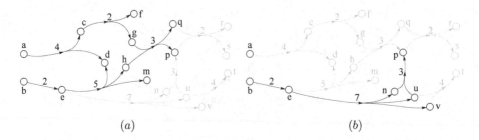

Fig. 3. Here we look for an "optimal" hyperpath $h(ab, p)$ for the hypergraph in Fig. 2. The hyperpath shown in (a) has size=16 and rank=10; the one in (b) has size=12 and rank=12. Hence, the choice is not unique, since it is based on the criterion of optimality.

empty hyperpath is zero, whilst the rank of a hyperpath defined by transitivity, that is $h(X, y) = \{(Z, y)\} \cup \bigcup_{z_i \in Z} h(X, z_i)$ is defined as follows:

$$\mathbf{rank}(h(X, y)) = w(Z, y) + \max_{z_i \in Z}\{\mathbf{rank}(h(X, z_i))\}$$

Examples of "optimal" hyperpaths according to the above metrics are in Fig. 3.

A Hypergraph for a Repository of Learning Components. Let us consider a Repository $\mathcal{R} = \{lc_1, lc_2, \ldots, lc_m\}$ of Learning Components, with the corresponding set of Learning Objectives $LO(\mathcal{R})$ and the set of Concepts $\mathcal{C}(\mathcal{R})$ used in LO. We can define a corresponding *Learning Hypergraph* $\mathcal{H}_\mathcal{R}$, according the following rules:

- the set of nodes coincides with the set of Learning Objectives: $N \equiv LO$; we recall that each learning objective lo with concept c and level l is denoted simply as c_l;
- for each learning component $lc_i = \langle C_i, RK_i, AK_i, E_i \rangle \in \mathcal{R}$ we introduce the hyperarc (RK_i, AK_i) whose weight is equal to the effort E_i;
- for each concept $C \in \mathcal{C}(R)$ and for each i, j such that $1 \leq j < i \leq k$, we introduce "implicit" hyperarcs (c_i, c_j) with weight 0.

The implicit arcs do not correspond to actual Learning Contents, but implement the assumption (stated in Sect. 2) that a competence possessed at a certain cognitive level implies the possession of competencies at lower levels in the same context (with zero effort):

$$c_i \Longrightarrow c_j \quad \text{for each level } j < i.$$

Note that an ontology, established among the concepts in KD, might introduce analogous implications, due to concepts which are conceptually related. As an example, if a concept c' *subsumes* a concept c'' (e.g., if c'' is a special case of concept c'), then one might assume that, if a learner reaches an educational goal c'_i (concept c' at level i), then (s)he reaches the educational goal c''_i as well (i.e., $c'_i \Longrightarrow c''_i$, for each level i). If this is the case, we can introduce an implicit arc from c'_i to c''_i for each $i = \{1, 2, \ldots, k\}$ with effort 0.

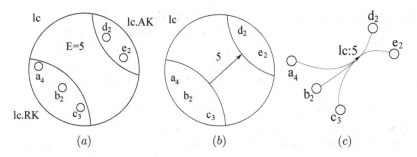

Fig. 4. Representation of a single learning component lc: (a) graphical representation of lc, characterized by a Required Knowledge $\{a_4, b_2, c_3\}$, an Acquired Knowledge $\{d_2, e_2\}$, and an Effort $E = 5$; (b) a simplified representation of the same lc; (c) the same lc represented as a directed hyperarc from $lc.RK$ to $lc.AK$.

Modeling Learning Paths with Hypergraphs. Adopting directed hypergraphs allows us to exploit the algorithms conceived for this model to find *Learning Paths* with certain characteristics from the current cognitive state of the learner to any possible target knowledge.

Let us consider a repository $\mathcal{R}$ of learning contents and a learner in a given state of knowledge $CS \subseteq KD$. A *(feasible) Learning Path* is a sequence $LP = \langle lc_1, lc_2 \ldots, lc_m \rangle$ such that each $lc_i \in LP$ has a required knowledge $RK_i \subseteq CS \cup AK_1 \cup AK_2 \cup \cdots \cup AK_{i-1}$, for $i = 1, 2, \ldots, m$. Intuitively, a feasible learning path is such that each learning component lc_i has a required knowledge that is part of the *current* cognitive state of the learner, which includes the initial cognitive state plus the acquired knowledge of the learning components *before* lc_i in the sequence. In the following, when no ambiguity arises, we refer only to feasible Learning Paths.

Let us consider a repository of Learning Components $\mathcal{R}$, a learner in a cognitive state $CS \subseteq KD$, and a target knowledge $TK \subseteq KD$. If we consider the Learning Hyperpath $\mathcal{H}_{\mathcal{R}}$, the following properties hold:

1. There exists a learning path LP from CS to TK in $\mathcal{R}$ if and only if there exists a hyperpath $CS \rightsquigarrow TK$ in $\mathcal{H}_{\mathcal{R}}$; furthermore, any topological order of the hyperpath $h(CS, TK)$ is a feasible learning path LP;
2. A learning path with minimum *total effort* (computed as the sum of the efforts of all the involved LCs) corresponds to a hyperpath with minimum **size**, and vice-versa;
3. If we suppose that more learning components can be taken in parallel, a learning path with minimum *timespan* corresponds to a hyperpath with minimum **rank**, and vice-versa.

Of course, in a realistic setting, we would impose a bound on the effort of parallel learning activities: this can handled by defining optimization criteria with constraints.

An example. In order to make more intuitive the use of the proposed model, we provide a small example of a repository of LCs modeled by a directed hypergraph. In Fig. 4 we can see the graphical representation of a single learning content lc; in particular we see the same lc depicted in three distinct ways: a general representation, a simplified one, and the corresponding hyperarc. A sample repository $\mathcal{R}$ is given in Fig. 5 which shows, respectively, the learning components included in this repository, and the corresponding Learning hypergraph $\mathcal{H_R}$. Beside the learning components, this hypergraph includes dashed arcs representing the implicit arcs at zero cost. Note that the third Learning Content, C, represents a course improving skill a from level 3 to level 5.

Suppose that a given learner with initial cognitive state $CS = \{a_4\}$ must reach the Target Knowledge $\{f_2, g_2\}$. This is possible by a learning path $\langle E, F \rangle$, with timespan 6 and total effort 6 (see Fig. 6(a)). On the other side, a less advanced learner with cognitive state $CS = \{a_3\}$ may follow $LP = \langle A, B, D, F \rangle$ (Fig. 6(b)), with a timespan 7 and effort 9. In this case, a learning path with smaller effort would be $\langle C, E, F \rangle$ (Fig. 6(c)), with effort 8, but timespan 7.

The computational cost of computing Learning Paths. The size of the description of a repository $\mathcal{R}$ corresponds to the size of the Learning Hypergraph. For each learning component lc_i we need to represent the required knowledge RK_i and the acquired knowledge AK_i, possibly sharing this representation among several learning components. The space requirement to represent n learning components is $O(n+s)$, with $s = \sum_i |S_i|$, where either $S_i = AK_i$ or $S_i = RK_i$ for some lc_i. In the model described above, given a repository $\mathcal{R}$ (with a description of size $|\mathcal{R}|$), an initial cognitive state CS, and a target knowledge TK, we can prove the following results:

1. finding a feasible Learning Path (or checking its absence) can be solved in linear time, that is $O(|\mathcal{R}|)$; the available algorithms are *incremental*, that is, the solution can be updated for small changes of the repository (this corresponds to finding any hyperpath from CS to TK [4]);
2. finding a Learning Path with minimum timespan can be solved in time $O(|\mathcal{R}| \cdot \log |\mathcal{R}|)$ (as finding a hyperpath with minimum rank [5]);
3. finding the hyperpath with minimum total effort is NP-hard (this is the complexity of finding a hyperpath with minimum size [3]).

We claim that the first two results can be stated (with the same time complexity), even if we consider the problem of finding any learning path (or a hyperpath with minimum timespan) with *filtering*, e.g., involving skill levels not larger than k. The third result is a lower-bound for the problem of finding a learning path with minimum total effort, within the considered model. Of course, there are approximated approaches to this problem (see, e.g., [11]), due to its reducibility to the well known *set covering* problem. A classification of optimization criteria for directed hyperpaths and the hardness of the related problems is given in [3].

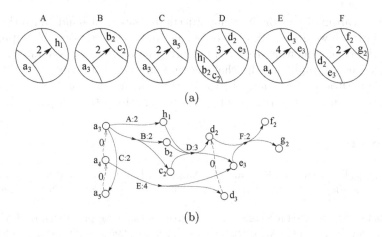

(a)

(b)

Fig. 5. (a) A repository of Learning Contents $\mathcal{R}$ with six learning components; (b) the corresponding learning hypergraph $HH_{\mathcal{R}}$ including a hyperarc for each learning component plus three implicit arcs with zero cost: these correspond to an implicit containment (for any concept c, an educational objective at level i implies an educational objective at a lower level, i.e., $c_i \Longrightarrow c_{i-1}$).

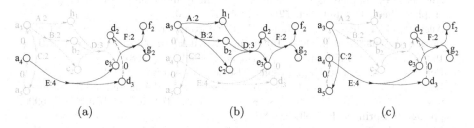

(a)   (b)   (c)

Fig. 6. Referring to the repository in Fig. 5, given a Target Knowledge $\{f_2, g_2\}$:
(a) a Learning Path from a Cognitive State $CS = \{a_4\}$ with effort=6 and timespan=6;
(b) a Learning Path from a Cognitive State $CS = \{a_3\}$ with timespan=7 (and effort=9);
(c) a Learning Path from $CS = \{a_3\}$ with effort=8 (and timespan=8).

4   Conclusions

Populating a repository (pool) with a huge number of learning objects and related connections might derive in long waiting times for the production of courses, as well as in long and even less sustainable delay in adaptation. We have shown some promising ways to find customized learning paths within repositories of learning objects through the use of directed hypergraphs. This opens the possibility of using algorithms and heuristics devised on such data structures, to ease the representational burden of large pools and the computational greed of certain operations, such as course content selection, learning object sequencing, and searching for optimal learning paths. These operations are notoriously of the highest computational complexity, and are usually disposed of by confiding in the limited cardinality of the learning objects repository at hand. With the presented approach we hope to devise better solutions to the problem, by improving the possibility of exploiting decades of algorithmic results developed in the area of directed hypergraphs for the challenging goal of a sustainable management of large repositories of learning objects. Further algorithmic problems are to be considered, such as the optimization of learning paths with multiple criteria.

References

1. Alimonti, P., Feuerstein, E., Laura, L., Nanni, U.: Linear time analysis of properties of conflict-free and general petri nets. Theor. Comput. Sci. **412**(4–5), 320–338 (2011)
2. Ausiello, G.: Directed hypergraphs: data structures and applications. In: Dauchet, M., Nivat, M. (eds.) CAAP 1988. LNCS, vol. 299, pp. 295–303. Springer, Heidelberg (1988)
3. Ausiello, G., Italiano, G.F., Laura, L., Nanni, U., Sarracco, F.: Structure theorems for optimum hyperpaths in directed hypergraphs. In: Mahjoub, A.R., Markakis, V., Milis, I., Paschos, V.T. (eds.) ISCO 2012. LNCS, vol. 7422, pp. 1–14. Springer, Heidelberg (2012)
4. Ausiello, G., Italiano, G.F., Nanni, U.: Dynamic maintenance of directed hypergraphs. Theor. Comput. Sci. **72**(2–3), 97–117 (1990)
5. Ausiello, G., Italiano, G.F., Nanni, U.: Hypergraph traversal revisited: cost measures and dynamic algorithms. In: Brim, L., Gruska, J., Zlatuška, J. (eds.) MFCS 1998. LNCS, vol. 1450, pp. 1–16. Springer, Heidelberg (1998)
6. Berge, C.: Graphs and Hypergraphs. Elsevier, Amsterdam (1973)
7. Bergenthum, R., Desel, J., Harrer, A., Mauser, S.: Modeling and mining of learnflows. In: Jensen, K., Donatelli, S., Kleijn, J. (eds.) ToPNoC V. LNCS, vol. 6900, pp. 22–50. Springer, Heidelberg (2012)
8. Bloom, B.E.: Taxonomy of Educational Objectives. D.McKay Company Inc., New York (1964)
9. De Marsico, M., Sterbini, A., Temperini, M.: A framework to support social-collaborative personalized e-learning. In: Kurosu, M. (ed.) HCII/HCI 2013, Part II. LNCS, vol. 8005, pp. 351–360. Springer, Heidelberg (2013)
10. Gallo, G., Longo, G., Nguyen, S., Pallottino, S.: Directed hypergraphs and applications. Discrete Appl. Math. **42**, 177–201 (1993)
11. Gallo, G., Pallottino, S.: Hypergraph models and algorithms for the assembly problem. Technical report 06/92, Dip. di Informatica, University of Pisa, Italy, Corso Italia 40, I-56125 Pisa, Italy (1992)
12. Li, H., Hasegawa, S., Kashihara, A.: A resource organization system for self-directed & community-based learning with a case study. In: Wong, L.-H. et al. (eds.) I. A.-P. S. for Computers in Education, Proceedings of the 21st International Conference on Computers in Education - ICCE 2013, pp. 329–338 (2013)
13. Limongelli, C., Sciarrone, F., Temperini, M., Vaste, G.: The lecomps5 framework for personalized web-based learning: a teacher's satisfaction perspective. Comput. Human Behav. **27**(4), 1285–1466 (2011)
14. Liu, X.-Q., Wu, M., Chen, J.-X.: Knowledge aggregation and navigation high-level petri nets-based in e-learning. In: International Conference on Machine Learning and Cybernetics, vol. 1, pp. 420–425 (2002)

15. Sun, X., Lu, Y.: Directed-hypergraph based personalized e-learning process and resource optimization. In: 2012 Fourth International Conference on Digital Home (ICDH), pp. 171–178, (Nov 2012)
16. Xuedong, S., Feng, Z.: Unified and integrated e-learning modeling supporting dynamic learning process optimization. In: Eighth International Conference on Fuzzy Systems and Knowledge Discovery (FSKD), vol. 4, pp. 2137–2141 (July 2011)

Computer Science Paper Classification for CSAR

Jiahui Quan[1](✉), Qing Li[2], and Minglu Li[1]

[1] Shanghai Jiao Tong University, Shanghai, People's Republic of China
{quan-jh,mlli}@sjtu.edu.cn
[2] City University of Hong Kong, Hong Kong, People's Republic of China
qing.li@cityu.edu.hk

Abstract. When researchers or students entering a new research field in computer science, they desire to know who the top scientists are and what the best papers are in this field, then they know to find whom to collaborate with or can find best papers in this area to read. In order to divide different research fields, it is very important to correctly classify all the papers in computer science. In this paper, we propose CSAR classification system derived from 2012 ACM Computing Classification System (CCS), and also propose a new weighted naive Bayes classifier to classify the papers in top publications by their research fields. The experiments show that the performance of proposed weighted naive Bayes classifier is better than the unweighted naive Bayes classifier and overwhelms the results of k-NN classifier.

Keywords: Text classification · Weighted naive Bayes classifier · CSAR classification system · Academic information platform

1 Introduction

Researchers or students desire to know the academic rankings or useful academic information in different research fields of computer science, so it is important to set up a academic platform to publish useful academic information. Computer Science Academic Rankings (CSAR) [1] is proposed to meet this need. CSAR is different from other online-learning platforms [2,3]. It's a ranking and recommended system for academic information. It can recommend accurate rankings of academic institutions, authors and publications to users, and provide an academic information exchange platform. One of CSAR's functions is to provide helpful academic information by research fields. In this paper, we propose CSAR classification system as a part of CSAR. CSAR classification system is derived from the 2012 ACM Computing Classification System (CCS) [4]. Since the paper data we collect are from multi-source, such as ACM Digital Library [5], IEEE Xplore Digital Library [6], Springer [7], and ACM CCS is only suitable for ACM papers, we propose CSAR classification system which is suitable for all papers in computer science. By now CSAR has utilized the paper data of Class A and Class B conferences recommended by China Computer Federation (CCF) [8]. CSAR also collects the citations from Google Scholar [9] and other useful information

© Springer International Publishing Switzerland 2014
Y. Cao et al. (Eds.): ICWL 2014 Workshops, LNCS 8699, pp. 34–43, 2014.
DOI: 10.1007/978-3-319-13296-9_4

[10] for these papers. So it integrates all the first-class academic information in computer science. Some of these papers belong to the conferences associated with ACM, so they already have CCS categories, while the others almost don't have. Our object is to assign normalized CSAR classification to all these papers correctly. After assigning the classification to all these papers, when querying the academic information in certain area, we can easily find out the papers we need.

Our contributions can be summarized as follows: (1) We propose CSAR classification system which is derived from 2012 ACM CCS. (2) We also propose a new weighted naive Bayes (weighted NB) classifier to classify the papers by their research fields. (3) When researchers query papers in certain research area, CSAR can return the related academic information in this area, such as the top-cited papers and its information. The rest of the paper is organized as follows: Sect. 2 reviews related work. Section 3 introduces CSAR classification system. Section 4 illustrates the proposed weighted NB classifier. In Sect. 5, we present the experimental results. Section 6 discusses the details of experimental results. Finally, we conclude the paper in Sect. 7.

2 Related Work

2.1 Computing Classification System

Previously, ACM has multi-version of computing classification system. The previous version is 1998 version [11]. With the rapid development of computer science, this version can not meet the needs of current classification requirements. Vesseya et al. [12] proposes a unified classification system in the computing disciplines that is based on five research-focused characteristics: topic, approach, method, unit of analysis, and reference discipline. But their research only focuses on three main disciplines: Computer Science, Software Engineering, and Information Systems. The CiteSeer^x project is based on the ACM Computing Classification System [13] which explores the ways to automatically expand the CCS ontology, but this latest work still use 1998 version CCS. As far as we know, no related work utilizes or improves the 2012 version CCS.

2.2 Text Classification Methods

Our proposed classification method discussed in Sect. 4 belongs to short text classification. Sriram et al. [14] give the scenario of Twitter to illustrate the classification of short text messages. They propose to use a small set of domain-specific features extracted from the author's profile and text. Their proposed approach effectively classifies the text to a predefined set of generic classes such as News, Events, Opinions, Deals, and Private Messages. Reference [15] addresses the issue of semi-supervised text classification by using Wikipedia knowledge. It utilizes both labeled and unlabeled data to construct classifiers. In [16], the authors employ the way of deriving latent topics from existing large corpus and propose an method to leverage topics at multiple granularity, which can model the short text more precisely.

2.3 Naive Bayes Classifier

Naive Bayes classifier has a wide range of applications, such as text classification, data mining [17], or the prediction for h-index [18]. Work in [19] explores the use of hierarchical structure to classify a heterogeneous collection of web pages. The author uses naive Bayes classifier and analyzes the feasibility of a web page classifier which exploits the hierarchical structure of categories. Wu et al. [20] propose a new Artificial Immune System based on Weighted Naive Bayes (AISWNB) classifier. AISWNB uses immunity theory in artificial immune systems to find optimal weight values for each attribute which can be obtained during the learning process.

3 CSAR Classification System

3.1 2012 ACM CCS

2012 ACM CCS is a hierarchical classification system in computing domain. The first and second level classification of CCS has 14 and 88 categories respectively. The deeper the levels are, the more subcategories they have. One paper with CCS classification may have major categories and minor categories (if any). These categories are specified by the paper authors.

3.2 CSAR Classification System

We found that 2012 ACM CCS has some defects in arranging categories. For example, *Operating systems* is an important category in computer science, but it's placed at the 4th level of CCS under *Contextual software domains*. This kind of arrangement is not so intuitive, and greatly affects the classification precision. Because the deeper level is, the more subcategories are, which greatly disperses the determination of categories. In other situation, category like *Network properties* is not suitable as the name of research field, so we should use deeper and more suitable subcategories such as *Network security* and *Network structure*.

We propose a hierarchical CSAR classification system for computer science. We rearrange some categories of CCS, and control the number of its levels to establish CSAR classification system (Since our purpose is to distinguish different domains, not the more detailed, the better). We mainly use 2nd level categories of CCS as the leaf nodes of our classification system, because they are not too general nor too detailed. But for the categories which need rearrangement, we may go deeper and put them at appropriate place. When we classify papers by domains, we just assign the leaf names of CSAR classification system as the paper classification. Figure 1 depicts part of the CSAR classification system. The leaves are the classification for the papers, which may be at 2nd level or deeper levels. We also change the positions of some classifications to make them more appropriate, such as *Operating systems*.

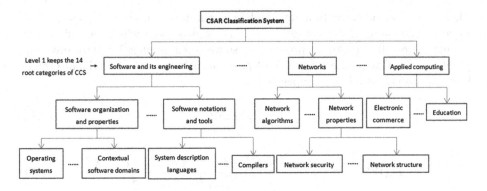

Fig. 1. Part of the CSAR classification system

4 Design of Weighted Naive Bayes Classifier

4.1 Principles Behind Naive Bayes Classifier

First we introduce the theory of naive Bayes classifier. Define W is the word variable, and C is the category variable. For one word w in document d and one category c, Bayes' theorem is defined as:

$$P(C = c|W = w) = P(C = c)\frac{P(W = w|C = c)}{P(W = w)} \qquad (1)$$

Define n as the total number of words in document d. According to Bayes' theorem, the probability of a document d belonging to a category c can be calculated as:

$$c = \arg max_c P(c|w) = \arg max_c P(c) \prod_{i=1}^{n} P(w_i|c) \qquad (2)$$

To calculate the parameter estimation of conditional probability, we apply maximum likelihood estimate:

$$L(c|w) = P(w|c) = \prod_{i=1}^{n} P(w_i|c) \qquad (3)$$

We use logarithm to transfer the continued multiplication to the continued sum. Now the maximum likelihood estimate can be written as:

$$\hat{c} = \arg max L(c|w) = \arg max \sum_{i=1}^{n} \ln P(w_i|c) \qquad (4)$$

The maximum likelihood estimate of prior probability $P(c)$ is:

$$P(C = c) = \frac{\sum_{i=1}^{m} I(c_i = c)}{m} \qquad (5)$$

where I is the indicator function, and m is the total number of papers. The value of maximum likelihood estimate could still be zero which can affect the calculation result of posterior probability, so we add a number $\lambda > 0$ to solve this problem. The Bayesian estimations of prior probability and conditional probability are shown as follows, respectively:

$$P_\lambda(C = c) = \frac{\sum_{i=1}^{m} I(c_i = c) + \lambda}{m + K\lambda} \tag{6}$$

$$P_\lambda(W^{(j)} = a_{ji}|C = c) = \frac{\sum_{i=1}^{m} I(w_i^{(j)} = a_{ji}, c_i = c) + \lambda}{\sum_{i=1}^{m} I(c_i = c) + S_j\lambda} \tag{7}$$

where K is the total number of categories, and S_j is the total number of unique words appear in the documents. We found that when $\lambda = 0.3$, the classifier has better performance in our experiment.

4.2 Weighted Naive Bayes Classifier

We propose a weighted NB classifier. Algorithm 1 illustrates the procedure of building prediction model. Before processing, we select all the papers with CCS categories, and convert their CCS categories into CSAR categories. We store all these papers in one file $CsarPaper$ and use it as the input of Algorithm 1. $Stopword$ stands for stopwords dictionary. The output is the prediction model $Model$ and validation set $ValidationtSet$ (all papers in one file).

Algorithm 1. Procedure of Building Prediction Model

Input:
$CsarPaper$, $Stopword$;
Output:
$Model$, $ValidationtSet$;
begin
    $line \leftarrow$ Read one line in $CsarPaper$;
    while $line > 0$ **do**
        Hash all words in $CsarPaper$ into digits;
        $Dict \leftarrow$ Add new words in $CsarPaper$ into dictionary;
        $TrainingSet \leftarrow$ Randomly choose 80 % $CsarPaper$;
        $ValidationtSet \leftarrow$ Randomly choose 20 % $CsarPaper$;
        $line \leftarrow$ Read one line in $CsarPaper$;

    $Model \leftarrow$ Compute and Save prediction model using $TrainingSet$;
    Output: $Model$, $ValidationtSet$

All words in papers with CCS categories are hashed into digits to save computation time and space. When building prediction model, Algorithm 1 computes the probability of each category and probability matrix for each category. Probability matrix stores all the category names and their probability data. The probability data include the words (in digits) and their probabilities.

When we have the prediction model, we can predict categories of papers in validation set, shown in Algorithm 2.

Algorithm 2. Procedure of Predicting Categories

Input:
Model, ValidationtSet;
Output:
PredictedCate, Precision, Recall, F_1 score;
begin

    Load prediction model *Model*;
    line ← Read one line in *ValidationtSet*;
    while *line* > 0 **do**
        Compute classification probability for each paper in *ValidationtSet* using *Model*;
        PredictedCate ← Find the category which the maximum probability belongs to;
        Compare *PredictedCate* with the *RealCate*;
        line ← Read one line in *ValidationtSet*;

    Compute *Precision, Recall, F_1 score*;
    Output: *PredictedCate, Precision, Recall, F_1 score*;

The paper information we use for classification includes paper titles, abstracts, and some extra information (conference session names and CSAR categories). In fact these fields show different importance, so when computing classification probability for each paper, we assign different weights to these fields. The weighted NB classifier tries to find the maximum value of Eq. 8. Here we just find one category with the highest score. Categorizing one paper into two or more classifications will be illustrated in our future work.

$$\max(\Psi(title_i, \alpha) + \Psi(abstract_i, \beta) + \Psi(extra_i, \gamma))$$
$$s.t.,$$
$$\alpha + \beta + \gamma = 3$$
(8)

where Ψ is the function that calculates the probability of each possible category, while $title_i$, $abstract_i$, and $extra_i$ represent the title, abstract, and extra information of i-th paper, respectively. α, β, and γ are the weights for title, abstract, and extra information, respectively. If α, β, and γ are all set as 1, it becomes unweighted naive Bayes (unweighted NB) classifier. We will give the assignments of them in Sect. 5.

4.3 Computational Complexity

The weighted NB classifier has a linear computational performance. If N is the number of paper samples, and M is the length of category table in CSAR classification system. The time complexity of training Bayes model is $O(MN)$, while the time complexity of predicting category is $O(M)$.

5 Evaluation

5.1 Experiment Overview

The experimental data are the 36344 papers from the Class A and Class B conferences recommended by CCF. There are totally 8834 papers with CSAR categories. We divide them into training set (7067 papers) and validation set (1767 papers). For the 27510 papers without CSAR categories, we use them as test set.

5.2 Comparative Algorithms

k-Nearest Neighbors (k-NN) algorithm is an efficient and commonly used classification algorithm, so we use it as a comparative algorithm. The k-NN algorithm compares each paper to be predicted with all the samples in the training set, so k is the number of all training samples, which is 7067. We define the similarity function as the number of common words both papers have. The more common words two papers have, the higher the similarity score is. We choose the category of the paper with the highest similarity score as the predicted category. Another comparative algorithm is unweighted NB algorithm.

5.3 Performance Evaluation

In our experiment, we compare our proposed weighted NB classifier with unweighted NB classifier and k-NN classifier. After some experiments, we empirically set the weights for α, β and γ as 1.1, 0.6 and 1.3, respectively. We use the same input for all the three methods. The total precision of classification is 79.01 % (weighted NB), 72.80 % (unweighted NB), 52.15 % (k-NN).

Now we check the precision of the three methods in some important categories, shown in Fig. 2. Weighted NB is still the best in the overwhelming majority situations. One important reason that weighted NB method is better than the other two methods is that the other two methods only utilize the statistics, while weighted NB wisely assigns the largest weight to the most important information.

We choose some categories to check the detailed precision, recall and F_1 score in weighted NB. Figure 3 depicts that the precision of these categories is generally good, but the recall is not always high. The F_1 score also reflects such phenomenon. We design the algorithm inclining to precision, not to recall. Because the purpose of us is to publish academic information by research fields, correctly

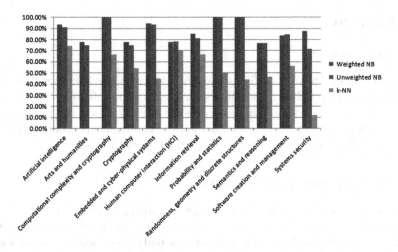

Fig. 2. Precision of some categories for weighted NB, unweighted NB and k-NN

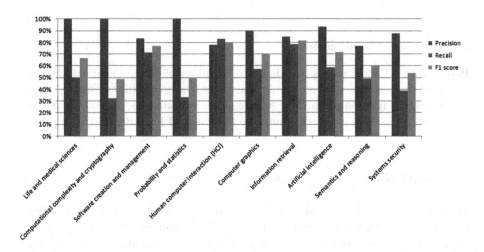

Fig. 3. The detailed performance of weighted NB classifier for some categories

mapping a paper to a category is more important than finding all potential categories of it (because some categories maybe wrong). So our algorithm mainly focuses on precision.

After evaluating the performance of the weighted NB classifier, we apply it to all the Class A and Class B papers. Now we can provide some helpful academic information by fields. When a researcher query academic information for certain area, CSAR can return the relevant academic information in this field, such as the top-cited papers in an area. The real returned results contain the information including conference name, year, authors, affiliations, authors' emails, reference information, URLs for cached full papers and other recommended information.

6 Discussion

6.1 Data Skew

In the experimental results, we found some categories had bad performance. Data skew should be responsible for it. Data skew means some categories have a lot of training samples, while others have very less. It greatly affects the classification results. If one category's hit rate is high, its training numbers is usually sufficient. Otherwise lack of sufficient training samples, the result is poor.

6.2 The Ambiguity of Classification

We found that even not hit, the predicted category may still have strong relations with the real categories. For example, the predicted category is *Machine learning*, and no such category in real categories, but there exists *Artificial intelligence* in real categories. We all know *Machine learning* is a branch of *Artificial intelligence*. They are strongly related, but our classifier doesn't hit.

6.3 Manual Classification

Papers with CCS categories are classified by humans, so the classification may be wrong or miss some categories. Although the low probability of wrong classification can be ignored when using a large number of samples, potentially missed categories in the real categories could be the cause of low hit rate that can not be neglected.

7 Conclusion

We propose a classification system for computer science called CSAR classification system, which is derived from 2012 ACM CCS, and propose a new weighted NB classifier to classify papers of top publications in computer science. Its performance is better than unweighted NB classifier and k-NN classifier. We also discuss the causes of unbalanced classification results and why we lose precision. We also apply weighted NB classifier to predict the categories of papers without CSAR categories. Now CSAR can provide academic information by research fields, and becomes a helpful academic platform leading you to the unfamiliar areas in computer science.

References

1. Shi, C., Quan, J., Li, M.: Information extraction for computer science academic rankings system. In: 2013 International Conference on Cloud and Service Computing (2013)

2. Zhao, J., Forouraghi, B.: An interactive and personalized cloud-based virtual learning system to teach computer science. In: 12th International Conference on Web-Based Learning (2013)

3. Kravcik, M., Wan, J.: Towards open corpus adaptive e-learning systems on the web. In: 12th International Conference on Web-Based Learning (2013)

4. 2012 ACM Computing Classification System. http://www.acm.org/about/class/class/2012

5. ACM Digital Library. http://dl.acm.org

6. IEEE Xplore Digital Library. http://ieeexplore.ieee.org/

7. Springer. http://www.springer.com

8. China Computer Federation. http://www.ccf.org.cn/sites/ccf/paiming.jsp

9. Google Scholar. http://scholar.google.com/

10. The DBLP Computer Science Bibliography. http://dblp.uni-trier.de/

11. Coulter, N., French, J., Glinert, E., Horton, T., Mead, N., Rada, R., Ralston, A., Rodkin, C., Rous, B., Tucker, A., Wegner, P., Weiss, E., Wierzbicki, C.: Computing classification system 1998: current status and future maintenance. Comput. Rev. **39**(1), 24–39 (1998)

12. Vesseya, I., Ramesha, V., Glassb, R.L.: A unified classification system for research in the computing disciplines. Inf. Softw. Technol. **47**(4), 245–255 (2005)

13. Kashireddy, S.D., Gauch, S., Billah, S.M.: Automatic class labeling for CiteSeerX. In: 2013 IEEE/WIC/ACM International Joint Conferences on Web Intelligence (WI) and Intelligent Agent Technologies (IAT), vol. 1, pp. 241–245 (2013)

14. Sriram, B., Fuhry, D., Demir, E., Ferhatosmanoglu, H., Demirbas, M.: Short Text classification in Twitter to improve information filtering. In: Proceedings of the 33rd International ACM SIGIR Conference on Research and Development in Information Retrieval (2010)

15. Zhang, Z., Lin, H., Li, P., Wang, H., Lu, D.: Improving semi-supervised text classification by using Wikipedia knowledge. In: The 14th International Conference on Web-Age Information Management (2013)

16. Chen, M., Jin, X., Shen, D.: Short text classification improved by learning multi-granularity topics. In: Proceedings of the Twenty-Second International Joint Conference on Artificial Intelligence, vol. 3, pp. 1776–1781 (2011)

17. Thirunavukkarasu, K.S., Sugumaran, S.: Analysis of classification techniques in data mining. Int. J. Eng. Sci. Res. Technol. 3740–3746 (2013)

18. Ibáñez, A., Bielza, C., Larrañaga, P.: Cost-sensitive selective naive Bayes classifiers for predicting the increase of the h-index for scientific journals. Neurocomputing **135**, 42–52 (2014)

19. Neetu: Hierarchical classification of web content using naive Bayes approach. Int. J. Comput. Sci. Eng. **5**(5), 402–408 (2013)

20. Wu, J., Cai, Z., Zeng, S., Zhu, X.: Artificial immune system for attribute weighted naive Bayes classification. In: The 2013 International Joint Conference on Neural Networks, pp. 1–8 (2013)

Supporting Educational Content Enrichment and Learning via Student-Created Definitions

Martin Svrček and Marián Šimko[✉]

Faculty of Informatics and Information Technologies,
Slovak University of Technology in Bratislava,
Ilkovičova 2, 842 16 Bratislava, Slovakia
{xsvrcekm, marian.simko}@stuba.sk

Abstract. Creating notes and annotations in educational content during learning helps students in better organization of learning materials. In addition, the provided content represents an interesting source of information for further processing, which can result into enrichment of the educational content or metadata. In this paper we report on new type of annotation - definition - in educational system ALEF – a mean for creating, accessing and rating definitions of key terms in a course by students themselves. We describe experiments conducted and present analysis of definitions provided by students of two courses at Slovak University of Technology.

Keywords: Definitions · Content enrichment · Annotation · Student collaboration

1 Introduction

Nowadays, utilization of elements of Web 2.0 in web-based education is de facto standard. Various educational systems allow students to tag, rate and/or comment on educational content they deliver, e.g. [2, 10, 16]. The student experience is being constantly improved. Richer system functionality on client-side gives a student more power, more competences and greater autonomy. The traditional role of a teacher in such environment has shifted and distinction between teacher and student blurs [4].

Collaboration in learning has many advantages and, in many scenarios, collaborative learning is more effective than individual learning [6]. In the context of collaborative learning, the Web has become a medium in which students ask for information, evaluate one another's ideas and monitor one another's work, regardless of their physical locations. These features are very important for the collaboration and make the web environment more interesting. There are many web-based educational systems, which support collaborative learning, either directly or indirectly, e.g. [5, 15, 16].

Interactive and collaborative web-based learning introduced multiple advancements that support learning experience. However, there are still many issues that are not paid much attention. When learning, students often encounter many new terms. And they want to or need to know what these terms mean – to acquire the new knowledge permanently or "just" to understand the context. They often need explanations, which should be linked to these terms and accessed instantly in case of need. In this paper,

© Springer International Publishing Switzerland 2014
Y. Cao et al. (Eds.): ICWL 2014 Workshops, LNCS 8699, pp. 44–54, 2014.
DOI: 10.1007/978-3-319-13296-9_5

we see *definitions* as a special type of in-text annotation that can be created by students. Our aim is to research how beneficial student-created definitions are for students and their learning experience. In addition, we want to explore the potential of student-created definitions for semi-automatic domain modeling and follow up the preceding research on this topic [7]. We take advantage of existing popular adaptive collaborative web-based educational system ALEF [15] and implement definitions as a new type of annotation within ALEF.

The rest of the paper is structured as follows. Section 2 covers related work. In Sect. 3 we describe our approach – definitions as proposed to support learning and their realization in the educational system ALEF. In Sect. 4 we report findings from a conducted experiment. In Sect. 5 we summarize the paper and conclude our work.

2 Related Work

Web 2.0 introduced a plethora of possibilities how to make student experience during learning better. Various forms of tools and learning helpers were developed starting with content taggers [1, 8, 9, 13], components and tools supporting social interaction and feedback [2, 5, 14], collaborative content creation [14, 15] and resulting into a learning-specific tasks supporters [2].

ALEF is a system with many features that support interactive collaborative learning [15]. It contains several specialized widgets facilitating various learning-specific activities. The activities include content tagging [13], discussions, educational content errors reporting, student questions creation [2], and external resources linking [12].

To mention relevant works related to tagging, SemKey represents a system with support for such functionality [9]. Tags offer more information and determine relationships between concepts and resources. The tags are used to enrich the content but also to enhance the search. SemKey uses other sources and thus solves the problems with similar tags. A hybrid recommender system in [8] uses tagging and concept maps as a basis for recommendation. Users can organize content by adding tags, they construct representation of concepts and concept maps. These activities represent their knowledge and skills. The collaborative tagging system OATS is a tool for efficient navigation and organization of educational content [1].

CoWeb is a collaborative learning environment based on the Wiki allowing editing and creating pages with the learning content [14]. Students can discuss their problems by adding comments to the educational content. The main objective of the system is to improve and accelerate learning through these features. COALE is collaborative and adaptive learning environment aimed at dynamic learning organization of teaching through personalized recommendations [5]. The users solves the task, discuss each other and the system (based on its activities) shows recommendations.

Nowadays, there are many educational interactive and/or collaborative web-based systems. Although they – in many cases – utilize various forms of interaction, or directly or indirectly benefit from collaboration during learning, there still is a space for supporting students during learning-specific tasks. In our case, we see the need of students to obtain instant information about the concepts (represented by relevant domain terms) during learning in an educational system. Our goal is to provide students definitions of these terms in one place without the need for search. We take advantage of implicit collaboration (such as rating, voting) for filtering and selecting the most useful definitions for students.

3   Definitions: Collaborative Learning Content Enrichment

We propose a new type of annotation within the educational system ALEF. This new type of annotation we refer to as *definition*. The definition annotation serves as an explanation of some concept. It consists of two parts: (1) a *term* being defined, and (2) the term's *explanation*.

The motivation behind considering definitions as annotations (and not in another form – e.g., a simple list of terms assigned to a course) is two-fold:

– Annotations in ALEF are created on per-document basis, i.e., we can track to what learning object an annotation was created. As a result, definition-learning object relationships may emphasize defined term's importance for the learning object.
– Students are familiar with user interface in ALEF which supports and facilitates work with annotations and are used to it. Various forms of other annotations are very popular among students using ALEF such as highlights, user questions or external resources [2]. Several UI components supporting annotation creation and accessing were developed, including in-text presentation, sidebar, filter and annotation widgets, and are available for developers.

By introducing definition annotations to ALEF, we expect students to have a convenient way to access, navigate in and acquire relevant domain terms – an important building block of knowledge about a subject domain. A scenario when a student does not fully understand important terms can be seen especially at the beginning of a course, when he or she just starts to learn. In this case, definitions are a great advantage. They provide an explanation of the concepts and, therefore, the student can better understand the intent of educational documents. Our approach constitutes an alternative to traditional forms of looking up for desired information.

When compared to full-text search, the advantage is speed of lookup in terms of number of actions – the elements of user interface (UI) for annotations in ALEF are suited to access annotations much faster, e.g., via specialized annotation widgets. In addition, in contrast with search results, definition lookup results in explicit information of term-explanation pairs and it is more suitable for scenarios where a student does not understand a term and wants to learn it directly, without the necessity to explore multiple search results. We will describe the mentioned UI for accessing definitions in more detail later. When compared to other type of annotation – tags, which represent an explicit form of information contained within a learning object and often overlap with relevant domain terms, definitions' advantage is that they contain explanatory part, which tags do not.

Another problem is the diversity of interpretations of terms. In a typical case, if a student does not understand some term, he looks for a solution on the Web. But on the Web, one can find the term to have several meanings in different domains. Therefore, it is very convenient to obtain information directly from the educational system, as the information there (provided or checked by teachers) are usually relevant.

Utilizing definitions by students is not the only advantage of our proposed concept. By *creating* definitions within educational content, students themselves contribute to learning process and strengthen their knowledge even more. Besides providing benefits to students, students' activity can bring value to the educational content as well. By creating definitions, students both: identify important terms for a learning object (as well as the whole course), and provide explicit explanations for such terms. This information can be used to improve domain model of the course (a form of metadata layer [2, 3] that is typically utilized in advanced content processing, e.g., information filtering or recommendation [8, 11]).

Now we describe definition annotations from two perspectives: (1) creating a definition, (2) accessing a definition.

Creating Definitions

To support creation of definitions, we considered two scenarios. In the first scenario, our intent is to encourage students to find term definitions within the educational system ALEF. In the second scenario, a student creates a definition "from the scratch". Based on the scenarios, we differentiate two definition types:

1. ALEF definition (AD) – a definition, where the source of explanation is learning content available within the educational system ALEF, i.e., explicit explanatory texts that can be added as definitions are already present in the content. To create ALEF definition, students select some text in the learning content and assign a definition to it. We support this type of annotation since definitions of many terms are often present within the educational content that is part of a course being learned. The important thing to note here is that although many definitions (i.e., terms with explanations) are already present in the content, they are often not explicit and students may have a problem to recognize them as domain relevant terms at all.

   In order to add definition from the educational content, a student selects text in a document and invokes Create definition dialog from popup menu (see Fig. 1, left) by clicking Add definition icon. Student fills definition name attribute and view type attribute (private/public). After confirmation, the system saves the added definition and displays it.

2. Own definition (OD) – a definition, where the source of explanation is outside ALEF, e.g., it originates from an external source somewhere on the Web.

   Students can use a set of dedicated forms (one is a part of annotation browser, see Fig. 1, bottom right) to fill all necessary attributes (term, explanation, private/public) and optionally associate it with some content.

Note that these two types of definitions are not explicitly differentiated in the UI. We differentiate them automatically based on actions that led to creating the annotation.

The advantage of adding ALEF definitions (AD) is that the quality of definition is high. In fact, it potentially is as high as the quality of underlying educational materials. However, this could be also considered disadvantage if the materials are not good or if they do not "fit" student knowledge level. Definitions created by students in such case may be confusing and "disorganized". Additional advantage is speed of creation. Creating ALEF definitions is fast as a student needs to perform only several mouse clicks (in the best case) or edit a definition to a minimal extent.

A definition created by a student on his own (OD) – by "producing" it himself or copying it from external source – has no minimal level of quality assured and has to be further evaluated. On the other hand, Own definitions have a greater potential to enrich educational content within the system and to introduce important information missed by students.

In order to make definitions have an educational value for students, we need to assure that they are not incorrect. This particularly applies for Own definitions (OD). For definitions added from external sources, it is important to evaluate their overall correctness. This can be done e.g., by employing student rating. We believe that ratings will allow students to determine the accuracy or inaccuracy of the definition.

The advantage of our concept of definitions is the concentration of structured domain relevant information in one place. If a student has all the necessary information in one place, he may not need to look for them on the Web. In this context, our aim is to make definition annotations to be accessed more easily: for this purpose we employed text highlighting and created a dedicated widget by utilizing ALEF's annotation framework.

Accessing Definitions

In ALEF, access to annotations is provided by means of four basic UI elements [2]:

1. *In-text interaction and presentation* – provides the ability to work with annotations directly in the educational text. Annotations may be set up to be visually differentiated (e.g., highlighted) directly in the text, which makes them easy to use.
2. *Sidebar* – provides the ability to view annotations directly next to the learning content (in a slim side strip). Hence, annotations do not interfere with text, but they are visibly assigned to it – marks where annotation occurs are created on per-line basis.
3. *Annotation browsers* – also known as "widgets". Enable to view and access all annotations of the same type in one place.
4. *Annotation filter* – allows students to manage what type of annotations they want to be visible during learning.

We used all the four basic elements (see also Fig. 8 in [2]) to implement user interface elements displaying and accessing definitions.

The most important UI element to interact with all definition annotations in a selected course is Definition widget (see Fig. 1, right). It allows filtering of annotations according to basic properties. Users can select from *my own/all* definitions (reflecting private/public attributes) and *document/course* definitions. Users then can search in pre-filtered results by using fast auto-complete textbox. After selecting particular definition (represented by a term) from the result list, all definitions provided by students to the term will be displayed. Each definition can be rated by clicking well known +/− buttons.

We consider the whole life cycle of definition as a collaborative process: one student creates a definition, others rate it. This can be viewed as a form of implicit collaboration [2].

It is important to note that in ALEF, several user actions can be set up to contribute to activity score maintained for each student. A comprehensive score computation engine has been created in ALEF. The engine derives user score in almost real time based on user actions in the system and configuration of user action importance coefficients set by a teacher. Note that we set these coefficients to have default values for definition-related actions, not particularly favoring these actions to be exploited by students to get higher score (cf. [2] for score computation).

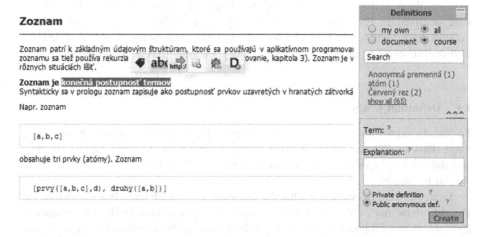

Fig. 1. Creating definition in ALEF: Selected text and popup window for adding definitions in the learning object named List (Zoznam) (on the left hand side). Definition widget (annotation browser for definitions) (on the right hand side). Content of the course is in Slovak language.

4   Evaluation

In order to evaluate our approach and confirm our assumptions, we need to perform several experiments in real world setting of educational system ALEF. Our aim is to collect definitions from students during learning in educational system ALEF, analyze them and asses their impact on learning process as well as assess usability and quality of provided definitions for potential domain model enrichment.

We have conducted an uncontrolled mid-term experiment involving two educational courses: Functional and Logic programming and Principles of Software Engineering at our faculty (the both courses contain supporting educational materials in ALEF). The experiment lasted about eight weeks – it started at about the half of the summer semester (April 16th 2014) and finished at the time of the final exams in those courses (June 12th 2014). We have expected students to be internally motivated to use definitions since this period includes the most mid-term exams as well as the final exams. During this period, our tool had been introduced to the students to better organize their learning material, to potentially help them better prepare for exams. In addition, the new feature in ALEF was intensively propagated to approach students, which did not use ALEF very often.

Our two basic research questions' groups in this evaluation were:

– *Definition usage.* Are definitions as a new type of annotations interesting for students? Do they attract them in terms of learning assistance?
– *Definition accuracy.* How accurate and correct definitions provide students? Are students able to filter out less accurate definitions collaboratively by rating them?

The questions actually represent quantitative and qualitative aspect of the evaluation. We present results of evaluation divided according to the two courses. 227 students were involved in the course Functional and Logic Programming (FLP), 42 students were involved in Principles of Software Engineering (PSE). Together 244 unique students were involved in both courses (25 students were involved in both courses). FLP or PSE consists of 113 or 159 explanatory learning objects, respectively.

4.1 Definition Usage

To find an answer to the first group of research questions, we explored the question usage statistics. We particularly focused on the number of added definitions. During the first half of the experiment, the students added 492 definitions (2.02 definitions per student in average).

First, we were interested in what the proportion of ALEF and Own definitions is. The data show that 74 % of all definitions were ALEF definitions (AD). The remaining 26 % were Own definitions (OD, see Table 1). These numbers confirm our expectations that students prefer to look for definitions within the educational system. Another interesting finding is that despite the higher difficulty of creating Own definitions when compared to ALEF definitions (in terms of number of actions that need to be performed), the students added in average one quarter of all definitions as Own definitions. This suggests that the students did not find terms considered to be domain relevant explained explicitly in the course material. They either did not find them at all or did not find them in a form explicit enough or formally expressed clearly enough to be added as ALEF definitions. This may be an indicator that some educational course parts should be improved or reformulated.

Second, we were interested in student rating behavior. Students can collectively determine which definitions are correct and which are not by rating them + or – (see Sect. 3). However, the students did not use the feature as much as we expected. They provided ratings to only 22 % of definitions, allowing us not to derive any significant conclusions. The small number of ratings could be explained by the following causes: (1) A small length of the experiment for the students to fully discover the potential of rating and to take advantage of it to promote correct definitions (and also improve owns score). No 'critical' mass of ratings was delivered by the students to efficiently filter between good and bad definitions. (2) The small number of multiple definitions of one term was present in the course, which did not motivated the students enough to differentiate between good and bad definitions of the term. (3) The definition-related actions' importance coefficients reflecting into activity points counting to the overall student score in ALEF were set incorrectly, motivating the students not enough to rate definitions. The causes 1 and 2 could be overcome by conducting a longer experiment

Table 1. Overall definition usage statistics.

	All def. [count]	ALEF d. (AD) [count | ratio]	Own d. (OD) [count | ratio]	Def. with at least one rating (+/−)	Students enrolled
PSE	347	240 | 0.69	107 | 0.31	59 | 0.17	227
FLP	145	125 | 0.86	20 | 0.14	48 | 0.33	42
Total	492	365 | 0.74	127 | 0.26	107 | 0.22	244

and by motivating students to rate definitions utilizing other means (e.g. by changing presentation of good and bad definitions). We can eliminate the cause 3 by adjusting weight of rating actions in ALEF based on comprehensive usage data analysis from the experiment.

In general, we consider the obtained evidence on definition usage very encouraging. We expect even more "creational" activity from students after definition rating will be adopted better. The aforementioned findings deal mainly with the quantity of the provided definitions. It is also important to evaluate the quality of the definitions to reveal their potential for both students and domain modeling.

4.2   Definition Accuracy

In order to evaluate the accuracy of definitions, we focused on two aspects of definitions and tried to answer the following questions: 1. To what extent the provided definitions represent relevant domain terms? 2. How accurate are explanations of the terms provided in explanation part of definitions?

To answer the first question, we compared the students' definitions with relevant domain terms from domain models in ALEF. A domain model in ALEF represents a form of semantic description of the educational content. It is used for advanced services in the system such as recommendation [11]. A domain model of each course consists of relevant domain terms, relationships of various types between them and mapping of relevant domain terms to learning objects. In our case, we took relevant domain terms and considered them to be the gold standard for comparison with the terms from the definitions created by the students. Domain models of courses in ALEF were created by domain experts independently of the current experiment. For this part of evaluation, we consider the relevant domain terms from both courses. The total number of relevant domain terms is 580.

After filtering definitions' terms, we obtained 394 unique definition terms. 225 are relevant domain terms. This makes precision of 0.57 and recall of 0.39. Again, the obtained numbers are very promising. We expect that the overall coverage of relevant domain terms by student-provided definitions can help students in acquiring domain relevant vocabulary and will make it possible to use definitions for navigating in the course. The obtained precision and recall confirm the potential of our approach towards at least partial enrichment of the domain model. The definitions' explanations would be an ideal candidate for an *intentional* description of learning concepts represented by relevant domain terms and may result in richer domain model allowing the educational system to provide more accurate services. However, we also need to assess the correctness of the explanations, which definitions include. This is one of the most important points of our verification.

In order to evaluate definitions' correctness, we let two domain experts to assess it. In this part of evaluation, we considered the Functional and Logic Programming course only. The domain experts rated the 110 definitions in the course in terms of three basic characteristics: correctness, conciseness and domain-related importance. Each of these characteristics was evaluated at interval of 1–5, where lower values represent more negative rating.

The average ratings of the experts are presented in Table 2. We consider the average correctness 3.86 to be highly satisfactory and it is in line with expectations resulting from the previous parts of the experiment. The average conciseness partially confirms our concern about the form of term explanations in the educational courses (note that 86 % of definitions were ALEF definitions, cf. Table 1). However, we again expect improvement in this aspect in line with the higher utilization of ratings by students.

The most important result of expert evaluation is, however, domain importance rating. Domain importance can be considered an a posteriori variant of precision measure from the gold standard evaluation, i.e., it assesses to what extent definitions (more precisely, terms that are defined) are domain relevant. The average value 4.58 is quite inconsistent with a finding from the previous part of the experiment as it is much more encouraging. It may suggest that the gold standard may not fit for this task ideally as it contains relevant domain terms at different level of granularity. This can also be an indication that the domain model can be really improved this way.

Table 2. The average values of the characteristics as rated by domain experts (1-worst, 5-best).

Characteristic	Correctness	Conciseness	Domain importance
Average rating	3.86	3.92	4.58

5 Conclusions and Future Work

In this paper we presented our approach to support educational content enrichment via definition annotations, which are created by students during learning. We described the core idea of our approach and provided description about its realization within educational system ALEF. We are not aware of similar approaches among the state-of-the-art and we consider the potential of definitions for both learning and metadata enrichment to be worth researching.

We evaluated our approach by conducting a real-world experiment involving students of two courses at Slovak University of Technology in Bratislava. The results are very encouraging and confirm the majority of expectations we had. In the context of usability, accuracy and relevance of the provided definitions, we have achieved very satisfactory results making definitions very promising tool to support learning. A task remaining to be finished is to prove that the students themselves can determine the accuracy of the definitions by means of "default" social interaction known from social networks, i.e., by rating. Due to the small number of definitions' ratings collected to date, we cannot accept this assumption yet. However, the rest of results allow us to draw the following conclusions. Definitions:

- are an interesting form of learning support in the educational system with a potential to be used with benefits by students intensively,
- when added by students, they are in most cases correct and have a true potential to help students in learning; information that students can gain from definitions provided by other peers will in most cases provide valuable and relevant information,
- indeed have the potential to enrich a domain model of a course, and, as a result, improve accuracy of services of the educational system that are based on the domain model, such as metadata-based recommendation of learning objects.

We see the great potential that our definitions bring into the educational system ALEF. They can significantly help students in order to understand the subject-matter. However, further experiments have to be conducted to provide stronger evidence on definitions' positive influence. Many additional research hypotheses should be formulated to study the impact on both learning process and automated domain model enrichment in more depth. Our further steps after the semester will involve qualitative evaluation and interviews with students. We will analyze the gathered data and will study rating behavior of students during learning in ALEF. This topic can be further extended into different research directions. They include incorporation of teachers in the various processes of definition manipulation or exploration of possibilities that enrichment of domain model poses.

Acknowledgments. This work was partially supported by grants No. VG1/0675/11, KEGA 009STU-4/2014, and APVV-0208-10.

References

1. Bateman, S., et al.: Oats: the open annotation and tagging system. In: Proceedings of the International Scientific Conference of the Learning Object Repository Research Network (2006)
2. Bieliková, M., et al.: ALEF: from application to platform for adaptive collaborative learning. In: Manouselis, N., et al. (eds.) Recommender Systems for Technology Enhanced Learning, pp. 195–225. Springer Science + Business Media, New York (2014)
3. Brusilovsky, P.: Developing adaptive educational hypermedia systems: from design models to authoring tools. In: Murray, T., Blessing, S., Ainsworth, S. (eds.) Authoring Tools for Advanced Technology Learning Environments, pp. 377–409. Springer, Berlin (2003)
4. Downes, S.: E-learning 2.0. ACM eLearn Mag. **10**(1), 93–103 (2005)
5. Furugori, N., et al.: COALE: collaborative and adaptive learning environment. In: Proceedings of the Conference on Computer Support for Collaborative Learning: Foundations for a CSCL Community, pp. 493–494. International Society of the Learning Sciences (2002)
6. Gokhale, A.A.: Collaborative learning enhances critical thinking. J. Technol. Educ. **7**(1), 22–30 (1995)
7. Harinek, J., Šimko, M.: Improving term extraction by utilizing user annotations. In: Proceedings of 13th ACM Symposium on Document Engineering, pp. 185–188 (2013)

8. Kardan, A.A., Abbaspour, S., Hendijanifard, F.: A hybrid recommender system for e-learning environments based on concept maps and collaborative tagging. In: Proceedings of the 4th International Conference on Virtual Learning ICVL, pp. 300–307 (2009)
9. Marchetti, A. et al.: Semkey: a semantic collaborative tagging system. In: Workshop on Tagging and Metadata for Social Information Organization at WWW, pp. 8–12 (2007)
10. Meccawy, M., Blanchfield, P., Ashman, H., Brailsford, T., Moore, A.: WHURLE 2.0: adaptive learning meets web 2.0. In: Dillenbourg, P., Specht, M. (eds.) EC-TEL 2008. LNCS, vol. 5192, pp. 274–279. Springer, Heidelberg (2008)
11. Michlík, P., Bieliková, M.: Exercises recommending for limited time learning. Procedia Comput. Sci. 1(2), 2821–2828 (2010)
12. Miháľ, V., Bieliková, M.: Domain model relations discovering in educational texts based on user created annotations. In: IEEE 14th International Conference on Interactive Collaborative Learning (ICL), pp. 542–547 (2011)
13. Móro, R., et al.: Towards collaborative metadata enrichment for adaptive web-based learning. In: Proceedings of the 2011 IEEE/WIC/ACM International Conference on Web Intelligence and Intelligent Agent Technology, vol. 3, pp. 106–109. IEEE CS (2011)
14. Rick, J., et al.: Collaborative learning at low cost: CoWeb use in English composition. In: Proceedings of the Conference on Computer Support for Collaborative Learning: Foundations for a CSCL Community, pp. 435–442. International Society of the Learning Sciences (2002)
15. Šimko, M., Barla, M., Bieliková, M.: ALEF: a framework for adaptive web-based learning 2.0. In: Reynolds, N., T-S, M. (eds.) KCKS 2010. IFIP AICT, vol. 324, pp. 367–378. Springer, Heidelberg (2010)
16. Su, A., et al.: A Web 2.0-based collaborative annotation system for enhancing knowledge sharing in collaborative learning environments. Comput. Educ. 55(2), 752–766 (2010)

2014 International Workshop on Peer-Review, Peer-Assessment, and Self-Assessment in Education

Using Peer Assessment
with Educational Robots

Dave Catlin[(✉)]

CEO Valiant Technology Ltd., 3, Grange Mills, Weir Road,
London SW12 0NE, UK
dave@valiant-technology.com

Abstract. Educational robots offer tremendous potential for providing exciting, dynamic learning experiences in K-12 Education. The constructionist notions of Piaget, Papert and others underpin the use of this technology. A problem exists in ensuring successful lessons using these paradigms. The root of that problem is the imagination, curiosity and creativity of students. How can that be given free reign while at the same time trying to meet the rigid demands of a school curriculum subjected to the hegemony of high-stake-testing? Seminal work by Black and Wiliams summarized what can be called good teaching practice – the key to resolving this conundrum. Their development of Assessment for Learning (AfL) strategies offers a way of structuring lessons while fostering essential intellectual freedom of the student. Peer assessment is a key part of AfL. This paper explains and illustrates how peer and self-assessment is an intrinsic aspect of educational robotic activities.

Keywords: Peer assessment · Self-assessment · Educational robots · Constructionism · Papert · LOGO · Turtles · Roamer · Assessment for learning · AFI · Black and Wiliams · TWR · Teaching with robots

1 Introduction

The aim of this paper is to explain the role of peer and self-assessment (PASA) in the successful use of educational robots. It is not a review of the value of PASA; it is about how PASA is applied with educational robots. The first part of the paper briefly summarizes relevant aspects of educational robotics. It describes some of the issues that effective use of technology has to address. It has been proposed that Assessment for Learning (AfL) will resolve these problems [1]. PASA is a key part of AfL methodology. The rest of this paper illustrates through examples how these assessment processes are a natural part of work with educational robots.

2 Educational Robots

In 1970, Seymour Papert invented the first educational robots called Turtles [2]. Students controlled the robot by writing programs in LOGO, a computer language developed especially for education. It is a constructionist tool, providing an environment aimed at helping students improve their ability to learn. It is also a philosophy of

© Springer International Publishing Switzerland 2014
Y. Cao et al. (Eds.): ICWL 2014 Workshops, LNCS 8699, pp. 57–65, 2014.
DOI: 10.1007/978-3-319-13296-9_6

education opposed to what Papert termed instructionism where the teacher acts as a dispenser of knowledge [3]. This does not mean the teacher should never tell children things; Papert called that idea silly [4]. What he suggested was the creation of microworlds: learning environments which were rich in ideas and challenges that motivated the children to become explorers of knowledge. LOGO and the Turtle were explorer's tools. The teacher becomes a guide whose purpose is to ensure the student maximizes their learning experience. It is wrong to think that because LOGO and Turtles have been around for a long time, that these are yesterday's ideas. Papert's work created a paradigm in the Kuhnian sense, that is still relevant today.

In 1989 the development in the UK of Roamer followed by PIP put a simplified derivative of LOGO into a Turtle. Students programmed these robots using on-board keypads. Modern robots like the current Roamer, still use the programming paradigm, but facilitate more natural interactions using HCI, HRI and tangible computing technologies. This paper focuses on these Turtle type robots, not the construction type robots like Lego (launched in 1999). There are overlaps, between the two types, but as a rule-of-thumb, TWR (teaching with robots) is the forte of Turtle type robots and TR (Teaching robotics) is the province of construction type robots.

Activities and robots that conform to Educational Robotic Applications (ERA) Principles provide the opportunity for students to be active learners in an environment that encourages thinking, creativity, curiosity and the development of imagination [5]. The claim is that they do this by providing students with concrete constructivist experiences which when linked to traditional teaching can enhance and deepen a student's understanding of curriculum content. ERA principles homogeneously combine to provide a community based learning environment which has the ideal mixture of Learner, Knowledge and Assessment elements [6]. The connection between ERA and PASA is made in the conclusions.

3 Praxis Problems

Clements and Sharma claim that if implemented correctly LOGO provides an educational environment that has few equals [7]. Yet improperly implemented, its results can be trivial. Others also report this inconsistency and discussed the various issues that affect the implementation of LOGO [8, 9]. Papert said of his creation, not everything done in the name of LOGO is in the spirit of LOGO [10]; essentially he is referring to people using constructionist tools in an instructionist way. When children are exploring things, they will get ideas and inspirations that were not in the teaching plan. You now have engaged enthusiastic learners. Whether their ideas are good or bad, the potential for learning is enormous. But the strictures of the curriculum urge you strangle this eagerness and move on.

The easy option is to shortchange our children and teach to test. It takes a lot of courage and confidence to implement the constructionist approach intrinsic in educational robots. Clements and Sharma point out; it also requires the buy in of administrators, curriculum developers, teachers and students. The teacher is the key. It is recognized that teaching is both an art and a skill. This has nothing to do with robots.

See the exemplar Fleet Circus – a design technology project run by an exceptional teacher Trevor Thompson [11]. This project perfectly illustrates a teacher nurturing the imagination and creativity of students and still delivering good test results. The challenge is how do you capture that? AfL offers an answer.

4   Assessment for Learning (AfL)

Professors Paul Black and Dylan Wiliam of Kings College, London claimed that governments judge school performance by treating them as though they were a black box [12]. They monitor what they put into schools (investment) and what they get out (return) measured by what has become called high stakes testing. Black and Wiliam's research focused what went on inside this black box, specifically what went on inside the classroom: the mechanics of what transforms input into output. How does a teacher interact with the student? What type of interactions will help raise standards? Clearly the answer is epitomized in Trevor Thompson. AfL essentially codifies his good practice. AfL consist of four elements – see Table 1 adapted from Smith [13].

Table 1. Elements of AfL

Element	Explanation
Learning intentions	The student's perspective on what they are learning
Success criteria	How will the student recognise when they have successfully completed the assignment
Quality interactions and feedback	Understanding in real time if the students understand or are confused by anything in the lesson. How the teacher responds to the feedback, interacting with student to help improve their educational experience
Peer Assessment and Self-Assessment	What students think about their work and the work of their classmates – conducted in a way that helps improve the quality of their understanding

5   Peer and Self-Assessment with Educational Robots (PASA)

5.1   Methodology

The section illustrates how PASA is an intrinsic aspect of educational robotics, and how a range of methods of implementing PASA can be integrated into educational robotic activities. These are presented through a series of activities. The activities are described and then the PASA element discussed. Most of these examples are supported with online materials which provide more information. The examples are drawn from Valiant Technology's research archive which contains over 30 years of work with schools all over the world. Although most of the activities relate to work done with the educational robot Roamer, the principles apply to any similar robot system. Moreover, the examples are not singular occurrences; they are representative of a wide range of exemplars. First let us look at some early research findings.

5.2   Early Research on Floor Turtles

Between September 1987 and December 1988 a National Floor Turtle project was run in the UK involving schools in 21 participating education districts [14]. This research used 350 Turtle type robots, all programmed from LOGO on the computer and supplied by different companies. It was done at a time before any academic concept of AfL or PASA existed. Some of its conclusions heralded the future:

- One of the difficulties faced by teachers was knowing when to intervene, and when to allow children the freedom to make and learn by their 'mistakes'.
- It was a feature of early work in project schools that teachers tended to set tasks for children to carry out, whilst they gained experience in the use of LOGO and the floor Turtle. Later, it was evident that teachers had gained sufficient confidence to permit children to initiate their own activities.
- The two most common areas where the participating teachers note improvement were in the children's involvement in their work and their interaction with each other. Greater self-confidence, fewer inhibitions, and more practical activity leading to easier discussions were all identified.

This illustrates four key issues:

- The nature of teacher involvement
- Ability of students to manage their work
- Students engagement
- The interaction between students and student confidence.

All of these points contribute to an environment that supports PASA.

5.3   Robot Activities and the Role of the Teacher

PASA is a natural aspect of most robotic activities. In the activity The Adventures of Myrtle the Turtle a scenario is set where the robot travels back in time and meets various people. In the process she helps invent geometry. In the first activity she meets a caveman trying to build a bridge across a river. She helps by swimming across the river and telling him how far she went. The children program the robot to move forward a number. The number represents the distance travelled by the robot. The student has to decide on a unit, estimate the distance, test that estimate with the robot. Chris Gregory explains, "*Practical measurement of length, weight, capacity, etc. is a common feature of early mathematics work. Unfortunately this often becomes the manipulation of standard units and the use of ready-made measuring devices.*" He goes onto explain how using a robot engages the students with all the basic facets of measurement from choosing units to deciding whether they have a viable answer given the practical context [15].

With robots students normally work in groups. Valiant's research has noted that even simple activities like this involve the students sharing, discussing and evaluating each other's ideas on an almost continuous basis.

The teacher's role in this process is that of observer and facilitator or guide. The notion of teacher as a facilitator or guide has become common currency.

The importance of observation is less prominent. Deputy head Anne Butler from Hotwells Primary School in Bristol, England stressed the value of stopping teaching and watching and listening to the children. Robot activities provide the teacher that opportunity. The interactions students to student and students to robot become public. The teacher can observe this and decide whether or not to intervene and what form that intervention should take. Sometimes the students simply need factual information or clarification. But on other occasions they need to think more deeply about an issue. The teacher can encourage this through a series of techniques called "effective questioning" [16]. The aim this type of interaction is not to get the pupils to providing answers, but to promote a debate amongst the group about a relevant area of knowledge. Another situation, where students present their thoughts to scrutiny of their peers.

5.4 Star Wars Activity

ICT teacher Nick Flint decided to use Roamer in a Star Wars Project. This activity took place at Maple Cross School in Rickmansworth, London. It was part of a week where the focus was on Art and Design, Math and English. The class consisted of Year 5 and Year 6 students (9–11 years old) [17].

A lot of robot projects involve significant amounts on non-robotic work. This particular project started with an Art and Design activity where the pupils made a Star Wars town. Valiant researchers visited on the day students were scheduled to script and produce robot videos. The students had never used the robot before, so they also had to learn how to program it. The classes were split into production groups. Initially each student was tasked with drafting an outline script for the video. The next part brought the team together in a script meeting. In this session each student presented their ideas, which was reviewed by the team. Following this assessment the group selected a script for development. In one case a team chose to amalgamate two ideas. The teams then spent the rest of the day learning to program the robot and producing the video [18].

PASA was a continuous aspect the day's interactions. Students were faced with problems, had ideas about solving them, shared their ideas and discoveries. The other team members reviewed the ideas provided feedback and eventually decided how to proceed. Three adults were involved working with the students, but their role was largely time management and answering technical questions when asked by the different teams. This type of scenario is common with robotic activities. An essential characteristic for success is an affirmative learning environment where students trust each other's comments and opinions. It is a positive aspect of peer assessment that it is easier to accept criticism from your fellow students, than it is from adults. Maple Cross had obviously worked hard on developing that attitude amongst its students. This did not mean the day was without it traumas. One child (who has a difficult home environment and noted personal problems) did get upset and destroyed his model building. What was impressive was the way the teachers and students dealt with the situation. After an hour the pupil was back on task receiving positive support from his peers.

After the event, Nick Flint set the students the task of writing a news article about the day. This idea represents a great opportunity to engage students in reflective thought. We plan to investigate how we can structure this type of task so that students do more than present a narrative of the day, but encourage them to assess their learning [19].

5.5   Self-Realization

In the late 1990s Professor Christian Sarralié of CNFEI in France reported working with adolescent students who had been brain damaged in automobile accidents. One student had lost the ability to perform simple arithmetical operations. He could not accept this situation and indeed in his mind he was a top performing math student, despite contrary evidence in his education record. The pliability of the brain and the nature of their condition meant that he could regain much of his mathematical ability. However, he reacted aggressively when teachers tried to engage him in basic primary school math. The teacher then gave him an activity using the Roamer robot. This required him to perform some basic arithmetical operations. The robot's non-judgmental neutrality acted as a mirror, reflecting his thinking [20]. His assessment of his mathematical knowledge radically transformed making him amenable to the learning process.

5.6   Internal Dialog Externalized

Valiant once received a report from a school in Northern Ireland that the teachers had noticed a young girl talking to the Roamer as if it were a pet. They realised from the conversation that the child was suffering abuse. They took appropriate action.

MIT's Sherry Turkle describes how our contact with the world and the concrete objects in it, evoke thoughts, feelings and emotions [21]. Turkle is also one of a number of researchers who have investigated how this phenomenon applies to robots [22]. It is an aspect of the ERA Engagement Principle that students form a bond with the robot. Even though they know it is a machine they act with it as if it were sentient. This phenomenon is not confined to young children. Turkle's research looked at robots as cyber-companions with the elderly. What Turkle has shown is that the dialog tends to reflect the child's inner concerns and struggles. For example one pupil who had a medical condition was persistently making sure the robot was well looked after. Although it is not strictly PASA, it does indicate mental processes which a skilled educational psychologist might be able to use to help a student. It is also an indication of the future potential of robots to become more than a passive peer reflecting a student's ideas.

5.7   Design Process, Inspiration and Show and Tell

The Dog House activity challenges the children to make a robot dog. This is a good example of the ERA Pedagogical Principle. It involves students in a range of different types of tasks: research on animals and dogs in particular, observation of dog behaviour, and analysis of data, mathematical modelling, programming, testing and debugging the programs. Creating a robot dog is like creating an animated sculpture. It is not a dog; it's a robot that makes you think of a dog [23].

This activity illustrates four ways educational robots engage PASA. The first two of these are inherent in the Design Process. All designs go through a recognizable set of phases, starting with the specification; what do I want to design? Gathering information, thinking of possible designs, evaluating these ideas, designing, making the design, testing and modifying and finally evaluating and reviewing the design. At each stage all previous decisions are reviewed. For example, do I get an idea that makes me want to change the specification? In the Dog House activity the students worked on individual projects, so this was an exercise in the students assessing their work and improving it based on those assessments. The dynamics would have been different if it was a group project and the process would be a peer assessment process.

Robots are highly visible and students notice what other students or groups are doing. It is quite natural for students to be inspired by the work of others. In the traditional classroom this might be deemed copying. In this environment it is learning. An excellent example in occurred in the Fleet Circus Project. Some of the boys had noticed the girls making characters out of Flymo clay. This made heavy figures they wanted for their design. They not only used the same materials, but they spontaneously 'subcontracted' the girls to help them make the parts they needed!

At the end of an activity like this you can hold a "Dog Show" – a show and tell experience where the students explain their research, ideas and design. Their fellow students can ask them questions and engage in a peer assessment process.

5.8   Project Management, Questionnaires and Plenary Sessions

In this activity students are presented with a scenario where a space craft has crash into a canyon. As a rescue organization students have to send their robots to the scene of the disaster and retrieve this expensive piece of hardware p24]. This will involve them building a structure that they can transport to the site. A variety of found materials are available to make the structure, but each item they use will cost a certain amount. The stronger materials are more expensive than the weaker materials. The activity breaks down into a number of different tasks which need to be completed simultaneously. This involves different team members working by themselves or in pairs on one task. They need to bring their work together. It is a chance to appoint a project manager, whose task is to oversee the completion of a viable solution. This affords the opportunity to review each other's effort, find integration problems and resolve them.

At the end of the task we used a questionnaire to gauge the student's reaction to the activity. The efforts in this example were restricted to handing out the forms at the end of the activity – the students filled them in as they were clearing up. Nothing particularly unusual in that, except it is missing a golden PASA opportunity. It is possible to make such efforts far more meaningful. First ensure the questionnaire endeavors to find out what the students felt they learnt. Stop all activity, and get each group to complete a single form. This immediately involves them in reviewing, discussing and sharing their experiences.

The final strategy is to allow time for an assessment plenary. This should be used with most activities not just the Space Craft Rescue project. In fact the Dog Show is an example, given a structure by the nature of the activity. In this case the teacher can lead the discussion, by choosing comments from the questionnaires and opening them up for the whole class to review and discuss.

6 Conclusions

Peer and Self-Assessment are intrinsic facets of educational robotic activities. Students normally work in groups and the practical and authentic nature of the activities provides an environment where sharing of ideas, the discussion of problems, the creation of solutions, the review and modification of those solutions is a continuous aspect of such activities. The teacher's role in this is that of guide and her main tool is effective questioning, which is a way of engaging groups of students to review each other efforts.

The cited examples illustrate how PASA relates to aspects of ERA:

- The Curriculum and Assessment Principle provides the most obvious connection with PASA. While Papert was focused on revolutionizing schools, this principle aims to integrate his core ideas into everyday teaching practice. Clearly a big part of that is assessment and designers of educational robotic activities find PASA is a convenient way of satisfying this requirement.
- The Practical Principle is really about getting the buy-in cited by Clements and Sharma. The PASA related observations made in the Turtling without Tears report have been consistently reported by teachers over the last 3 decades. Teacher's constantly seek ways of creating situations where students are able to engage in PASA experiences and find robots a useful way of succeeding in this effort.
- Another persistent observation of robot activities is their ability to connect students with the Sustainable Learning (Lifelong Learning) Principle. The proclivity of robots to involve group work provides the opportunity to develop cognitive, social, personal and emotional traits. The Star Wars activity is an example of how educational robots create the opportunity for student interactions to assume the beneficial characteristics of PASA.

Consciously applying PASA ideas to educational robotic activities is relatively new. This review of a few historical examples of work done with robots is typical of experiences with educational robots. It reveals that over the last 3 decades, the latent and unreported contribution of PASA to the success of this technology. It is now clear that there is great potential for these ideas to enhance the effectiveness of the technology. This requires a partnership between PASA research and design. The latest Roamer for example, has been developed so that it is capable of far more than acting as a mirror. The limitation is not technological, but an understanding of how robots can be more active PASA agents.

References

1. Catlin, D.: Maximising the effectiveness of educational robotics through the use of assessment for learning methodologies. In: 3rd International Conference on Teaching Robotics, Teaching with Robotics. Riva La Garda, Italy. (2012)
2. Papert, S.: Mindstorms: Children Computers and Powerful Ideas, p. Vii. Basic Books, New York (1980)
3. Papert, S.: The Children's Machine, p. 86. Basic Books, New York (1993)

4. Papert, S.: The Children's Machine, p. 139. Basic Books, New York (1993)
5. Catlin, D., Blamires, M.: The principles of educational robotics applications (ERA): a framework for understanding and developing educational robots and their activities. In: Constructionism 2010, Paris (2010)
6. Bransford, J.D., Brown, A.L., Cocking, R.R. (eds.): How People Learn: Brain, Mind, Experience and School. National Academy Press, Washington DC (2000)
7. Clements, D.H., Sarama, J.: Research on logo: a decade of progress. In: Cleborne, D.M., Johnson, D.L. (eds.) LOGO: A Retrospective, pp. 9–46. The Hayward Press Inc. New York and London (1997)
8. Bull, G., Bull, G.: The evolution and future of LOGO. In: Maddux, C.D., Johnson, D.L. (eds.) LOGO: A Retrospective, pp. 47–59. The Haworth Press, New York and London (1997)
9. Hopkins, J.L.: Turtle politics. In: Maddux, C.L., Johnson, D.L. (eds.) LOGO: A Retrospective, pp. p61–70. The Haworth Press, New York and London (1997)
10. Papert, S.: Introduction? What is LOGO? Who Needs It? In: LOGO Philosophy and Implementation, pp. v–xvi. LCSI (1999)
11. Catlin, D., Thompson, T., Year 6 Students, Fleet School, Class of 1998. Fleet School Circus Project. Valiant Technology Ltd (1998). http://podcast.roamer-educational-robot.com/other-projects/. Accessed 11 April 2014
12. Black, P., Wiliam, D.: Inside the black box: v. 1: raising standards through classroom. NFER Nelson, London (2006)
13. Smith, I.: Assessment and Learning: Pocketbook. Teachers' Pocketbooks, Alresford (2007)
14. Mills, R., Staines, J., Tabberer, R.: Turtling Without Tears. National Council for Educational Technology (1989)
15. Gregory, C.A.: Adventures of Myrtle the Turtle: Measure a River (1991). http://goo.gl/LZr1WR. Accessed 12 May 2014
16. Wragg, E.C., Brown, G.A.: Questioning in the Primary School. Routledge, London and New York (2001)
17. Catlin, D.: Star Wars Roamer. Valiant Technology Ltd, May 2013. http://goo.gl/0tOZYZ. Accessed 15 May 2014
18. Coode, A.: Maple Cross Star Wars Video. Nick Flint and Maple Cross Year 5 and 6 Students Class of 2013, April 2013. http://goo.gl/OM1uXh. Accessed 15 May 2014
19. Flint, N.: Children of Maple Cross Primary School, Star Wars in Rickmansworth. 10 May 2013. http://goo.gl/6GjiRg. Accessed 13 April 2014
20. Sarralié, C.: The Roamer: an object for readapting in the case of adolescents with a cranial trauma (1998). http://goo.gl/zU3ND0
21. Turkle, S.: Evocative Objects: Things We Think with. MIT Press, Cambridge (2007)
22. Turkle, S., Taggart, W., Kidd, C.D., Daste, O.: Relational artifacts with children and elders: the complexities of cybercompanionship. Connect. Sci. **18**(4), 347–361 (2006)
23. Catlin, D.: In the Dog House. Valiant Technology Ltd., 16 April 2014. http://goo.gl/sOZbvo. Accessed 15 May 2014
24. Catlin, D.: Spacecraft Rescue. Valiant Technology, 2012 July 2014. http://goo.gl/XKoF9H. Accessed 14 May 2014

Peer Assessment in Engineering Group Projects: A Literature Survey

Evangelia Triantafyllou$^{(\boxtimes)}$ and Olga Timcenko

Department of Architecture, Design and Media Technology,
Aalborg University Copenhagen, Copenhagen, Denmark
{evt,ot}@create.aau.dk

Abstract. Peer review has proved to be beneficial in project-based environments by involving students in the process and encouraging them to take ownership of their learning. This article reviews how peer assessment has been employed within group work for different engineering programs. Since the administrative burden is one of the common reported challenges of peer assessment, computer assisted peer assessment is also briefly reviewed. Finally, opportunities and challenges in applying peer assessment in a project-based creative engineering program are presented based on the review of the literature.

Keywords: Peer assessment · Problem-based learning · Group work · Project-based learning · Engineering education · Mathematics · Literature survey

1 Introduction

Peer assessment has been deployed at various educational levels and curriculum areas. Topping defined peer assessment as "…an arrangement in which individuals consider the amount, level, value, worth, quality, or success of the products or outcomes of learning of peers of similar status" [27]. Various studies have proven peer assessment effective in promoting the development of teamwork and other professional skills in undergraduate students, in fostering the ability to critically evaluate their own learning and in helping students to develop a sense of ownership of their learning [1, 24].

Problem-Based Learning (PBL) is a teaching and learning approach that has been proved to benefit from peer assessment methods. PBL is a student-centered instructional approach, in which learning begins with a problem to be solved. Students need to acquire new knowledge in order to solve the problem and therefore they learn both problem-solving skills and domain knowledge. The goals of PBL are to help the students "…develop flexible knowledge, effective problem solving skills, self-directed learning, effective collaboration skills and intrinsic motivation." [11]. When PBL supports group work is also called project-based learning. While working in groups, students try to resolve the problem by defining what they need to know and how they will acquire this knowledge. This procedure fosters the development of communication, collaboration, and self-directed learning skills.

Our research efforts take place at Aalborg University, Denmark, where all programs are based on PBL that supports group work. Our main interest is to improve the PBL approach in mathematics education for creative engineering (e.g. Media Technology).

© Springer International Publishing Switzerland 2014
Y. Cao et al. (Eds.): ICWL 2014 Workshops, LNCS 8699, pp. 66–71, 2014.
DOI: 10.1007/978-3-319-13296-9_7

Such disciplines are more related to arts and humanities, and constructed in specific opposition to the technology and science. Typically, students in such studies lack basic skills in mathematics and do not relate to standard applications of mathematics.

We hypothesize that peer assessment techniques can help such students because they may force them to think on different problem solving techniques and they may increase engagement in mathematics. As an attempt to ground our hypothesis, the present article reviews how peer assessment has been employed within group work for different engineering programs. Since the administrative burden is one of the common reported challenges of peer assessment, computer assisted peer assessment is also briefly reviewed. Finally, opportunities and challenges in applying peer assessment in a project-based creative engineering program are discussed.

2 Peer Assessment in Group Work and Projects

A large number of authors have discussed the benefits and limitations of peer assessment in group work and projects [7, 9, 26]. This chapter starts with a brief review of studies within peer assessment in group work that focused on improving challenges of this learning approach. Then, we present studies that were conducted in project-based engineering education. We describe these studies using Topping's elements of a typology [27] as their descriptors to the extent the information provided by the authors allows us to do so.

2.1 Challenges of Group Work

Although group work is assumed to have positive effects on student learning, experiences from educational practice indicate that it can also introduce problems for both students and teachers, such as students who only maintain an appearance of being actively involved and students who let others do the work, also called free riders [23]. Research attempted to eliminate such problems by introducing peer assessment in group work. Initially, there was much attention on the problem of differentiation of individual contributions in group projects. Earl applied a peer assessment scheme for evaluating students' contribution to group performance based on communication skills in a Mathematics Modeling course [4]. In the same curriculum area, Goldfinch introduced an assessment technique, which also focused on easing the administrative burden of peer assessment for the lecturer, and on taking measures against an observed problem whereby over-generous students effectively penalized themselves. Kommula employed both quantitative and qualitative methods to assess the role and contribution of individual team members in a mechanical engineering program [14].

Later on, researchers put much effort on the problem of free riders in group work. Brooks and Ammons introduced a group evaluation instrument for peer assessment in an undergraduate business course in order to mitigate free-rider problems and improve students' perceptions about group work [2]. Elliott reported on an action research approach to the development and evaluation of a self- and peer assessment strategy. This approach was designed to promote student participation in group projects in a post-graduate program in clinical health sciences [5].

2.2   Peer Assessment in Engineering Projects

In the field of engineering, group work has been extensively introduced in the context of problem- or project-based learning [13]. With the aim to evaluate the teaching and learning outcomes in a first-year project-based engineering course, Neal et al. [18] used peer assessment with multiple marking techniques in a first year undergraduate engineering design course. They involved 123 students completing both individual (35 % of mark) and team (65 %) assessment tasks. The individual marks were awarded using Calibrated Peer Review (CPR) [22]. This method involved students marking three exemplar papers and then an actual paper, in order to calibrate student's marks. Students received marks for both their own work and the review of other's work. The group marks were given anonymously. Neal et al. incorporated this type of assessment in order to eliminate fears among students related to free riders and additional work, which is not recognized. In order to address biases, they applied the normalization factor technique [3]. This technique involves multiplying the mark awarded to a student's team (given by the instructor) by students' mark awarded by peer assessment (a normalization index) in order to get individual marks. Based on this assessment procedure, they were able to draw useful conclusions for diversity and predictability of students' performance.

Hersam et al. designed a nanotechnology engineering course employing collaborative group learning, interdisciplinary learning, problem-based learning, and peer assessment [10]. This course was given to 19 senior undergraduate students and junior graduate students, and peer assessment was employed in order to simulate working environments, where professionals are asked to evaluate one another through peer review. Group work was assigned in place of homework and peer assessment was used in order for the students to evaluate group activities and the final project. The group activity scores were 100 % determined by peer assessment. For final projects, the student-generated score made up 20 % of the total score. Since group work grades accounted for the 40 % of the overall grade, and final project grades accounted for the 30 % of the overall grade (the rest 30 % was determined by a final exam), 46 % of the overall course grade was determined by peer assessment. Hersam et al. found that students engaged in substantial and meaningful peer assessment and they expressed enthusiasm for the assigned group activities, which were evaluated solely by peer asssessment.

Fagerholm and Vihavainen [6] developed a tacit skills assessment framework for master students' software engineering capstone projects (from external partners) aiming at providing a decision support utility for evaluating students' teamwork proficiency. This framework consisted of an online questionnaire and used nine indicators for both self- and peer assessment of tacit skills. Within this framework, the questionnaires are filled in by students, the project coach, and the external partner. Data from the questionnaire is analyzed to provide an overall grade based on a given weighting (set by the instructor), or to indicate students that have been free-riding. Fagerholm and Vihavainen evaluated their framework with data from 18 bachelor's and 11 master's level projects (176 students), where it has been found to provide reasonable support for teachers in evaluating tacit, social, and teamwork skills. They concluded that their framework eased administrative burden for teachers and it helped to eliminate rater bias. Moreover, its dimensions were well understood, and it matched teachers' expert ratings.

Maskell introduced peer assessment within an embedded systems design course for second-year undergraduate students [17]. He aimed at eliminating the added burden upon staff that assessment in problem-based and self-directed learning introduces and at improving assessment as proposed by students in previous years (i.e. absence of individual marks, assessment criteria and expectations of staff not clearly defined, delayed and not appropriate feedback from lecturers). He negotiated assessment criteria with the students and introduced peer assessment for an individual assignment, which made up 20 % of the final mark. The peer assessment process involved each student in a group assessing anonymously two assignments and then the group as a whole ranking each of them. Maskell used also a peer performance index to account for individual variations in the final group report. While the outcomes of this study were successful, Maskell pointed out that peer assessment should be introduced into early years before students form rigid views on the teaching style and the assessment format, if it is to be accepted as a valid assessment technique. Moreover, he emphasized the importance of providing a mix of assessment strategies in order to maintain certain minimum standards.

3 Computer Assisted Peer Assessment

One of the most important practical concerns in peer assessment is the burden of manual work in collecting and analyzing peer assessment data. Online questionnaires, semi-automated analysis tools and mobile technology have been introduced in order to remove much of this manual work [12, 25, 30]. Moreover, complete systems have been developed for self- and peer assessment management. Freeman and McKenzie described such a system, called SPARK, which facilitated self- and peer assessment and emphasized fairness in group work assessment [8]. SPARK^{PLUS} not only allows self- and peer assessment of group work, but also allows students to self and peer assess individual work. Moreover, it allows for judgment improvement through benchmarking exercises and it has been found efficient in calibrating academic standards amongst teaching staff in large classes [29]. In the same direction, Ohland et al. introduced the CATME system that focuses also on reducing teacher workload by providing auto-mated peer- and self-assessment. Moreover, CATME provides a set of tools that place emphasis on handling group dynamics, group formation, and use behavioral anchors in the assessment [20]. The SMARTER extends CATME and attempts to link educational research with teaching faculty actions to enhance learning of teamwork skills [19]. Finally, WebPA is an online peer-moderated marking system [16]. It is designed for giving individual marks to students working in groups and doing group-work, whose outcome of earns an overall group mark.

4 Discussion

The review of studies that adopted peer assessment revealed various benefits when this approach is adopted within project-based engineering. Firstly, it encouraged student involvement and responsibility and has been used efficiently to minimize the number of free riders by encouraging students to reflect on their role and contribution to the process of the group work. Secondly, it minimized confusion about assignment outcomes and expectations by introducing concrete assessment criteria, and contributed to the assignment of individual marks among group members. Thirdly, peer assessment proved to be a valid process that resulted in substantial and meaningful feedback to students. Finally, it resulted in students being involved in the process and being encouraged to take ownership of this process [28].

However, we can foresee some challenges peer assessment may introduce in project-based environments. Firstly, peer evaluation may have a negative impact on a PBL environment, which promotes a cooperative and non-judgmental atmosphere among group members [21]. In a PBL learning environment, students should feel free to make hypotheses, to ask questions and request clarification of challenging points. On the other hand, peer assessment promotes judgmental attitudes that may create tension among group members. Secondly, students may feel or even be ill equipped to undertake the assessment [15]. This is one of our biggest concerns, since creative engineering students lack basic skills in mathematics.

Based on the aforementioned strengths of peer assessment, we argue that mathematics education in creative engineering can greatly benefit from peer assessment. Nevertheless, a carefully designed framework is required in order to minimize challenges introduced by this method. This requires that students get familiar with the concepts and elements of assessment against specified criteria from the beginning and that they are provided with guidance on how to judge others' contributions. Finally, students should be continuously assisted to build a set of criteria that match the learning outcomes with regards to the output and process of the group work.

References

1. Boud, D., Falchikov, N.: Rethinking Assessment in Higher Education: Learning for the Longer Term. Routledge, London (2007)
2. Brooks, C.M., Ammons, J.L.: Free riding in group projects and the effects of tim-ing, frequency, and specificity of criteria in peer assessments. J. Educ. Bus. **78**, 268–272 (2003)
3. Cinar, Y., Bilgin, A.: Peer assessment for undergraduate teamwork projects in petroleum engineering. Int. J. Eng. Educ. **27**, 310–322 (2011)
4. Earl, S.E.: Staff and peer assessment - measuring an individual's contribution to group performance. Assess. Eval. High. Educ. **11**, 60–69 (1986)
5. Elliott, N., Higgins, A.: Self and peer assessment – does it make a difference to student group work? Nurse Educ. Pract. **5**, 40–48 (2005)
6. Fagerholm, F., Vihavainen, A.: Peer Assessment in experiential learning assessing tacit and explicit skills Agile software engineering capstone projects. In: 2013 IEEE Frontiers in Education Conference, pp. 1723–1729 (2013)
7. Freeman, M.: Peer assessment by groups of group work. Assess. Eval. High. Educ. **20**, 289–300 (1995)
8. Freeman, M., McKenzie, J.: SPARK, a confidential web–based template for self and peer assessment of student teamwork: benefits of evaluating across different subjects. Br. J. Educ. Technol. **33**, 551–569 (2002)

9. Goldfinch, J., Raeside, R.: Development of a peer assessment technique for obtaining individual marks on a group project. Assess. Eval. High. Educ. **15**, 210–231 (1990)
10. Hersam, M.C., Luna, M., Light, G.: Implementation of interdisciplinary group learning and peer assessment in a nanotechnology engineering course. J. Eng. Educ. **93**, 49–57 (2004)
11. Hmelo-Silver, C.E.: Problem-based learning: what and how do students learn? Educ. Psychol. Rev. **16**, 235–266 (2004)
12. Isabwe, G.M.N., Reichert, F., Carlsen, M.: Rethinking practices of Assessment for Learning: Tablet Technology Supported Assessment for Learning Mathematics, pp. 155–159. University of Agder, Norway (2013)
13. Kolmos, A.: Reflections on project work and problem-based learning. Eur. J. Eng. Educ. **21**, 141–148 (1996)
14. Kommula, V.P., Oladiran, M., Uziak, J.: Self and Peer Assessment in Engineering Students Group Work (2009) 937
15. Langendyk, V.: Not knowing that they do not know: self-assessment accuracy of third-year medical students. Med. Educ. **40**, 173–179 (2006)
16. Loddington, S., Pond, K., Wilkinson, N., et al.: A case study of the development of WebPA: an online peer-moderated marking tool. Br. J. Educ. Technol. **40**, 329–341 (2009)
17. Maskell, D.: Student-based assessment in a multi-disciplinary problem-based learning environment. J. Eng. Educ. **88**, 237–241 (1999)
18. Neal, P., Ho, M., Fimbres-Weihs, G., et al.: Project-based learning for first-year engineering students: design of CO_2 sequestration. Australas. J. Eng. Educ. **17**, 39–54 (2011)
19. Ohland, M.W., Layton, R., Loughry, M., et al.: SMARTER Teamwork: System for Management, Assessment, Research, Training, Education, and Remediation for Teamwork (2010)
20. Ohland, M.W., Loughry, M., Carter, R., et al.: The Comprehensive Assessment of Team Member Effectiveness. CATME), A New Peer Evaluation Instrument (2006)
21. Papinczak, T., Young, L., Groves, M.: Peer assessment in problem-based learning: a qualitative study. Adv. Health Sci. Educ. **12**, 169–186 (2007)
22. Robinson, R.: calibrated peer review™: an application to increase student reading & writing skills. Am. Biol. Teach. **63**, 474–480 (2001)
23. Salomon, G., Globerson, T.: When teams do not function the way they ought to. Int. J. Educ. Res. **13**, 89–99 (1989)
24. Sivan, A.: The implementation of peer assessment: an action research approach. Assess. Educ. Princ. Policy Pract. **7**, 193–213 (2000)
25. Søndergaard, H., Mulder, R.A.: Collaborative learning through formative peer review: pedagogy programs and potential. Comput. Sci. Educ. **22**, 343–367 (2012)
26. Stanier, L.: Peer assessment and group work as vehicles for student empowerment: a module evaluation. J. Geogr. High. Educ. **21**, 95–98 (1997)
27. Topping, K.: peer assessment between students in colleges and universities. Rev. Educ. Res. **68**, 249–276 (1998)
28. Topping, K.J.: Peer assessment. Theory Pract. **48**, 20–27 (2009)
29. Willey, K., Gardner, A.: Investigating the capacity of self and peer assessment activities to engage students and promote learning. Eur. J. Eng. Educ. **35**, 429–443 (2010)
30. Wu, C., Chanda, E., Willison, J.: Implementation and outcomes of online self and peer assessment on group based honours research projects. Assess. Eval. High. Educ. **39**, 21–37 (2014)

Peer-Review from Learners' Perspective

Elisabeth Katzlinger[1]([⊠]) and Michael A. Herzog[2]

[1] Johannes Kepler University Linz, Linz, Austria
elisabeth.katzlinger@jku.at
[2] Magdeburg-Stendal University of Applied Sciences, Stendal, Germany
michael.herzog@hs-magdeburg.de

Abstract. Within the framework of a broad four-year study with 550 participants in the fields of e-business and business informatics that was conducted at a German and an Austrian university, different media-based learning methods and their effects were compared. In order to be able to draw comparisons with other learning methods, a game-based learning scenario (Beer Game), a case study that was worked on in interuniversity groups and documented in a Wiki as well as peer-review were factored into the study. This article focuses on different pedagogical and technical varieties of implementation of a peer-review learning scenario as well as the qualitative analysis of students' feedback and improvement suggestions. Compared with other media-based learning scenarios, the peer-review method was rated surprisingly positive in most respects. However, the suggestions for improvement analyzed for the present study mainly concerned a lack of anonymity in courses with a small number of participants, a lack of knowledge on the part of the reviewers, a wish for more reviews, the possibility to defend one's paper after the review and a wish for examples what good peer reviews look like. Furthermore the study mirrors the progress that was achieved in the recent past of the peer-review tools.

Keywords: Peer review · Virtual collaborative learning · e-business education · Cross teaching · Peer learning · Peer assessment

1 Introduction

Although it is a scientifically well researched and critically discussed method of academic quality assurance, in literature little empirical material is available on the use of peer-reviews in the context of academic teaching. Peer-review is hardly recognized as an activating pedagogical instrument, which supports the method of inquiry-based learning and may contribute to a significant increase of learning successes by using additional feedback processes. A scientific study that verifies the qualitative as well as quantitative effects of the method and which also takes a differentiated look at the design of the learning scenario, could contribute to a broader use of the learning method. One goal could be the development of an empirically supported guideline for academic teachers on how this method could be applied best in different disciplines and with different students.

Current empirical research in the field of higher education didactics addresses diversity aspects. Students differ from each other regarding their qualifications as well

© Springer International Publishing Switzerland 2014
Y. Cao et al. (Eds.): ICWL 2014 Workshops, LNCS 8699, pp. 72–81, 2014.
DOI: 10.1007/978-3-319-13296-9_8

as their learning styles. As with other learning scenarios, different students benefit differently from peer-review as a learning method.

Since 2010, the Cross Teaching Study has investigated different media-based learning methods concerning their acceptance and effect. How do different students handle the different learning scenarios and how successful are they in their endeavors? In this study, peer-review plays an important role in connection with self-determined learning. When comparing the learning methods from the angle of the diversity of students, differences concerning demography, occupation, study progress and learning style are taken into consideration. The tools for the peer-review in the learning management systems have clearly improved in recent years. However, whether the changes in the peer-review process have positive or negative effects, also stands in need for further examination.

2 Peer-Review as a Method in Research and Teaching

Self-organized learning increasingly finds its way into higher education. Thereby the learners themselves can – and have to – decide on constitutive elements of their learning process, such as learning locations, study time, learning tasks or learning methods. Among these learning methods are working with e-portfolios or the peer-review method (Hornung-Prähauser 2010, p. 261f). In both cases, students receive feedback on their papers not only from their teacher or tutor, but from other learners too. As far as the procedure is concerned, students have to hand in their own papers first, before being assigned a paper for reviewing. After that, students could be provided the opportunity to integrate the feedback of their peers into their papers as a second step in the learning process.

One of the current methods in academic quality assurance is peer-review; it is one of the key elements of self-regulation in science. Researchers of equal competence review and comment on the papers of peers (Reinmann 2010, p. 218; Neidhardt 2010, p. 280). After a revision phase, in which the comments are considered and incorporated, the paper is turned in again. The aim of this process is a sensitive, valid and reliable measurement of research performance, although the method has not remained undisputed (Münch 2009, p. 297).

As peer-review is an accepted method of academic quality assurance, it seems useful to prepare students for their role as future reviewers. In the English-speaking world, feedback of learners and peer-review are mainly used as teaching and learning methods in master courses (Hoidn 2010, p. 260).

Reviewing and evaluating papers requires that the reviewer closely deals with the content of the relevant paper, which in turn means a benefit for his/her own work as well. The study of Breuer (2010) shows that peer-review leads to mutual support among the learners. Peer-review in the sense of mutual reviewing and assessing is applicable in courses with many participants, as it is a scalable learning method – the number of reviewers rises with the number of submissions (Sharples et al. 2012, p. 33).

The increase of communication, collaboration and peer interaction among the learners is a target for new learning approaches; the learners are encouraged to cooperate and interact (Ge 2011). These forms of learning are self-directed, flexible, problem solving (Ehlers et al. 2010) and provide a concept of self-organized learning that increasingly finds its way into higher education. This includes teaching and learning methods that aim at the self-determination of the learning process (tasks, methods, learning locations, study time, etc.) on the part of the students and involves learning methods such as e-portfolio work or peer-review (Hornung-Prähauser 2010).

Electronic peer-review is a learning method that can improve the quality of education. When students assess their co-students' work, the process becomes reflexive: they learn by teaching and by assessing. Peer assessment is interactive and dynamic as students assess, critique and make value judgments on the quality and standard of other learners' work, and provide feedback to the authors (Nagel et al. 2010).

Especially to improve social competences peer-review has the potential to increase cognitive, social, affective and transferable skills, and also include higher levels of critical thinking (Trautmann 2009). The development of critical thinking is enhanced through discussion and feedback. Peer reviewing other students' papers help the learners to improve their own work and they benefit from the feedback. In Trautmann's (2009), study the students pointed out that they gain new perspectives through seeing both good and bad examples in the work of fellow students.

The role of teachers and learners in traditional learning contexts is fixed, the teacher is responsible for the content and the learning process, the learner has a more passive role. Evaluation and assessment is the exclusive right and task of the teacher. Nevertheless, evaluating someone else's work can be a very useful for the learning process of the evaluator (Zenha-Rela et al. 2006).

Peer-review may be part of the e-portfolio work; thereby the e-portfolios are not only assessed by teachers, but also by peers who give feedback to their fellow students. This enables students to integrate their peer's suggestions and correct their work; a procedure that is commonly used within the scientific world as papers are revised and comments of reviewers are considered in the final publications. The comment function of weblogs can also be used as another form of peer-review (Liou et al. 2009).

3   Approach

Since October 2010, via the ERASMUS teaching staff exchange program, a collaboration has been established between the Department of Economics of the Magdeburg-Stendal University of Applied Sciences, Germany and the Department of Data Processing in Social Sciences, Economics and Business of the Johannes Kepler University Linz, Austria. For this collaboration certain courses from the field of e-business are interconnected. In addition, students were questioned online about the different learning methods (interuniversity case study, peer-review, game-based learning – Beer Game) and their media use simultaneously. In total, 551 students have participated in the study since 2010; 367 from Magdeburg-Stendal and 184 from Linz. Altogether 273 questionnaires of students, who participated in the peer-review, were evaluated (Table 1).

The gender ratio in this study is 67:33 concerning the students from Linz, and – more balanced – 48:52 with more female students participating in Magdeburg in the peer-review study. The average age of the students from Linz is higher than the average age of the students from Magdeburg, which is probably due to the different

Table 1. Average age and gender ratio of the whole study (N = 273)

	Number of men	Age	Number of women	Age	Total number	Age
Linz (Austria)	83	27,4	40	26,2	123	27,0
Magdeburg (Germany)	72	25,0	78	22,9	150	23,9
Total	155	26,3	118	24,0	273	25,3

position the course has within the curricula of the two universities on the one hand and mirrors the high ratio of working students in Linz, where 58 % of students work 16 h or more a week, while in Magdeburg this ratio stands at 26 %.

4   Implementation

The implementation of the electronic peer-reviews was realized in the learning management system, Moodle. For the first reviews of the present study, the activity "peer-review", an additional module of Moodle 1.8, was used. This module is basically equipped with necessary functions for peer-review; however, usability and process operation have weaknesses (Herzog et al. 2012). The advancement of this module is found as "Workshop" under activities in Moodle versions 2 with many options, from which many different fields of application arise. The workshop activity permits peer assessments, where the learners mutually assess each other on the one hand and are assessed by their teachers on the other hand.

For the present study, peer-review was applied and subsequently compared as a learning method in different courses of different topics from the field of e-business at the University of Linz and Magdeburg-Stendal University. In the course "IT-Ethics" of the masters program, Digital Business Management students chose to work on one case study on the topic of IT-ethics. In the course "Business and Internet", students received a short case-description on the topic of e-procurement, where different goods had to be procured and students had to choose an adequate scheme of classification for the goods as well as corresponding procurement methods. In the courses on business informatics and process management, process models developed by students were subjected to peer-review. In some courses, the peer-review was directly used as a basis for grading, whereas in other courses it was used as an ungraded feedback-method. With the aid of the feedback, students could revise their papers and subsequently submit them again.

Preconditions for the implementation of the solution. The workshop activity runs through several different phases that are processed consecutively (see Fig. 1). Overlapping of the single phases is basically provided for, however only in exceptional cases useful.

Preparation phase. In the preparation phase, the individual options for the workshop activity are chosen, for example, mutual assessment or group mode. Furthermore, it can be specified whether it should be a "blind review", or the teacher is able to trace back,

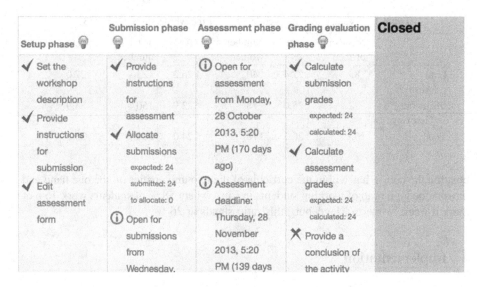

Fig. 1. Workshop-activity in Moodle

who assessed whose paper. In addition, in this phase, the time schedule for the activity is determined.

Learners receive concrete instructions and tasks, how to review their peers. One or more files (papers, models, figures, presentations, videos etc.) can be submitted. In order to lead the learners towards their activity, a model submission can be provided, which the learners can review for testing purposes. Experience has shown that learners are rather unfamiliar with giving feedback; thus for useful peer-review support of the learners is necessary.

To work out the criteria for the assessment requires diligence from the teacher. The individual criteria may be weighed differently. The reviewers award points for each criterion and give feedback in the form of comments.

Submission phase. After the preparation phase, the teacher activates the submission phase, in which the learners turn in their papers. In this phase, it is of great importance that the deadlines for submission are met, as late submissions can hardly be considered during the distribution process for the peer-review.

Assessment phase. After the submission of the papers, the teacher initiates the distribution of papers to reviewers. The papers are assigned either randomly, manually by the teacher or in a time-controlled way. Additionally in this phase, it is specified how many papers each reviewer has to assess. The reviewers award points for each of the predefined criteria and can furthermore give feedback in the form of a comment on each criterion.

Grading phase. In case of conflicts for example, one of the papers is assessed very inconsistently or contradictorily, the teacher is able to intervene and decide after the end of the assessment phase. The grading and the transfer of the weighted points (gradebook) have to be initiated by the teacher.

5 Evaluation and Findings

For the present study, feedback of the learners was analyzed. Within the framework of the survey, learners had the possibility to give feedback on the peer-review in general and also to make concrete comments or suggestions for improvement. 83 of the 273 learners participating in the peer-review courses gave an additional qualitative feedback, which shall be analyzed below.

In general the learners rated the peer-review positively; 77 % of them rated it as a very good or good learning method. Their feedback mainly concerned suggestions for improvement either relating to the method itself or to how the method could be applied more efficiently.

In the following the statements of the students are clustered and assigned to specific topics:

A lack of anonymity in courses with a small number of participants. Students remarked that especially in courses with a small number of participants anonymity could not be guaranteed. Even if the reviewer does not know the authors' names, students usually know each other.

> *"There is no real anonymity in small classes – all the students know each other and you don't want to hurt these people and so you often don't evaluate them critically enough. However, I can well imagine it for a large class."*

Assessing peers. A number of responses addressed the issue of the assessment of learners through learners, which was regarded as a difficult task. Students remarked that they did not want to be responsible for the bad marks of their colleagues. To get the chance of giving feedback was appreciated; having to assess their colleagues in a way that influences their marks was however regarded with skepticism.

> *"It is difficult to assess a colleague fairly, as you don't want to "spoil somebody else's chances"."*
> *"I realized that it is difficult to mark objectively."*
> *"I found it really hard to mark my colleagues' work."*
> *"I don't think it's good to give the real marks. Peer-review yes, but marking no, because you don't want to spoil someone else's marks. Maybe to give a suggestion for the mark, but the tutors should do the real grading. So you can hand over the responsibility and the assessments will be more realistic."*

One of the students thought that students assessed each other more critical than teachers would assess the students.

> *"Students tend to assess their colleagues more critical than a professor would do. This could be prevented if students were relieved from the pressure of expectation that is associated with this task."*

Possibility to defend the paper. Students expressed their wish for a possibility to defend their papers several times. In some of the courses, students were allowed to correct their papers after the peer-review. Students, who attended these courses, achieved significantly better results concerning the final assessment of their papers.

"There is no possibility to defend your paper. This means that you are forced even more to float with the current and do what you think will be assessed best – so there is no improvement compared to the other methods of assessment."

"There is no possibility to criticize the results of the assessment! To get a bad mark just because someone else didn't do the peer-review carefully should not affect my result but the result of the person, who didn't do his job right."

Lack of knowledge on the part of the reviewer. Many responses addressed the issue of a lack of knowledge on the part of the reviewers, which became obvious especially in connection with one of the tasks given (Modeling with Lindner Diagram). In this connection students also expressed their wish for a general discussion of the task.

"As this method presupposes that all participants carefully deal with the task, which was not the case, I'm not convinced 100 %. This led to unqualified results."

"General discussion before the assessment with the students. Partly (factually) wrong assessments were made. Probably this could be prevented in the future by discussing it in advance."

Wish for more than one review. In order to mitigate the lack of knowledge of some of the reviewers, students expressed their wish for at least three reviews.

"I received many reviews, which, however, differed very much from each other, with the result that I achieved a lower total score."

"From my point of view the biggest problem with the peer-review is that you only get 2 opinions from two colleagues and you don't really know whether they really became acquainted with the topic before and thus are able to assess my paper "correctly". I really appreciated that they reviewed it again."

"In order to be sure to eliminate any "outliers" and to get a better, more correct overall picture of the assessment each submission should be reviewed by more than only two or three persons."

Assessment criteria before starting to write the paper. Much of the feedback concerned the incorporation of the peer-review into the whole course process. Students expressed the wish that the review criteria should be discussed before starting work and that examples of good works should be provided.

"The criteria for the peer-review appeared nowhere while we worked on the texts."

"It would be helpful if we had examples of good works towards which we could turn in fulfilling our tasks. Otherwise everyone has his own opinion about the task and thinks the opinion of the other one is wrong, although both opinions could be right with the right reasoning."

"The topic or the task you get for the peer-review could be discussed in some more detail in advance in order to get more information and suggestions how the task should be completed."

Yes/No Assessment. The first peer-reviews were realized in the learning management system Moodle 1.9. In this version the reviewers did their assessments on the basis of a list of criteria. Each criterion could be answered by either yes or no. The feedback revealed that students are critical of this mode.

"Some people did not get the assessment system with the tick marks right. Maybe this could be adjusted better."

Positive feedback. In the feedback students expressed their approval of the peer-review method, especially when it came to their learning success.

"The peer-review is good in order to get feedback on the projects you worked on. You get information on what you did well and what could be improved."

"I think the peer-review is good, as you could see how others completed the task given and you could see where and how you could improve your own work or where you did better than the others. Nevertheless I think that some didn't really make an effort in regards of the assessment of others."

"Because of the peer-review you really had to become acquainted with the topic, which was really interesting and which led to a consolidation of what was learned, at least in my case."

"A really interesting way of learning. May definitely be applied more often."

"Interesting experience."

"It was fun to try this method and to gain new experiences through this approach."

"Good exercise, very practical."

Different methods compared to each other. Within the framework of the survey, students rated the following different learning methods on the basis of a four-grade scale ([1] poor … [4] very good): Case study, peer-review and game-based learning. They rated their appropriateness as learning methods, personal learning outcome, enjoyment to work with the method, the cost-benefit-ratio and the method in general. Results are presented in Fig. 2.

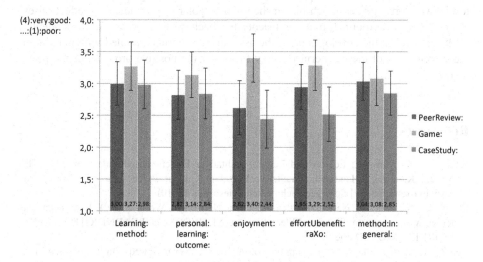

Fig. 2. Students rating learning methods

84 % of the students rated the peer review method as very good or good. Of course students rated the game-based learning scenario best in all points, especially when it comes to enjoyment. On the other hand students differed more in peer-review enjoyment while they rated the method in general comparatively homogenious.

6 Conclusion

The students, whose feedback was analyzed for the present study, basically rated the peer-review positively, although they are not used to assessing their colleagues in their daily routine at university and especially not to really influence their fellow students' marks. However, giving feedback was widely appreciated.

Students usually do not get to know their fellows' work or papers, which is why the peer-review is a good opportunity to see how their colleagues completed the tasks given and estimate their own standpoint.

To give well-founded feedback requires a careful preparation and thoroughly involving oneself into the subject matters. Even if students frequently doubt the factual assessment quality of their colleagues in their feedback on peer-review as a learning method, critically dealing with the comments and feedback of their colleagues still means a learning effect, even if these comments are considered as unjustified or wrong.

One surprise in the study was the consistently positive rating of peer review as a learning method compared to other media-based learning scenarios. Especially opposite to the game based approach, peer-review is strongly reglemented and structured in a way people usually find to be not the easiest method.

Apart from students view, preparation and completion of peer-review is time-consuming for teachers. In a process where students received feedback from their peers first and could upload an improved version later for grading, learning impact and results where recognized much higher then in a singular peer review. The effect raises again if there is additional, multiple teacher feedback in the process. As the students' feedback reveals, the development of the assessment criteria combined with maximum transparency about these criteria is a key factor for the positive progress of the peer-review.

References

Breuer, F., Schreier, M.: Lehren und Lernen qualitativer Forschungsmethoden. In: Mey, G., Mruck, K. (Hrsg.) Handbuch Qualitative Forschung in der Psychologie. VS Verlag für Sozialwissenschaften | Springer Fachmedien Wiesbaden (2010)

Ehlers, U., Steinert, A.: Networked Learning in a Networked World (2010). http://netzwerk lernen.wikispaces.com/file/view/Ehlers_Steinert_NETWORKED+LEARNING+IN+A+NET WORKED+WORLD.doc

Ge, Z.: Exploring e-learners' perceptions of net-based peer-reviewed English writing. Int. J. Comput. Support. Collab. Learn. 6(1), 75–91 (2011)

Herzog, M.A.; Katzlinger, E.: Peer Review als aktivierende Lernmethode in der universitären Lehre. Moodlemoot 23. 2. 2012, Linz (2012)

Hoidn, S.: Lernkompetenzen an Hochschulen fördern. VS Verlag für Sozialwissenschaften | Springer Fachmedien Wiesbaden (2010)

Hornung-Prähauser, V., Wieden-Bischof, D.: Theorie und Praxis zu E-Portfolios in der Hochschule. In: Hugger, K.-U, Walber, M. (Hrsg.) Digitale Lernwelten. Konzepte, Beispiele und Perspektiven, pp. 245–268. VS Verlag für Sozialwissenschaften | Springer Fachmedien Wiesbaden (2010)

Liou, H.-C., Peng, Z.-Y.: Training effects on computer-mediated peer review. System **37**(2009), 514–525 (2009)

Münch, R., Baier, C.: Die Konstruktion der soziologischen Realität durch Forschungsrating. Berliner J. für Soziologie **2009**(19), 295–313 (2009)

Nagel, L., Kotzé, T.G.: Supersizing e-learning: What a CoI survey reveals about teaching presence in a large online class. Internet High. Educ. **13**, 45–51 (2010)

Neidhardt, W.: Selbststeuerung der Wissenschaft: Peer Review. In: Simon, D., Knie, A., Hornbostel, S. (Hrsg.) Handbuch Wissenschaftspolitik, pp. 280–292. VS Verlag für Sozialwissenschaften | Springer Fachmedien Wiesbaden (2010)

Reinmann, G., Sippel, S., Spannagel, C.: Peer Review für Forschen und Lernen. Funktionen, Formen, Entwicklungschancen und die Rolle der digitalen Medien. In: Mandel, S., Rutishauser, M., Seiler Schiedt, E. (Hrsg.) Digitale Medien für Lehre und Forschung, pp. 218–229. Waxmann Verlag, Münster (2010)

Sharples, M., McAndrew, P., Weller, M., Ferguson, R., FitzGerald, E., Hirst, T., Mor, Y., Gaved, M., Whitelock, D.: Innovating Pedagogy 2012: Open University Innovation Report 1, Milton Keynes: The Open University (2012)

Trautmann, N.M.: Interactive learning through web-mediated peer review of student science reports. Educ. Technol. Res. Dev. **57**(5), 685–704 (2009)

Zenha-Rela, M., Carvalho, R.: Work in progress: self evaluation through monitored peer review using the moodle platform. In: 36th ASEE/IEEE Frontiers in Education Conference, San Diego, CA, Session T2D, pp. 26–27 (2006)

Formative Self-assessment to Support Self-driven Mathematics Education at University Level

Giovannina Albano[1,2(✉)] and Leke Pepkolaj[1]

[1] DIEM – Dipartimento di Ingegneria dell'Informazione,
Ingegneria Elettrica e Matematica Applicata,
University of Salerno, Fisciano – SA, Italy
galbano@unisa.it, leke.zefi@alice.it
[2] CRMPA - Centro di Ricerca in Matematica Pura e Applicata,
Fisciano – SA, Italy

Abstract. In this paper we discuss how to exploit the use of the module Quiz, available in any e-learning platform, to improve mathematics competencies of engineering students. The use of quizzes aims to improve the learning process during its progress. Our use of self-assessment has combined with traditional lectures, as benefit, since it allows self-driven recovery learning paths. Much attention has been paid to construct effective close-ended questions apt to actually evaluate competencies and not only contents. Quizzes are also used as an effective tool to improve learning and overcome incorrect beliefs.

Keywords: Mathematics · Quiz · Learning paths

1 Introduction

In this paper we discuss the use of the module Quiz to support mathematics education in a blended learning setting. At university level, where large groups of students are involved in traditional lectures (about 200 per class in our case), the possibility of automatic assessment and feedback, given by the module Quiz, allows to equip the students with learning experiences which should be unaffordable in traditional settings. It has been possible to set up recovery learning paths based on formative self-assessment, which join features from both guided-learning and self-regulated learning. In fact, for each meaningful topic of linear algebra a course consisting of quizzes with a multi-level structure has been designed. The student can freely choose one course for the self-assessment. Then, according to its outcome, further quizzes are suggested, which can differ for level of difficulty or which can suggest a finer analysis of the failure based on comprehension tests. Quiz-base courses have been implemented in the platform IWT[1] and its massive use has been planned for next term at the Faculty of Engineering of the University of Salerno.

---

[1] http://www.momanet.it/index.php/it/soluzioni/e-learning-training

© Springer International Publishing Switzerland 2014
Y. Cao et al. (Eds.): ICWL 2014 Workshops, LNCS 8699, pp. 82–91, 2014.
DOI: 10.1007/978-3-319-13296-9_9

2 Theoretical Framework

2.1 Errors vs Mistakes

Even if, often "error" and "mistake" are used as synonymous, we distinguish between them and thus we provide their meaning in the context of our work. The first one derives from deep incomprehension or gap and make evident problems of cognitive nature. The second one usually derives from lack of attention or suitable control, it consists in incorrect habits or automatisms developed in incorrect manner [8]. In mathematics, errors occur more frequently handling problems, which require to use more contents and rules in a sequence to be discovered by the student herself, whilst mistakes occur during exercises, which require to execute well-defined sequences of operations.

2.2 Classification of Errors and Mistakes

In this section we present a classification of errors and mistakes, which we have derived from a review of literature [6, 9] and considered suitable as basis of our generation of the quizzes.

We consider only the errors classifiable; being the ones whose paternity is recognizable, as in the following list:

- E1 – inappropriate use of the data. This kind of error concerns incorrect associations or stiffness in the elaboration of the information needed to give an answer. They can be caused by difficulties in: reading, the student does not read the key words or the symbols in the statement of the questions; decoding, the student does not know the meaning of words and symbols in the text of the questions; coding, the student understands the data of the problem but she is not able to write them correctly in the semiotic system more suitable to get the answer;
- E2 – linguistic deficiency. It means that students are not able to understand and to manipulate mathematical objects by means various type of semiotic representations, both at syntactic and semantic levels [4]. This kind of error is very relevant from mathematics education point of view [5];
- E3 – cognitive and metacognitive deficiency. This kind of error can be caused by lack of contents or of competencies [7];
- E4 – incorrect logical deduction. This kind of error is caused by the application of inappropriate rules or strategies.

Among the mistakes, we have distinguished the following ones:

- M1 – lack of control and feedback. The students do not give a step-by-step solution to the problem but they give only the final outcomes, they do not check their product with respect to theoretical concepts and results, they do not make any comment to their product which can be useful to the reader in order to understand their solution process;
- M2 – technical mistakes. The students make incorrect calculus;
- M3 – Harlow *error factors*. The students make a correct procedure which does give a correct answer but which is not what required by the given problem;

- M4 – lack of answer to some questions. The students relinquish some questions corresponding to topics they did not study;
- M5 – coding mistakes. The students do not order the answers or do not make any reference to the related question, they solve subsequent questions without taking into account the relations among them, they do not put their name on the worksheets or do not number the pages;
- M6 – a priori evaluation of the difficulties. The students are not able or do not pay attention to evaluate the difficulties of each question or problem, which also includes to be able to choose the easier solution strategy.

3 Methodology

In this section, we present the methodology used in designing the recovery-learning path. The underpinning idea is based on a multi-level structure as shown in the following figure:

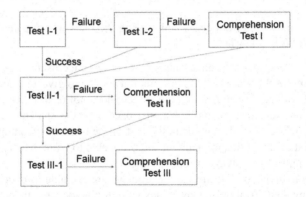

Fig. 1. Structure of the recovery learning path for each topic.

For each topic, we have distinguished three levels of difficulty.

If the student is successful in performing the test, then she can access to the upper level, otherwise she is guided towards a comprehension test [3]. At first level, after a failure to the first test, a further analogous test is presented, in order to avoid non-cognitive reasons for the negative outcome (anxiety, fortuitousness, etc.).

After a comprehension test, the student goes to the next level. This is because the aim of such kind of tests is not to assess the student's knowledge but they aim to put the attention to the reasons of the previous failures, giving the students the tools, the keys to overcome them. Thus, the comprehension tests address the following points:

- Understanding the problem. To face this point, the test includes questions aimed to make clear to the student the data and the text of the problem. Errors E1 and E2 are particularly addressed: the first one, because of the importance of reading the problem in order to make clear which is the "environment" in which the problem lies; the second one, because of the importance of being able to coordinate various semiotic systems used in mathematics both to understand and to solve. It is also important to help students to recall the definition of the objects involved into the problem and their properties, which can be exploited to get the solution.

– Understanding the solution. The errors E3 and E4 are the focus in this case.
– Understanding why some given solutions are incorrect. In this case, given a problem and an incorrect solution, students are required to find the reason of the incorrectness. At a lower level, this can be done indicating punctually the incorrect piece and asking for an explanation, then at a higher level, also the former is required to the students. All kind of mistakes can be addressed here.

4   An Application to a Case Study

The methodology described in the previous section has been applied to the case of the module of Linear Algebra for engineering undergraduates.

A partition of the whole course program devises eight main topics: matrices, linear systems, vector spaces, Euclidean spaces, homomorphisms, diagonalization, 2D and 3D analytic geometry. Tests according to the multi-level structure in Fig. 1 have been created. Let us see in more details in the following.

4.1   Analysis of the Protocols

In order to implement a recovery-learning path, the first activity done has been the analysis of the students' products. Thus the starting point has been the protocols of the written exams, which consist in solving six problems regarding the last six topics previous cited (matrices and linear systems are considered as instrument for making linear algebra and thus their assessment is implicitly included in all the problems).

For each problem the main errors/mistakes have been detected, according to the classification given in Sect. 2.2. Let us see some samples.

The following figure shows an error of type E4.

The given question requires to decide if a given vector, that is the last row of the matrix in Fig. 2, belongs to the vector space generated by the vectors constituting the first three rows of the matrix. The student notes that the last row is proportional to the third ones, then she concludes that the last vector is linear dependent from the previous ones (correct!) but at the same time she uses this information to make an

Fig. 2. Linear dependence of a vector

incorrect deduction, answering that the given vector does not belong to the given vector space! This is an example of incorrect logical deduction, which can suggest that the student misses the relation between being linear dependent, being generated by vectors and belonging to a vector space.

In some cases, there is a doubt on the reason of the incorrectness. For instance, in Fig. 3 the student uses the brackets indicating the dimension of the null-space. It can be interpreted as a linguistic deficiency, which is E2, which means that the student is aware that the dimension of a vector space is a number (and in this case it is correct that is 0) but she is not aware of the meaning of the use of the brackets, which indicate a set. A further interpretation could suggest the hypothesis that the student does not distinguish the difference between a number, i.e. 0, and a singleton consisting of the number 0 (so going towards E3).

Fig. 3. Dimension of the null-space

The following sample shows a frequent case where the student does not pay attention to the text of the problem (E1), going directly to the questions, and so she answer correctly to a different problem (M3).

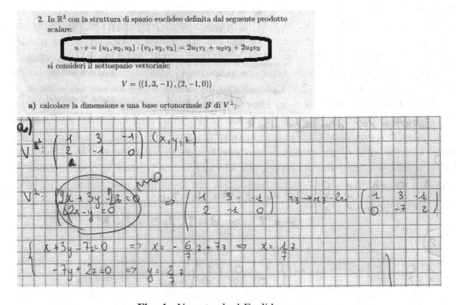

Fig. 4. Non standard Euclidean space

The problem concerns the Euclidean space related to the given dot product (see box in Fig. 4) and asks for the dimension and a basis of the vector space orthogonal to given V. The student applies a solution procedure which is correct with respect the standard dot product but incorrect with respect the given dot product!

In most of the cases, errors and mistakes occur and interact along the solution, as shown in the following sample. The first box in Fig. 5 shows how the student computes the dimension of the vector space W, given by its Cartesian representation.

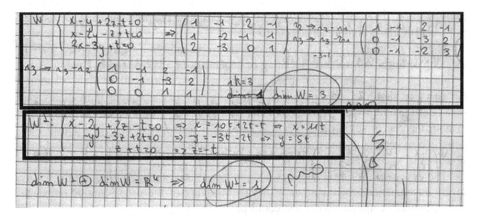

Fig. 5. Vector spaces - dimension

As you can see, her conclusion on the value of the requested dimension is incorrect, since she poses dim W equal to the rank of the matrix instead of its complement with respect to 4 (first box). This could highlight cognitive deficiency (E3). Just after this, the student consider the echelon form of the previous given linear system as the Cartesian representation of the space orthogonal to W (second box), making evident that there is no control on what she is doing (metacognitive level in E3). Moreover she make also technical mistakes (M2) writing the second coefficient of the first equation.

The same student, going ahead in answering to another question of the same problem, does not take into account the previous computation and solves again the linear system representing W. As shown in Fig. 6, this time she poses dim W = 1

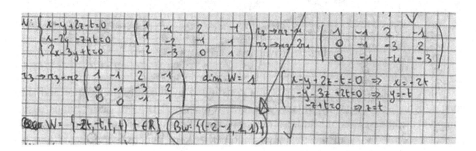

Fig. 6. Vector spaces – basis

(correct!) without giving any justification (M1), and without any cross control with the previous outcomes (metacognitive level in E3). Finally, she finds a basis consisting in one vector which is coherent with the dimension of W just calculated, but not coherent with the previous one, which could also suggest a cognitive deficiency (definition of dimension – E3).

4.2   Samples from the Tests

In this section, we want to sketch how we have exploited the previous analysis in order to prepare suitable comprehension tests.

The error seen in Fig. 2 suggests questions investigating on various topics, such as meaning of linear dependence, meaning of generators of a vector space, conditions for a vector to belong to a vector space, and the relation among all of them. Comprehension tests should contain questions addressing each of the notions individually and then questions involving all of them contemporarily. The questions can be formulated in both theoretical setting and practical cases. For instance, at first consider abstract definition of generators and then ask for verifying that a given vector is generated by a given set of vectors according to given coefficients.

The error seen in Fig. 3 suggests comprehension questions focusing on the nature of the mathematical objects at stake and the meaning of the used semiotic representation. Suitable comprehension test could be:

Let X be a vector subspaces in R^4. Are the following sentences true or false?

- dim X = {0} is incorrect because the dimension of a vector space is not a set;
- dim X = (0, 1, 3, −1) is correct because (0, 1, 3, −1) is a vector in R^4
- dim X = ½ is correct because the dimension of a vector space is a number
- dim X does not exist is incorrect because the dimension of a vector space is the number of the element in a basis, thus it is 0 or a positive integer number.

Analogous error is shown in Fig. 7:

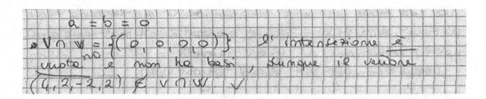

Fig. 7. Trivial space and empty set

where the student get the intersection constituted by the only null vector and she concludes in words that the intersection is the empty set! In both the previous case, comprehension tests should address the conversion among different semiotic system (verbal vs symbolic) and the treatment (number vs set), which is considered key in mathematics learning [4].

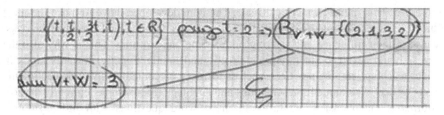

Fig. 8. Dimension and basis of a vector space

The comprehension tests should also include questions presenting incorrect pieces of solutions, asking for finding which the error/mistake is, and why it is so. To this aim, the students' protocols have been used. For instance, a question could present the piece shown in Fig. 8 and could ask for deciding which is incorrect among the two box and for detecting the reason of the error:

- There is inconsistency between the dimension and the number of the vectors in the basis, as the dimension of a vector space is the number of vectors of each basis of the vector space;
- The number of the vectors in the basis is correct and the dimension is incorrect, since the description of the vectors in V + W is made using 1 parameter, thus the dimension of V + W is 1;
- The dimension of V + W is incorrect since from the parametric description of V + W is not possible to compute 3 linear independent vectors corresponding to any three assignment of the unique parameter t.

The error in Fig. 4 suggests focusing on the scope of the problem. In fact, here the reason of the error can be ascribed to the fact that the student does not read the whole problem, but she goes directly to the punctual question. Comprehension tests should include questions that draw attention to the environment in which the question has been posed. For instance, it can be required to compute the norm of a vector or the Cartesian representation of the vector space orthogonal to a given V according to various dot product, so that the student has to apply the same abstract procedure in each case that becomes specific according to the environment of the exercise.

As the comprehension tests should supporting the student in confirming correct acquired knowledge and in overcoming incorrect beliefs, they have been implemented as true/false questionnaires where the reasons of the answers' correctness or not is explained and then the focus for the student is not to pass the test but to improving her learning understanding why she failed.

5   Advantages of the Quiz-Based Recovery Learning Path

The quiz-based recovery-learning path consists in groups of questions with automatic evaluation of the answers. The admissible formats for the items include multiple choice, true/false, matching, fill-in, cloze-procedure, short answer, numerical answer. Apart from short answer and numerical answer items, the other formats only require the learners to select their answer out of a prearranged set, and not to construct the answer themselves. This might be a critical issue. The item developers have to make the most of the benefits, exploiting the opportunities as much as possible, and to reduce the risks, because of their influence and steering on teaching and learning. This is why also the quizzes should avoid to steer (even indirectly and unintentionally) towards kinds of dubious teaching/learning practices, such as focusing on contents only or neglecting the aspects related to semiotic representations and language (for example, currently in most platforms is much easier and faster to insert word questions with little symbolic expressions and no images).

Apart the educational benefits of testing [10], let us recall the following concerning the use of the quizzes [1]:

- *Self-sufficiency:* the possibility of automatic assessment and feedback offered by the selected-response items makes them particularly suitable to large groups of students, such as undergraduates. They allow equipping the students with learning experiences which should be unaffordable in traditional settings. Automatic assessment and immediate feedback are indispensable requisites of the feasibility and the sustainability of such activities.
- *Flexibility:* the students can tailor training activities according a chosen level of dimension and difficulties. For instance, to make a quiz with a little number of random questions or it is possible to construct a sequence of quiz of growing difficulties so to allow the students to face the difficulties gradually. This affects the affective aspects too, as the student has the possibility of doing activities apt to her avoiding the frustration that can be derived from too many failures.
- *Challenge:* the chance to repeat more and more the quiz appears fundamental for the self-assessment since it should improve student's knowledge and at the same time reduce the need of tutoring (Valenti, in [2]). On the other hand, the chance of getting immediate feedback can motivate the student to go on and improve his marks, repeating more times the quizzes. Moreover, the CAA offers the student reporting tools able and useful to monitor her progress and make comparison between her outcomes and the ones' of her classmates [2].
- *Self-efficacy:* to get immediate feedback about some aspects of their learning may greatly affect the so-called sense of self-efficacy. The chance of trying and making mistakes without the judgment of another human may help some students to grow more confident and to develop a more positive attitude towards their products.
- *Learning:* students could even use sets of questions as a means to learn: the interaction with the resources could be used to add some piece of knowledge. Using resources of this kind might prove somewhat risky, such as to induce some students to neglect the skills related to argumentation, as some kinds of items might prove harder to develop and implement than others.

6   Conclusions

This work would support with a case study the assumption that close-ended questions can be used in a meaningful way for the formative self-assessment and thus the quiz module available in e-learning platform can be a powerful tool for supporting mathematics learning, not only at level of contents but also at a deeper level such as comprehension. Recovery learning paths can be designed starting from the analysis of the incorrect answers, which are so considered in a positive view, consisting in quizzes. Tests, especially the comprehension ones, become a meaningful learning activity and they have no more considered as evaluation tools. Even if some drawbacks of the use of closed-ended question can remain, a careful use as described in the paper allows proposing recovery activity to large groups of students, which is the case of undergraduates, exploiting many benefits derived by the automatic feedback.

References

1. Albano, G., Ferrari, P.L.: Mathematics education and e-learning: meaningful use of the quiz-modules. In: Faggiano, E., Montone, A. (eds.) Proceedings of ICTMT11 (International Conference on Technology in Mathematics Teaching), pp. 53–58. Università degli Studi di Bari Aldo Moro (2013)
2. Bartalini, T.: Quality of learning and teaching mathematics with Computer Aided Assessment. Ph.D. thesis in computer science, Università degli Studi di Firenze, Italy (2008)
3. Conradie, J., Frith, J.: Comprehension tests in mathematics. Educ. Stud. Math. **42**, 225–235 (2001)
4. Duval, R.: The cognitive analysis of problems of comprehension in the learning of mathematics. Educ. Stud. Math. **61**(1), 103–131 (2006)
5. Ferrari, P.L.: Mathematical language and advanced mathematics learning. In: Johnsen Høines, M., Berit Fuglestad, A. (eds.) Proceedings of the 28th Conference of the International Group for the Psychology of Mathematics Education, vol. 2, pp. 383–390. Bergen University College Press, Bergen (2004)
6. Movshovitz-Hadar, N., Zaslavsky, O., Inbar, S.: An empirical classification model for errors in high school mathematics. J. Res. Math. Educ. **18**(1), 3–14 (1987)
7. Niss, M.: Mathematical competencies and the learning of mathematics: The Danish KOM project. In: Gagatsis, A., Papastavridis, S. (eds.): 3rd Mediterranean Conference on Mathematical Education, 3–5 Jan 2003, pp. 115–124. Hellenic Mathematical Society, Athens (2003)
8. Pellerey, M.: L'eredità di Luigi Calonghi nella ricerca pedagogico-didattica (2012). http://www.giombattistaamenta.it/wp-content/uploads/2012/12/Pellerey-Leredita%CC%80-di-Luigi-Calonghi1.pdf
9. Radatz, H.: Error analysis in mathematics education. J. Res. Math. Educ. **10**(3), 163–172 (1979)
10. Roediger III, H.L., Putnam, A.L., Smith, M.A.: Ten benefits of testing and their applications to educational practice. In: Mestre, J.P., Ross, B.H. (eds.) Psychology of Learning and Motivation, vol. 55. Elsevier Inc., San Diego (2011)

A Survey of Methods for Improving Review Quality

Edward F. Gehringer$^{(\boxtimes)}$

Department of Computer Science,
North Carolina State University, Raleigh, USA
efg@ncsu.edu

Abstract. For peer review to be successful, students need to submit high-quality reviews of each other's work. This requires a certain amount of training and guidance by the review system. We consider four methods for improving review quality: calibration, reputation systems, meta-reviewing, and automated meta-reviewing. Calibration is training to help a reviewer match the scores given by the instructor. Reputation systems determine how well each reviewer's scores track scores assigned by other reviewers. Meta-reviewing means evaluating the quality of a review; this can be done either by a human or by software. Combining these strategies effectively is a topic for future research.

Keywords: Student peer review · Reputation systems · Calibration · Meta-review

1 Introduction

Classroom peer review began to be studied about 1970. A common technique was for students to exchange papers with a partner, and then make comments on the partner's work. Students were shown to benefit [1] from the feedback they received, and also from the feedback they gave. As reviewees, they profited from seeing whether their classmates understood their work, and from feedback on how to improve it. As reviewers, they benefited from seeing someone else's work as readers would see their own work, and thinking metacognitively about what constituted a good piece of work.

In the last 20 years or so, a variety of web-based peer-review applications have been developed for use in education. Basic peer-review functionality is to accept a submission from a student, and then, once the review period begins, to present that submission a few other students, who are asked to read the work and comment on its quality. Usually, reviewers are asked to fill out a rubric. Depending on the system, students may also be asked to assign the submission a numeric score, rate it on several rubric criteria, or rank it against the other students' work that they have reviewed.

2 Quality Control

It is important to assure that students do a careful job of reviewing. Particularly if they are new to the material, they may not have a clear idea of what constitutes good work. So, review systems employ various means to insure good reviewing.

© Springer International Publishing Switzerland 2014
Y. Cao et al. (Eds.): ICWL 2014 Workshops, LNCS 8699, pp. 92–97, 2014.
DOI: 10.1007/978-3-319-13296-9_10

2.1 Calibration

One of the most widespread methods for review quality assurance is *calibration*. It was pioneered by Calibrated Peer Review [2] at the end of the 1990 s. An instructor provides three samples of work that might be submitted for a particular assignment. One of them is a model solution; the others have specific shortcomings. Before being allowed to review real student work, students are asked to review all three of the sample submissions. How well they do on reviewing these establishes their reviewer competency index (RCI) [3] and determines how heavily their review is counted in assessing their peers.

Calibration has been used by several other systems, notably in the Coursera MOOC platform [4]. In the Coursera approach, students grade a submission that has already been graded by staff. If the student-assigned grade is "close enough" to the staff-assigned grade, students are allowed to proceed to assessing peers; if not, they repeat the process with another submission. They iterate through the process until they come "close enough"—a maximum of five times—after which they proceed to reviewing student work, regardless of the accuracy of their training assessments.

2.2 Reputation Systems

An RCI is a form of *reputation*. Reputations are often computed for participants in web-based review outside the classroom (e.g., for product reviews). Several algorithms exist for computing reputations from review scores themselves [5–7]. The simplest of these uses two metrics, leniency and spread. Leniency indicates how the scores of this reviewer compare with the scores of other reviewers who review the same work. A reviewer is more lenient if (s)he assigns higher scores than other reviewers do. Spread is a measure of the tendency of a reviewer to assign different scores to different work. A reviewer who assigns all 4 s on a Likert scale of 1 to 5 would have a spread of 0. Generally, a higher spread is better, because it indicates that the reviewer is discriminating between good and bad work.

The first reputation algorithm was developed by Hamer [5], developer of the Peerwise application [8]. In this system, reviews are weighted in a fashion that is inversely proportional to the difference in scores assigned by this reviewer to a particular submission and the average of the scores assigned to the submission by all reviewers.

In peer-review systems, reputations can be used either to give credit to students for careful reviewing, or to weight peer-assigned grades. If students are assigned grades based on reviews they are given, then the scores of reviewers who appear to be doing a careful job (median leniency, "large enough" spread) should be given more weight than reviewers who appear to be doing a cursory job of assessment. The SWoRD system [9] calculates a reputation based on leniency, spread, and agreement of a reviewer with other peer reviewers who have reviewed the same material. It uses these reputations both to give credit for reviewing and to weight peer reviews in assigning grades.

CrowdGrader [10] has an interesting twist on review weighting. It drops the lowest grade and the highest grade before calculating an average of the rest of the grades.

This approach, similar to that used in Olympic competitions, is used to derive the "consensus grade" for a submission, which is one of three factors used to compute a student's grade.

Summative peer *grading* is much more controversial than (formative) peer review, because it substitutes the judgments of inexperienced students for that of the presumably expert course staff. There is, of course, a middle ground: Course staff can look at the peer-assigned grades and use them to inform, but not determine, a student's final grade. One way to do this is to look at low scores that the reviewers have assigned to rubric criteria on a particular piece of student work, and read the prose feedback that the reviewers have given on each of those criteria. If the reviewer has a good reason for the low score, then the reviewer's assessment can be factored into the student's grade.[1] This allows the instructor or TA to be in charge of grading, but locate relevant issues much more quickly than (s)he could without the peer reviewers' assistance.

Still, in classes that are *really* large—MOOCs, for example—there is no alternative to peer grading (for work that cannot be machine-scored). Coursera seems to be the MOOC platform that has taken the most scholarly approach to peer review. They studied two MOOCs with a total of more than 64,000 students [4, 11]. For peer-reviewed assignments, each student assessed 5 peers, including one peer submission that was also graded by the staff. These student-and-staff-graded submissions were called "supernodes"; each was graded by the staff and 1/3 of the students in the class. The researchers' Model 1 made no use of reputation in assigning scores to students. It was found that up to 20 % of the student grades were more than 10 % from the student's "true" grade ("true" grades were assigned either by staff grading or crowd-sourcing; it didn't make much difference which of the two was used).

Next, each student was assigned a reputation based on how accurately they scored their supernode submission. The researchers added these reliabilities to Model 1 to weight student-assigned scores in computing reviewees' grades. This produced impressive gains; now 94 % of the student-assigned grades were within 10 % of the "true" grade. Their Model 2 allowed grading reputations to be cumulated over different assignments. Model 3 took into account a student's score on the assignment as well, on the assumption that students who do good work are also good graders. Both of these models did slightly better than the weighted Model 1. Model 3 scored 95 % of the students' work within 10 % of its "true" grade.

2.3 Meta-Reviewing, Manual and Automated

Reputation systems represent an algorithmic approach to determining grading reliability. It's also possible, of course, for humans to assess grading reliability. In this approach, known as *meta-reviewing*, a human is presented with a submission and a corresponding review. The metareviewer may be either a student or a TA or instructor. It is possible to incentivize students to perform metareviews by giving them credit for

---

[1] In principle, one could also do this with *high* scores associated with rubric criteria, but high scores tend to be much more common than low scores, and a high score may just be indicative of an inexperienced reviewer's inability to find anything wrong with the work on a particular dimension.

doing so [12]. The Expertiza system [13] allows an assignment to include a metareview period that follows the review period. Metareview scores can be used to deriving weighting factors, just as reputation systems would do. They can also be used to give students credit for reviewing; the score for an assignment then contains components for a the quality of the work and the quality of the reviewing.

One interesting approach is to automate the metareview process. It is possible [14] to input the review and the work being reviewed to a natural-language processing system. The system can then compute metrics for factors such as review relevance, type of content (e.g., detecting problems, giving advice), coverage, and review tone (whether the words used have positive or negative implications). This feedback can be presented to the reviewer when the review is about to be submitted. The reviewer can use the feedback on the review to improve the review before submission.

2.4 Helpfulness Ratings

A fourth approach is taken by Mobius/SLIP (http://www.mobiusslip.com/), which has students rank the helpfulness of the reviews they have received. This is called the "double-loop mutual assessment" approach. In the first loop, the students review the artifacts they are presented with. In the second loop, they review the reviews. The application displays a slider, onto which students can drag the various reviews in any order, except that they cannot drag two reviews onto the exact same position on the slider. Students see where they rank on average, but not where any particular individual ranked them. This is to prevent retaliation. The instructor, of course, sees the rating results from both loops, and can use them to determine the student's grade. The practice in Mobius/SLIP is to assign almost as much weight to reviewing as to submitted work.

CrowdGrader [10] allows students to rate the reviews that they receive on a scale from –2 (incorrect, completely unhelpful) to +2 (very helpful). The lowest feedback score received by a particular reviewer is dropped; then the remaining feedback scores are averaged, with negative scores being weighted twice as heavily as positive scores. The resulting *helpfulness grade* is one of three components used in determining a student's grade in CrowdGrader (the other two are the *consensus grade* (Sect. 2.2), and the *accuracy grade*, measuring how much the scores assigned by this student differ from the scores assigned by other students to the same work).

Both Mobius/SLIP and CrowdGrader take pains to prevent students from retaliating against reviewers who have assigned them low scores. Mobius/SLIP uses ranking, so a student who is dissatisfied with all the grades (s)he as received still has to rate one of the reviews as #1. CrowdGrader drops the lowest feedback grade before determining the helpfulness score. Thus, a student won't be able to retaliate against a single unfavorable reviewer, but may be able to retailiate against all but one who assigned low scores.

2.5 Rating vs. Ranking

Some systems use rating of reviews (each artifact is rated with a numeric score on a set of rubric criteria), while others use ranking (the "best" is ranked one, second best, two, etc.). Both approaches have advantages and disadvantages. Advantages of the rating approach include (i) the score that a student receives depends only on that student's work, and not on whether the other students assessed are weak or strong; and (ii) it is easier to use detailed rubrics, where students rate a submission on a variety of criteria (it would require a lot more "page-flipping" to effectively rank them on the same criteria). The ranking approach avoids the common problem of students rating submissions uniformly highly, which is the easy way out, because it doesn't require a deep understanding and avoids negative reactions from reviewees.

3 Conclusion

Various strategies have been developed to improve the quality of student reviews, and hence, the quality of feedback to students. For formative review, a good rubric is important. Future work can focus on improving the reliability of review criteria, and giving students automated feedback on the quality of a review they are about to submit, thus helping them to give better feedback. For summative review, peer-assigned grades are not yet an acceptable substitute for instructor-assigned grades. The most promising strategies for improving it include tuning the calibration process, and assigning additional reviewers to work that has not yet received enough quality reviews to be able to determine a reliable score.

References

1. Topping, K.: Peer assessment between students in colleges and universities. Rev. Educ. Res. 68(3), 249–276 (1998)
2. Chapman, O.L.: Calibrated peer review (TM). Abstracts of Papers of the American Chemical Society, vol. 217, pp. U311–U311. 1155 16TH ST. Am. Chemical Soc., NW, Washington, DC 20036 USA (1999)
3. Margerum, L.D.: Application of calibrated peer review (CPR) writing assignments to enhance experiments with an environmental chemistry focus. J. Chem. Educ. 84(2), 292 (2007)
4. Kulkarni, C., Wei, K.P., Le, H., Chia, D., Papadopoulos, K., Cheng, J., Klemmer, S.R.: Peer and self assessment in massive online classes. ACM Trans. Computer-Human Interact. (TOCHI) 20(6), 33 (2013)
5. Hamer, J., Ma, K.T., Kwong, H.H.: A method of automatic grade calibration in peer assessment. In: Young, A., Tolhurst, D. (eds.) Proceedings of the 7th Australasian Conference on Computing Education. ACM International Conference Proceeding Series, Newcastle, New South Wales, Australia, vols. 42, 106, pp. 67–72. Australian Computer Society, Darlinghurst (2005)
6. Cho, K., Schunn, C.D., Wilson, R.W.: Validity and reliability of scaffolded peer assessment of writing from instructor and student perspectives. J. Educ. Psych. 98(4), 891–901 (2006)
7. Lauw, H.W., Lim, E.-P., Wang, K.: Summarizing review scores of "unequal" reviewers. In: 2007 SIAM International Conference on Data Mining, Minneapolis, 26–28 April, pp. 539–544 (2007)
8. Denny, P., Hamer, J., Luxton-Reilly, A., Purchase, H.: PeerWise: students sharing their multiple choice questions. In: Proceedings of the Fourth international Workshop on Computing Education Research, pp. 51–58. ACM, September 2008

9. Cho, K., Schunn, C.: Scaffolded writing and rewriting in the discipline: a web-based reciprocal peer-review system. Comput. Educ. **48**, 409–426 (2007)
10. de Alfaro, L., Shavlovsky, M.: CrowdGrader: a tool for crowdsourcing the evaluation of homework assignments. In: Proceedings of the 45th ACM Technical Symposium on Computer Science Education (SIGCSE '14), pp. 415–420. ACM, New York (2014). http://doi.acm.org/10.1145/2538862.2538900, doi:10.1145/2538862.2538900
11. Piech, C., Huang, J., Chen, Z., Do, C., Ng, A., Koller, D.: Tuned models of peer assessment in MOOCs. In: Proceedings of the 6th International Conference on Educational Data Mining, Memphis, TN, July 2013
12. Gehringer, E., Peddycord, B., Grading by experience points: an example from computer ethics. In: Proceedings of the Frontiers in Education 2013, Oklahoma, Oct 2013
13. Gehringer, E.F.: Expertiza: information management for collaborative learning. In: Monitoring and Assessment in Online Collaborative Environments: Emergent Computational Technologies for E-Learning Support, pp. 143–159 (2009)
14. Ramachandran, L.: Automated assessment of reviews, Ph.D. dissertation, North Carolina State University (2013). http://www.lib.ncsu.edu/resolver/1840.16/8813

2014 International Workshop on Mobile and Personalized Learning

Bridging in-and-out Class Learning: Mobile Seamless Mandarin Learning

Yu-Ju Lan[1(✉)], Yao-Ting Sung[2], and Kuo-En Chang[3]

[1] National Taiwan Normal University,
Taipei, Taiwan, R.O.C.
yujulan@gmail.com
[2] Department of Educational Psychology and Counseling,
National Taiwan Normal University, Taipei, Taiwan
sungtc@ntnu.edu.tw
[3] Department of Information and Computer Education,
National Taiwan Normal University, Taipei, Taiwan
kchang@ice.ntnu.edu.tw

Abstract. This study aimed at bridging CSL students' learning both inside and outside the classroom. Mobile seamless learning technology was used to enhance their Mandarin performances. Forty-one overseas Chinese students participated in this study. The Mandarin Chinese performances was collected and analyzed to determine the effects of mobile seamless learning on Mandarin Chinese learning by overseas Chinese students. Analysis of the results showed that overseas Chinese students were benefited from connecting the gaps between inside and outside the classroom learning.

Keywords: Chinese as a second language (CSL) · Seamless learning · Mobile technology · Mandarin Chinese

1 Introduction

Mandarin Chinese learning has been a popularly global topic in recent years [1]. For learning Mandarin Chinese, many people go to the countries in which Mandarin Chinese is the dominative or mainly used language, such as China, Taiwan, and Singapore. Taiwan has been one of the most popular countries for learners of Mandarin as a second language (L2), especially for overseas Chinese students, from all over the word because of the Chinese tradition and culture reserved in the Asia Pacific island [2, 3].

According to Swain [4], the opportunity for L2 learners doing target language output not only enhances their L2 fluency but also helps them aware the status of their interlanguage. Furthermore, Lave and Wenger [5] argued that effective L2 learning involves activity, context and culture, whereby L2 knowledge needs to be presented in authentic contexts. To acquire L2 knowledge whether outside or inside the classroom requires meaningful tasks in authentic situations. Due to the dynamically interactive process of language learning, both Long [6] and Krashen [7] emphasized the importance of social interaction happened in authentic contexts to L2 learners acquiring the target language. Thus, how to provide the overseas Chinese students opportunities

© Springer International Publishing Switzerland 2014
Y. Cao et al. (Eds.): ICWL 2014 Workshops, LNCS 8699, pp. 101–105, 2014.
DOI: 10.1007/978-3-319-13296-9_11

pursuing them to apply what they learned inside the classrooms to social interaction in real world context is the main concern of this study.

The aim of the study, thus, was to enhance the orally interactive performances of the overseas Chinese students by applying mobile seamless technology supported cooperative task-based learning. The lessons learned from the study will be an important example for expanding the learning contexts from in class to the outdoor worlds for the overseas Chinese students, and will also add to the knowledge pool of research on technology enhanced language learning (TELL).

2   Methods

2.1   Participants

The participants were 41 overseas Chinese students from Australia (mean age, 17.1 years; 17 males and 24 females). Most of them knew few Mandarin Chinese, neither spoken nor written. English was their shared first language (L1). These students voluntarily enrolled in a six-week course of Mandarin Chinese provided by the university in which the author teaches. During the six-week period, they learned basic Mandarin Chinese knowledge and culture topics for 4 weeks, while in the first week they were usually administered placement test and introduced the surrounding of the campus and engaged in a one-week field trip in the last week.

2.2   Research Design

The approach of dependent groups, paired-sample t test, was adopted in this study. Quantitative data were collected and analyzed. The performance of Mandarin Chinese language was administered before and after the teaching process. The scores of the performance test were analyzed via dependent-samples t-test to evaluate the improvements made by the students due to the use of mobile seamless technology in their Mandarin language learning.

2.3   Instruments

Mobile Mandarin learning platform (MobileMan). MobileMan was developed by the author aiming at providing FL/L2 learners a seamless platform to bridge the learning happened in and out of the classrooms. It supports them doing both individual and cooperative learning. While doing individual learning, the functions of location based service and context awareness abilities of MobileMan allow the learners using mobile devices to scan QR codes and access the just-meet materials for where they are. Figure 1 shows the screen shots of MobileMan when the attending overseas Chinese students doing campus exploration. On the other hand, when doing cooperative learning, first, FL/L2 learners collected information during the exploring process. Then, they work together and discuss to solve the problems assigned by their teachers.

Fig. 1. Left: the visiting spots with learning materials; right: the learning material for learners exploring one representative building (the Commons) on the campus.

Mandarin communication performance online test. The aim of this test consisting of 21 items was to determine the communication abilities of the participating overseas Chinese students, such as "可以刷卡嗎? (1) 只能付現金 (2) 一共3000元 (3) 不可以帶外食. (Could I pay by card? (1) Cash only. (2) It is 3000 NTD. (3) Please no outside food or drink.)" All of the items were first confirmed by two content experts and then uploaded to an online test system developed by the author. In order to focus on oral communication, all the test items were audio format only. Figure 2 shows the screen shot of the online test.

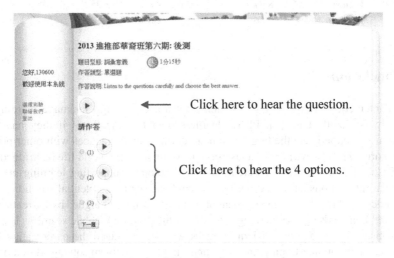

Fig. 2. Item example of Mandarin language performance test.

2.4 Procedures

This study lasted for six weeks, two hours per week. The pretest of Mandarin communication performances was administered followed by the training on the operation of the MobileMan system in the first week. From the second week, all the students were grouped into small exploration groups of 3 or 4 overseas Chinese students to do 2 units of campus exploration for 4 weeks. In each unit, the basic words and sentences needed for later exploration were taught first. Then the exploration mission was interpretation and assigned to each group. After getting the mission, all the overseas Chinese students went out of the classroom and explored the campus or its neighborhood. Each of them collected and shared information while exploring. After exploration, they got together to discuss and figure out the answers to the problems. Finally, all the groups reported their exploration results in front of the whole class. In the last week, the posttest of identical performance test was administered again.

3 Results

The online Mandarin communication performance test was administered to all the participants before and after completion of the two units of seamless learning of campus exploration. Table 1 lists the means and standard deviations for the online Mandarin communication performance test plus the results of the t-test analysis. As the data shown in Table 1, the overseas Chinese students made significant improvements after using MoblieMan for seamless Mandarin learning ($t = -3.252$, $df = 40$, $p = 0.002 < 0.01$, effect size = 0.46).

Table 1. Means and standard deviations (SDs) for the Mandarin communication performance test and t-test analysis (n = 41)

Test	Mean	SD	t
Pretest	8.07	2.62	-3.252^*
Posttest	9.46	2.98	

4 Conclusions

"Social interaction" is the key component in learners' foreign language learning as argued by Meltzoff et al. [8]. FL/L2 learners only become fluent if they have the opportunity to experience the target language during social practices with other people in real world [7]. How will FL/L2 classroom learning and real world life be bridged and support social practice in it? To create a new "ecology" supporting learning practice and social interactions across scenarios and contexts seems a potential solution.

In order to achieve higher engagement of social interactions as argued by Larreamendy-Joerns and Leinhardt [9], the learning activities in the proposed mobile seamless learning was established with a series of inquiry tasks which encouraged the participating CSL learners engaging in questioning, making connection, and problem solving. Based on the results obtained from the current study, the participating overseas Chinese students made significant improvement in the Mandarin communication performances test. They also enjoyed the inquiry and exploring process based on their answers to the interview.

To put it in a nutshell, the proposed mobile seamless learning system, MobileMan, successfully played the role in stimulating the participating overseas Chinese students engaging in social interaction in real contexts and consequently improved their Mandarin oral practices and learning motivation. Future research should aim at providing CSL learners with adapted learning and scaffolding materials as well as a more unconscious seamless platform to optimize the learning switching from context to context.

Acknowledgments.   The author would like to thank the Ministry of Science and Technology, Taiwan, R.O.C., for financially supporting this research under Grant No. NSC 101-2511-S-003-031-MY3. She is also thankful that this research is partially supported by the "Aim for the Top University Project" of National Taiwan Normal University (NTNU), sponsored by the Ministry of Education, Taiwan, R.O.C., the "International Research-Intensive Center of Excellence Program" of NTNU and the Ministry of Science and Technology, Taiwan, R.O.C. under Grant No. NSC 103-2911-I-003-301.

References

1. Ramzy, A.: Get ahead, learn mandarin: China's economic rise means the world has a new second language—and it isn't English (2006). http://clta-gny.org/article/GetAhead.htm
2. Jiang, X.M.: The current situation and reflection of TCFL. Paper presented at 2007 Multicultural and Ethnic Harmony International Conference, Taiwan, Taipei (2007). http://r9.ntue.edu.tw/activity/multiculture_conference/file/2/3.pdf. Accessed 23–24 Nov 2007
3. Lan, Y.J.: Does second life improve Mandarin learning by overseas Chinese students? Lang. Learn. Technol. **18**(2), 36–56 (2014)
4. Swain, M.: Three functions of output in second language learning. In: Cook, G., Seidelhofer, B. (eds.) Principle and Practice in Applied Linguistics: Studies in Honor of H.G. Widdowson, pp. 125–144. Oxford University Press, Oxford (1995)
5. Lave, J., Wenger, E.: Situated Learning: Legitimate Peripheral Participation. Cambridge University Press, Cambridge (1991)
6. Long, M.H.: The role of the linguistic environment in second language acquisition. In: Ritchie, W.C., Tej, K.B. (eds.) Handbook of Second Language Acquisition, pp. 413–468. Academic Press, San Diego (1996)
7. Krashen, S.D.: Second Language Acquisition and Second Language Learning. Pergamon Press, New York (1981)
8. Meltzoff, A.N., Kuhl, P.K., Movellan, J., Sejnowski, T.J.: Foundations for a new science of learning. Science **325**(5938), 284–288 (2009)
9. Larreamendy-Joerns, J., Leinhardt, G.: Going the distance with online education. Rev. Educ. Res. **76**(4), 567–605 (2006)

A Meta-Analysis of the Effects of Learning Languages with Mobile Devices

Yi-Shian Lee[1]([⊠]), Yao-Ting Sung[2], Kuo-En Chang[3],
Tzu-Chien Liu[4], and Wei-Cheng Chen[5]

[1] Aim for the Top University Project Office,
National Taiwan Normal University, Taipei, Taiwan
bill.net.tw@yahoo.com.tw
[2] Department of Educational Psychology and Counseling,
National Taiwan Normal University, Taipei, Taiwan
sungtc@ntnu.edu.tw
[3] Department of Information and Computer Education,
National Taiwan Normal University, Taipei, Taiwan
kchang@ice.ntnu.edu.tw
[4] Graduate Institute of Learning and Instruction,
National Central University, Taoyuan, Taiwan
ltc@cc.ncu.edu.tw
[5] Research Center for Psychological and Educational Testing,
National Taiwan Normal University, Taipei, Taiwan

Abstract. Language learning has undergone rapid changes over the past several years from computer-assisted learning to more recently, mobile devices. Mobile devices have become useful learning tools that can potentially be applied in both various settings. This study adopted 44 peer-reviewed journal articles published between from 1993 to 2013 to demonstrate that mobile assisted language instruction provided meaningful average improvement with an overall mean effect size of 0.54. The current analyses revealed few statistically significant findings when applied into some moderators.

Keywords: Mobile-assisted language learning · Meta-analysis · Ubiquitous learning

1 Introduction

The use of information technology to support teaching and learning effectiveness has been developing since the seventies and can be roughly divided into three stages. The desktop stage (1970–1980), where computer labs or a classroom computer were used to assist in teaching and learning; the laptop stage (1990–2010), where the emphasis was on getting laptops into the hands of children in one-to-one programs; and the current mobile device (2010 to present) stage, where handhelds bring accessibility and ubiquity that allow for learning without constraint. To date, there have been no clear-cut conclusions showing that continued advancements in information technology have led to more efficient and effective education practices. Additionally, As computer-assisted

© Springer International Publishing Switzerland 2014
Y. Cao et al. (Eds.): ICWL 2014 Workshops, LNCS 8699, pp. 106–113, 2014.
DOI: 10.1007/978-3-319-13296-9_12

learning has been a focus of educational research for years, language learning has also been a major field of research with computer technology since the 1960s. Despite its limitations, the benefits of computer technology, technology can be very beneficial remains limited in its ability to assist in language learning.

In recent years, a large body of literature has attempted to develop alternative learning tools for computer-assisted learning. The emergence of wireless technology and mobile device innovations has received a great deal of attention from the field of education. M-learning integrates electronic learning (e-learning) materials with mobile devices, such as Personal Digital Assistants (PDAs), tablet PCs, mobile phones, and e-book readers. Mobile devices offer portability, social interactivity, context sensitivity, connectivity, and individuality, features that desktop and laptop computers might not offer [1, 2]. Mobile devices have made possible rich, real-time, collaborative learning, inside and outside the classroom [3, 4].

In examining the overall effectiveness of mobile devices in language learning, most review research has been performed using the qualitative method. Some described and summarized ways mobile devices have been used in teaching and learning [5, 6] and other relevant trends, while some have tried to point out problems encountered when mobile devices are used in learning and teaching [7, 8]. However, it is difficult to evaluate the actual effectiveness of mobile devices overall and the specific moderator variables using the qualitative approaches above. As such, this study employed meta-analysis to organize and quantify studies on the effectiveness of mobile devices in language learning. This study seeks to address the following questions: 1. To overview the use of mobile devices in language learning, including types of mobile devices and software, and environments, etc. 2. To view the overall effectiveness of integrating mobile technology into education on language learning. 3. To compare differences among the effects of each moderator variable on language learning.

2 Method

2.1 Data Sources and Search Strategy

This research employed electronic searches, manual searches, and reference list checking to retrieve relevant literature for the meta-analysis. For electronic searches, the main databases were the Education Resources Information Center (ERIC), the Institute of Science Index (ISI), and the Social Sciences Citation Index (SSCI). The keywords searched were the following: (1) mobile-device keywords, including mobile, wireless, ubiquitous, wearable, portable, handhelds, mobile phone, personal digital assistant (PDA), palmtop, pad, web pad, tablet pc, tablet computer, laptop, e-book, digital pen, pocket dictionary, and clickers; (2) learning keywords including teaching, learning, training, and lecture. Manual searches included the major journals of educational technology and e-Learning, such as the Language Learning & Technology, Computer Assisted Language Learning, Recall, Computers & Education, Journal of Computer Assisted Learning, and British Journal of Educational Technology.

2.2   Search Results

Initial screening stage: This study began the first stage on January 10th, 2014. We found 721 abstracts published between 1993 and 2013 (ERIC 303 ISI 418) that had to do with mobile learning and language. After researchers read each article and main text, they judged whether or not the article had to do with mobile device and language education, and whether or not to select it for this study. 288 total articles were selected.

Experimental screening stage: The second stage screened studies by research method. True experiments, including equivalent group pre- and post-test designs, equivalent group post-test designs, and randomly paired post-test designs; and quasi-experiments, including non-equivalent pre- and post-test designs and counterbalanced designs [9–11], were included in the analysis range.

Meta-analysis standards screening stage: There are three standards in this screening stage. The first is whether or not the study is suitable for this study's purpose, i.e. does it compare mobile devices in teaching situations. Therefore the experimental group must deal with mobile devices, and the control group had to use traditional teaching methods (no mobile devices or simply used desktops). The second is that all of the results must have been presented in a way that meets the standards for a meta-analysis [12]. The third is that at least some of the measured variables have to do with learning achievement.

2.3   Outcome Variable Selection, Effect Size Determination, and Coding

This study used the dependent variable of learning achievement scores for the analysis of effect size. There were several ways of measuring student achievement, such as standardized tests, teacher-created tests, and tests designed by the researcher. Additionally, because some research included the effects of mobile devices on cooperative learning, the dependent variables of cooperative behaviors, such as frequency of peer interaction [13, 14] were included for analysis, too. It is worth mentioning that although some research mentioned experimental results for cooperative learning, they lacked some data and thus could not be analyzed. For example, some study [15] did not provide details about the means and standard deviations for the cooperative learning experimental and control groups.

When creating the effect sizes of each article, we followed literature [16] to integrate the effect sizes within an article: (a) a single study with identical outcome variables with two or more effect sizes (for example, test scores and grades in school); (b) a single study with identical outcome variables that underwent multiple experimental treatments (such as two experimental groups with a single control group); (c) a single study with identical outcome variables measured separately over periods of time (ex, posttests); and (d) a study that did not provide the overall statistical results of the students, and thus the statistical results of various subgroups need to be integrated. This study uses information found in literature [12, 16] to calculate Hedges's g for all of the effect indicators.

The codebook included the following variables: research name, research sample, research design, hardware used, software used, languages, and environments. This study handled missing values by coding the value as 0 [17], indicated it was not mentioned in the literature.

2.4 Data Analysis

This study used two formulae to calculate the effect sizes of articles. For the experimental research with random assignment and without a pre-test, Cohen's d (formula 1) was used to get effect sizes.

$$d = \frac{\bar{X}_E - \bar{X}_C}{\sqrt{\frac{(n_C-1)s_C^2+(n_E-1)s_E^2}{(n_C+n_E-2)}}} \tag{1}$$

where $\bar{X}_E$ represents the mean scores of the experiment group, $\bar{X}_C$ represents the mean scores of the control group, n_C represents the sample size of the control group, n_E represents the sample size of the experiment group, s_C^2 represents the variance of the control group, and s_E^2 represents the variance of the experiment group. Moreover, this Hedge's g can be obtained through formula 2, where N represents the total sample size.

$$g = [1 - 3/(4 \times N - 9)] \times d \tag{2}$$

3 Results

3.1 The Overall Effect Size for Learning Achievement

This study integrated 44 research articles (k) and their corresponding 200 effect sizes (es) of learning achievement into an overall mean effect size. In most situations, the effect of using mobile devices on learning achievement is more positive than traditional methods, and only in the minority of cases did traditional methods have stronger performances. Hence, the overall mean effect size was 0.539, the 95 % confidence interval was between 0.377 and 0.702. In other words, learners using a mobile device performed significantly better overall than learning using paper or desktops, and can be understood as those who used mobile devices learned about 70.51 % more than those who did not.

The Q statistics show that the effect sizes in the meta-analysis were heterogeneous ($Q_{total} = 82.653$, $z = 6.500$, $p < .001$), which indicates that there are differences among the effect sizes that have some source other than subject-level sampling error (see Table 1). These other sources are likely diversity of researched design, hardware used.

Table 1. Learning achievement overall effect size

Effect size			95 % CI		Homegeneity test	
n of es	g	SE	Lower	Upper	Q_{total}	df
200	0.539	0.083	0.377	0.702	82.653***	43

CI = confidence interval, *** $p < .001$.

3.2 The Effect Size of Learning Achievement for Moderator Variables

This study shows the effect size for the moderator variables such as research design, software used, hardware used, languages, and environments. According to Cohen's [18] effect size strengths, 0.80 and above is large, 0.20 and below is small, and around 0.50 is medium strength. This study uses this standard as a basis for its interpretations.

Research design. Table 2 shows the learning achievement effect size in different research designs for mobile learning. Quasi-experimental studies ($g = 0.721$, $z = 7.067$, $p < .001$) attends high-end medium effect size and true-experimental ($g = 0.185$, $z = 1.301$, $p > .05$) attends small effect size. The heterogeneity test resulted in a Q_B that achieves significance ($Q_B = 9.377$, $p = .002$), which shows that the two types of research design categories have significant difference.

Table 2. Research design effect size summary statistics

Category	k	g	z	95 %CI
1.Quasi-experimental	29	0.721	7.067***	[0.521–0.921]
2.True-experimental	15	0.185	1.301	[−0.094–0.464]
Q_B				9.377**
df				1

CI = confidence interval, ** $p < .01$, *** $p < .001$.

Software used. Table 3 indicates the effect size for teaching-oriented software ($g = 0.588$, $z = 5.374$, $p < .001$) was more than general purpose software ($g = 0.473$, $z = 3.722$, $p < .001$). After conducting Q analyses, Q_B not achieved significance at the .05 level ($Q_B = 0.473$, $p > .05$), which means that the various categories did not have significantly different average effect sizes. In other words, what kind of software is used matters, as it does not significantly influence the effect size of the experiment.

Table 3. Software used effect size summary statistics

Category	k	g	z	95 %CI
1.General-use	18	0.473	3.722***	[0.224–0.722]
2.Specially-designed	26	0.588	5.374***	[0.374–0.803]
Q_B				0.473
df				1

CI = confidence interval, *** $p < .001$.

Hardware used. Table 4 shows the effect sizes for the usage of different hardware types in mobile learning. Handheld devices ($g = 0.732$, $z = 7.117$, $p < .001$) attends high-end medium effect size and laptops ($g = 0.180$, $z = 1.287$, $p > .05$) attends small effect size. The Q_B was significant ($Q_B = 10.055$, $p = .002$), which indicates that the effect sizes among the various categories were be different significantly from one another.

Table 4. Hardware used effect size summary statistics

Category	k	g	z	95 %CI
1.Handhelds	30	0.732	7.177***	[0.530–0.933]
2.Laptops	14	0.180	1.287	[−0.094–0.455]
Q_B				10.055**
df				1

CI = confidence interval, ** $p < .01$, *** $p < .001$.

Language. Table 5 shows the effect size for different language, among which the largest effect size was Spanish ($g = 0.567$, $z = 1.678$, $p > .05$), closely followed by English ($g = 0.554$, $z = 6.166$, $p < .001$) and Chinese ($g = 0.381$, $z = 1.135$, $p > .05$). The Q statistical analysis revealed that Q_B not achieved statistical significance ($Q_B = 0.365$, $p > .05$), which means that the effect sizes for each of the categories was not significantly different from the other language.

Table 5. Language effect size summary statistics

Category	k	g	z	95 %CI
1.English	37	0.554	6.166***	[0.378–0.729]
2.Chinese	3	0.381	1.135	[−0.277–1.039]
3.Hebrew	1	0.366	0.704	[−0.653–1.385]
4.Spanish	3	0.567	1.678	[−0.095–1.230]
Q_B				0.365
df				3

CI = confidence interval, *** $p < .001$.

Environments. Table 6 shows that mixed or unrestricted had the largest effect ($g = 0.781$, $z = 5.710$, $p < .001$), followed by classroom ($g = 0.4$, $z = 3.616$, $p < .001$). Comparatively, outside ($g = 0.388$, $z = 1.239$, $p > .05$) had medium-end low effects. Q statistical analyses found Q_B not be significant ($Q_B = 4.958$, $p > .05$), which shows that the different categories' effectiveness do not have be difference significantly.

Table 6. Environments effect size summary statistics

Category	k	g	z	95 %CI
1.Classroom	25	0.400	3.616***	[0.183–0.616]
2.Outside	3	0.388	1.239	[−0.226–1.001]
3.Mixed/unrestricted	16	0.781	5.710***	[0.513–1.050]
Q_B				4.958
df				2

CI = confidence interval, *** $p < .001$.

4 Conclusions and Future Work

The effect of mobile devices has increasingly received attention in language learning as mobile devices are expected to eventually take over the role of desktops in language education. Nevertheless, very little research using meta-analyses has been devoted to examining mobile devices in language education. By investigating empirical research published in peer-reviewed journals with mobile devices in language education, it was found that they have a medium strength of effect, indicating that mobile devices are more effective than traditional or desktop computers in language learning.

A future research will focus on the functionality and applicability of language learning teaching-oriented software should be further expanded to allow for easy modification and flexibility that allows instructors to customize language teaching/learning materials. Second, specialized development training in mobile assisted language programs needs to be provided to language educators.

References

1. Attewell, J., Webster, T.: Engaging and supporting mobile learners. In: Proceedings of M-Learning 2004: Mobile Learning Anytime Everywhere, London, pp. 15–20 (2004)
2. Chinnery, G.M.: Emerging technologies going to the mall: mobile assisted language learning. Lang. Learn. Technol. 10(1), 9–16 (2006)
3. Norris, C., Soloway, E.: Envisioning the handheld centric classroom. J. Educ. Comput. Res. 30(4), 281–294 (2004)
4. Tatar, D., Roschelle, J., Vahey, P., Penuel, W.: Handhelds go to school. IEEE Comput. 36 (9), 30–37 (2003)
5. Frohberg, D., Goth, C., Schwabe, G.: Mobile learning projects – a critical analysis of the state of the art. J. Comput. Assist. Learn. 25(4), 307–331 (2009)
6. Fleischer, H.: What is our current understanding of one-to-one computer projects: a systematic narrative research review. Educ. Res. Rev. 7(2), 107–122 (2012)
7. Godwin-Jones, R.: Emerging technologies mobile apps for language learning. Lang. Learn. Technol. 15(2), 2–11 (2011)
8. Kukulska-Hulme, A., Shield, L.: An overview of mobile assisted language learning: from content delivery to supported collaboration and interaction. ReCALL 20(3), 271–289 (2008)
9. Ary, D., Jacobs, L.C., Razavieh, A.: Introduction to research in education, 6th edn. Wadsworth, Belmont (2002)
10. Best, J.W., Kahn, J.V.: Research in Education, 9th edn. Allyn and Bacon, Boston (2003)
11. Cohen, L., Manion, L., Morrison, K.: Research methods in Education, 5th edn. Routledge Falmer, London (2000)
12. Lipsey, M.W., Wilson, D.B.: Practical Meta-Analysis. Sage, Thousand Oaks (2000)
13. Lan, Y.J., Sung, Y.T., Chang, K.E.: A mobile-device-supported peer-assisted learning system for collaborative early EFL reading. Lang. Learn. Technol. 11(3), 130–151 (2007)
14. Lan, Y.J., Sung, Y.T., Chang, K.E.: Let us read together: development and evaluation of a computer-assisted reciprocal early English reading system. Comput. Educ. 53(4), 1188–1198 (2009)
15. Zurita, G., Nussbaum, M.: Computer supported collaborative learning using wirelessly interconnected handheld computers. Comput. Educ. 42(3), 289–314 (2004)

16. Borenstein, M., Hedges, L.V., Higgins, J.P.T., Rothstein, H.R.: Introduction to Meta-Analysis. Wiley, Chichester (2009)
17. Bernard, R.M., Abrami, P.C., Lou, Y., Borokhovski, E., Wade, A., Wozney, L., Wallet, P.A., Fiset, M., Huang, B.: How does distance education compare with classroom instruction? A meta-analysis of the empirical literature. Rev. Educ. Res. **74**(3), 379–439 (2004)
18. Cohen, J.: Statistical Power Analysis for the Behavioral Sciences, 2nd edn. Erlbaum, Hillsdale (1988)

educoco: A Mobile Social Learning Platform for Project-Based Learning and Collaboration

Shih-Pang Tseng[1](✉) and Ti-Chih Chen[2]

[1] Department of Computer Science and Entertainment Technology, Tajen University,
Pingtung, Taiwan
tsp@tajen.edu.tw
[2] Education Business Division, United Daily News, Taipei, Taiwan
tichih.chen@udngroup.com

Abstract. Learning is a social behavior. The important issue to design a learning management system is how to effectively use the technologies to improve the collaborative learning. Due to the drawbacks of Facebook, the authors proposed a new social networking service, *educoco*, for K-12 education in Taiwan. The characteristics of teachers are specially strengthened in *educoco*, and the learning activity is project-based. Now, there are more than 10000 users in Taiwan.

Keywords: Social-learning · K-12

1 Introduction

People can adapt the environment or the society better by learning new knowledges, skills, and so on. In the past twenty years, the development of e-learning [1] means that more traditional learning activities have been shifted into the cyberspace successfully. Furthermore, more innovative learning activities are developed via the new information and communication technologies. Especially, due to the development of smart mobile technologies, the people can learn anywhere without the limitation of classroom and desktop. Today, the varied types of e-learning are widely applied on different kinds of educations, from the primary education to the continuing education.

The learning activities of human being do not only access the content from the learning media, but also communicate with the other people. Since interactions among peers can effectively trigger the individual learning behavior [2], the learning management system (LMS) should be designed to encourage these interactions. Therefore, learners can efficiently use this type of LMS to engage with each other learners and with their teachers, share knowledges and experiences, work and learn collaboratively [3]. This paper proposes a new mobile social learning platform, *educoco* [4], which designs and implements for project-based learning and collaboration. Moreover, *educoco* has been used to a great degree in Taiwan.

ⓒ Springer International Publishing Switzerland 2014
Y. Cao et al. (Eds.): ICWL 2014 Workshops, LNCS 8699, pp. 114–121, 2014.
DOI: 10.1007/978-3-319-13296-9_13

The remainder of the paper is organized as follows. The related works are in Sect. 2. Section 3 introduces why to design the *educoco*. The detail of the *educoco* are in Sect. 4. Conclusion is given in Sect. 5.

2   Related Works

The learning theory describes the generalized learning objectives and approaches. When the instructors design what to learn and how to learn, the learning theory can provide general and essential guides. In addition, the designer of learning management system can decide the functional specifications of LMS according to the learning theory. Moodle [5] claimed its design guided by the *social constructivism* [6]. In Moodle, there are some functions which support the learners collaborative interaction with environment to construct their knowledge. However, Moodle is still a more traditional course-centered LMS, not a collaboration-centered one.

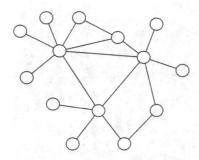

Fig. 1. An example of the social network among learners [7].

The connectivism [7] is proposed by George Siemens in 2005. In contrast with the previous theories, learning is considered as the social activity, not only the individual activity. And knowledge is constructed in cooperation with others in the social process. The social context of learning, such as the social network among learners and instructors, is the most important issue in connectivism. Figure 1 shows an example of the social network among learners. The connectivism pays less attention on the organization of learning contents. In e-learning, the connectivism focus on how to effectively use the Internet technology to improve the collaborative learning.

A web blog [8] is a personal discussion or informational site published on the Internet. Blogging can be as a potential social learning activity. Kubincová et al. [9] proposed a work to show that incorporating well organized peer review rounds into the process significantly increased learners' participation. Anther work, proposed by Ercan Top [10], shows that the pre-service teachers had positive feelings about the collaborative learning; and they had moderate feelings related to sense of community in the classes which incorporated blogs.

3   Motivation

Facebook [11] is an online social networking service since February 4, 2004. Relative to the various web blog sites, Facebook is a huge, but centralized-controlled site with more than 1 billion users. Due to the popularity of Facebook, there are many work which apply Facebook as a social learning tool. Roblyer et al. [12] proposed a work about Facebook behavior comparison of faculty and student in higher education. This work indicate that students are much more likely than faculty to use Facebook and are significantly more open to the possibility of using Facebook and similar technologies to support classroom work. This work shows the potential of Facebook as a social learning tool. Tower et al. [13] proposed a successful application of Facebook to improve nursing students' perception of efficacy. Kabilan et al. [14] proposed another successful case which shows that students believed Facebook could be as an online environment of learning English. These above two works are both in higher education.

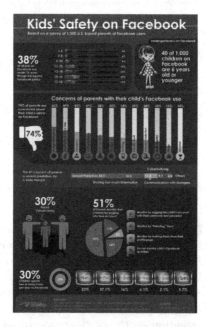

Fig. 2. MinorMonitor Surveys 1,000 Parents of Children on Facebook, Shares Results on Realities, Parental Concerns [15].

Although there are some successful cases of Facebook as a social learning tool, Facebook is designed as a popular generalized social service originally. Some drawbacks of Facebook are indicated in education, especially K-12. According the survey of 1,000 parents of children under 18 years old who use Facebook [15], 74 % of parents are concerned about their children's safety on Facebook, with the majority worrying about sexual predators, at 56 %. Figure 2 shows the detail of this survey.

One important issue is that all user are equivalent in Facebook. The teachers are without any privileges on the activities and contents in Facebook. The pedagogic behaviors of teachers are still important, even in the cyberspace. Therefore, some educational social networking service are proposed. Popescu et al. [16] proposed the Lintend platform, an educational social networking service.

4   educoco

educoco, shown as Fig. 3 is a social networking service implemented by Education Business Division of United Daily News, Taipei, Taiwan. Because of the drawbacks of Facebook, which is not suitable for K-12, *educoco* is designed for K-12 education in Taiwan. The characteristics of teachers are specially strengthened in *educoco*. Figure 4 shows the privileges of the teacher, such as assigning a mission and choosing the contents.

Fig. 3. The Homepage of educoco (http://educoco.udn.com)

The social relationship, called by *circle*, is the kernel of *educoco*. Figure 5 illustrates the circles in *educoco*.

- **Class Circle:** the relationship is only organized by the teacher. The students must have the invitation from the teacher to join class circle. It is the basic relationship in *educoco*.
- **Friend Circle:** the relationship can be organized by the student, but limited in the same class circle.
- **Mission Circle:** the relationship is organized by the teacher. When the teacher assign a mission, the teacher should organize a mission circle with a small group students to complete the mission.

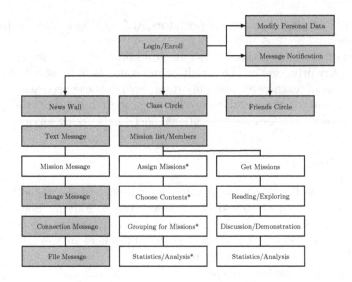

Fig. 4. The system architecture of *educoco*. The function denoted by * are only for teachers.

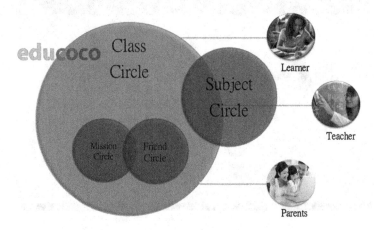

Fig. 5. The various circles in *educoco*

– **Subject Circle:** the relationships are among the class circles. The different class circles can share the learning contents with the same subject.

A *mission* is one learning activity with some specific learning objective which should be accomplished by the collaboration of the mission circle. There are two types of missions, reading and miscellaneous missions. The students in the specific reading mission circle should read the contents assigned by the teacher at first. The reading can give the student a basic prior knowledge to discover new knowledge of related topics. Next, the student is encourage to explore the relative information in Internet. Thirdly, the student should share his/her finding and

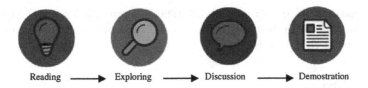

Reading ⟶ Exploring ⟶ Discussion ⟶ Demonstration

Fig. 6. The process of reading mission

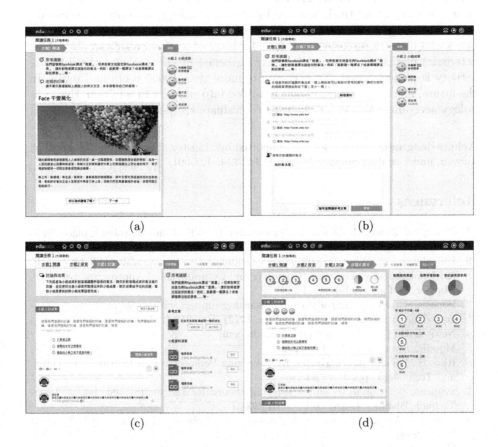

(a)   (b)

(c)   (d)

Fig. 7. (a) Reading (b) Exploring (c) Discussion (d) Demonstration

discuss each other. At last, the students in the same mission circle complete the mission by demonstrating their finding and summary in *educoco*. Figure 6 shows the process of reading mission, and Fig. 7 illustrates the functions to complete the mission. The teacher can monitor the students' behaviors of the mission circle. In addition, *educoco* provides the statistic analysis of the students' behaviors in mission circles.

educoco is launched on March 7, 2014 by United Daily News in Taiwan. There are more than 10000 users until June, 2014. The student/teacher ratio is about

5. In *educoco*, there are already about 1900 different circles, and about 1200 missions. In average, a new version of *educoco* would be announced to improve the functions or to fix the bugs.

5   Conclusion

Learning is a social behavior. The important design issue of learning management system is how to effectively use the Internet technology to improve the collaborative learning. Due to the drawbacks of Facebooks, the authors proposed a new social networking service, *educoco*, for K-12 education in Taiwan. The characteristics of teachers are specially strengthened in *educoco*, and the learning activity is project-based. Now, there are more than 10000 users in Taiwan. In the future, more types mission will be added into *educoco*. In addition, the technology acceptance model will be used to evaluate the performance of *educoco*.

Acknowledgment. This work was supported by Ministry of Science and Technology, Taiwan, under contact number MOST 103-2632-E-127-001.

References

1. Zhang, D., Zhao, J.L., Zhou, L., Nunamaker Jr., J.F.: Can e-learning replace classroom learning? Commun. ACM **47**(5), 75–79 (2004)
2. Dillenbourg, P.: What do you mean by collaborative learning? In: Dillenbourg, P. (ed.) Collaborative-Learning: Cognitive and Computational Approaches, pp. 1–19. Elsevier, Oxford (1999)
3. Popescu, E.: Providing collaborative learning support with social media in an integrated environment. World Wide Web **17**(2), 199–212 (2014)
4. News, U.D.: (2014). http://educoco.udn.com/
5. Moodle: About moodle, June 2014
6. Kim, B.: Social constructivism. In: Emerging Perspectives on Learning, Teaching, and Technology, pp. 1–8 (2001)
7. Siemens, G.: Connectivism: a learning theory for the digital age. Int. J. Instr. Technol. Distance Learn. **2**(1), 3–10 (2005)
8. Blood, R.: Weblogs: a history and perspective. Rebecca's Pocket (2000). Accessed 7 Sept 2000
9. Kubincová, Z., Homola, M., Bejdová, V.: Motivational effect of peer review in blog-based activities. In: Wang, J.-F., Lau, R. (eds.) ICWL 2013. LNCS, vol. 8167, pp. 194–203. Springer, Heidelberg (2013)
10. Top, E.: Blogging as a social medium in undergraduate courses: sense of community best predictor of perceived learning. Internet High. Educ. **15**(1), 24–28 (2012). (Social Media in Higher Education)
11. Facebook, I.: (2014). http://facebook.com/
12. Roblyer, M., McDaniel, M., Webb, M., Herman, J., Witty, J.V.: Findings on facebook in higher education: a comparison of college faculty and student uses and perceptions of social networking sites. Internet High. Educ. **13**(3), 134–140 (2010)
13. Tower, M., Latimer, S., Hewitt, J.: Social networking as a learning tool: Nursing students' perception of efficacy. Nurse Educ. Today **34**(6), 1012–1017 (2014)

14. Kabilan, M.K., Ahmad, N., Abidin, M.J.Z.: Facebook: an online environment for learning of english in institutions of higher education? Internet High. Educ. **13**(4), 179–187 (2010). (Special Issue on Web 2.0.)

15. MinorMonitor: Minormonitor surveys 1,000 parents of children on facebook, shares results on realities, parental concerns (2012)

16. Popescu, E., Ghita, D.: Using social networking services to support learning. In: Wang, J.-F., Lau, R. (eds.) ICWL 2013. LNCS, vol. 8167, pp. 184–193. Springer, Heidelberg (2013)

Investigating the Effectiveness of Video Segmentation on Decreasing Learners' Cognitive Load in Mobile Learning

Pei-Yu Cheng[1], Yueh-Min Huang[1(✉)], Rustam Shadiev[1],
Chih-Wei Hsu[2], and Shao-Tsu Chu[3]

[1] Department of Engineering Science,
National Cheng Kung University, Tainan, Taiwan
{b770416, rustamsh}@gmail.com, huang@mail.ncku.edu.tw
[2] Graduate School of Digital Living Technology,
Ksu Shan University, Tainan, Taiwan
luch76912s76912@gmail.com
[3] Department of Information and Communication,
Ksu Shan University, Tainan, Taiwan
shaotsu@mail.ksu.edu.tw

Abstract. Researchers have recommended that watching a video for learning purpose can increase learners' motivation and interests effectively. On the other hand, related studies suggest that lengthy videos need to be segmented in order to decrease learners' cognitive load. Following abovementioned suggestions, this study administered mobile video lectures for students and investigated how videos of various lengths influence students' cognitive load and learning performance. Forty freshmen students of one technological university participated in this study; they were randomly assigned into the experiment group and the control group. Segmented video was demonstrated for the experimental group while the control group watched non-segmented video. Results of this study indicate that students in the experiment group had better learning performance and they were less cognitively overloaded compared to students of the control group. Results also showed that the experiment group had less work load compared to the control group. Based on research findings, this study suggests that using segmentation strategy for creating mobile video learning material can help not only to reduce cognitive load but also to increase learning performance.

Keywords: Video · Segmentation · Cognitive load · Learning performance

1 Introduction

In recent years, information technology-based instruction becomes an important issue as learning has transformed from traditional face-to-face learning to digital and personalized learning. With the rapid development of the information technology and prevalence of the internet, technology is being employed for learning in very diverse ways.

For example, applications of mobile technology [1, 2] and E-book [3] for instruction showed that teaching material with the support of the technology can be not

© Springer International Publishing Switzerland 2014
Y. Cao et al. (Eds.): ICWL 2014 Workshops, LNCS 8699, pp. 122–129, 2014.
DOI: 10.1007/978-3-319-13296-9_14

only presented differently compared to traditional teaching material but also rapidly. Moreover, combining multimedia learning can effectively trigger learners' learning motivation and enhance their learning performance [4].

According to related studies, video is an effective teaching material [5], and it has been successfully applied to many subjects [6–10]. Learning through videos can enhance learners' learning motivation and comprehension of teaching material [10]. Regarding preview or review of the lessons, video learning material can be effective for learners [11]. However, based on the Theory of Multimedia Learning [12], humans cannot deal with too much information at once. When a video is too long, learners may not be able to deal with all presented in video information and become cognitively overloaded [12]. According to related studies, excess length and content of video tend to negatively influence learning [13]. Hence, the measure to avoid cognitive load when watching video is an important issue. Some researchers argue that by segmentation, video is divided into fragments and it can effectively lower work memory and extraneous cognitive load [12–14]. Furthermore, video segmentation does not negatively influence learning [15]. It provides learners with time for processing information, and indirectly enhances learners' learning performance [15].

Informed by related research, this study measured cognitive load and learning performance by employing Cognitive load questionnaire [16] and NASA Task Load [17]. In other words, this study explored the effects of videos of various lengths on learners' cognitive load and the relationship between cognitive load and learning performance.

The purpose of this study was to explore the literature on the effects of length of video on students' cognitive load in mobile learning process. Furthermore, this study aimed to analyze the relationship between cognitive load and learning performance.

2 Literature Review

2.1 Video Learning

According to the related research, multimedia video draws learners' attention [18]. For learners, in particular who watch multimedia video for the first time, it will enhance their concentration [19]. Learning by video can strengthen learners' learning motivation and help learners comprehend teaching material [10]. Hence, based on related studies, video is a kind of effective teaching material [5]. For preview or review of lessons, video learning can be effective for learners [11].

In modern online learning environment, learning by video is the mainstream. In recent years, video websites become popular and learners can watch many videos from internet. Some popular OpenCourseWare (MOOCs) in the world, such as Harvard University's Edx, MIT 's OCW, Stanford University's iTunesU, provides video courses for learning various subjects [20].

Researchers have pointed out that when a video is too long, learners may not be able to deal with all information presented, and Cognitive overload may take place, which negatively influences learning [5, 15]. According to the recent research on Open-CourseWare (MOOCs), short videos are more attractive for learners. It is suggested that the length of teaching video material should be within 6 min to avoid learners' cognitive load [21]. Other studies indicated that segmenting video into fragments can effectively lower work memory processing and extraneous cognitive load [12]. Ayres and Paas argued that segmentation of animation or control by learners may lower learners' cognitive load [22]. Segmentation does not negatively influence on learning, it may also provide learners with some time for processing information, and indirectly enhances learners' learning performance [15].

2.2 Cognitive Load

According to related literature, multimedia teaching material should be designed with consideration of learners' cognitive load [23, 24]. When multimedia teaching material is properly arranged and designed, it enhances comprehension in learning [25, 26]. At early stage of development, the theory of cognitive load was called mental work-load, and was originally not applied to education [27]. Sweller introduced the theory of cognitive load to academia [28]. Sweller classified cognitive load into three kinds as follows: intrinsic cognitive load, extraneous cognitive load and germane cognitive load [16]. From the perspective of learning, three kinds of cognitive load are shown below:

- Intrinsic cognitive load: it is based on effect of difficulty of teaching material. Intrinsic cognitive load cannot be changed by instructional design and it can only lower the difficulty of teaching material.
- Extraneous cognitive load: in learning process, learners consume cognitive resources for learning activities which will not enhance the performance. For instance, regarding great number of hyperlink connections in digital teaching materials, learners who are unfamiliar with computer should learn the operation by some cognitive resources. However, operational process cannot increase their understanding of learning content.
- Germane cognitive load: as extraneous cognitive load, it is related to learning activities when learners process cognitive resources. The difference is that germane cognitive load helps learners understand learning content. For instance, examples are adopted to explain the concepts. Although learners must process some cognitive resources, and it helps probe into learning content.

Common measurement of cognitive load is the following: Subjective Techniques, Physiological Techniques, Task and Performance-Based Techniques [29]. Subjective Techniques is based on scale of questionnaire. Since it is convenient and rapid, it becomes the most common measurement. Physiological Techniques aims to measure the change of physical figures, such as heartbeat, eye movement, brain waves, etc. Since the devices are expensive and there are many restrictions on wearing the instrument, it is less adopted. Task and Performance-Based Techniques measure cognitive load by learners' learning performance and difficulty of tasks. For instance, increase of secondary task tends to result in interference of primary task, so it is rarely used.

In order to find the effects of videos of various lengths on students' cognitive load in learning process and the relationship between cognitive load and learning performance, this study adopts subjective measurement to evaluate learners' cognitive load and workload in learning process by scales, explores the difference of cognitive load between experimental group and control group, and analyzes the difference and learning performance.

3   Research Design

3.1   Participants

This study investigated how videos of various lengths affect students' cognitive load and their learning performance. Participants in this study were freshmen students in one technological university (N = 40); they were randomly assigned into the experiment group and the control group.

3.2   Experiment Procedure

Figure 1 shows the experimental flow of this study. Before the experiment, this study distributed pretest to subjects to find if there is significant difference between two groups. After the subjects filled out the questionnaire, the researcher conducted experiment on two groups, and played an instructional video on mobile devices. In the experimental group, the instructional video was segmented into three fragments, and

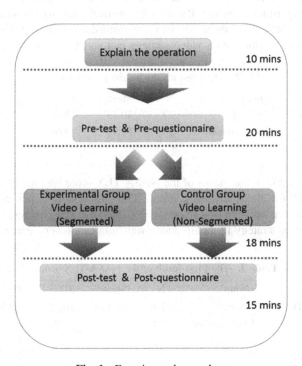

Fig. 1. Experimental procedure

the video was played for three times. There was one-minute stop after a video was playing for five minutes. For the control group, the video was not segmented and there were no any stops in the video, except after it played for 15 min, there was a three-minute pause. Once the experiment ended, the subjects completed tests and filled out the questionnaire in fifteen minutes. The questionnaires and tests were then retrieved when time is up.

4   Result and Discussion

This study used the pre-test scores as covariate for t-test analysis to avoid any inter-action effects from the pre-test on the students' learning outcomes. As listed in Table 1, the pre-test mean for the control group was 50.00, and 55.75 for the experimental group. The results did not reach a level of significance, t = 1.315, p > .05. It suggests that homogeneity of two groups of variables is supported.

Table 1. The t-test results for the pre-test scores.

	Group	N	Mean	SD	t
Pre-test	Control	20	50.00	12.67	1.315
	Experimental	20	55.75	14.89	

According to Table 2, the post-test mean for the control group ware 50.33, and 60.99 for the experimental group. Results of statistical analysis showed a significant difference in learning performance between two groups, t = −2.197, p < .05. This result suggests that using segmentation video strategy can enhances learning performance.

Table 2. The t-test results for the post-test scores

	Group	N	Mean	SD	t
Post-test	Control	20	50.33	15.06	2.197*
	Experimental	20	60.99	15.64	

*p < .05

As listed in Table 3, the means of the NASA-TLX score was 63.33 for the control group, and 54.99 for the experimental group. The t-test results shows that there was a significant difference between two groups, t = −2.569, p < .05. This result suggests that using segmentation strategy in mobile video watching can lowers learner's workloads.

Table 3. The t-test result of the NASA-TLX scores

	Group	N	Mean	SD	t
NASA-TLX	Control	20	63.33	10.27	−2.569*
	Experimental	20	54.99	10.06	

*p < .05

As listed in Table 4, the control group students' cognitive Load were significantly higher than the experimental group students, t = −6.082, p < .001). That is, the students who learned with the segmented video learning strategy had lower cognitive load than those who learned with non-segmented strategy.

Table 4. The t-test of the cognitive loads between the two groups

	Group	N	Mean	SD	t
Cognitive Load	Control	20	4.63	0.82	−6.082***
	Experimental	20	3.16	0.70	

***$p < .001$

According to the analytical result, the experimental group had superior learning achievement to the control group. A comparison of cognitive load and workload revealed that the average of cognitive load and workload of experimental group is lower than control group. This suggested that the experimental group perceived lower mental load and workload than control group in mobile video watching. Based on the results, this study infers that segmented video learning strategy can effectively lower learners' cognitive load and workload in learning process, thus enhancing learning achievement.

5 Conclusion

5.1 Conclusion

Based on the findings, of this study concludes:

- Videos of various lengths have different effects on students' cognitive load in learning process:Length of video influences learners' time to deal with all information, thus resulting in cognitive overload and negatively influences learning. Currently, the Ministry of Education of Taiwan has adjusted and put emphasis on information technology based instruction and instructional method of flipped classroom. This demonstrates the importance of this study.
- Different lengths of mobile video had significantly different effects on students' cognitive load and learning performance.

5.2 Limitation

This study has certain limitations, such as manpower, funds, and time, and thus, it proposes the following suggestions:

- A larger sample size and different age groups can be included in the future studies.
- Ages are segmented for analysis and cross-comparison.
- Future research can obtain objective evidence by using sensing technology (Eye-tracking and EEG) to assess physical conditions of learners such as visual attention and cognitive processes in the brain in order to compare with subjective evidence.

Acknowledgment. This research is partially supported by the "International Research-Intensive Center of Excellence Program" of NTNU and National Science Council, Taiwan, R.O.C. under Grant no. NSC 103-2911-I-003-301, NSC 102-3113-P-006-019-, NSC 100-2511-S-006-014-MY3, and NSC 100-2511-S-006-015-MY3.

References

1. Huang, Y.-M., Huang, S.-H., Wu, T.-T.: Embedding diagnostic mechanisms in a digital game for learning mathematics. Educ. Technol. Res. Dev. **62**(2), 187–207 (2013)
2. Huang, Y.-M., Chiu, P.-S.: The effectiveness of a meaningful learning-based evaluation model for context-aware mobile learning. Br. J. Educ. Technol. (2014)
3. Liang, T.-H., Huang, Y.-M.: An investigation of reading rate patterns and retrieval outcomes of elementary school students with e-books. J. Educ. Technol. Soc. **17**, 218–230 (2014)
4. Sever, S., Oguz-Unver, A., Yurumezoglu, K.: The effective presentation of inquiry-based classroom experiments using teaching strategies that employ video and demonstration methods. Aust. J. Educ. Technol. **29**, 450–463 (2013)
5. Pryor, C.R., Bitter, G.G.: Using multimedia to teach inservice teachers: impacts on learning, application, and retention. Comput. Hum. Behav. **24**, 2668–2681 (2008)
6. Yang, J.C., Huang, Y.T., Tsai, C.C., Chung, C.I., Wu, Y.C.: An automatic multimedia content summarization system for video recommendation. J. Educ. Technol. Soc. **12**, 49–61 (2009)
7. Bolliger, D.U., Supanakorn, S., Boggs, C.: Impact of podcasting on student motivation in the online learning environment. Comput. Educ. **55**, 714–722 (2010)
8. Hill, J.L., Nelson, A.: New technology, new pedagogy? Employing video podcasts in learning and teaching about exotic ecosystems. Environ. Educ. Res. **17**, 393–408 (2011)
9. Facer, B.R., Yen, C.-J.: Academic effectiveness of podcasting: a comparative study of integrated versus supplemental use of podcasting in second language classes. Comput. Educ. **58**, 43–52 (2012)
10. Kay, R., Kletskin, I.: Evaluating the use of problem-based video podcasts to teach mathematics in higher education. Comput. Educ. **59**, 619–627 (2012)
11. Star, J.R., Strickland, S.K.: Learning to observe: using video to improve preservice mathematics teachers' ability to notice. J. Math. Teach. Educ. **11**, 107–125 (2008)
12. Mayer, R.E., Chandler, P.: When learning is just a click away: does simple user interaction foster deeper understanding of multimedia messages? J. Educ. Psychol. **93**, 390 (2001)
13. Moreno, R.: Optimising learning from animations by minimising cognitive load: cognitive and affective consequences of signalling and segmentation methods. Appl. Cogn. Psychol. **21**, 765–781 (2007)
14. Hasler, B.S., Kersten, B., Sweller, J.: Learner control, cognitive load and instructional animation. Appl. Cogn. Psychol. **21**, 713–729 (2007)
15. Spanjers, I.A., van Gog, T., Wouters, P., van Merriënboer, J.J.: Explaining the segmentation effect in learning from animations: the role of pausing and temporal cueing. Comput. Educ. **59**, 274–280 (2012)
16. Sweller, J., Van Merrienboer, J.J., Paas, F.G.: Cognitive architecture and instructional design. Educ. Psychol. Rev. **10**, 251–296 (1998)
17. Hart, S.G., Staveland, L.E.: Development of NASA-TLX (Task Load Index): results of empirical and theoretical research. Adv. Psychol. **52**, 139–183 (1988)
18. Chandler, P.: Dynamic visualisations and hypermedia: beyond the "Wow" factor. Comput. Hum. Behav. **25**, 389–392 (2009)

19. Sweller, J.: Instructional design consequences of an analogy between evolution by natural selection and human cognitive architecture. Instr. Sci. **32**, 9–31 (2004)
20. Kop, R., Fournier, H., Mak, J.S.F.: A pedagogy of abundance or a pedagogy to support human beings? Participant support on massive open online courses. Int. Rev. Res. Open Distance Learn. **12**, 74–93 (2011)
21. Guo, P.J., Kim, J., Rubin, R.: How video production affects student engagement: an empirical study of MOOC videos. In: Proceedings of the First ACM Conference on Learning@ Scale Conference, pp. 41–50. ACM, (2014)
22. Ayres, P., Paas, F.: Can the cognitive load approach make instructional animations more effective? Appl. Cogn. Psychol. **21**, 811–820 (2007)
23. Cooper, G.: Research into cognitive load theory and instructional design at UNSW (1998). Accessed 8 August 2003
24. Paas, F., Renkl, A., Sweller, J.: Cognitive load theory and instructional design: recent developments. Educ. Psychol. **38**, 1–4 (2003)
25. Balluerka, N.: The influence of instructions, outlines, and illustrations on the comprehension and recall of scientific texts. Contemp. Educ. Psychol. **20**, 369–375 (1995)
26. Schuster, D.A., Carlsen, W.S.: Scientists' teaching orientations in the context of teacher professional development. Sci. Educ. **93**, 635–655 (2009)
27. Jex, H.R.: Measuring mental workload: problems, progress, and promises. Adv. Psychol. **52**, 5–39 (1988)
28. Sweller, J.: Cognitive load during problem solving: effects on learning. Cogn. Sci. **12**, 257–285 (1988)
29. Wierwille, W.W., Eggemeier, F.T.: Recommendations for mental workload measurement in a test and evaluation environment. Hum. Factors J. Hum. Factors Ergon. Soc. **35**, 263–281 (1993)

2014 International Workshop on Open Badges in Education

Supporting Self-regulated Learning Through Digital Badges: A Case Study

Stefania Cucchiara, Alessandra Giglio^(✉), Donatella Persico,
and Juliana E. Raffaghelli

National Research Council of Italy – Institute for Educational Technologies,
Genoa, Italy
{cucchiara,giglio,persico,raffaghelli}@itd.cnr.it

Abstract. Self-regulated learning (SRL) takes place when individuals plan, monitor and evaluate their own learning experiences. Learning assessment plays a crucial role in this process because it provides an excellent basis for the above three phases of SRL; however, the identification, design and implementation of meaningful assessment activities is not easy and some technological affordances for an SRL-sensitive assessment design still need to be explored. Although Digital Badges are already considered an instrument that could provide good answers to the complex problem of assessment for learning, their potential for SRL support is rather under-explored. This paper puts forward a proposal on the role that Digital Badges can play in supporting SRL. The proposal consists in a "badge ecosystem", developed for a course on "Scientific Information for Biomedical Research", aimed at differentiating among different levels of competence to facilitate learners in making better informed decisions on how to go about in their learning process. The conclusions discuss the expected advantages and shortcomings of the proposed ecosystem.

Keywords: Digital Badges · Self-regulated learning · Assessment · Learning design · Lifelong learning

1 Introduction

Aim of this paper is to present a case study on how Digital Badges can be used to support self-regulation in an online course. Such a course intends to develop professional competence among adult learners in a knowledge-intensive domain. Professional learning, in this context, is intended as an ongoing process, whereby a specific training initiative should provide participants not only with domain related skills but also with transversal competences needed to deepen the acquired expertise in a lifelong perspective. In such a perspective, transversal competences are deeply connected with those needed to self-regulate one's own learning. Learning assessment plays a crucial role in the self-regulated learning (SRL) process because it makes learners aware of their level of competence, a necessary condition to make autonomous decisions during the three main phases of SRL: forethought, execution and monitoring, and self-evaluation of the learning experience [24].

In this case study, we assume that, in order to develop professional knowledge, a course should aim to promote SRL related to the course content. Consequently, Digital

© Springer International Publishing Switzerland 2014
Y. Cao et al. (Eds.): ICWL 2014 Workshops, LNCS 8699, pp. 133–142, 2014.
DOI: 10.1007/978-3-319-13296-9_15

Badges were considered as a key instrument to implement a suitable assessment strategy. Along the study, we will focus on the opportunities for self-regulation offered by the course design and on how these opportunities are completed by the badge ecosystem. Section 1.1. introduces the concept of SRL, which is one of the pivot concepts in our article. Moreover, it briefly summarizes the connections between SRL and the emerging discussion on Digital Badges. Section 2 focuses on the description of the course and on how Digital Badges are introduced as a part of the assessment strategy. Section 3 provides a detailed explanation of the pedagogical and technological affordances of our Digital Badges ecosystem, and proposes an approach for the evaluation of the model. The conclusions discuss the expected advantages and shortcomings of the proposed ecosystem.

1.1 Self-regulated Learning and Digital Badges

Self-Regulated Learners are individuals who actively and consciously control their own learning from cognitive, affective, motivational and behavioral points of view [7]. SRL is of crucial importance for lifelong learning and professional learning [11, 14]; therefore a key issue in Technology Enhanced Learning (TEL) research is how to develop learning environments that take advantage of technological affordances to foster the practice and the development of SRL abilities [3, 4, 10]. A well-known, consolidated model [23] describes SRL as a cyclic process consisting of (1) forethought, (2) execution and monitoring, and (3) self-evaluation. Recently, the culture of openness in education and the idea of connectivism [20] have brought to the forefront learning experiences where adult learners have to take control of their learning processes. In particular, learners have to: (a) identify their learning objectives, (b) choose among different learning activities and digital tools, (c) dynamically plan and shape their own learning experience in virtual, open environments. In this process, a key role is played by assessment and the way it stimulates learners to take control of their learning and reflect on their own achievements [16]. Using technology can facilitate assessment for SRL through the accessibility and affordability of multi-media production tools combined with web 2.0. It also allows learners to choose the media that best accommodate their content and best suit their presentation preferences to produce their artefacts. Early examples of Technologies for self-monitoring and self-evaluation include eRubrics [19] and ePortfolios [5]. However, some critical aspects of ePortfolios are the complex way in which materials are presented and the lack of impact beyond the personal sphere; indeed, the technological affordances could be used to generate standards that are the base to permit learning recognition [8, 15]. Digital Badges move one step forward in the implementation of such a social vision of assessment in lifelong learning. They consist in sets of icons, implemented in technological learning environments, which can be issued by institutions promoting educational initiatives and displayed by users to show their learning achievements [13]. The badges should be portable, linked to open pathways of learning, and hence transparent to both the organization that releases them, and to those willing to know about the learners' achievements. Due to their early stage of development and testing, empirical evidence of how Digital Badges could implement assessment strategies supporting the development of competences for lifelong learning is still quite limited [12]. Studying the connections between open Digital Badges and self-regulation could increase our possibilities to implement strategies for assessment promoting skills for lifelong learning.

2 The Case of the "Scientific Information for Biomedical Research" Course

This study has been carried out in the context of the Science & Technology Digital Library Project (S&T DL), one of the initiatives of the Italian Digital Agenda for the exploitation of ICTs in order to foster growth, innovation and competitiveness, in line with the European Digital Agenda (EU Strategy 2020).

The course "Scientific Information for Biomedical Research" (in the following, SIBR2014) has been designed to support the users of the S&T DL system. In particular, the SIBR2014 course addresses young researchers and technologists of the life science sector, as well as non-tenure track employees of the National Council of Research of Italy (CNR). This online training initiative aims to provide participants with basic knowledge and skills about scientific information and communication, and to raise awareness on the issues of digital scholarship and open culture as new trends in professional context [17]. In this domain, we distinguish among three levels of goals based on Bloom's taxonomy [1, 6] including: knowing (relating to the level 1 of Bloom's taxonomy), using and comprehending (relating to levels 2 and 3), creating and reflecting (relating to levels 4–6).

In line with the aim of supporting the practice and development of SRL, course participants are offered the possibility to choose: (a) which contents and modules to follow, (b) how and when to participate, (c) whether to participate individually or in collaboration with others. Moreover, information about the content map and the assessment strategy are provided to participants, to support the forethought, monitoring and evaluation phases of SRL.

The content domain of the course consists of three main areas, namely "information retrieval and management", "dissemination", and "evaluation" of scientific information. The course structure features one module for each of the above mentioned areas, plus an introductory and a conclusive module. Since there are no prerequisite relationships between them, participants are free to plan their own personalized learning path through the modules.

The "information retrieval and management" module intends to promote skills related to the use of databases in searching and retrieving bibliographic resources both in well-known generalist databases (Web of Science, Scopus and Google Scholar) and in some disciplinary databases (Medline/PubMed and the Cochrane Library).

The "dissemination" module refers to skills related both to the choice of criteria to publish research work and to the use of social networks for sharing it.

The "evaluation" module refers to the most common indices to evaluate articles, journals and researchers' scientific production; it also encompass the skills to calculate them, with a critical eye on the chosen methods.

As it happens with many professional content domains, this one is far from being consolidated in all of its parts: although there are important, relatively stable knowledge areas and skills to be learned, there are also wide areas of content that are still debated among experts and need to be appraised critically by participants. In relation to these areas, participants need to develop their own ideas or, at least, become aware of the different positions of the experts of the field. Examples of these critical aspects are the debate on the value of bibliometric indicators for the evaluation of research, the discussion of proprietary data-banks versus open science, the value of social networks for researchers.

Each course module has been designed following a Problem-based-learning (PBL) approach [2, 18, 21], rooted in constructivist pedagogical principles. According to PBL, a problem is the starting point of the learning process. This approach has had a great impact on medical education and training for the past 40 years, because it is based on active learning - even in small groups - with clinical problems used as stimulus for learning [9]. According to Colliver (op. cit.), PBL is a challenging and motivating approach; therefore, it has a greater effectiveness for the acquisition of knowledge and problem-solving skills.

In this perspective, some authentic problems were identified for each module of the course in order to stimulate participants to work on their solution, either individually or collaboratively, using given available resources. In order to achieve the learning outcomes, in each module participants are provided with: (a) an initial question that introduces the problem, (b) some content to be read and (c) a series of activities that lead to the solution of the problem.

At the end of each module, a video with an expert interview is proposed. In this video, the expert presents the most debatable aspects of the module content, giving food for thought to participants and inviting them to discuss such aspects in a web-forum.

As said before, the course design and the assessment strategy has been tailored on the base of SRL principles, such as the possibility to choose among several possibilities and that of self-assessing one's own competence at any time, with the explicit intent to promote self-regulation skills. In this vein, badges have been introduced as a part of the assessment strategy, which is explained in the following section.

3   A Badge Ecosystem for SIBR2014

3.1   Pedagogical Design of SIBR2014 Badge Ecosystem

As The Mozilla Foundation and Peer 2 Peer University state in their working document on Open Badges for Lifelong Learning, "badges can play a crucial role in the connected learning ecology by acting as a bridge between contexts, making these alternative learning channels and types of learning more viable, portable, and impactful." [22, p. 5].

The assessment strategy of the SIBR2014 course was developed with a badge ecosystem that takes into account the validation both of hard (technical, operative) and soft (interpersonal, behavioral) skills. For each of the problems tackled in the three modules described in Sect. 2, a specific assessment activity is provided. Each assessment activity leads to the achievement of a Digital Badge. Therefore, we designed a "structure" where course contents, activities and expected learning outcomes are clearly aligned and explicit to learners. Such a "structure" is composed of: (a) a Knowledge Map of the contents of the course as described in the prior section; (b) a Competence Map, with three levels of competence as mentioned in Sect. 2; (c) the assessment activities, aligning with the Knowledge and the Competence Map, where for every competence and level there is a specific type of assessment activity; (d) the badge ecosystem, consisting on one badge per type of competence (as explained later). Figure 1 introduces the Competence Map, whereas Fig. 2 shows the assessment activities, and Fig. 3, the Badge Ecosystem.

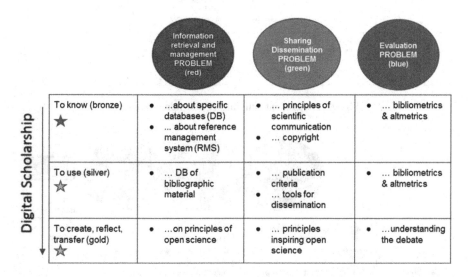

Fig. 1. The Competence Map (Color figure online)

Each module is identified by a color (red, green and blue) and the relevant badges feature the same colors to recall the content of the module; equally, icons to identify the level of the competence were selected (the bronze, silver and golden stars).

The total amount of badges in our badge ecosystem is twelve.

For each module, participants can achieve the bronze badge of "informed participant" by searching and acquiring the information and knowledge of that particular, disciplinary field (Bloom's Knowledge level); participants can also achieve a silver badge of "competent participant" by comprehending and using new information they acquired (Bloom's Application and Comprehension level); participants can reach the higher, gold badge by creating, reflecting and transferring knowledge and competencies they got from the learning path of the whole module (Bloom's Judge, Analysis and Synthesis levels). Two more badges are issued to participants that show specific abilities in working in a more individual or social dimension: being an individual or a collaborative-oriented learner reflects the ability to self-regulate one's own learning at an individual level or in a socio-constructivist context.

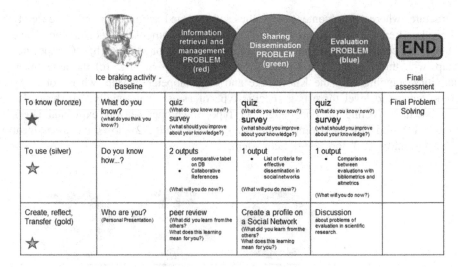

Fig. 2. Assessment activities (Color figure online)

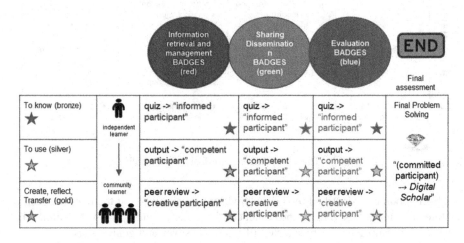

Fig. 3. The badge ecosystem (Color figure online)

A final, diamond badge is issued to participants that proved ability to solve a final, complex problem; it accounts for most of the issues discussed into each module and certifies the completion of the course. Moreover, the diamond badge aims to demonstrate that the overall professional identity as "Digital Scholar" lies on more than the sum of specific (hard or soft) skills. All of the badges here presented are meant to be issued by completing some peer or individual activities that are validated by the tutor of the course itself.

As a result of the assessment strategy combined with the badge ecosystem, we hypothesize that self-regulation can be triggered in terms of: (a) self-monitoring of the individual achievements, as well as planning of further actions against the scheme of desired learning outcomes; (b) awareness of the areas in which the learning achievements are weaker, in order to plan one's own learning activities aimed at reaching the desired learning outcomes. In fact, our SIBR2014 badge ecosystem's main objectives, aligned with the ones declared by The Mozilla Foundation, are:

- Capturing of the Learning Path: our Digital Badges have the double function of validating parts of the learning process and, simultaneously, attesting participants' progress, so that they can easily monitor their own learning resume.
- Achievement Signaling: participants can review their progresses on their profile homepage by looking at the badges they achieved. The system can also be used as a base for official recognition for the training.
- Motivation: using a Digital Badges ecosystem can be a strategy to increase participants' motivation in progressing along the learning path and to self-assess one's own learning by comparing their performance with those of their peers.

3.2 Technical Specifications for Developing SIBR2014's Badge Ecosystem

Our SIBR2014 badge ecosystem is intend to be interoperable and exportable to different professional platforms and contexts. In order to achieve a full interoperability, we decided to follow The Mozilla Foundation Open BadgeKit guidelines to issue our badges[1]. This kind of tool helps our badge ecosystem to be easily exported by participants that can "knit (their) skills together" (http://openbadges.org/) and that can use them as evidence of their knowledge and skills in the disciplinary field of the course. Technically speaking, our Digital Badges operate in a WordPress[2] platform using the BadgeOS Plugin[3], that allows to connect the plugin with Mozilla Backpack (via Credly, a sort of achievement repository).

Each badge of the SIBR2014 course is designed in a common-based way: each badge has a graphic icon with different colors that helps recognizing easily and quickly the module and the competence level (in its variation of bronze, silver and gold background) of the badge itself. Moreover, each badge has a description section in which both the participants' achievements and the workload path are declared.

At the bottom of the description page, an "evidence section" is presented, where participants can find documents, files and interaction pieces justifying the achievement of the badge itself. This feature allows participants to demonstrate their achievements with concrete artifacts, like in ePortfolio systems.

3.3 The Evaluation of the Badge's Ecosystem SIBR2014: a Proposal

As mentioned earlier, the proposed badge ecosystem entails an isomorphic structure that connects the "course objectives", the "Competence Map", the "assessment system"

---

[1] http://badgekit.openbadges.org/

[2] http://wordpress.org/

[3] https://badgeos.org/

Table 1. Badge ecosystem: evaluative approach

Badge's functionality	SRL connected processes	Evaluation methods	Expected results
Capturing Validate prior learning Trace participant progress	− Prior skills visibility enables recognition of one's own learning gaps and need to focus − Awareness of progress on the ongoing learning activities allows the learner to self-monitor and compare achievements with goals initially set	Analysis of learners engagement with Badges (low/high) Survey (embedded on the personal space) Interviews	Learners adopting badges will: − Improve their goal setting ability and their planning of learning activities − Better monitor the ongoing learning activities
Signaling Review progresses Reflect	− The badges show the types of competences required in the field of digital scholarship, and support the learner in selecting those competences that she considers appropriate to develop − The final badge (diamond) represents more than the mere sum of achievements allows the learner to consider the "big picture" (becoming a digital scholar) and self-evaluate		Learners adopting badges will: − Self-evaluate the learning experience connecting it with future experiences
Motivating Award achievements	− Promote the motivational base of SRL through "gamification": challenge, achieve, show		Learners adopting badges will be stimulated to participate in specific learning activities to achieve the relevant badges

and the "set of badges". The evaluation of the badge ecosystem should lead to the identification of the key issues enabling SRL. Our evaluative approach to the proposed badge ecosystem is shown in Table 1. Column 1 contains the "badge functionalities", whereas column 2 connects the functionalities with the expected SRL processes, and column 3 introduces the type of methods that could be adopted to evaluate the impact of badge functionalities on the SRL process. Finally, column 4 anticipates the results we expect to find in terms of learning outcomes.

4 Conclusions

In this paper, the Digital Badge ecosystem of the SIBR2014 course is illustrated to demonstrate how Digital Badges can be used to promote SRL, a key component in the framework of Skills for 21st Century. In particular, in our ecosystem, badges should support not only self-evaluation, the third phase of Zimmerman's SRL model [23], but also the other two phases, namely forethought and monitoring. Specifically, badges allow participants to monitor their own learning process, comparing and evaluating their goals and achievements with those of other participants. The badge ecosystem is aligned to course contents, participants activities, assessment tools, and also to the competence levels acquired by participants.

Hopefully, running this course will provide us with data about how course participants take advantage of badges and use them to self-regulate their learning, as well as with feedback about the limits and problems connected to the course learning design and assessment strategies.

References

1. Anderson, L.: Bloom's Taxonomy : A Forty-Year Retrospective. NSSE; Distributed by the University of Chicago Press, Chicago (1994)
2. Azer, S.A.: Problem-based learning. Challenges, barriers and outcome issues. Saudi Med. J. **22**(5), 389–397 (2001)
3. Bartolomé, A., Bergamin, P., Persico, D., Steffens, K., Underwood, J. (eds.): Self-regulated learning in technology enhanced learning environments: problems and promises. In: Proceedings of the STELLAR-TACONET Conference, Barcellona, 1 Oct 2010. Shaker Verlag, Aachen (2011)
4. Beishuizen, J., Steffens, K.: A conceptual framework for research on self-regulated learning. In: Carneiro, R., Lefrere, P., Steffens, K., Underwood, J. (eds.) Self-regulated Learning in Technology Enhanced Learning Environments: A European Perspective, pp. 3–20. Sense Publishers, Rotterdam (2011)
5. Blackburn, J.L., Hackel, M.D.: Enhancing self-regulation and goal orientation with ePortfolios. In: Jafari, A., Kaufman, C. (eds.) Handbook of Research on ePortfolios. Idea Group Reference, Hershey (2006)
6. Bloom, B.S.: Taxonomy of Educational Objectives: The Classification of Educational Goals, Part 2. Pennsylvania State University, McKay (1956)
7. Boekaerts, M., Pintrich, P., Zeidner, M.: Handbook of Self-regulation. Elsevier, San Diego (2005)
8. Clark, J.E.: The digital imperative: making the case for a 21st-century pedagogy. Comput. Compos. **27**(1), 27–35 (2010)
9. Colliver, J.A.: Effectiveness of problem-based learning curricula: research and theory. Acad. Med. **75**(3), 259–266 (2000)
10. Dabbagh, N., Kitsantas, A.: Supporting self-regulation in student-centered web-based learning environments. Int. J. E-Learn. **3**(1), 40–47 (2003)
11. Dettori, G., Persico, D.: Fostering Self-regulated Learning Through ICT. IGI Global, New York (2011)
12. Gibson, D., Ostashewski, N., Flintoff, K., Grant, S., Knight, E.: Digital badges in education. Educ. Inf. Technol. (2013). doi:10.1007/s10639-013-9291-7

13. Halavais, A.M.C.: A genealogy of badges. Inf. Commun. Soc. **15**(3), 354–373 (2012)
14. Littlejohn, A., Milligan, C., Margaryan, A.: Charting collective knowledge: supporting self-regulated learning in the workplace. J. Workplace Learn. **24**(3), 226–238 (2012)
15. Martí, M.C., Ferrer, G.T.: Exploring learners' practices and perceptions on the use of mobile portfolios as methodological tool to assess learning in both formal and informal contexts. Procedia Soc. Behav. Sci. **46**, 3182–3186 (2012)
16. Nicol, D.J., Macfarlane-Dick, D.: Formative assessment and self-regulated learning: a model and seven principles of good feedback practice. Stud. High. Educ. **31**(2), 199–218 (2006). doi:10.1080/03075070600572090
17. Raffaghelli, J., Valla, S. Cucchiara, S., Giglio, A., Persico, D.: Exploring researchers' discourses about producing, disseminating and evaluating scientific information on the web. The case of biomedical sciences. In: Proceedings of the 6th International Conference on Education and New Learning Technologies, Barcelona (2014, in press)
18. Savery, J.R.: Overview of problem-based learning: definitions and distinctions. Interdisc. J. Probl.-Based Learn. **1**(1), 9–20 (2006)
19. Serrano-Angulo, J., Cebrián de la Serna, M.: Study on the impact on student learning using the eRubric tool and peer assessment. In: Mendez-Vilas, A. (ed.) Education in a Technological World: Communicating Current and Emerging Research and Technological Efforts, pp. 421–427. FORMATEX, Badajoz (2011)
20. Siemens, G.: Connectivism: a learning theory for the digital age. eLearn space – blog. http://www.elearnspace.org/Articles/connectivism.htm (2004). Accessed 2 May 2014
21. Strijbos, J.W., Martens, R.L., Jochems, W.M.G.: Designing for interaction: six steps to designing computer-supported group-based learning. Comput. Educ. **42**, 403–424 (2004)
22. The Mozilla Foundation, Peer 2 Peer University, The Mc Arthur Foundation: Open badges for lifelong learning. Exploring an open badge ecosystem to support skill development and lifelong learning for real results such as jobs and advancement. Working Document. https://wiki.mozilla.org/images/b/b1/OpenBadges-Working-Paper_092011.pdf (2012). Accessed 3 March 2014
23. Zimmerman, B.J.: Models of self-regulated learning and academic achievement. In: Zimmerman, B.J., Schunk, D.H. (eds.) Self-regulated Learning and Academic Achievement: Theory, Research and Practice, pp. 1–25. Springer, New York (1998)
24. Zimmerman, B.J.: Developing self-fulfilling cycles of academic regulation: an analysis of exemplary instructional models. In: Schunk, D.H., Zimmerman, B.J. (eds.) Self-regulated Learning. From Teaching to Self-reflective Practice, pp. 1–19. The Guildford Press, New York (1998)

Improving Teacher Awareness Through Activity, Badge and Content Visualizations

Sven Charleer$^{(\boxtimes)}$, Jose Luis Santos, Joris Klerkx, and Erik Duval

Department of Computer Science, KU Leuven, Leuven, Belgium
{Sven.Charleer,JoseLuis.Santos,Joris.Klerkx,Erik.Duval}@cs.kuleuven.be

Abstract. This paper introduces LARAe (Learning Analytics Reflection & Awareness environment), a teacher-oriented dashboard that visualizes learning traces from students, badges and course content. We also present an evaluation of the dashboard in a course on Human-Computer Interaction. The LARAe teacher dashboard provides a detailed overview of group and individual activities, achievements and course outcomes. To help visualize the abundance of traces, badges are used to abstract essential aspects of the course such as course goals and social activity. This paper reports our work on LARAe, presents the course in which we evaluated our approach with students and teachers, and analyses our first results that indicate that such an environment can help with teacher awareness.

Keywords: Learning analytics · Learning dashboards · Collaboration · Reflection · Awareness · Information visualization · Open badges

1 Introduction

Feedback and collaborative discourse, between student and teacher, among students and even with external parties, leads to significant gains in learning [1]. Traditional tools for such discourse are exams, discussion fora, self-assessment and peer evaluations, but also (micro-)blogging (Twitter, Wordpress, Facebook) can help students share and reflect on their work, collaborate, discuss and learn from peers [7]. These activities leave behind a multitude of learner traces that reflect progress of students [17]. Reflecting on those traces can help learners to understand what is the optimal setting and context in which they learn best. Teachers on the other hand can, among other things, use those traces to find out which student is struggling with what content. Information visualization offers effective ways to explore this abundance of data, find new insights, and tell compelling stories.

In previous work, we have developed visualization tools such as StepUp!, SAM and TinyARM [17]. These tools used basic graphical representations such as bar charts, line charts and parallel coordinates to present all traces of all users. Evaluations have shown that they can provide a broad insight on student activities, but also that the abundance of information is overwhelming for students [13].

© Springer International Publishing Switzerland 2014
Y. Cao et al. (Eds.): ICWL 2014 Workshops, LNCS 8699, pp. 143–152, 2014.
DOI: 10.1007/978-3-319-13296-9_16

Our work presented in this paper goes one step further and provides students and teachers with Open Badges[1] as abstractions of essential aspects of the course such as achieving particular course goals or social activity. This paper introduces LARAe, a large display visualization for teachers that combines these abstractions through badges with its underlying raw data (e.g. amount and content of blogposts of a student) to provide deep-level awareness of all student activities, achievements and outcomes.

The remainder of this paper is structured as follows: Sect. 2 discusses relevant examples of learning dashboards and the use of badges in learning. The context of our evaluation, including course design and badge methodology, is presented in Sect. 3. Section 4 then elaborates on the LARAe dashboard. Section 5 presents preliminary results of the evaluation, followed by a discussion on improvements and conclusions in Sect. 6.

2   Background and Related Work

Similar to the Quantified Self[2] movement, which focuses on collecting user traces and using the data for self-improvement, Learning Analytics can help understand and optimize learning and the environments in which it occurs [15]. By tracking learner activities (which in our context include software development with a shared source repository, blogging, time tracking, posting on a discussion forum, etc.), these learning traces [4] can be visualized on interactive dashboards, helping students and teachers become more aware of their activities [13].

These visualizations can help teachers evaluate and improve course activities, structure and materials [11,12]. The data is also valuable for detecting and predicting problematic students [18] or imbalanced group activity [8], allowing for quick intervention.

Fig. 1. An interactive tabletop application allowing collaborative reflection through badge visualizations. The lack of content and context makes it difficult to interpret the data.

---

[1] http://openbadges.org
[2] http://quantifiedself.com

These data can be presented in many ways [16]. Badges, which can represent abstractions of learning traces, bring with them many benefits and uses: The creation process of the badges can influence the design of the course [6] and hence create clearer goals for both student and teacher. Badges can be used as feedback and are proven to directly impact behavior and motivate students in off- and online courses [6,9,13]. Skill recognition can be brought outside the classroom to support life long learning by using badges as certifications in e.g. Massive Open Online Courses [5,6].

The meaning of data might get lost through abstraction. Teachers and students can misinterpret the information when it is limited to e.g. activity count, grades and course goals. Previous work [3] has shown that there is a need for context and content to enrich the badge data (Fig. 1). Following the visual information-seeking mantra of "Overview first, zoom and filter, then details-on-demand" [14], the dashboard presented in this paper uses both badges and an overview of activity to give teachers a gateway to the content, retaining a sense of context and providing access to the details.

3 Case: Course on HCI

We evaluated our LARAe dashboard following a user-centered rapid prototyping approach, where we first rely on paper prototypes to gather initial feedback on early ideas and then gradually develop more functional digital prototypes in rapid iteration cycles. The concrete evaluation context was a course on Human-Computer Interaction (HCI) for computer science master students, taught in 2013, with 26 students.

3.1 Course Environment

The course focused on the design, development and evaluation of a recommendation application, i.e. a tool that enables humans to recommend resources to other humans (as opposed to recommender systems). It was taught to 26 engineering students between the ages of 20 and 25. Students worked in groups of 3 and improved their application through iterative development. The course includes face-to-face studio sessions. All presentations, course material and reports are publicly accessible online, through Slideshare, the course wiki[3] and the student group blogs. Twitter with a course specific hashtag (#chikul13) is used to share opinions, questions and comments about the course. In total, 142 blog posts, 549 blog comments and 548 tweets were generated during the course.

3.2 Capturing and Exposing Learning Traces

Our back-end system consists of a tracking service, Data Store and Badge Rewarding System.

---

[3] http://ariadne.cs.kuleuven.be/wiki/index.php/Chi_2013

To collect Learning Analytics data, the tracking service collects blog posts and comments from the course blogs through their RSS[4] feeds. It connects to the Twitter API[5], to collect course related tweets which are identified by the #chikul13 hashtag. The tracking service supports multiple sources, from RSS feeds to proprietary APIs such as the weSPOT Inquiry system[6] [10].

These learning traces are stored in the Data Store which also exposes the data through a RESTful web service [13].

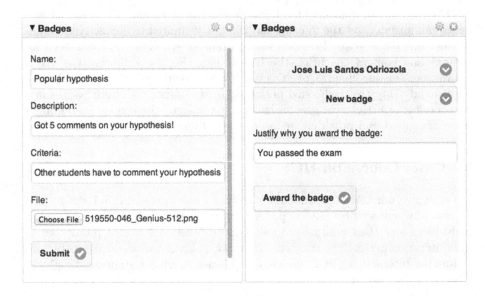

Fig. 2. Example of the Badge Award widget for weSPOT Inquiry system. Left: Creation of a badge. Right: Awarding a badge to a student.

The Badge Rewarding System allows for both automatic and manual assignment of badges to students. The Badge API[7] facilitates the development of applications on top of the Badge Rewarding System, e.g. applications for teachers to define and assign badges (Fig. 2). The source code is available at https://github.com/jlsantoso/stepup/tree/chicourse/OpenBadgesAPI. Section 3.3 will further explain the badges deployed in the HCI course and the automatic awarding of badges.

3.3   Abstracting Traces Through Badges

Summarizing data and relating them to important aspects, such as intended learning outcomes, can be achieved with badges. To define what badges we use

---

[4] http://en.wikipedia.org/wiki/Rss
[5] https://dev.twitter.com/docs/api
[6] http://inquiry.wespot.com
[7] http://wespot.net/en/apis

in our HCI course, we worked together with the teacher to identify the most important activities. Blogs and Twitter play a big role in the course as they are indicators of commitment and collaboration, so we want to reward posting of tweets and blog posts. For example, badges are awarded for a specific number of tweets, posts, and comments. Badges can also indicate a certain level of quality of the content of a blog post which can be derived from the number of comments it receives, by students, teachers and externals participants in the course (This particular course follows an open approach that enables anyone to comment on the content, discussions, activities and results in the course). Inactivity is a behavior that students should avoid. This is translated into a negative badge. Furthermore, some badges are allocated individually and some are assigned to teams. In total, 51 different kinds of badges are defined. The full list together with an explanation of their meaning can be found at http://navi-hci.appspot. com/badgeoverview.

Badges are automatically assigned bi-weekly. Certain activity in the tracked data will trigger the assignment of a badge when requirements are met and a mail is sent to the student with information on the awarded badge. This badge data is also stored and accessible through a REST service, creating an open data framework on which other tools can easily be developed. Furthermore, we follow the Mozilla Open Badges Standard[8] for describing the badges, so that our framework is interoperable with other systems such as the Learning Management Systems Moodle[9] and Blackboard[10]. On top of that, students can choose to publish their awards on social networks if they like to do so.

4 The LARAe Dashboard

On top of these services, we develop our learning dashboards to deliver visualizations that help get insights about how learners interact with content and with other learners, teams and external users.

The dashboard is presented on a large desktop, an interactive whiteboard or a touch display and consists of 6 main information areas (see Figs. 3 and 4):

1. **Student-Badge Matrix:** With student names on the horizontal axis and badges on the vertical axis, the matrix gives an overview of how many times a specific student has been awarded a specific badge. Larger circles denote that a badge has been awarded more often to a particular student.
2. **Activities/Badges Over Time:** This view consists of 5 graphs. The first graph displays the total activity of all students over time by day. These activities are split up in the next 3 graphs: blog posts, blog comments and tweets. The last graph shows the number of badges awarded each day. The bars of these bar charts are interactive. Clicking or touching a bar will update the *Activity List.*

---

[8] http://openbadges.org
[9] http://moodle.org
[10] http://blackboard.com

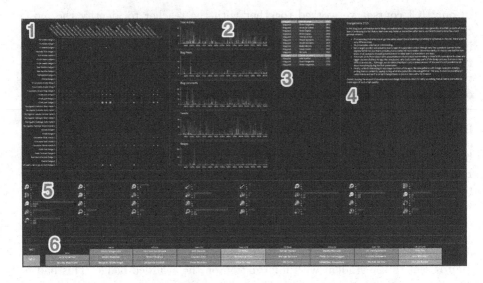

Fig. 3. Overview of information areas of the LARAe dashboard.

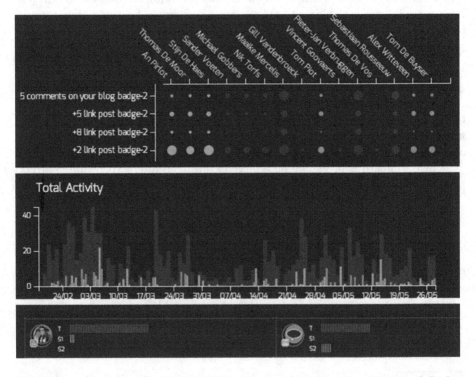

Fig. 4. Zooming in on the Student-Badge Matrix, Activities Over Time and Badge Overview graphs.

3. **Activity List:** This list contains the activities done or badges awarded on the selected day of the bar chart. These items are selectable and will update the Activity Details Field.

4. **Activity Details Field:** This fields shows the content that is linked to an activity. In the case of blog activity, it will provide the user with the content of the blog post or comment. A tweet activity will display the related tweet. The field can also present more information on badges, such as the name and description.

5. **Badge Overview:** The Badge Overview is another visualization of the awarded badges and facilitates student or group comparison (see Fig. 4 for details). T represents the total number of badges awarded to the class. S1 and S2 stand for Set 1 and Set 2 and display the number of badges awarded to the sets of selected students (see *Filter Area*). Clicking on a badge provides the user with a description of the badge.

6. **Filter Area:** A number of filtering options are available in the *Filter Area*. Students can be selected from the list and can be assigned to Set 1 (blue) and Set 2 (red). All other areas will be updated with the cumulative data of the selected students in each set, in the corresponding set color (see Fig. 4): the *Student-Badge matrix* will highlight the selected student, the *Activities Over Time* will show the subset of data as an overlay on top of the total data, the *Badge Overview* will show the total number of badges awarded in Set 1 and Set 2, and the *Activity List* will highlight activities done by the selected students. The time slider allows the user to modify the time range of the data displayed on the dashboard.

The dashboard is a web application developed using HTML5, Javascript, D3.-js[11] and crossfilter.js[12]. The backend is created with Node.js[13] and MongoDB[14].

5 Preliminary Evaluation Results

Our initial evaluations serve to gather feedback about perceived usefulness and effectiveness of the dashboard. We also wish to understand how users interacts with the visualization e.g. which information areas attract most attention and why, whether the visualization can provide insights and if badges enriched with context and content prove to be an added value for teachers.

We evaluated LARAe with 6 people with teaching responsibilities. 3 out of 6 participants were involved in the teaching of the HCI course. Participants used a 27" high resolution screen and a trackpad to interact with the dashboard.

Using the think-aloud protocol, the participants were asked to explore the different information areas of the dashboard. They freely interacted with the visualizations and attempted to make sense of the data. Once a participant got

---

[11] http://d3js.org

[12] http://square.github.io/crossfilter/

[13] http://nodejs.org/

[14] http://www.mongodb.org

stuck, a scenario was provided to explore the dashboard further. The evaluation ended with 49 5-scale Likert questions (1 - Strongly disagree, 5 - Strongly agree) covering clarity, usefulness and effectiveness of the different information areas and a SUS questionnaire.

The SUS score was 76 (SD = 7) [2]. This matches the observations during the evaluations: 5 out of 6 participants understood each information area without help and covered all scenarios without external input. From the survey, questions about the general clarity of each area were all rated positively (M = 4.0, SD = 0.9).

Participants found the ability to compare students and groups of students very interesting. Survey results averaged 4.0 (SD = 0.6) for perceived effectiveness regarding activity comparison and 3.5 (SD = 0.8) regarding badge comparison. This sparked interest for a deeper analysis and led users to search for links between activities, badges and grades. The comparison was usually done between the best and lowest graded groups (scores were presented next to student names, omitted from Fig. 3 for student privacy). The survey revealed that most users considered LARAe useful for understanding class achievements and activities (M = 3.8, SD = 0.8); participants started their analysis by exploring the Student-Badge Matrix, typically by first looking for high and low achievers. The Activity Over Time graphs were used afterwards to analyze the activity and recognize periods of student/group inactivity.

All participants agreed that the dashboard improves their general awareness of the activities (M = 4.0, SD = 0.6) and the badges awarded (M = 4.1, SD = 0.4). Because it provides access to activity, achievement and student-generated data (blog posts, comments, tweets), the dashboard was considered beneficial to use in discussions and evaluations of course outcomes among teaching staff (M = 4.0, SD = 0.9) and with students (M = 4.0, SD = 0.6).

6   Conclusion and Future Work

Learning dashboards provide a means of visualizing the abundance of learner traces that are left by students and teachers during a course. We presented our experiment of simplifying the data through badges that emphasize the more important student activities and course goals. We also explained how the LARAe dashboard improves teacher awareness of activity and achievements. As the dashboard was perceived useful as an evaluation and discussion tool, we will perform further evaluations using more collaborative settings (e.g. interactive tabletops, interactive whiteboards), among teachers but also together with students.

While LARAe already facilitates access to the student-generated content (blog posts, comments and tweets), we believe visualizing the learning traces through abstractions like badges and using them as a gateway to content can help both teachers and students with the task of keeping track of and learning from the large amount of data they generate. We will therefore further research how we can improve teacher and student awareness regarding outcomes.

Acknowledgements. The research leading to these results has received funding from the European Community's Seventh Framework Programme (FP7/2007–2013) under grant agreement No 318499 - weSPOT project.

References

1. Black, P., Wiliam, D.: Assessment and classroom learning. Assess. Educ. Principles Policy Pract. **5**(1), 7–74 (1998)
2. Brooke, J.: Sus - a quick and dirty usability scale. Usability Eval. Ind. **189**, 194 (1996)
3. Charleer, S., Klerkx, J., Santos, J.L., Duval, E.: Improving awareness and reflection through collaborative, interactive visualizations of badges. In: Kravcik, M., Krogstie, B.R., Moore, A., Pammer, V., Pannese, L., Prilla, M., Reinhardt, W., Ullmann, T.D. (eds.) ARTEL@EC-TEL. CEUR Workshop Proceedings, vol. 1103, pp. 69–81. CEUR-WS.org (2013)
4. Duval, E., Verbert, K.: Learning analytics. E-Learning Educ. 1(8) (2012)
5. Goligoski, E.: Motivating the learner: Mozilla's open badges program. Access Knowl. Course J. **4**(1), 1–8 (2012)
6. Higashi, R., Abramovich, S., Shoop, R., Schunn, C.: The roles of badges in the computer science student network. In: 2012 Games+Learning+Society Conference, Citeseer (2012)
7. Lin, W.J., Liu, Y.L., Kakusho, K., Yueh, H.P., Murakami, M., Minoh, M.: Blog as a tool to develop e-learning experience in an international distance course. In: Sixth International Conference on Advanced Learning Technologies, pp. 290–292. IEEE (2006)
8. Martinez Maldonado, R., Kay, J., Yacef, K., Schwendimann, B.: An Interactive teacher's dashboard for monitoring groups in a multi-tabletop learning environment. In: Cerri, S.A., Clancey, W.J., Papadourakis, G., Panourgia, K. (eds.) ITS 2012. LNCS, vol. 7315, pp. 482–492. Springer, Heidelberg (2012)
9. McDaniel, R., Lindgren, R., Friskics, J.: Using badges for shaping interactions in online learning environments. In: IEEE International Professional Communication Conference, pp. 1–4. IEEE (2012)
10. Mikroyannidis, A., Okada, A., Scott, P., Rusman, E., Specht, M., Stefanov, K., Boytchev, P., Protopsaltis, A., Held, P., Hetzner, S., Kikis-Papadakis, K., Chaimala, F.: weSPOT: A personal and social approach to inquiry-based learning. J. Univ. Comput. Sci. **19**(14), 2093–2111 (2013)
11. Raca, M., Dillenbourg, P.: System for assessing classroom attention. In: Proceedings of the Third International Conference on Learning Analytics and Knowledge, LAK '13, pp. 265–269. ACM, New York (2013)
12. Rivera-Pelayo, V., Munk, J., Zacharias, V., Braun, S.: Live interest meter: learning from quantified feedback in mass lectures. In: Proceedings of the Third International Conference on Learning Analytics and Knowledge, LAK '13, pp. 23–27. ACM, New York (2013)
13. Santos, J.L., Charleer, S., Parra, G., Klerkx, J., Duval, E., Verbert, K.: Evaluating the use of open badges in an open learning environment. In: Hernández-Leo, D., Ley, T., Klamma, R., Harrer, A. (eds.) EC-TEL 2013. LNCS, vol. 8095, pp. 314–327. Springer, Heidelberg (2013)
14. Shneiderman, B.: The eyes have it: a task by data type taxonomy for information visualizations. In: IEEE Symposium on Visual Languages, pp. 336–343. IEEE (1996)

15. Siemens, G., Long, P.: Penetrating the fog: Analytics in learning and education. In: EDUCAUSE, Boulder, CO, USA, vol. 46, pp. 30–32 (2011)
16. Silius, K., Tervakari, A.M., Kailanto, M.: Visualizations of user data in a social media enhanced web-based environment in higher education. In: Global Engineering Education Conference, pp. 893–899. IEEE (2013)
17. Verbert, K., Duval, E., Klerkx, J., Govaerts, S., Santos, J.L.: Learning analytics dashboard applications. Am. Behav. Sci. **57**(10), 1500–1509 (2013)
18. Wolff, A., Zdrahal, Z., Nikolov, A., Pantucek, M.: Improving retention: Predicting at-risk students by analysing clicking behaviour in a virtual learning environment. In: Proceedings of the Third International Conference on Learning Analytics and Knowledge, LAK '13, pp. 145–149. ACM, New York (2013)

Revisiting the Wikinomics Concept: Towards New Methodological Approaches

Athanasios Priftis[1(✉)], Theo Bondolfi[1], and Yves Boisselier[2]

[1] Ynternet.org, Geneva, Switzerland
thanasis.priftis@ynternet.org, theo.bondolfi@zen3.org
[2] MAC Team, Brussels, Belgium
yb@mac-team.eu

Abstract. Wikinomics is a well-established socioeconomic term. This paper draws from the ongoing work of the Wikinomics European Lifelong Learning project. It revisits the term's definition and attempts to re-frame it, using collaborative training and educational approaches, that include sustainable network building and an open badges use scenario. The open badges scenario has been launched through an open communication process with the Mozilla Open Badges initiative and is based on a methodology aiming to connect the Wikinomics project learning outcomes, with the ECVET framework approach.

Keywords: Wikinomics · Collaboration · Education · Open badges · ECVET

1 Introduction

The Wikinomics project is an effort to create and transfer innovation on collaborative methodologies and open innovation, at national, European and international level. It builds on the WikiSkills project[1] that developed a training material, a facilitator methodology and a network of practitioners on the wiki-culture, at European level, in both education and training sectors. The tools and methodologies deployed by the Wikinomics project include the organisation of collaborative events, framed as wiki-thons and seek solutions base-camps for business, VET institutions and associations, as well as, local TEDx events. All of these actions are connected with the WikiAngels European network of practitioners and the, aforementioned, results of the WikiSkills project.

2 Context

The financial crisis has accelerated the pace of economic restructuring, displacing many workers from declining sectors to unemployment due to a lack of the skills required by expanding sectors, while the 'Agenda for new skills and jobs' initiative highlights the need to upgrade skills and to boost employability[2]. As mentioned in the Council

---

[1] The WikiSkills EU project website is available at http://wikiskills.net/the-project.
[2] European Commission, 'Agenda for new skills and jobs' initiative (2010), available at http://ec.europa.eu/social/main.jsp?catId=958.

© Springer International Publishing Switzerland 2014
Y. Cao et al. (Eds.): ICWL 2014 Workshops, LNCS 8699, pp. 153–161, 2014.
DOI: 10.1007/978-3-319-13296-9_17

conclusions on the role of education and training in the implementation of the Europe 2020 strategy[3], it is important to "strengthen the capacity to anticipate and match labour market and skills needs, as well as to deliver the right mix of skills, including transversal competences".

Meanwhile, on Wikipedia and other Internet citizen collaborative initiatives, a new way of learning is self-developing, organically. By supporting synergistic collaborative opportunities, wiki environments have proved to provide rich learning outcomes in a wide range of educational environments and levels. This is, mainly, the result of a commons driven participation, coupled with free open source production, as well as licensing, culture. However, trainers rarely understand, or use collaborative methods for their courses, or publish their content under free licenses, missing out on key opportunities to handle dynamic pedagogical methodologies in the digital age.

In this context, the Wikinomics project aims at setting free-culture and wiki methodologies as the basis for an innovative pedagogical methodology. A way of developing key-competences required for the future labour market needs, including creativity, innovation, collaboration, ICT literacy, communication in mother tongue and foreign languages, learning to learn, social and civic awareness, sense of initiative and entrepreneurship. It has a focus on vocational education (also known as vocational education and training or VET) that prepares people for specific trades, crafts and careers at various levels. Craft vocations are usually based on manual or practical activities, are traditionally non- academic and related to a specific trade, occupation or vocation. They are sometimes referred to as technical education, as the trainee directly develops expertise in a particular group of techniques.

3   Introduction to the Term Wikinomics

Tapscott and Williams [5] and Leadbeater [2] are the experts that introduced and framed the socio-economic term "wikinomics", internationally. They, essentially, described a new world of web-based economics where cultural values such as participation, collectivism and creativity are its foundation. These values not only form the new business models of the digital economy, but their declared cultural roots suggest an ideological paradigm shift: a move towards a restructuring of post-industrial societies and economies.

The basic principle of this transformation is the following: the new services are created by crowds of (mostly) anonymous users who define their own informational, expressive and communication needs. This process is often called 'mass creativity' or 'peer production'. As a result, the conventional hierarchical business model of producer–consumer is rapidly replaced by the so-called 'co-creation' model [3]. Mass creativity, peer production and co-creation are blurring the distinction between collective (non-market, public) and commercial (market, private) modes of production, as well as between producers and consumers.

---

[3] COUNCIL OF THE EUROPEAN UNION, Council conclusions on the role of education and training in the implementation of the Europe 2020 strategy (2011), available at http://www.consilium.europa.eu/uedocs/NewsWord/en/educ/119282.doc.

In both works of Wikinomics [5] and We-Think [2] 'mass collaboration' and 'communal creativity' shape the way in which people will work and live in the future. The Internet and the World Wide Web, with the software and service infrastructures built on them, enable people to participate in the economy by being creative: 'smart firms' better harness this collective capability, in order to spur innovation and growth. In these events, consumers become workers, devoting some of their time, effort and imagination to developing products for one another.

3.1 Wikinomics Limits

The wikinomics described above has often been dismantled as a subtle form of exploitation of unpaid labour: its main idea being the outsourcing of labour to globally distributed customers and collaborators that act as prosumers so that labour and other costs are reduced. In this line of thinking, exploitation expands to the realm of spare time, as prosumers, as a tendency, deliver unpaid surplus value. In other words, companies can design and assemble products with their customers, and in some cases customers can do the majority of the value creation. This trend is not a novel form of management and organization and it connected with the goal of an increasing competitive advantage and the reduction of humans to economic reason in the last instance [1].

Another space of criticism, that the established wikinomics approach creates, is the promotion of certain form of individualism. Treating subjects as anonymous information organisms can be quite problematic, as to how empower and enforce a culture of sharing within innovative structures of collaboration [7]. As Fred Turner [6] has analysed, the key to this seamless concatenation of communalist thinking and good business sense was the ability of its propagandists to speak within multiple registers simultaneously: the discourses of economy as well as the discourse of friendship and community-building.

4 The Wikinomics Project Approach

The Wikinomics project recognizes the contradictions and tensions described above. Its fundamental concept is to go beyond them by adopting a positive learning and experimenting approach. It acknowledges the field of technical education as the cornerstone and the primary testbed of its efforts. It aims that the trainee reuses its outcomes and has an opportunity to develop expertise in a particular group of techniques. It integrates free culture and wiki-based methodologies to achieve autonomy and collaboration both of the trainer and the trainee.

Most importantly the Wikinomics project content creation, evaluation and dissemination process embody the existence of a community of practices among VET and other training actors, both at a European and international level. This is more a transnational network that is coined under the name of WikiAngels, striving to act as platform of experimentation and research and to adopt new socio-economical and pedagogical models.

The Wikinomics partners, on their own, wouldn't be enough to provide a larger scale transition in new pedagogical approaches, collaborative tools and open innovation practices. WikiAngels and other experts networks give feedback, evaluate and reuse project's outcomes at various occasions. The WikiAngels network provides a new interface with companies and other organizations and expands the area of Wikinomics targets to various domains.

4.1   The WikiAngels Network

The main carrier of this concept is the WikiAngels European network. WikiAngels are people of various expertise that create events, collaborations and services aiming at shifting current practices towards more collaborative learning and working. They share and collaborate on a wide range of skills to develop a wikinomics culture and, at the same time and have access to the project's resources (learning material, contacts, events) so as to foster their own business process. Thus, the WikiAngels network is an integrated part of the Wikinomics project in order to contribute to the exploitation of the project's outcomes.

The initial goals of this structure includes, a role of:

- A multiplier of open resources with a commons' driven, collaborative agenda.
- A provider of sustainable impact on the project's target groups.
- A network with commitment to self – sustainability.

WikiAngels are the motivators and the implementers behind the tools and methodologies deployed by the Wikinomics project, regarding wiki-thons, seek solutions basecamps, as well as, local TEDx events. These action are a part of their autonomous Business Process in which they introduce the idea of continuity between people, content and software in dynamic context of collaboration. This is to be completed by a, under development, matrix of competences on how to share the acquired customers between the available experts and, at the same time, support the common WikiAngels work. The WikiAngels network[4] is designed to remain open to various experts' participation. The availability of their expertise will be related to the open ended activities (basecamps, wikithons, presentations) that are being implemented.

4.2   Wikinomics Innovation Transfer to a VET and ECVET Context

ECVET is currently recognized as one of the key issues in education and training (VET) in Europe and every year numerous seminars and workshops are organized by the European Commission to discuss and share best practices on the topic. However, the studies[5] carried out within the ECVET Digital Platform[6] project show that the development of the ECVET system in Europe is still at its early stages: There's seems to be a relevant lack of awareness about ECVET's main features and objectives also

---

[4] The WikiAngeks network presentation is available at http://wikiskills.net/get-started/hire/.

[5] European Centre for the Development of Vocational Training, WORKING PAPER No 16. Trends in VET policy in Europe 2010–2012, Progress towards the Bruges communiqué.

[6] The ECVET Digital Platform is available at http://www.ecvet-projects.eu/default.aspx.

among VET professionals and in some EU Countries the policy and regulatory frameworks are still under preparation. At the same time, several VET organizations and institutions all over Europe are showing an increasing interest toward the issue and start to set up specific projects (mainly funded by European Programs), which is an excellent precondition for a successful implementation of ECVET.

The first ECVET component to be tackled within the Wiknomics Project is the learning outcomes and standards. This implies developing a shared understanding, between core and boundary project partners, of what 'learning outcomes' means, how the approach impacts on education and training systems, and how learning outcomes are developed and written: learning outcomes reflect professional standards, intersecting with occupational and educational standards.

The second crucial ECVET characteristic is that it is multi-purposed: it addresses European learning mobility, within education and training systems and portability of qualifications and learning outcomes for entering to another education and training level or system. Developing mobility appears as a huge task that prompts stakeholders to develop appropriate narratives and reflect on setting up strategies for mobility in VET. The Wikinomics approach is to address the above, mainly through the:

- matching wiki skills with new VET training approaches,
- pilot application of wiki practices and adapting them to ECVET,
- disseminating key concepts of wiki culture, at a European level,
- support informal learning tools and outcomes at various countries,
- introduce new pedagogical methods such as collaborative learning and teaching (including multi-stakeholders involvement).

As we will describe later in this paper, the Open Badges approach is a key effort in order to provide a useful and functional synthesis of these actions.

4.3   Methodologies Towards Wikinomics Key-Competences

Wikinomics project methodologies towards key competences understanding and acquisition reflect on students and trainers realities. Students no longer enter the classroom with the idea that all knowledge will come from the teacher with his/her books and methods. Students work connected with a vast amount of data available and with stakeholders well beyond the immediate training/teaching staff (such as socio-economic actors). The various learning competences need to be associated with context related experiences at all levels. In this sense, the Wikinomics project adopts a step-by-step pedagogical approach, accessible to all competences levels, taking particular attention to early ones.

The second key competences methodologies focus area is team competences. Collaborative working and market oriented results are often missing in educational programs. Thus, the Wikinomics project has a focus on the development of team working methodologies that could be applied to EU Lifelong Learning key competences, primarily, on:

- digital competence, dealing with the confident and critical use of Information Technology for work, leisure and communication,

- learning to learn, meaning the ability of individuals to organise their own learning through being aware of their own learning processes or needs,
- interpersonal, intercultural and social competences, civic competence, covering all forms of behavior that empower individuals to participate in an effective and constructive way in social and working life, and particularly in increasingly diverse societies, and to resolve conflict where necessary,
- entrepreneurship, involving the ability to turn ideas into action through creativity, innovation and risk taking as well as planning and management of projects in order to achieve objectives.

There has been a substantial work done in the area of wiki competences during the WikiSkills project. As a result of the WikiSkills analysis a set of 10 competences have been identified which can be fostered by the adoption of the wiki culture, which are named Key Wiki Competences (KWC).[7] The correspondence of this framework with the Key Competences for Lifelong Learning proposed by European Parliament and the Council is also demonstrated. However, this correspondence is not equivocal, either in its interpretation, or in its composition of competences.

5   Using an Open Badges Approach for ECVET, a Scenario

According to various ECVET resources,[8] the essential actions that can make, the ECVET credit transfer process, a successful reality include the:

- Development of Learning Outcomes (which are the backbone of the whole system).
- Assessment (which should be done using the proper tools and methods for assessment which are quality assured).
- Recognition (which should be lined with a framework).
- Transparency (where all actions and processes should be transparent).
- Transferability (which is vital if it is to allow mobility and accumulation of credits).
- Mobility (which is after all one of the aims of this project).

The unitisation of qualifications has gained momentum with the development of credit arrangements based on learning outcomes and with the progress made in recognition and validation of non-formal and informal learning. Within the Wikinomics project, a unit is a component of a qualification, consisting of a coherent set of knowledge, skills and competence that can be assessed and validated. Defining and building of units, reflecting on the links between modules and units, creating guidelines and framework conditions for developing ECVET units are issues to be further researched, along with award of credits and allocation of credit points.

---

[7] The Wiki Key Competences have been identified in Deliverable 2.3. Pedagogical Framework for Wiki Uses, available at: http://wikiskills.net/wp-content/uploads//D2.3_WikiSkills_Pedagogical_Framework_v2.pdf.

[8] The European Credit System for Vocational Education and Training ECVET - Get to know ECVET better- Questions and Answers; Revised February 2011.

The Wikinomics project is integrating this approach by launching an open communication process with the Mozilla Open Badges initiative. The goal of this initiative is twofold: the first reason is the need to enrich our understanding and practices of a modern, wiki culture, modular evaluation system for key-competences, as well as, VET culture and strategies. More specifically, the Wikinomics project attempts to integrate a "badges" approach in order to identify a series of international criteria regarding the acquisition and evaluation of competences developed through the use of free-culture and wiki methodologies. This is inline with the connected learning ecology approach used within the Mozilla Open Badges project.[9]

The second reason has to do with the networking of Wikinomics partners and sharing outcomes with a vibrant international community that adopts its own unitisation, evaluation and qualification strategies. It is crucial for our common work with various Wikinomics stakeholders and end-users, to explore and initiate innovative ways on the design, use and reproduction as a part of larger VET system deployment.

The Mozilla Web Literacy Map[10] contains the competencies and skills that Mozilla and our community of stakeholders believe are important to pay attention to when getting better at reading, writing and participating on the web. It is part of Mozilla's ongoing goal to create a generation of webmakers – those who can not only elegantly consume but also write and participate on the web. It is fair to say that the Mozilla learning, web literacy legacy is under development as most of the content on skills and competencies will appear during the next two years time.

Wikinomics, on the other hand, deploys a framework of ECVET key-competences developed through the use of free-culture and wiki methodologies. This happens, mainly, by conducting a series of collaborative wiki-based learning scenarios in which VET trainers adopt specific learning and training activities in order to achieve shared results and learning outcomes. This is based on the WikiSkills pedagogical approach, scenarios and experience.

These two approaches (Mozilla Open Badges and Wikinomics) seem different, firstly on the way they advance skills acquisition, learning and training and, secondly, on the mechanisms they use to approach the interested groups and implement their educative goals. At this point we would like to propose a situation where both systems are used, in such a way that their strong points become more evident.

This scenario could be based on the assumption that every person that wants to acquire an open badge on a "technology item" receives an initiation to complete, a short, step-by-step, question and answer questionnaire on free Internet culture. A teaser, with good use tips and collaborative examples that would give to the participants, access, to a larger learning environment: there, they could get in touch with various free culture elements, including licenses schemes, knowledge resources, entrepreneurship opportunities, participation in actions with potential social and economic impact.

---

[9] Open Badges for Lifelong Learning Exploring an open badge ecosystem to support skill development and lifelong learning for real results such as jobs and advancement, Working document available at https://wiki.mozilla.org/images/5/59/OpenBadges-Working-Paper_012312.pdf.

[10] The Mozilla Web Literacy Map (https://wiki.mozilla.org/Learning/WebLiteracyStandard).

This synergistic approach would try to address questions, such as:

- How small changes in behavioral use can improve online behavior and collaboration?
- How do such issues evolve in communities?
- What would be the learning outcome of each of these points?

Digital literacy, in this case becomes the initiator for a more fundamental behavioral approach. Actors on digital skills learning, often, tend to adopt a "mechanistic" approach on digital skills acquisition, meaning that they privilege a specific set of technical knowledge while avoiding more difficult tasks like culture and behavior change. There is a need and space for an action that would use social awareness techniques, in order to document and highlight the protagonists, and their stories, at the time of their digital learning and practice.

5.1   Qualification Profiles, Unit Design and Assessment Within Open Badges

As already mentioned, the Wikinomics project has identified the key competences to be addressed, as well as, their description in levels, with the aim of defining three (3) different qualification profiles for each competence. These levels of proficiency are "beginner", "intermediate" and "expert", and describe what a person should know, understand and is able to do to develop each competence. These qualification profiles can be applied to all VET professional families and is inline with the Open Badges qualification profiles.

Qualifications are described using units of learning outcomes so as to be able to relate the outcomes of assessed or evaluated learning experiences in a common methodology. A unit is a component of a qualification, consisting of a coherent set of knowledge, skills and competences of the established learning outcomes. The units are based on learning outcomes and are built both in an academic and a professional approach. In this chart the competences exposed are exposed following the KSAVE model[11] and by levels of proficiency, including: introduction, thinking on objectives, creating the initial content, introducing quality criteria, organising self and peer evaluation, publishing and diffusing.

The synergistic approach that the project adopts facilitates a stealth assessment scenario [4], as well as, the introduction of assessment indicators that are closer to an Open Badges approach. These indicators need to be addressed both in a self and peer evaluation contexts.

---

[11] KSAVE model proposes to understand learning as a sum of Knowledge, referred to the references to specific knowledge or understanding requirements, Skills, which are processes that curriculum framework are designed to develop and finally, Attitudes, Values and Ethics, referred to the behaviours and aptitudes that someone exhibit in relation to each of the skills. For more info, please visit http://atc21s.org/wp-content/uploads/2011/11/1-Defining-21st-Century-Skills.pdf.

6 Conclusions: Enriching the Wikinomics Approach

In this paper, we emphasized on the Wikinomics project focus on collaboration with various VET actors in all project phases (learning outcomes and units writing, pilot teaching and evaluation), in order to appropriate and propose an Open Badges methodology. Wikinomics brings together, in collaborative events fostered by the Wiki-Angels network, various stakeholders with a focus on learning and acting on a wikinomics basis, including:

- VET teachers, trainers and students.
- Wiki culture experts.
- Business and associations.
- A transnational open badges community.

In this sense, we can rethink the term "wikinomics" and its early description: assuming the need for better training, connecting training and labour permits us to better address wikinomics limits. The Wikinomics project recognises the key role that teachers, trainers, students, as well as, other socio-economic stakeholders play in this procedure: they do not only implement policies but also drive change and progress in VET and the need for learners to acquire collaborative and entrepreneurship skills.

References

1. Fuchs, C., Blachfellner, S., Bichler, R.M.: The urgent need for change: rethinking knowledge and management. In: Stary, C., Barachini, F., Hawamdeh, S. (eds.) Knowledge Management: Innovation, Technology and Cultures - Proceedings of the 2007 International Conference on Knowledge Management. Series on Innovation and Knowledge Management, vol. 6, pp. 293–307. World Scientific, New Jersey, London, Singapore (2007)
2. Leadbeater, C.: We-Think: Mass Innovation, Not Mass Production. Profile Books, London (2007)
3. Prahalad, C.K., Ramaswamy, V.: The Future of Competition: Co-creating Unique Value with Customers. Harvard Business School Press, Boston (2004)
4. Shute, V.J., Kim, Y.J.: Formative and stealth assessment. In: Spector, J.M., Merrill, M.D., Elen, J., Bishop, M.J. (eds.) Handbook of Research on Educational Communications and Technology, 4th edn. Lawrence Erlbaum Associates, Taylor & Francis Group, New York (2013)
5. Tapscott, D., Williams, D.: Wikinomics: How Mass Collaboration Changes Everything. Portfolio, London (2006)
6. Turner, F.: From Counterculture to Cyberculture: Stewart Brand, the Whole Earth Network and the Rise of Digital Utopianism. Chicago University Press, Chicago (2006)
7. Van Dijck, J.: The Culture of Connectivity: A Critical History of Social Media. Oxford University Press, Oxford (2013)

Awarding a Community Membership Badge - Teachers' Development of Digital Competences in a cMOOC

Niklas Karlsson[1]([⊠]), Linda Bradley[2], and Anna-Lena Godhe[1]

[1] University of Gothenburg, Box 100,
405 30 Gothenburg, Sweden
niklas.karlsson@bioenv.gu.se,
anna-lena.godhe@ait.gu.se
[2] Chalmers University of Technology,
Forskningsgången 6, 412 96 Gothenburg, Sweden
linda.bradley@chalmers.se

Abstract. In this article the badge given in connection with a cMOOC designed by and for teachers is explored. *Digitala skollyftet* aimed to raise the digital competence amongst teachers in Swedish schools. The participants in *Digitala skollyftet* could apply to be awarded a badge for their participation. The awarding process, as well as the participation, of a small group of people who were awarded badges is analysed. Blog-posts were taken as evidence when applying for badges and blogging thereby became an important way to participate. Blogs can be regarded as exhibition spaces where the blogger exhibits and reflects on their learning process. Results show that there is a difference in how the blogs are designed, depending on the level of experience from the blogger. To a large extent, forums, such as Facebook and Twitter, are used as performance spaces, which facilitate the interaction and discussion with other participants.

Keywords: MOOC · Teacher development · Digital competence

1 Introduction

In recent years, there have been suggestions that Massive Open Online Courses (MOOCs) would arise as a new way of gaining knowledge and competencies. MOOCs have been portrayed both as a threat and an opportunity to universities [1]. However, there are different types of MOOCs and the ones classified as cMOOCs are based on community building and interaction [8] rather than xMOOCs, which are similar to the structure of traditional academic courses with a set starting and finishing point. This article concerns a national cMOOC held in Sweden, *Digitala Skollyftet,* aiming to raise teachers' digital and social media competencies. A badge was designed for the MOOC, which could be achieved after fulfilling a number of steps in the process of participating in the MOOC activities.

Since MOOCs are not very common in Sweden, particularly not cMOOCs, there was a general concern amongst the organizers that the participants may need some structure to get involved. Therefore, a starting point in November 2013 was established

© Springer International Publishing Switzerland 2014
Y. Cao et al. (Eds.): ICWL 2014 Workshops, LNCS 8699, pp. 162–171, 2014.
DOI: 10.1007/978-3-319-13296-9_18

and weekly hangouts were arranged where different issues were discussed and "experts" were invited to take part in the discussions. *Digitala skollyftet* may therefore be considered as a hybrid which was constructed with a connectivist pedagogical model in mind, but which also incorporated features from xMOOCs in order to give a skeletal structure which the participants could relate to.

The aim of this article is to explore the Digitala Skollyftet badge and the evidence given to be awarded with the badge in order to investigate what the badge entails and how it functions as an assessment of the involvement in the cMOOC. The awarding process is explored in order to elucidate the function of the badge as a form of assessment. The badge is regarded as a community membership badge [13]. Earlier research [9] indicates that it is difficult to assess the involvement in a cMOOC without constraining the autonomy of the participants. The requirements and design of this badge will be explored and the participation of some of those who were awarded with the badge will be analysed further.

In order to get a badge, the applicants had to present evidence of their engagement in the MOOC. The evidence predominantly consisted of blog-posts. This evidence presented by applicants and the feedback given on the applications are analysed to explore whether these blogs predominantly are utilized as a space for interaction with others or as a space for presenting your achievements. Furthermore, the feedback given on the applications are analysed to explicate how the badges function as a form of assessment.

1.1 *Digitala Skollyftet*

During the autumn of 2013, an internet site, *Digitala skollyftet*, was set up as a basis for a cMOOC designed by and for teachers addressing three cornerstones; digital competence, sharing-is-caring and school development. Four teachers, who have previously been involved in another initiative called *Skollyftet* in Sweden, set up the site and planned for the MOOC. *Skollyftet,* which is well-known among teachers in Sweden, originates from an attempt to counteract negative media coverage of Swedish schools and aims to emphasize positive aspects and changes in the Swedish educational system. On Twitter, a number of Swedish teachers actively post information and discuss school issues on a daily basis. Every Thursday night there is an hour-long discussion on a particular subject in what is called #skolchatt. Similar discussion forums have been created for those who work in pre-school and for headmasters, for example.

Over one thousand teachers enrolled in *Digitala skollyftet*. However, to enroll in a MOOC, particularly a cMOOC, does not mean committing to anything. Enrollment is free and open and there are no predefined expectations for participation [11]. Since the MOOC is open, participation is possible whether being enrolled or not. Therefore, the number of people who enrolled has little, or no, relation to the number of active participants. As McAuley et al. put it "participation in a MOOC is emergent, fragmented, diffuse, and diverse" [11].

Digitala skollyftet aimed to facilitate user engagement and the loose structure of the MOOC contained suggestions of weekly tasks which the participants could engage in. The participants were asked to present themselves and make attempts at finding other participants in digital environments and networks. *Digitala skollyftet* was based on user engagement, offering a number of online tasks in which the participants could engage actively by interacting with others, contributing with posts in digital environments and social forums such as Twitter and Facebook, as well as setting up their own blogs. However, participation in a cMOOC like this does not necessarily mean actively interacting and posting, but could also consist of following the flow of events connected to the MOOC and receiving information through others by reading what they post as well as discussions in different forums.

1.2   The *Digitala Skollyftet* Badge

On the site *Digitala skollyftet* there is a certain page where the badge is presented and explained. The page includes a badge manual with basic information of what a badge is and more detailed descriptions of what applies to the *Digitala skollyftet* badge. There are links to a slide presentation created by the organizers, as well as to pages where open badges are explained. On the pages, badges are explained as a certificate for "abilities, achievements, participation, education, experience, interest etc. It is a way to digitally verify informal learning and works as a complement to formal qualifications such as credits from higher education and teacher diploma" [3]. It is also stressed that the badge contains easily accessible digital information about what it represents and that the badge is possible to display publicly in social media and on your own sites.

One of the organisers states in a blog post [13] that the *Digitala skollyftet* badge is a community membership badge and that the peer assessment involved in awarding badges is particularly suitable since the community is characterized by networks of peers, rather than the hierarchical relationship between teachers and students. Furthermore, "all members in the community, not only expert members, are skilled in recognising the community membership of new members" [13]. Peer evaluation is regarded as a valuable contribution in building the community and not as a separate assessment process.

For those who fulfill the criteria for a specific badge, it becomes "a receipt and a recognition of the learning experience which it represents" [3]. The specific criteria for the *Digitala skollyftet* badge are related to the three cornerstones in the MOOC; digital competence, sharing-is-caring and school development, which are here also called the three key competences that distinguish the participants in *Digitala skollyftet* and the Online Community of Educators (*det Utvidgade Kollegiet*). Those who receive a *Digitala skollyftet* badge show their competence in using digital tools for communication, learning and creation. Furthermore, they show competence in "sharing-is-caring" since they learn from others and teach others in the Online Community of Educators. Finally, they show competence in school development since they use their skills in a way that supports the development of their role within the school [3].

In connection to the criteria for the badge the aim of the badge is further explained as recognition of the contribution to the Online Community of Educators. This is regarded as a sense of belonging, to which a learning experience is connected.

"We use our skills with digital tools to communicate, learn and create knowledge together in a non-hierarchical spirit of "sharing-is-caring" and this knowledge is re-invested in the schools to create sustainable school development" [3].

A brief description of the awarding process is given on the page where the badge is explained. When applying for a badge, a short application form is filled in which includes a link to the "project" that meets the criteria for the badge. A short description of what the project is about is also required. The application should be sent to someone who already has a *Digitala skollyftet* badge and that person will give feedback on the project and award the badge.

The awarded badges are displayed on a page together with a short explanation of the badge (similar to the descriptions at the *Digitala skollyftet* site) [3]. The awarded badges can be accessed either by clicking on an image of the creator or through the list of short descriptions of badges further down on the page. The descriptions consist of an image of the creator, the title of the project, a description of the project and a link to the evidence, predominantly blog posts. By clicking on the title of the project a page is accessed where the creator of the badge states "steps taken" and "lessons learned" [3]. Further down on this page, the feedback given on this particular badge is displayed. The feedback is arranged in kudos, questions and concerns. Positive comments are given in the kudos section and more critical questions and concerns in the other sections. Sometimes the creator of the badge has made improvements which are displayed along with a new URL. This may be followed by further feedback from the person awarding the badge.

2   Theoretical Framing

MOOCs are often associated with connectivist perspectives on learning. *Digitala skollyftet* to some extent resembles the MOOC Connectivism and Connective Knowledge (hereafter CCK08), since both explore connectivist notions of knowledge building. In previous research [9, 10], the participants learning experiences in CCK08 have been explored in relation to the connectivist principles of autonomy, diversity, openness, and connectedness and interactivity [4]. 'Autonomy' means that learners have a choice of where, when, how, with whom, and even, what, to learn. 'Diversity' is related to there being a diverse population in the network in order to avoid group-thinking [12]. 'Openness' concerns the free flow of information and is supposed to encourage a culture of sharing and a focus on knowledge creation where there are no barriers between "in" and "out" [9]. 'Connectedness' and interactivity are considered to be what makes all this possible. Knowledge emerges as a result of connections, according to the connectivist perspective [2]. Though the CCK08 contained the connectivist principles, paradoxes also arose which constrained "the possibility of having the positive experiences of autonomy, diversity, openness and connectedness/interactivity normally expected of an online network" [9]. It could therefore be put into question whether it is possible to combine the connectivist principles, which are based on online networks, with MOOCs. To emphasize the network aspects, and downplay the course aspects, the organisers of *Digitala skollyftet* tended to refer to the MOOC as a Massive Open Online Community, rather than Course.

To frame participatory activities, Goffman's [5] concept of presentation of self may be used as a way to identify user interaction. For activities of participation, online performance has been used in investigating notions of front and back stage activities

[6]. However, as Hogan [6] points out, Goffman´s dramaturgical approach focuses on situations which are framed in time and space. Online environments, on the other hand, are often asynchronous and therefore less dependent on time and space. Hogan prefers the metaphor of exhibition, rather than Goffman´s metaphor of stage play, when considering online environments. Hogan distinguishes between performance spaces online where actors perform with each other and exhibition spaces where artifacts will be submitted by individuals in order to show to others [6]. This distinction will be used to further identify different ways in which it is possible to participate in MOOCs like *Digitala skollyftet*.

3 Method

The method for collecting data incorporates a number of different datasets which will be synthesized in the analysis in order to illuminate different aspects of the MOOC as well as of particular aspects of it, such as badges.

The empirical data consist of surveys, shown in Table 1, and open online resources, such as blogs, Twitter, and Facebook. These have been mined for data which concerns *Digitala skollyftet*. Tweets containing the hashtag *#digiskol* have been collected as well as posts on Facebook concerning *Digitala skollyftet*. Collecting data from social media is difficult and an area of research which is still very much at an exploratory stage when it comes to how to collect and analyse data, as well as ethical aspects of how to use data [7].

Table 1. An overview of the conducted surveys

Survey 1, October 2013	Questions regarding the participants workplace, work experience and basic information about their use of social media. Consent given to participate in the study. 438 persons agreed to further participate in the study
Survey 2, November 2013	In-depth questions about the use of ICT and social media in and outside the workplace. 140 persons answered the survey
Survey 3, February 2014	Open-ended questions about their participation in the MOOC. 97 persons answered the survey
Survey 4, April 2014	Additional survey sent to 10 persons who had taken a badge and 10 persons who had actively participated in the MOOC (based on answers in previous surveys) but not taken a badge. Open-ended questions about badges. 9 persons answered the survey

All in all, 66 persons answered survey one, two and three, 10 of these persons were also awarded with the *Digitala skollyftet* badge. In the entire MOOC, 47 persons were awarded the *Digitala skollyftet* badge, disregarding the organizers, and two of these applied to two badges. The fourth survey was carried out in order to focus on questions about badges and addressed participants who had actively taken part in the MOOC as well as the ten persons who had been awarded with badges.

The analysis in this article focuses on open online data connected to the badge such as blog-posts and application to the badge. The answers in the final survey are also central to the analysis, whereas the other surveys and other online data are regarded as secondary information sources on which additional information about the participants are based.

4   Results

In this section, the total number of badges will briefly be mapped out, considering the content of them but also how the participants represent themselves and present their participation in the MOOC. Thereafter, the focus will be on the ten persons who were awarded with badges and who answered the surveys in this study.

4.1   Representation in Applications for Badges

This section analyses how the persons who have been awarded with a *Digitala skollyftet* badge represent themselves when applying for the badge. It should be pointed out that the analysis concerns the application for the badge and no extensive analysis of the evidence which the applicants attach to the application has been undertaken.

When ta king into account the open information in the application for the badges in *Digitala skollyftet*, it becomes clear that applying for the badge involves the presentation of self as well as of what is claimed to have been done in order to meet the criteria for the badge [3]. Representations of self and knowledge are intertwined so that the presentation of self may reveal how knowledge is viewed and vice versa. Some general characteristics of the presentations will be illuminated in order to highlight both differences and similarities in the presentations. These characteristics are pointed out to exemplify differences and similarities and no hierarchical order of presentation or participation is intended. The feedback given on the applications will also be regarded in the analysis.

There is a natural focus on what the persons themselves have done when they present the evidence for meeting the criteria of the badge. However, differences in focus can be distinguished where students and colleagues are emphasized to different extents. Some applicants predominantly focus on their own achievements; in the skills they have acquired in handling digital tools or in the enlarged network which they have established through participating in the MOOC. It is not always clear how their personal gains are put into practice in the work with students or how they are shared and spread with other colleagues. In other applications, the work with students is in focus and how personal gains are used in practices in the classroom are exemplified. Claiming a blog created by the teacher together with the students is an example of evidence, where the applicant emphasizes how skills and knowledge are utilized together with students and aimed at improving their classroom practices. Some applications stress how the MOOC has enabled them to share and spread knowledge with colleagues. In most applications, networking, as in participating in different forums in social media, is mentioned and the applicants increased participation in these forums is put forward as a personal gain. However, in some cases networking is in focus and the applicants convey how they have contributed to creating networking spaces, such as EdCamps and Teachmeets for teachers. Both EdCamps and Teachmeets can be characterized as "unconferences", where it is up to participants to set the agenda and where the goal is to share and discuss ideas and concerns regarding educational issues[1].

Whereas the presentation of self and of evidence for the badge in one sense illuminates the autonomous paths of the different applicants, there are also signs of how these paths interconnect and draw on each other. A handful of Facebook groups and a couple of groups in Google+ are mentioned by several applicants as important sources for both information sharing, discussions and reflections. Some groups are concerned with particular content, such as flipped classrooms or formative assessment. Others appear to be of a more general character where the members have found other participants to engage with. Some applications, such as Pearls and Pinterest, are mentioned by several persons as tools which they have become accustomed to and used in different ways, to display their engagement in the MOOC or to display the work of students.

Initially it was the organizers who awarded the badges, but gradually those who have been awarded with badges also started to give feedback to others. Apart from the organizers, 12 persons have given feedback on applications. Most of them have given feedback on a couple of applications but one person has given feedback on as many as nine applications. The feedback given on applications predominantly consists of positive comments on the work that the applicant has done. If issues are asked they mainly concern what thoughts the applicant have in regards to developing for example a blog. Concerns are seldom raised. When they are, they mainly concern that the evidence given should be a particular text or page where it is stated how the criteria for the badge have been met, rather than giving an entire blog as evidence. Different persons giving feedback have requested this kind of evidence. These requests show signs of interconnectedness since when giving feedback, one of the newly awarded participants raise the same concern as has previously been given on his/her own application. Questions are raised in connection to a few applicants and they mainly concern how the person claiming the evidence for being awarded with a badge, has interacted with others. These questions can be regarded as a way to attempt to highlight the importance of sharing your experience as well as your concerns in social media. Thereby, the questions aim to downplay that personal gains are being focused in the evidence for the badge, and simultaneously highlight the importance of sharing and the use of social media as a forum for mutual distribution of knowledge, rather than somewhere where you, primarily, boost your own achievements and knowledge.

4.2 Participation

In this section the focus will be on the ten people who have answered the surveys in this study and who have also been awarded with a *Digitala skollyftet* badge. The evidence which these ten participants have enclosed in their application for the badge consists of blog-posts. Therefore, the blogs in question and their content and structure

---

[1] For further information http://en.wikipedia.org/wiki/Unconference.

are taken into account in the analysis. The analysis will be based on the answers in the surveys and the application for the badge, including the evidence which was given for being awarded with the badge.

The evidence given to be awarded with the badge generally consisted of a blog-post. To a large extent, the content of the blogs reflects the journey of the blogger. At least, six of the ten blogs were started in connection with *Digitala skollyftet* and these bloggers can therefore be regarded as novice bloggers. The blogs, at least initially, serve as a way to present the blogger as a participant in *Digitala skollyftet*. The blogs are also a space where the bloggers' engagement in the MOOC is displayed. Blog-posts commonly concern the different digital tools the bloggers have tried out. There are also more reflective posts where some dilemma is considered or a text or film-clip which has been found on social media is discussed. These novice blogs typically have a few comments from other participants in *Digitala skollyftet*. Often the same person comments more than once and the blogger may also respond to the comments. The participants regularly comment on each other's blogs and often they do so since they share a common interest or work with the same subject or the same age-group of students. Networking, on these blogs, appear to present an opportunity to engage with those that you regard as similar to yourself in one way or another, rather than seeking out differences.

A couple of the blogs are class-blogs. This means that the blogs are used by the blogger, as a teacher, and their students to display what they do in school and to engage parents and others who may be interested. The focus of these blogs becomes what is done in the classroom and the blogs mainly address an audience consisting of the students and their parents. This could be regarded as another type of sharing-is-caring which may not be the intention of the MOOC but which serve a clear purpose for using digital tools. These blogs facilitate openness towards those who are not in the classroom so that they can follow and engage in classroom activities.

A few blogs started before *Digitala skollyftet* and these bloggers are therefore more experienced. To a large extent, the content on these blogs are reflections on activities that the bloggers have done in the classroom or things that they are planning to do, or would like to do. Two bloggers stand out as experienced both in blogging and in regularly engaging in social media and the Online Community of Educators. These two blogs are somewhat different in character compared to the others. There are fewer comments on these blogs and the blog-posts appear to display the bloggers' ability or expertise in different areas rather than their experiences or learning process in the MOOC.

The structure of a MOOC is sometimes portrayed as non-hierarchical since there are not supposed to be any teachers or experts. However, structures where some participants take on, or are given, the role of expert can be discerned from the difference in both content and structure of the blogs of these participants. Though the building of a community of peers may be the vision of a MOOC, the reality may be that structures of more-capable peers are inevitable. However, these structures should not be seen as negative, but rather as a way in which participants learn from each other and where more-capable peers can be regarded as assets since they may scaffold the experiences of newcomers.

The two expert bloggers and participants, highlighted in the previous paragraph, expressed a particular interest in the badge as a phenomenon in their answers in the surveys. Two of the other ten mentioned badges but did so because they thought that the process of being awarded with the badge had been complicated and difficult. The experiences bloggers thereby displayed familiarity and curiosity concerning badges as a phenomenon, while several of the others said that they had little or no knowledge of badges prior to the *Digitala skollyftet*.

When being asked whether they considered the badge to be a form of assessment and/or feedback, the answers convey that the badge was mainly considered as a form of feedback which also served as evidence for having participated in the course. Giving feedback to others when awarding badges was by some seen as positive and a way to promote a more open and less personal climate, others pointed out the risk of the criteria being interpreted differently or subjectively.

5 Conclusion

The persons who were awarded with a badge in *Digitala skollyftet* utilize their blogs as an exhibition space where their own journey through the MOOC is exhibited and reflected upon. However, there appears to be a difference in how this exhibition space is used by novice bloggers and more experienced ones. Those who are more experienced bloggers use their blog as an exhibition space where they display their views and knowledge on certain issues. These blogs have few comments from other participants. Since the less experienced bloggers have more comments on their blogs and engage in exchanges with others through the comments to a greater extent than the experienced bloggers, these blogs become hybrids which serve as both an exhibition and a performance space.

Mak et al. [10] explore the participants' use of blogs and forums in the MOOC CCK08. They come to the conclusion that blogs are used mainly as a personal space for learning and reflection. Forums, on the other hand, are largely used for interaction, discussion and sharing of ideas with others. Hogan [6] makes a similar distinction between exhibition spaces and performance spaces. Comparing interactions on Facebook and Twitter in *Digitala skollyftet,* the discussions on Facebook more closely related to classroom issues whereas discussions on Twitter generally regarded broader issues. Engaging in forums on Facebook may be a first step when attempting to use social media in your profession, having your own blog and using Twitter may be a next step, which most of the persons awarded badges have taken.

The connectivist principles of autonomy, diversity, openness, and connectedness and interactivity were by Mackness et al. [9] found to be constrained in the MOOC. Learner autonomy and assessment are, for example, regarded as difficult to simultaneously achieve. The comments given on applications for badges were generally positive and the participants conceived them as feedback on their participation rather than assessment. The badges can then be regarded as awards for participation rather than assessment of that participation. Largely omitting critical comments in the award process can be a way to overcome the paradoxes involved when applying connectivist principles to a MOOC.

References

1. Beaven, A.: Using MOOCs in an academic english course at university level. In: Beaven, A., Comas-Quinn, A., Sawhill, B. (eds.) Case Studies of Openness in the Language Classroom, 1st edn, pp. 217–227. (2013). http://Research-publishing.net
2. Bell, F.: Connectivism: its place in theory-informed research and innovation in technology enhanced learning. Int. Rev. Res. Open Distance Learn. **12**(3), 98–119 (2011)
3. Digitala Skollyftets Badge (2013). http://www.digitalaskollyftet.se/digitala-skollyftet-badge
4. Downes, S.: Connectivism: A Theory of Personal Learning (2008). http://www.slideshare.net/Downes/connectivism-a-theory-of-personal-learning
5. Goffman, E.: The Presentation of Self in Everyday Life. Anchor Books, New York (1959)
6. Hogan, B.: The presentation of self in the age of social media: distinguishing performances and exhibitions online. Bull. Sci. Technol. Soc. **30**(6), 377–386 (2010)
7. Horst, H., Miller, D.: Digital Anthropology. Bloomsbury, London (2012)
8. Jobe, W., Östlund, C., Svensson, L.: MOOCs for professional teacher development. In: Searson, M., Ochoa, M. (eds.) Proceedings of Society for Information Technology and Teacher Education Conference. AACE, Chesapeake (2014)
9. Mackness, J., Mak, S.F.J., Williams, R.: The ideals and reality of participating. In: MOOC. Networked Learning Conference, Denmark (2010)
10. Mak, S.F.J., Williams, R., Mackness, J.: Blogs and forums as communication and learning tools. In: A MOOC. Networked Learning Conference, Denmark (2010)
11. McAuley, A., Stewart, B., Siemens, G., Cormier, D.: The MOOC Model for Digital Practice (2010). http://davecormier.com/edblog/wp-content/uploads/MOOC_Final.pdf
12. McRae, P.: Echoing voices – emerging challenges for educational practice on the internet. In: Reeves, T., Yamashita, S. (eds.) Proceedings of World Conference on E-learning in Corporate, Government, Healthcare, and Higher Education, pp. 2622–2629 (2006)
13. Mörtsell, S.: Using P2PU to Badge Swedish Educators' MOOC (2014). http://info.p2pu.org/2014/02/11/using-p2pu-to-badge-swedish-educators-mooc/

Exploring the Potential of Open Badges in Blog-Based University Courses

Hans Põldoja[✉] and Mart Laanpere

Institute of Informatics, Tallinn University, Tallinn, Estonia
{hans.poldoja,mart.laanpere}@tlu.ee

Abstract. Recent developments with personal learning environments and open online courses have led educators to experiment with opening up their formal higher education courses. In these courses, the online learning activities take place in open learning environments based on various Web 2.0 tools such as blogs. Although this type of courses have a number of pedagogical benefits, they also raise issues related to private grading of students' works and recognizing the learning of informal participants. This paper presents our exploratory study on addressing these issues by introducing open badges to master's level course that takes place in a blog-based learning environment. Students' perspectives on using open badges were evaluated through focus group interviews. The results of the study indicate, that badges could have a potential in formal higher education, if they are used more widely and provide an explicit choice of personal learning paths for learners.

Keywords: Open badges · Assessment · Blog-based courses

1 Introduction

One of the recent trends in education is the blending of formal and informal learning. This is supported by introducing social media, personal learning environments and various open educational practices to formal higher education [1, 2]. Students can enrich their learning experience by using open educational resources from other universities and taking part in Massive Open Online Courses.

In many cases, such developments have led university lecturers and professors to increase the degree of openness in their courses. One approach is to move online learning activities to open learning environments that are based on social media and Web 2.0 tools such as blogs. The use of blogs in online courses provides a number of pedagogical benefits such as motivating learners, enhancing the development and expression of ideas, fostering interaction, collaboration and group work, inviting feedback from other learners, and enriching the learning environment [3]. The use of blog-based learning environments also allows educators to open up their course for informal participants or members of professional communities who are not officially enrolled to the course.

Open blog-based courses in formal higher education raise also a number of issues that are not present in traditional courses. For example, blog-based learning environments typically lack special features that support private feedback and grading of

© Springer International Publishing Switzerland 2014
Y. Cao et al. (Eds.): ICWL 2014 Workshops, LNCS 8699, pp. 172–178, 2014.
DOI: 10.1007/978-3-319-13296-9_19

students' submissions. Sending all grades by e-mail could often cause too much additional work for the facilitator and disconnects grades from the learning environment. Setting up a learning management system in parallel with blogs, just for grading, would be also cumbersome. Another issue is related to recognizing the learning outcomes of informal participants. As they are not officially enrolled, they cannot receive credits or a certificate from the university. Also, it is common that these informal learners complete only part of the course assignments.

In this study, we explored the potential of open badges as a possible solution for these issues. Section 2 gives a short overview of open badges and their current use in higher education. In Sect. 3, we describe the context of our study. The fourth section provides some empirical data on the students' perspectives. The article ends with a list of discussion items and some ideas for future research on open badges.

2 Open Badges and Their Use in Higher Education

Mozilla Open Badges is a web technology that allows to recognize and verify learning. Developed by the Mozilla Foundation, it is an open system that allows any organization or educator to start issuing digital badges. Badges are digital images that have built in data about the issuer, criteria, and evidence. Learners can collect earned badges to their digital backpack and display them on various profiles in social media.

As the open badges originate from the open source and open education community, the most well known implementations are related to informal learning [4]. There is still little research on integrating open badges to formal higher education. Based on current studies, we identified four potential emerging badge design patterns:

- *Composite badges* can be achieved by completing multiple assignments. For example, "Introduction to Openness in Education" course by David Wiley [5] provides only three different badges: OpenEd Overview Badge, OpenEd Researcher Badge, and OpenEd Evangelist Badge. In order to achieve the overview badge, the learner has to do a basic blog post on each of the topics. The researcher's badge requires a more in-depth posts in three of the topics.
- *Activity-based badges* can be awarded automatically based on measurable learning activities. Erik Duval's course on Human-Computer Interaction provides badges that promote activity, quality and results [6]. Activity badges are based on a number of entries posted to Twitter and WordPress. Quality badges are related to the external activity on students' works (e.g. comments and retweets). Results' badges can be achieved by completing certain milestones or assignments.
- *Grade-based badges* are based on the grades that the learners have received. Rughiniş and Matei [7] describe a course where learners can achieve "Bronze", "Silver" and "Gold" badges based on their grade point average. In addition to these, the learners can earn a "Perfectionist" badge by having all scores above 90 %.
- *Hierarchical badges* are divided to several levels, some of which may be composite badges based on lower level badges. Randall, Harrison, and West [8] propose a hierarchical badge system where the badges are divided into lower level, project level, and course level. If students have earned all the lower level and project level badges, they are automatically awarded with course level badge.

Santos et al. [6] found out that the students considered badges that promote achieving learning outcomes as the most important. These were followed by badges related to quality. Badges related to quantity were seen as less important. Their study also involved group badges and badges that have a negative connotation. Group badges were considered more important than individual badges. Students also turned a lot of attention to avoid achieving negative badges. Rughiniș and Matei [7] concluded that badges have an important role for focusing learners' attention on important learning outcomes. Randall et al. [8] pointed out that while it is relatively straightforward to provide badges for achieving concrete skills, there is a challenge to design badge systems for more conceptual achievements, such as gaining new knowledge, understanding, or attitudes.

3   Design and Implementation of Badges in a Blog-Based Course

Our first study on using open badges was carried out between February and May 2014 in the "Creating Digital Learning Resources" course for the educational technology master students. It is a 3-credit course that is conducted over 15 weeks. This year 19 learners participated the course, one of them was an informal participant. During the course there are four classroom meetings (4 × 4 h), the rest of the learning activities take place as an online course. The course is divided into six topics that last for 2 weeks: (1) learning objects and repositories, (2) authoring tools, (3) computer-based assessment, (4) new technologies for creating digital learning resources, (5) copyright and open educational resources, and (6) quality of digital learning resources. The first week is left for the introduction and last two weeks for completing the assignments.

The online part of the course involved using personal blogs by each student and facilitator. In this format the teacher is posting course assignments and reading material to the course blog. The students will post their responses to the assignments in their personal blogs and comment each other's works. In our course there were six blogging assignments — one for each topic. In addition to these assignments, the students were expected to develop one digital learning resource as a group assignment and to write a literature review.

Considering the current badge design patterns for formal higher education courses, we recognized that all of these lacked focus on learning outcomes. The Estonian higher education system has a strong focus on outcome-based assessment, therefore in our context the open badges should be also directly linked to learning outcomes. We propose *outcome-based badges*, as another possible badge design pattern.

The "Creating Digital Learning Resources" course has 7 learning outcomes: 5 of the learning outcomes are related to basic knowledge of the course topics, 1 is related to practical authoring skills, and 1 to deeper analyzing skills. The relationship between learning outcomes, assignments and badges is displayed on Fig. 1. There is 1:1 relationship between most of the learning outcomes and assignments, but some learning outcomes are related also to 2 or 3 different assignments. Our badges are divided into three levels: (1) basic knowledge badges, (2) skills badges, and (3) advanced knowledge badges. There is 1:1 relationship between the blogging assignments on 6 main topics and basic knowledge badges on these topics. The group assignment on developing a digital learning resource can lead into one of three badges depending on the type of a learning resource: "Content package author", "Assessment test author", and "e-Textbook author". The literature review can lead to advanced knowledge badge on one of the six main topics of the course.

When designing the badges, we realized that the current Mozilla Open Badges Infrastructure does not have a good way for specifying the "weight" of the badge. The estimated amount of work for each blogging assignment was 5 h, while we reserved 20 h for the literature review. Therefore, we decided to introduce the concept of weight. The weight of basic knowledge badges was 10 points, while skills badges and advanced knowledge badges were worth 20 points. Final grades of the course were calculated based on the weight of received badges. In order to receive grade A, the students had to collect six basic knowledge badges (60 points), one skills badge (20 points), and one advanced knowledge badge (20 points).

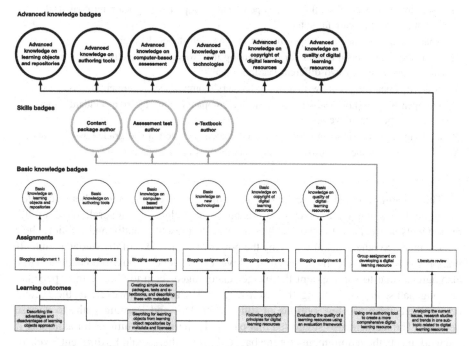

Fig. 1. Relationship between learning outcomes, assignments and badges

For issuing the badges we used WPBadger plugin for WordPress. This provided a simple and private way inform students, whether their work was accepted. The students were introduced to Mozilla Backpack and recommended to use WPBadgeDisplay plugin on their personal blogs. However, the majority of students used free WordPress. com hosting platform that do not allow users to add additional plugins. In that case, they could share a link to the badge collection in their Backpack.

4 Students' Perspectives on Open Badges

In order to understand students' perspectives on the use of open badges, we prepared 8 questions for the semi-structured focus group interviews with the students (see Table 1). Due to the exploratory approach of our study, the focus group interview was preferred to alternative methods (e.g. online survey, individual interviews). The interview topics included impact of badges to learner's motivation and self-regulation, reliability and validity of badges as assessment instrument, suitability of badges for formative vs. summative assessment. The sample included 15 students who were present on the final meeting of the course. For the interviews, they were divided into 2 focus groups in order to increase the likelihood of hearing everyone's opinion.

Table 1. Questions for the semi-structured focus group interviews

To what extent the use of open badges influences the learning motivation?
How and to what extent does the use of open badges support setting learning goals and choosing a suitable learning path?
To what extent does the use of open badges increase self-directed learning?
How reliable are the open badges for representing the progress and results of learning? Is the same badge earned by two different learners equal?
What do the open badges show first of all: learners' competences or something else?
Do the open badges show learners' performance compared with objective standard, other learners, or personal development?
What are the pros and cons of open badges compared with verbal and graded assessment?
What could be realistic scenarios for using open badges outside the course?

The students pointed out feeling of recognition and confirmation about accepted assignments, as the main benefits of using open badges. In general, most of the respondents appreciated the way badges allowed to present proudly and publicly their achievements to others, acknowledging the power of vanity. One of the students said: "If there is a possibility to collect something, I want to achieve all possible badges". They also agreed, that to some extent the badges encouraged them to choose their personal learning paths, thus enhancing their self-regulated learning. However, in the current course there were too few options of different badges and learning paths to choose between. The learners also suggested that pass/fail criteria is too limited for assessing if the work meets the requirements for the badge. Instead, there could be different levels of badges for the same assignment. The students admitted, that they see little value in badges, if these are used as a one-time experiment in one course. The badges would become more valuable, if several courses would have a possibility to earn badges. Also, they found the simple visual design of badges in the current course unattractive.

As for future possibilities, all respondents agreed that badges could have a larger potential in higher education, once they become an integral part of assessment and recognition system on the level of the master's programme. The students proposed several ideas for potential improvements, which should be considered by the open badges community when designing the next generation solutions. First, a greater choice of alternative learning paths, visualized as a sequence of open badges, should be provided to learners in order to increase their self-regulation. Second, open badges could be of help in bridging informal and formal education, both as tokens for recognizing the prior learning in the beginning of the university course, but also as means for presenting the course achievements outside of formal education context (e.g. in person's CV when applying for a new job). Third, the facilitators could offer larger variety of badge types designed with distinct visual styles, including badge types associated with social or motivational aspects, e.g. badges issued for the most active participants in online discussions or the most creative visualizations. The students also pointed out a need for a tool for visualizing their personal learning path as a sequence of open badges and monitoring the progress in achieving badges. Some respondents played with the idea of student-designed or student-awarded open badges that could be used for peer assessment.

Although our focus group interview suffered from the "cold start" issue that is typical for many experimental studies in technology-enhanced learning, we consider that the results of our first exploratory study can serve as a valuable input for further discussion in the community of open badges. We encourage the community to expand the notion and implementation patterns of open badges as a tool for bridging formal and informal education. We propose that open badges could be useful in all three types of assessment: assessment of learning, assessment for learning and assessment as learning [9].

5   Conclusions

In this paper, we shared some insights from our first exploratory study on using open badges in formal higher education. Comparing the related works, we indicated four existing badge design patterns for higher education courses. In our study, we took outcome-centered approach and proposed *outcome-based badges* as another possible badge design pattern. The results of the empirical study indicated a number of limitations with our first implementation of open badges. However, the learners agreed that open badges could have a potential in formal higher education, if they provide greater choice for learners.

This exploratory study raised several questions for further research on open badges in higher education. What are the consequences of combining outcome-based badges with other types of badges? How easy will it be for the students to prioritize which badges they should get? How to find a balance between representing the achievements and gamifying the learning experience? Also, there is a need for user-friendly tools for issuing badges and planning personal learning paths for earning badges.

References

1. Dabbagh, N., Kitsantas, A.: Personal learning environments, social media, and self-regulated learning: a natural formula for connecting formal and informal learning. Internet High. Educ. **15**, 3–8 (2012)
2. Peña-López, I.: Heavy switchers in translearning: from formal teaching to ubiquitous learning. On Horiz. **21**, 127–137 (2013)

3. Goktas, Y., Demirel, T.: Blog-enhanced ICT courses: examining their effects on prospective teachers' ICT competencies and perceptions. Comput. Educ. **58**, 908–917 (2012)
4. Ahn, J., Butler, B.S., Alam, A., Webster, S.A.: Learner participation and engagement in open online courses: insights from the Peer 2 Peer University. J. Online Learn. Teach. **9**, 160–171 (2013)
5. Wiley, D.: Assignments: Introduction to Openness in Education. https://learn.canvas.net/courses/4/assignments
6. Santos, J.L., Charleer, S., Parra, G., Klerkx, J., Duval, E., Verbert, K.: Evaluating the use of open badges in an open learning environment. In: Hernández-Leo, D., Ley, T., Klamma, R., Harrer, A. (eds.) EC-TEL 2013. LNCS, vol. 8095, pp. 314–327. Springer, Heidelberg (2013)
7. Rughinis, R., Matei, S.: Digital badges: signposts and claims of achievement. In: Stephanidis, S. (ed.) HCI International 2013 - Posters' Extended Abstracts, pp. 84–88. Springer, Berlin Heidelberg (2013)
8. Randall, D.L., Harrison, J.B., West, R.E.: Giving credit where credit is due: designing open badges for a technology integration course. TechTrends **57**, 88–95 (2013)
9. Earl, L., Katz, S.: Rethinking Classroom Assessment with Purpose in Mind: Assessment for Learning, Assessment as Learning, Assessment of Learning. Manitoba Education, Citizenship and Youth (2006). http://www.edu.gov.mb.ca/k12/assess/wncp/

Design Principles for Digital Badge Systems

A Comparative Method for Uncovering Lessons in Ecosystem Design

Nate Otto[✉] and Daniel T. Hickey

Center for Research on Learning and Technology,
Indiana University, Indiana, USA
nate@ottonomy.net, dthickey@indiana.edu

Abstract. This paper describes a method for studying programs that issue Open Badges to recognize learning. The Design Principles Documentation (DPD) Project followed the development of 30 educational programs that planned to issue open digital badges to recognize "lifelong learning" accomplishment. The DPD Project's aim was to formulate general design principles based on the practices observed among the 30 research subjects. Analysis yielded 37 principles across four researcher-selected functions of digital badge systems: recognizing learning, assessing learning, motivating learning, and studying learning. This work describes this research methodology and its affordances for uncovering relationships between different elements of badge system design and between those elements and the larger project contexts in which they operate.

Keywords: Open badges · Digital badges · Design principles

1 Introduction

Digital badges, as a technology used to credential learning achievement, serve a variety of functions within a learning ecosystem and in turn require supporting practices to support program goals and serve earner interests.

Open Badges are a subset of digital badges that follow the Open Badges Infrastructure (OBI) standard originally set out by the Mozilla Foundation [7]. In programs that use badges to recognize learning, each badge is a symbolic representation of specific achievements. Each Open Badge consists of an image packed with computer-readable metadata. Through the symbolism of the selected image and the information embedded in it as structured metadata, each badge makes specific claims about earners and can marshal collections of evidence to support those claims. Badge earners may share these claims with various audiences, and those audiences in turn may examine the metadata and evidence to make decisions about the validity of those claims from their own perspective.

Open Badge programs establish the claims they want to make with badges and build programs to control the social and technical practices through which badges are issued to the earners who participate in their programs. The collections of practices that

© Springer International Publishing Switzerland 2014
Y. Cao et al. (Eds.): ICWL 2014 Workshops, LNCS 8699, pp. 179–184, 2014.
DOI: 10.1007/978-3-319-13296-9_20

control what badges mean to each issuer and how they are issued are what are often referred to as "badge systems."

Badge systems in education encompass the goals, badge definitions, procedures, and technology particular to a learning program, and they are situated within that program's particular context. For example, when the arithmetic practice site *BuzzMath* describes its goal of fostering "inspiration and motivation in mathematics education" where students "master concepts based on the Common Core Mathematics Standards for Middle School," the badge system they build contains badges defined around that goal and procedures structured around the technical infrastructure of its parent company's self-paced online learning environment [1]. The same goal implemented for in-person learning would result in a system that may share features around what claims the badges would make about earners but would consist of a vastly different set of practices mediating how badges would be issued and what evidence would be available to back up their claims. Some of the practices implemented in a self-guided online context would not be appropriate to implement for students in the same room as their instructors.

2   The Design Principles Documentation Project

In order to better understand what factors affect which practices are appropriate in a given context, the MacArthur Foundation commissioned the Design Principles Documentation (DPD) Project at Indiana University in concert with the *Badges for Lifelong Learning Initiative*, a grant program that funded 30 projects to award open digital badges across many different educational contexts. These grants, part of a series of Digital Media and Learning (DML) grant competitions, encompassed programs across a wide spectrum of educational niches from formal classrooms at middle school through post-secondary levels to informal learning environments in museums, libraries, after-school programs, online learning platforms and more.

From these 30 projects, the DPD Project drew a collection of specific practices for using badges to recognize learning. Using open digital badges in learning in 2012 was uncharted territory, and the DPD Project set out to capture major features of the design processes at each of these projects as they moved to implement badge technology in each of their contexts. The goal of this research was to uncover lessons about the factors that make certain practices appropriate in particular contexts.

To capture the developing knowledge about what challenges and opportunities arise from specific combinations of contextual factors and badge system practices the DPD Project chose to characterize each project's specific practices in terms of general design principles, abstracted from their contextual factors. For example, BuzzMath's practice to "recognize developing mastery of Common Core skills" is an example of the general principle "use badges to map learning trajectory." This approach echoes Design-based Research (DBR) methods in its focus on how complex interaction between different elements of learning systems are designed to support learning [2].

The balance of this paper will describe the DPD Project's research methodology and the limitations and affordances of this method for comparing badge systems and drawing out lessons about the appropriateness of specific practices within specific program contexts. The DPD Project's Interim Report details the general design principles uncovered among the subject programs and begins highlighting relevant literature in educational disciplines [4]. Future papers will focus on findings that arose from this process.

3 Capturing Badge System Design Principles

3.1 Four Functions of Digital Badge Systems

Design Principles Documentation Project researchers selected four functions of digital badge systems to analyze, based on initial research about digital badges and previous educational literature related to credentialing systems. Grant and Shawgo's bibliography of badge related research shows common strands around credentialing, assessment, and motivation, and the works referenced demonstrate a variety of research methods used to interrogate learning systems [3]. Correspondingly, the DPD Project selected (a) *recognizing learning* (credentialing), (b) *assessing learning*, (c) *motivating learning*, and (d) *studying learning* as four components of well-considered badge systems. Each of these fields has a rich literature that certainly offers insights that will be relevant to developing and studying badge systems.

The imposition of this frame onto the study allowed DPD researchers to leverage deep veins of research, but it should not be interpreted to mean that the system designers at each of the badge projects designed their systems specifically to perform these four functions. In fact, very few projects intended or implemented any systematic practices to serve the function of studying learning.

At their core, badges in educational programs serve as credentials to recognize learning. Each badge makes claims about earner's learning, participation, or achievement. These *recognizing* claims require corresponding *assessment* practices for two reasons: (1) to make the critical decision about whether or not to issue the badge, and (2) to collect the appropriate evidence that could back up that claim and ensure that audiences would respect its validity. Each of the practices developed to serve these first two functions have complex implications for student motivation and can be analyzed from a variety of motivation perspectives. These include including formal theories such self-determination as well as the "folk" theories of motivation that may be most relevant in the minds of badge system designers.

3.2 Identifying Specific Practices

The process of identifying general design principles for badge systems began with an investigation of the specific practices designed for each project under study. An individual project's practices are system design features that take into account the contextual affordances of their setting, the goals of the project, and the underlying theories of learning from which they arise. Describing them entails capturing these different foundational factors as well as the design decisions made in their light.

The primary source material for identifying specific practices among the 30 DML subject projects was their grant proposal documents. Research team members scanned proposals for each project, which consisted of initial ideas as well as one or two revisions, and pulled out quotations that described specific goals or plans for implementation as well as those that indicated the overall theoretical orientation underlying those plans. Each practice was named with a descriptive moniker, aiming to concisely capture its most important features.

The collection of the specific practices intended for each project arose mostly from analysis of the proposal documents, but initial interviews with each project team were conducted as their badge systems begin implementation. These interviews mostly focused on the changes that had already occurred between proposal and first implementation, but the information gathered here also fed into the researchers' understanding of the initial set of principles as they asked questions about each of the project features they were beginning to understand. From this base of knowledge, the process of formulating general design principles began.

3.3   Formulating General Design Principles

In the functions of recognizing learning, assessing learning, and motivating learning, general principles began to take shape when DPD researchers clustered similar practices [6], and when all were accounted for, gave each principle a descriptive name. Often, well-defined sub-categories of each general principle emerged. For example, related practices that serve the *recognizing learning* purpose of "use badges to map learning trajectory" among the subject group performed this task either by tracking student progression through a series of leveled badges or along "routes or pathways" defining an order in which they may be earned. These sub-categories were formalized as "specific principles," which connected the specific practices embedded in each project's context to the general principles.

Defining principles for studying learning was more theoretical, because few projects intended or implemented systematic practices for studying what was happening in their badge systems [5].

4   Intended, Enacted, and Formal Practices

The DPD Project tracked the development of practices from their initial conception in the grant proposals to how each was first implemented in its project's context and how it evolved when the project reached the end of its grant period and came into some kind of steady continuing state, even if that steady state consisted of discontinued operation, possibly meaning the end of the badge program altogether. This process of practice evolution was defined across three distinct phases, and the DPD Project endeavored to map each program's progression to capture the story of their practices in terms of phases named for *intended, enacted,* and *formal (continuing)* practices. Most details about intended practices arose from projects' initial grant proposals, and the DPD Project captured project leaders' thoughts about how these evolved into enacted and formal practices by conducting interviews.

5 Conclusions

The process of collecting similar practices into general principles allowed rich comparison between projects and the identification of common challenges. Findings about the interaction between program contexts and design principles may be expanded into many future papers.

As an example of possible findings that arose from comparison, two DML competition winners planned to create badge systems to recognize learning in the area of modern agriculture, the UC Davis *Sustainable Agriculture and Food Systems* major and *Sweet Water AQUAPONS*, a high school program in Milwaukee and Chicago. Despite this similar purpose, each program made drastically different choices of practices to *recognize learning*. Where they both used the general principle "use badges to map learning trajectory," they chose opposing specific principles, with *AQUAPONS* choosing to "level badges" where *SA&FS* opted to use badges to "provide routes or pathways."

Though they had differed in recognition principles, thee projects converged in their choices of assessment practices, when analyzed in terms of the general principles that each specific practice represents. Both projects chose to "use e-portfolios" for assessment where badge evidence, including self-reflection was critical to the process. Both projects ran into technical difficulty implementing practices that the DPD Project identified with the specific principle "foster discussion around artifacts" (which falls under the "use e-portfolios" general principle), yet both were so determined to make that a formal part of their badge system that they each made significant changes to their online platforms to ensure that they would be able to enable discussions within their community. Analysis in terms of general principles can show the interaction between practices designed to serve different functions within the system. This pairing of *AQUAPONS* and *SA&FS* shows the necessity of adequate technical infrastructure to support the assessment practices needed to back up the claims made by badges and the social practices desired for motivating participation.

Without the framework relating these specific practices to the same general principles, researchers may have missed the connection between these significant changes across the two badge systems. DPD Project researchers hope that future badge systems may be able to take advantage of this information and recognize that significant investment supporting social interaction in portfolio platforms may be necessary to enact practices aimed to allow formative peer feedback on work related to earing badges.

Future research using this methodology may derive a different set of design principles from badge programs developed with early stage Open Badges technology, but the general approach may prove fruitful to gain similar lessons from badge programs yet to be developed. At this stage the DPD Project's primary goal is sharing out the principles, practices, and case studies via a project website [8].

Acknowledgements. This work was made possible by continuing funding and support from the MacArthur Foundation. Contributions to the development of the research and methodology described here were made by Rebecca Itow, Katerina Schenke, Cathy Tran, Andrea Rehak, and Christine Chow.

References

1. BuzzMath.: BuzzMath DML Stage 1 Proposal (2012). http://dml4.dmlcompetition.net/Competition/4/badges-projects.php%3Fid=2852.html
2. Cobb, P., Confrey, J., diSessa, A., Lehrer, R., Schauble, L.: Design experiments in educational research. Educ. Res. **32**(1), 9–13 (2003)
3. Grant, S., Shawgo, K.E.: Digital Badges: An Annotated Research Bibliography v1 (2013). http://www.hastac.org/pages/digital-badges-annotated-research-bibliography-v1
4. Hickey, D.T., Itow, R., Schenke, K., Tran, C., Otto, N., Chow, C.: Badges Design Principles Documentation Project January Interim Report. Indiana University (2014). http://iudpd.indiana.edu/JanuaryReport
5. Hickey, D.T.: Research Design Principles for Studying Learning with Digital Badges, 7 July 2013. http://www.hastac.org/blogs/dthickey/2013/07/07/research-design-principles-studying-learning-digital-badges
6. Itow, R.: Badges Design Principles Database Project: Update on Principles, 9 May 2013. http://www.hastac.org/blogs/rcitow/2013/05/19/badges-design-principles-database-project-update-principles
7. Mozilla Foundation and Peer 2 Peer University.: Open Badges for Lifelong Learning: Working Paper, 27 August 2012. https://wiki.mozilla.org/images/5/59/OpenBadges-Working-Paper_012312.pdf
8. Design Principles Documentation Project. (n.d.). Design Principles Documentation Project. http://dpdproject.info/

2014 International Symposium on Knowledge Management & E-Learning

Pedagogical Issues of Online Teaching: Students' Satisfaction with On-Line Study Materials and Their Preferences for a Certain Type

Blanka Frydrychová Klímová and Petra Poulova[✉]

University of Hradec Kralove,
Rokitanskeho 62, Hradec Kralove, Czech Republic
{blanka.klimova,petra.poulova}@uhk.cz

Abstract. Education has dramatically changed thanks to the implementation of new technologies into a learning process in last years. Such education place higher demands on teachers since they must have not only good pedagogical skills but usually also good managerial and technical skills. Unfortunately, there are not many empirical studies addressing pragmatic issues such as the form of online study materials. Thus, the purpose of this article is to discover what kind of online study materials students prefer so that the teacher could adjust his/her online teaching materials to student's needs.

Keywords: Education · E-learning · Empirical study · Research · Study material

1 Introduction

During the past 20 years education has dramatically changed thanks to the implementation of new technologies into a learning process. Therefore, pedagogues have had to redefine some of the strategies and concepts of teaching and learning. This has been done in terms of enriching classroom activities, reorganizing course structures, and providing learners with more autonomous as well as more learner-centered opportunities for learning.

In addition, Beldarrain [1] claims that educators must face the challenge of meeting the needs of a diverse population that is more mobile and technology-savvy than any previous generation. The 21st-century learner requires educational opportunities not bound by time or place, yet allow interaction with the instructor and peers. Thus almost every institution of higher education runs besides the traditional, face-to-face classes also online courses. Chickering and Ehrmann [2] provide seven principles for implementing new technologies in online education programs. Online learning can integrate emerging technologies for either synchronous or asynchronous modes by applying these seven principles. Regardless of delivery method, technology should:

1. Encourage contact between students and faculty.
2. Develop reciprocity and cooperation among students.

© Springer International Publishing Switzerland 2014
Y. Cao et al. (Eds.): ICWL 2014 Workshops, LNCS 8699, pp. 187–194, 2014.
DOI: 10.1007/978-3-319-13296-9_21

3. Use active learning techniques.
4. Give prompt feedback.
5. Emphasize time on task.
6. Communicate high expectations.

Undoubtedly, such courses place higher demands on their creators since they must have not only good pedagogical skills but usually also good managerial and technical skills. Nevertheless, the pedagogical skills are probably the most important in designing and running such courses.

In the Czech Republic teachers have always tried to follow ever relevant classical principles of the Czech teacher of nations - Jan Amos Komensky (respectively John Amos Comenius) to maintain and increase the quality of their teaching. His principles advocate learning by doing. They can be used for any form of instruction and they are particularly useful in designing courses. These principles can be outlined as follows:

- to proceed from easier issues to more complicated/difficult ones;
- to be aware of the meaning of subject matter not only memorize it thoughtlessly;
- to teach and learn things thoroughly and systematically;
- to transfer subject matter into practice,
- to facilitate learning;
- to make learning pleasure/fun; to engage students actively into the learning process;
- to make instruction universal [3].

The above principles are in fact thoroughly reflected in the electronic education. See, for example, Cerna [4] who demonstrates all these principles in the description of the exploitation of an on-line course of the subject Czech Language I, II, which is aimed at the teaching of foreign students, particularly the ERASMUS students at the Faculty of Informatics and Management (FIM) of the University of Hradec Kralove, Czech Republic.

Although there is no particular pedagogical approach recommended for online courses, Komensky's principles are worth following [5]. The whole course should be divided into separate lessons, with the structure of each lesson following these basic learning steps:

- informing of objectives;
- presenting content;
- assessing performance; and
- providing feedback.

Thus, the particular structure of each lesson should possess the following structure:

- Title;
- Goal – a short statement motivating the participants to study the particular lesson;
- Prerequisites – previous knowledge required to master the lesson;
- Skills to be learnt – a description of the knowledge to be gained in the par-ticular lesson;
- Body – the content in the form of texts, exercises and questions;
- Tasks, quizzes or assignments – ways in which understanding can be as-sessed in order to provide feedback.

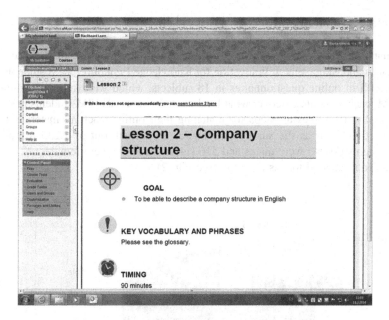

Fig. 1. A structure of a lesson [6].

See Fig. 1 below.

Moreover, to make online courses more effective Bednarikova [7] suggests implementing the so-called ACCEL model when running online courses. ACCEL is an educational model for interactive online education with the ICT support and it has the following five pillars:

1. activity, which requires an active and thinking approach from students;
2. co-operation, which supposes that participants will be involved into discussions, joint assignments and projects;
3. conformity, which means an adjustment to students' requirements, needs and possibilities;
4. entrance, which means that the study enables a qualitative entrance to information sources; and
5. life styles, which means that the study is adjusted to students' life style, their time and financial possibilities; independence on place and time.

Particularly, the interactivity of online materials is an important issue in their design [8]. As Jung [9] claim, expanded interactivity is especially important in overcoming one of the shortcomings of traditional distance education, that is, a lack of interpersonal interaction.

Unfortunately, there are not many empirical studies addressing pragmatic issues such as the form of online study materials. Thus, the purpose of this article is to discover what kind of online study materials students prefer so that the teacher could adjust his/her online teaching materials to student's needs.

2 Field Experience

In January of 2013, within FIMINO project (Study Programmes of the Faculty of Informatics and Management Innovation for Knowledge Economy), FIM students were asked to fill in online questionnaires in 18 subjects, which were supported online so that FIM teachers could discover what kind of study materials FIM students prefer and consequently, take relevant steps for matching their online teaching materials to student's needs. As far as the survey sample was concerned, out of 2,233 respondents 1,695 students (76 %) were males and 516 students (20 %) were females. 22 students (1 %) did not respond to this question (see Fig. 2).

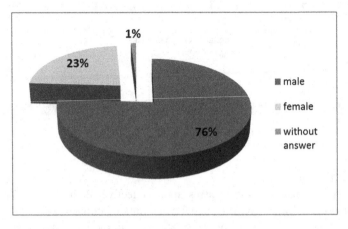

Fig. 2. Respondents' sex.

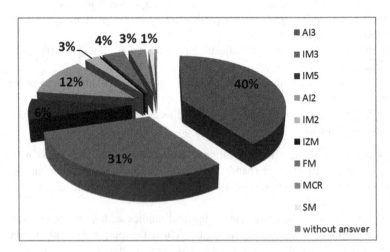

Fig. 3. Students' fields of study.

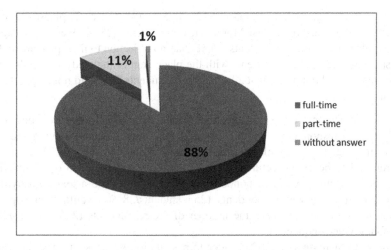

Fig. 4. Respondents' form of study.

As Fig. 3 shows, most of the respondents studied Applied Informatics - AI (1,157 students/52 %). The second biggest group consisted of students of Information Management – IM (890 students/40 %). Only 88 students of Financial Management (FM) and 20 students of Sport Management (SM) participated in the survey. A vast majority of these students were full-time students (1,968 respondents/88 %) while only 247 respondents (11 %) were part-time/distant students. Ten students (1 %) did not respond to this question. See Fig. 4 below.

In the survey students were asked the following two questions about the study materials:

1. Were you satisfied with the placement of the study materials in your e-courses?
2. Which study materials do you prefer?

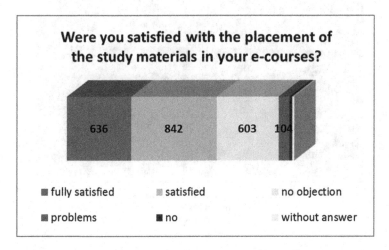

Fig. 5. Students' satisfaction with the study materials in e-courses.

Question 1: As Fig. 5 demonstrates, 842 students (38 %) were pleased with the placement of the study materials. Moreover, 636 students (28 %) were fully satisfied with their placement and 603 students (27 %) had no objection to their placement. Only 104 respondents (5 %) had problems with the placement of the study materials and 27 respondents (1 %) did not like it at all. Finally, 21 students (1 %) did not respond to this question.

Question 2: When answering this question, students could tick more than one option. Therefore, 443 respondents (49 %) reported that they favoured having the study materials in printed forms while most of the respondents (646 students/71 %) said that they preferred to be given lecture materials online, e.g. in the form of a PowerPoint lecture. 506 students (56 %) responded that they would desire a text with hypertext links and pictures. Fewer respondents (253 students/28 %) would then appreciate animated texts and almost the same number of the respondents (245 students/27 %) would fancy video sequences.

In order to increase students' chances to pass their e-subjects successfully, the so-called *study guide* was created and implemented into each new e-subject. This guide should serve as an introduction and motivation into the e-subject. Moreover, it provides information about the subject; its goal, instruction how to study, instruction about the organization of tutorials, subject requirements, or links to other sources.

Surprisingly, only 63 % of students read the guide, while 1,029 respondents (46 %) considered the guide useful and 388 respondents (17 %) read the guide but they did not consider it useful. More than one third of respondents (778 students/35 %) did not read it at all and 19 respondents (1 %) thought that there had not been any guide although it was created for all e-subjects. 19 respondents (1 %) did not answer this question (Figs. 6 and 7).

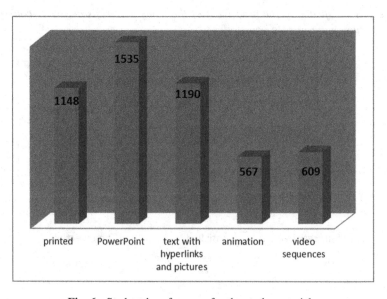

Fig. 6. Students' preferences for the study materials.

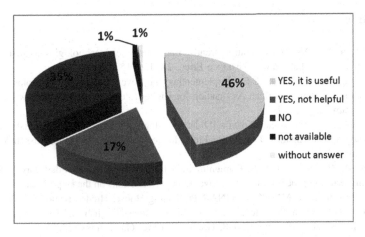

Fig. 7. Did you read the study guide of your e-subject?

3 Conclusion

As this research showed, a majority of respondents (838 students/93 %) welcomed a possibility of having their study materials online. The explanations might be as follows:

- students can access the online study materials anywhere and at any time;
- they can check all the information already given to them during their face-to-face classes;
- they do not have to waste their time on looking for the desired information else-where; or
- they do not have to be stressed during the lecture during which they do not understand everything or they do not manage to take all the notes because they can find this information in the online course afterwards.

Furthermore, this survey also indicated that students were not satisfied with the ordinary printed materials any more, but they would prefer to be offered various online texts with multimedia components, such as PowerPoint lectures; animations or video sequences. O'Daniel, [8] claims that online materials appeal to all sorts of learners while text appeal to just a few. Therefore, teachers/creators of online study materials should include multimedia components in their study materials because it is known that multimedia can concurrently affect more senses at one time. As Lindfors [10] points out, multimedia can provide a sensory and real learning experience; it presents a greater potential for learning. Sperling [11] also emphasize their facilitation role in the orga-nization of the online texts. In addition, as Mbarha [12] state, multimedia instructional materials have been recognized for enabling the understanding of complex engineering and IT decision-making situations. They have been also identified as an important tool for managers and students in their efforts to connect and apply classroom theory-based learning with the analysis of real-world problems. Finally, Mayer [13] emphasizes that multimedia instructional materials promote deeper learning.

References

1. Beldarrain, Y.: Distance education trends: integrating new technologies to foster student interaction and collaboration. Distance Educ. **27**, 139–153 (2006)
2. Chickering, A., Ehrmann, S.E.: Implementing the seven principles: technology as lever [Electronic version], American Association for Higher Education (1996). http://www.tltgroup. org/programs/seven.html
3. Comenius, J.A.: The Great Didactic [Didactica Magna]. Translated into English and edited with biographical, historical and critical introductions by M.W. Keatinge. Russell & Russell, New York (1967)
4. Cerna, M.: Reflection of J. A. Comenius didactic principles in a blended way of language teaching/learning process. In: Semradova, I. (ed.) Reflections on the Exploitation of a Virtual Study Environment. MILOS VOGNAR Publishing House, Hradec Kralove (2010)
5. Klimova, B.F., Cech, P.: E-learning in teaching business English. In: Sbornik prispevku ze seminare a souteze eLearning 2008, Hradec Kralove, Gaudeamus (2008)
6. A Structure of a Lesson. http://oliva.uhk.cz/webapps/portal/frameset.jsp?tab_tab_group_id=_2_1&url=%2Fwebapps%2Fblackboard%2Fexecute%2Flauncher%3Ftype%3DCourse%26id%3D_1507_1%26url%3D
7. Bednarikova, I.: Tutor a jeho role v distancnim vzdelavani a v e-learningu. Univerzita Palackého, Olomouc (2013)
8. O'Daniel, M.: Online versus Printed Materials, Computimes, Malaysia, 1 (2001)
9. Jung, I., Choi, S., Lim, C., Leem, J.: Effects of different types of interaction on learning achievement, satisfaction and participation in Web-based instruction. Innovations Educ. Teach. Int. **39**(2), 153–162 (2002)
10. Lindfors, J.: Children's Language and Learning. Prentice-Hall, Englewood Cliffs (1987)
11. Sperling, R.A., Seyedmonic, M., Aleksic, M., Meadows, G.: Animations as learning tools in authentic science materials. J. Instrum. Media **30**(2), 213–221 (2003)
12. Mbarha, V., Bagarukayo, E., Shipps, B., Hingorami, V., Stokes, S., et al.: A Multi-experimental study on the use of multimedia instructional materials to teach technical subjects 1, J. STEM Educ. Innovations Res. suppl. Special Edition 24–37 (2010)
13. Mayer, R.E.: The promise of multimedia learning: using the same instructional design methods across different media. Learn. Instr. **13**(2), 125–139 (2003)

An Architecture of a Gamified Learning Management System

Jakub Swacha[(⊠)]

University of Szczecin,
Institute of Information Technology in Management,
Mickiewicza 64, 71-101 Szczecin, Poland
`jakubs@uoo.univ.szczecin.pl`

Abstract. The growing popularity of using gamification in education, and especially in e-learning, propels interest in Learning Management Systems that incorporate gamification mechanisms. This paper describes the architecture of a Learning Management System that is gamified by design, focusing at its key components. It also discusses the requirements for an LMS due to introduction of game-based elements and the role of specific LMS components in implementing them.

Keywords: Gamification · Learning management system · E-learning platform

1 Introduction

Gamification is "the use of design elements characteristic for games in non-game contexts" [5]. It aims "to influence behaviour, improve motivation and enhance engagement" [14, p. 4]. In recent years, gamification has been widely adopted in various areas including business [15], science [11], social networks [1], tourism [21], and, last but not least, training and education [10]. Although the benefits of gamification can be exploited even in a traditional teaching process [12], it is especially helpful in the online learning and teaching [4].

Implementing gamification means adoption of game-based rules which are often complex [16, pp. 130, 196], so it is much more practical to use software at least to track learners' achievements, make necessary calculations, and trigger relevant feedback, rather than having the instructor manage all such tasks. In this aspect, e-learning platforms create a perfect opportunity for implementing gamification: instructors and learners are accustomed to using this kind of software, its key features include tracking learners' activity, and the only missing element are the gamification mechanisms.

The recent versions of the most popular learning management systems enable many gamification mechanisms (see e.g., the rule system and badge system in Claroline [3] or the conditional activities and badges in Moodle [13]), but we have found that many instructors consider them as either too complicated or requiring too much effort (and as still insufficient by some others).

A Learning Management System that is gamified by design, i.e., having the basic gamification mechanisms implemented at its core and allowing as complex game-based rules as the instructor needs, could be a good solution to this problem. In this paper we

© Springer International Publishing Switzerland 2014
Y. Cao et al. (Eds.): ICWL 2014 Workshops, LNCS 8699, pp. 195–203, 2014.
DOI: 10.1007/978-3-319-13296-9_22

describe the architecture of such a system, focusing at its main components. We start, however, with introducing game-based elements and matching them to LMS requirements, and then listing classic LMS components and specifying their role in the implementation of gamification.

2 System Components

2.1 Game-Based Elements

There is a number of game elements that can be exploited in gamification; here, we shall use a quite extensive list provided by Werbach and Hunter [19]. They organize the elements into three levels, which, in decreasing order of abstraction, are: dynamics, mechanics, and components.

The dynamics include: constraints (limitations or forced trade-offs), emotions, narrative (storyline), progression (player's development), and relationships (social interactions). The mechanics include: challenges (tasks that require player's effort), chance (randomness), competition, cooperation, feedback (information about player's progress), resource acquisition, rewards, transactions (between players), turns (sequential participation by alternating players), win states (ultimate game objectives). The components include: achievements, avatars, badges (proofs of achievements), boss fights (extremely hard challenges), collections (of items or badges), combat, content unlocking, gifting, leaderboards, levels, points, quests, social graphs, teams, and virtual goods. Table 1 shows how an LMS architecture can support respective game elements.

Table 1. Support for game elements in an LMS.

Element	Implemented in	Support by LMS
Dynamics		
Constraints	Course content	Definable rules, scripts for complex rules
Emotions	Course content	Embedding multimedia content
Narrative	Course content	Scripts for interactive storyline with multiple paths and endings
Progression	LMS	Registering student's progress in various aspects
Relationships	LMS	Synchronous and asynchronous communication tools
Mechanics		
Challenges	LMS and Course content	Delivering interactive material (possibly scripted), registering student's progress in solving individual challenges, triggering success/failure events
Chance	LMS and Course content	Assigning random challenges to students, randomized puzzle content

(Continued)

Table 1. (*Continued*)

Element	Implemented in	Support by LMS
Competition	LMS and Course content	Challenges for two students (duels), Sequences of challenges for many students (tournaments)
Cooperation	LMS and Course content	Challenges for groups of students (teams), Registering student's effort in helping other students
Feedback	LMS and Course content	Delivering information on progress in current activities (including rule-based scripted messages), Access to information on current student's status and past activities
Resource acquisition	Course content	Scripts handling resource acquisition, exchange or loss, Persistent storage of additional data (defined by course author) related to course progress
Rewards	Course content	Definable rewarding rules, scripts for complex rules
Transactions		See Resource acquisition
Turns	Course content	Turn-based challenges, Scripts checking challenge progress and passing control among the participating students
Win states	Course content	Definable win/draw/loss rules, scripts for complex rules
Components		
Achievements	Course content	Definable achievement rules, scripts for complex rules
Avatars	LMS	Uploadable student's image
Badges	LMS and Course content	Assigning images to achievements, Access to badges from outside the LMS (e.g., via Open Badges [7])
Boss fights	Course content	Setting up predefined and random hard challenges
Collections	Course content	Definable sets of items or badges, Scripts handling completing a collection
Combat		See Challenges
Content unlocking	LMS and Course content	Definable rules, scripts for complex rules
Gifting		see Resource acquisition
Leaderboards	LMS	Delivering information on current and all-time rankings
Levels	LMS and Course content	Registering student's level progress, Definable rules for attaining next level, scripts for complex rules

(Continued)

Table 1. (*Continued*)

Element	Implemented in	Support by LMS
Points	LMS and Course content	Persistent storage of student's point counter, Definable rules for acquiring/losing points, scripts for complex rules
Quests	LMS and Course content	Assigning sets of challenges to students, Definable quest requirements, scripts for checking complex requirements
Social graphs	LMS	Delivering information on student's network of contacts
Teams	LMS	Setting up teams, Joining/leaving teams, Communication between teams and among team members
Virtual goods	Course content	See Resource acquisition

2.2   Learning Management System Components

There are various approaches to define the architecture of a Learning Management System. The two probably best-known models are those proposed in the Jisc paper devoted to the technical framework to support e-learning [20, p. 3–5], and the *SCORM 2004 Handbook* [17, p. 3]. Yet for the purposes of this discussion, both these models are too simple on a general level, and too complicated if the details had to be considered. For this reason, we shall use a description of an LMS architecture by Avgeriou et al. who identify the following subsystems as specific to LMS [2, p. 192]:

- Main subsystem (master component that initializes and launches everything else),
- User management (registration in system, in courses and in groups, groups creation, authentication, access control with different views, student tracking, student profile management),
- Courseware authoring (web page editing, design templates),
- Courseware delivery (WWW server and client, delivery of hypermedia pages concerning e-book, glossary, index, calendar, course description etc., personalization per user),
- Assessment (on-line quiz or exam, project deliverables, self-assessment exercises),
- Searching (applies to all learning objects through metadata),
- Course management (creation, customization, administration and monitoring of courses),
- Study toolkit (private & public annotations, highlights, bookmarks, print out, offline studying, notepad, log of personal history, adaptive navigation and presentation, intelligent tutoring systems),
- System Administration (new course, back up, security, systems operation check, resource monitoring etc.),
- School Administration (absences records, grades records, student registrations),
- Help desk (on-line help, user support).

Table 2. Implementation of gamification in individual LMS components.

Component	Role
Main subsystem	Access to gamified system components, e.g. competitions and leaderboards
User management	Access to information on individual student's current progress and achievements
Courseware authoring	Defining point awards, achievements and other rules (e.g. regarding storyline forks, content unlocking, level-up conditions), Setting up challenges, quests, and contests, Editing scripts (for various purposes)
Courseware delivery	Delivering interactive learning material (possibly scripted), Synchronizing student's progress stored client-side (temporary) and server-side (persistent)
Assessment	Delivering interactive environment for challenges (including turn-based and team), Triggering predefined scripts, Checking success/failure conditions (automatic assessment), Synchronizing student's progress stored client-side (temporary) and server-side (persistent)
Searching	Searching over information on student's achievements and ranking
Course management	Access to information on course group members' current progress and achievements
Study toolkit	Access to information on individual student's past activities
System Administration	Backup of data on course progress and achievements
School Administration	Defining rules for conversion of points/levels/badges into grades
Help desk	On-line help regarding rules of play

Table 2 shows the role of each of the classic LMS components listed above in the implementation of gamification.

3 Gamified Learning Management System Architecture

3.1 Design Considerations

The general idea behind the architecture is that it should satisfy users with both low and high requirements in the aspect of gamification. For the former, the basic gamification mechanisms should be easily available when configuring all the key course elements, such as course progress, exercises, and assessment. For the latter, the instructor should not be limited to a predefined set of mechanisms, or events that trigger them. The only technically feasible way of meeting the second requirement is to allow embedding instructor-written scripts that would implement gamification mechanisms of any level of sophistication, that would be triggered by the instructor, specified actions of the students, or certain system events.

For both this reason and the need for automatic assessment of submitted exercise solutions, the scripting environment should be an important element of the gamified LMS architecture [18].

Web application seems to be the most natural way of implementation of a system conforming to this architecture. For this reason, actually two separate scripting environments should be considered. In order to reduce burden on the server and allow for immediate response to users' actions, most scripts should be executed client-side. Note that currently this does not pose a problem anymore, as client-side scripting environments for various programming languages are available (see e.g. references [6, 8, 9]). Still, some scripts (e.g., performing automatic assessment or implementing certain gamification rules) have to be executed server-side. So, a sandboxed environment for executing them is also required.

The learning environments should be persistent in the sense that students quitting the learning session should be able to return later to exactly the very course point at which they had left. For this reason alone the client-side state of the course progress (possibly affected by client-side scripts) should be reflected in the server-side state, which is considered persistent (as it is stored in the system's database) and available to the instructor.

3.2   Gamified LMS Architecture

Figure 1 shows the key components of the Gamified LMS architecture, grouped into Core Services, Automation Services, Administrator- and Instructor-level management modules, and Presentation modules.

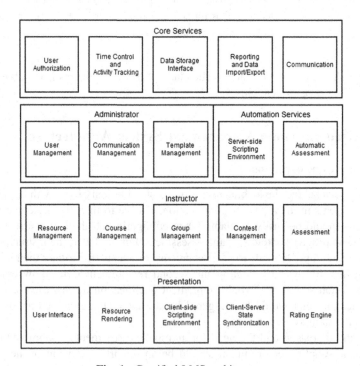

Fig. 1. Gamified LMS architecture.

The Core Services include modules that provide services supporting the remaining modules. User Authorization allows users to sign in and out, and verifies user access rights to all the functions and resources of the system. Time Control triggers events scheduled for specific points in time, whereas Activity Tracking records all the user actions as well as automatically triggered events (prescheduled or being a result of a rule execution). Data Storage Interface provides access to all kind of data stored by the system, constrained only by access rights, regardless of the actual database/storage technology used. Reporting and Data Import/Export provides collections of data (acquired through Data Storage Interface) in specified range and formatted according to specified report template or specific file format requirements. It may also be used to import data collections from external files. Communication redirects messages between instructors and students using embedded or external communication services.

There are three modules envisaged specifically for the system administrator. User Management allows to register and unregister users, as well as check and set their roles and privileges. Communication Management allows to configure communication services, as well as retract messages sent by users (provided it is technologically feasible). Template Management allows to import and configure templates used in various parts of the system (e.g., for GUI, reports, or resource rendering).

The Automation Services consist of Server-side Scripting Environment (SSE) that allows programming scripts to be run server-side in a virtual sandbox, and Automatic Assessment which automatically checks the exercise results. The latter may use the SSE in case of more complex types of exercises, especially programming exercises, to run instructor-written scripts verifying the correctness of the submitted solutions. SSE can also be used to run the actual exercise solutions (in case of programming exercises) to obtain their results, and time/memory usage measurements, as well as instructor-written scripts defining advanced gamification rules.

There are five modules envisaged specifically for the instructor (course administrator). Resource Management is for dealing with all types of resources in the system, including learning materials in any format, various types of tests and quizzes, exercises, and scripted interactive lessons. It allows to import and export them to/from the system, edit their respective metadata, search for relevant resources (based on the metadata), as well as (whenever technologically feasible) edit (or at least configure) the resources. Course Management allows to combine resources into courses, import and export the courses to/from the system, edit their respective metadata, as well as define and set relevant gamification, assessment and grading rules.

Group Management allows to define, duplicate and modify groups of students, assign them courses, set their course schedule, confirm or modify relevant gamification, assessment and grading rules, and configure in-group communication. Contest Management allows to prepare (by writing contest description, selecting appropriate resources, choosing contest rules and students/groups eligible to take part, as well as sending them invitations), run (by collecting submissions and checking deadlines), and finalize (by evaluating the submissions and informing about the winners) contests. Assessment allows to review exercise solutions, check Automatic Assessment results, fill-in final grades – or automatically calculate them according to grading rules; it should also trigger relevant gamification rules.

The remaining five modules are for the purpose of presentation of the course to the users. The User Interface module handles menus, dialog boxes, and other user controls of the system, displaying them in accordance with the chosen template. The Resource Rendering module takes care of displaying various resources embedded in courses, taking into consideration their configuration and the template used. Depending on the resource type, it may require generation of respective HTML code. If there are scripts embedded in resources (that apply some gamification rules, or provide dynamism or interactivity), they are executed using the next module: Client-side Scripting Environment. As the small steps of course progress are happening client-side only, another module is needed (Client-Server State Synchronization) to pass relevant information from the client to the server after some progress is made, or to recover a client-side session from a state stored server-side. Finally, Rating Engine module is responsible for showing rating controls for lessons, exercises and messages, and gathering feedback from the users.

4   Conclusion

The growing interest in using gamification in e-learning has not yet found an adequate answer in a form of a Learning Management Systems that would make it easy to incorporate gamification mechanisms of various kind in the courses. In this paper, an architecture of a Learning Management System specialized to fulfil this goal has been proposed. It aims to satisfy instructors in any area of education with both limited and extensive gamification plans. The former may quickly and easily implement basic gamification mechanisms (such as points, badges, and leaderboards) in their courses, and the latter obtain an ability to customize the game rules according to their own ideas thanks to unrestricted scripting.

The proposed architecture is web-based, and does not impose implementation using specific programming language or database technology. It reduces the computational burden on the server, moving most of data processing to the client. An important part of it is providing separate scripting environments for the server and client sides and a mechanism to synchronize data between them. Although the Learning Management Systems based on the architecture can be used to organize and manage gamified courses on any subject, its ample scripting capabilities make it especially attractive for programming courses.

A system conforming to the architecture presented in this paper is currently under development as an open-source project supervised by this author.

References

1. Alves, F.P., Maciel, C., Anacleto, J.C.: Guidelines for the gamification in mobile social networks. In: Meiselwitz, G. (ed.) SCSM 2014. LNCS, vol. 8531, pp. 559–570. Springer, Heidelberg (2014)
2. Avgeriou, P., Retalis, S., Skordalakis, M.: An architecture for open learning management systems. In: Manolopoulos, Y., Evripidou, S., Kakas, A.C. (eds.) PCI 2001. LNCS, vol. 2563, pp. 183–200. Springer, Heidelberg (2003)

3. Claroline CoreBundle. Rule system. https://github.com/claroline/CoreBundle/blob/master/Resources/doc/sections/rules.md
4. de-Marcos, L., Domínguez, A., Saenz-de-Navarrete, J., Pagés, C.: An empirical study comparing gamification and social networking on e-learning. Comput. Educ. **75**, 82–91 (2014)
5. Deterding, S., Dixon, D., Khaled, R., Nacke, L.: From game design elements to gamefulness: defining "gamification". In: Proceedings of the 15th International Academic MindTrek Conference, pp. 9–15. ACM, New York (2011)
6. Foord, M.: Try Python: Interactive Python Tutorial in the Browser. http://www.trypython.org/
7. Goligoski, E.: Motivating the Learner: Mozilla's Open Badges Program. Access Knowl. Course J. **4**(1), (2012). http://ojs.stanford.edu/ojs/index.php/a2k/article/view/381
8. Guo, P.J.: Online Python tutor: embeddable Web-based program visualization for CS education. In: Proceeding of the 44th ACM Technical Symposium on Computer Science Education, pp. 579–584. ACM, New York (2013)
9. Helminen, J., Malmi, L.: Jype – a program visualization and programming exercise tool for Python. In: Proceedings of the 5th International Symposium on Software Visualization, pp. 153–162. ACM, New York (2010)
10. Kapp, K.M.: The Gamification of Learning and Instruction: Game-Based Methods and Strategies for Training and Education. Pfeiffer, San Francisco (2012)
11. Khatib, F., DiMaio, F., Foldit Contenders Group, Foldit Void Crushers Group, Cooper, S., Kazmierczyk, M., Gilski, M., Krzywda, S., Zabranska, H., Pichova, I., Thompson, J., Popović, Z., Jaskolski, M., Baker, D.: Crystal structure of a monomeric retroviral protease solved by protein folding game players. Nat. Struct. Mol. Biol. **18**(10), 1175–1177 (2011)
12. Kumar, B., Khurana, P.: Gamification in education – learn computer programming with fun. Int. J. Comput. Distrib. Syst. **2**(1), 46–53 (2012)
13. Managing a Moodle course. Tracking progress. http://docs.moodle.org/26/en/Managing_a_Moodle_course
14. Marczewski, A.: Gamification: A Simple Introduction. Lulu, Raleigh (2012)
15. Rauch, M.: Best practices for using enterprise gamification to engage employees and customers. In: Kurosu, M. (ed.) HCII/HCI 2013, Part II. LNCS, vol. 8005, pp. 276–283. Springer, Heidelberg (2013)
16. Schell, J.: The Art of Game Design: A book of lenses. Morgan Kaufmann, Burlington (2008)
17. SCORM 2004 Handbook. Version 1.04. The e-Learning Consortium, Japan (2006)
18. Swacha, J., Baszuro, P.: Gamification-based e-learning platform for computer programming education. In: Reynolds, N., Webb, M. (eds.) Learning While We Are Connected, vol. 1, Research papers, pp. 122–130. Wydawnictwo Naukowe UMK, Toruń (2013)
19. Werbach, K., Hunter, D.: For the Win: How Game Thinking Can Revolutionize Your Business. Wharton Digital Press, Philadelphia (2012)
20. Wilson, S., Olivier, B., Jeyes, S., Powell, A., Franklin, T.: A Technical Framework to Support e-Learning, Jisc, UK (2004). http://www.jisc.ac.uk/uploaded_documents/Technical%20Framework%20feb04.doc
21. Xu, F., Weber, J., Buhalis, D.: Gamification in tourism. In: Xiang, Z., Tussyadiah, I. (eds.) Information and Communication Technologies in Tourism 2014, pp. 525–537. Springer, Heidelberg (2013)

A Survey of E-learning Content Aggregation Standards

Ricardo Queirós[1]([✉]) and José Paulo Leal[2]

[1] ESEIG/IPP (Polytechnic Institute of Porto),
CRACS and INESC-TEC, Porto, Portugal
`ricardo.queiros@eu.ipp.pt`
[2] CRACS and INESC-TEC, Faculty of Sciences,
University of Porto, Porto, Portugal
`zp@dcc.fc.up.pt`

Abstract. As e-learning gradually evolved many specialized and disparate systems appeared to fulfil the needs of teachers and students, such as repositories of learning objects, authoring tools, intelligent tutors and automatic evaluators. This heterogeneity raises interoperability issues giving the standardization of content an important role in e-learning. This article presents a survey on current e-learning content aggregation standards focusing on their internal organization and packaging. This study is part of an effort to choose the most suitable specifications and standards for an e-learning framework called Ensemble defined as a conceptual tool to organize a network of e-learning systems and services for domains with complex evaluation.

1 Introduction

The last two decades witnessed an impressive evolution in e-learning. Several types of e-learning systems appeared, from monolithic architectures to service oriented services aiming to cover the needs of different user profiles (e.g. staff, teachers, content authors, students). One of such system types is the Learning Management System (LMS) used to manage learning and track students progress. This proliferation of e-learning systems raises interoperability issues which are being considered by standardization institutions. These institutions have been creating standards and specifications for learning content, such as educational metadata or course structures.

The ultimate goal of this paper is to gather information on e-learnisng standards. For this study were selected several e-learning content aggregation standards focusing on the organization and package of those resources for dissemination purposes.

The aim of this research is to select the most suitable specifications and standards for an e-learning framework called Ensemble [1]. The Ensemble framework is a conceptual tool to organize a network of e-learning systems and services for domains with complex evaluation. It is based on content and communication specifications and aims at fostering the use best-of-bread tools for each domain.

© Springer International Publishing Switzerland 2014
Y. Cao et al. (Eds.): ICWL 2014 Workshops, LNCS 8699, pp. 204–214, 2014.
DOI: 10.1007/978-3-319-13296-9_23

2   Content Aggregation Standards

The concept of educational resource, course, student, summary or grade must be formally described in order to be shared among all the systems in an educational institution. For instance, the difficulty to reuse a course in schools with LMSs from different vendors (or even from the same vendor) is an apt example of the problems found currently in the majority of the LMSs. These interoperability issues affect the flexibility of the teaching-learning process and lead to a decrease of end user satisfaction and learning success [2].

The need for educational resources sharing among learning systems and authoring tools motivated the development of common formats to encapsulate learning resources into units of instruction. These formats apply structure and learning taxonomies so that the structure of the units of instruction and their behaviour (sequencing of activities) can be uniformly represented, interchanged and reproduced across heterogeneous environments. Content aggregation formats should be neutral and allow the encapsulation of separate resources ranging from a single educational resource to entire courses. At the same time can be complemented with definitions of how content is presented to the learner and the conditions under which a piece of content is selected, delivered, or skipped during presentation.

In this study dozens of standards and specifications were found. For the sake of terseness only the most prominent [3] are detailed (Fig. 1).

2.1   IMS Content Packaging

Packaging the learning resources complements content description and is crucial to facilitate the deployment, storage and reuse of learning resources. One of the earliest efforts was from the Aviation Industry Computer-Based Training Committee (AICC). The AICC association developed in 1998 a content package format called AICC HACP consisting of four comma separated ASCII files that define details about the learning content referenced by an URL. In 2000 the IMS Global launched the IMS Content Packaging (IMS CP). An IMS CP learning object (Fig. 2) assembles resources and meta-data into a distribution medium, typically an archive in ZIP format, with its content described in a manifest file at the root level. The manifest a file named imsmanifest.xml - adheres to the CP schema and contains the following sections:

- Metadata - describes the package as a whole;
- Organizations - describes the organization of the content within a manifest;
- Resources - contains references to resources (files) needed for the manifest and metadata describing these resources;
- Sub-manifests - defines sub packages.

Meta-data information in the manifest file usually follows the IEEE LOM schema, although other schemata can be used. These meta-data elements can be inserted in the metadata section of the manifest to describe the learning

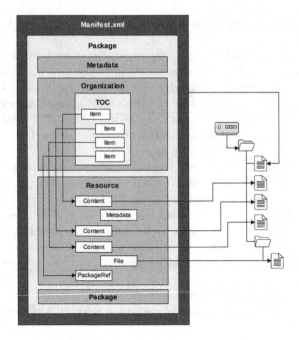

Fig. 1. IMS CP structure.

object as a whole or can be included in the resources section to describe each resource of the package. The IMS CP specification includes a manifest section called Organizations to design pedagogical activities and articulate the sequencing of instructions. By default, it uses a tree-based organization of learning items pointing to the resources (assets) included in the package.

2.2   ADL SCORM

The Sharable Content Object Reference Model (SCORM) was created by the Advanced Distributed Learning initiative (ADL) with the first production version launched in 2001. It is an application profile for content packaging that extends the IMS CP specification with more sophisticated sequencing and Contents-to-LMS communication. It defines communications between client side content and a host system called the run-time environment, which is commonly supported by learning management systems. The latest version of this specification is SCORM 2004 (4th edition) from 2009. Despite its popularity and dissemination SCORM continues to have many problems:

- Complexity - many people reported several interoperability issues between content (SCO) and host LMS;
- Scope - it relies on JavaScript and browser-based content neglecting mobile Apps, classroom based training, simulation and game-based training, and so on;

- Authoring - developing SCORM based solutions that work with mobile devices and work offline is difficult;
- Dependence - The content requires some form of Learning Management System (LMS) to host and manage the content;
- Communication - very limited in terms of learner tracking data that can be recorded/reported.

In order to address these issues, ADL and Rustici Software - a leader in the industry of e-learning interoperability software - developed the Tin Can API specification. The Tin Can API is an open source specification that allows learning content and learning systems to communicate recording and tracking all types of learning experiences. These learning experiences are recorded in a Learning Record Store (LRS) that can be a traditional LMS or an independent system.

In a technical view, the Tin Can API is a Representational state transfer (REST) web service that uses JavaScript Object Notation (JSON) as data format. The web service allows software clients to read and write experiential data in the form of statement objects. These statement objects are in the form of actor verb object. The format of these statements is based on Activity Streams (<Actor, Verb, Object> or I did this.). In this format, the Actor is the agent the statement is about, like a learner, mentor, teacher, or group. The verb describes the action of the statement, such as read, passed, or taught. And the object is what the Actor interacted with, like a book, a test, or a class. There is also a built in query API to help filter recorded statements.

To send and receive statements from an LRS, the Tin Can Api uses four sub-APIs. They are the statement, state, agent profile, and activity profile APIs. These are handled via RESTful HTTP methods (GET, PUT, POST, DELETE). For more information on these sub-APIs, see the xAPI specification (https://github.com/adlnet/xAPI-Spec/blob/master/xAPI.md).

Using this approach, Tin Can can capture everything you can capture today in SCORM, but it also provides much more flexibility by enabling the addition of new nouns, verbs, and objects. The record keeper for these learning events is the Learning Record Store (LRS). This could be an LMS with extended support for Tin Can, but necessarily An LRS on its own can simply provides the repository with learning events. To be of much use it also needs to include a way of extracting data through reports. The LRS can be located anywhere and the content when it is created in cloud service. Furthermore, the LRS doesnt need to know in advance anything about the content location, type or even the identity of the learner consuming.

With the Tin Can specification the teaching-learning process resolves the interoperability issues found in prior versions of SCORM, since it completely decouples content from host LMS, it enables content authors to build in any way they like (not only with JavaScript) and it supports disconnected scenarios which is an useful feature in mobile learning.

Recently the specification was re-branded to eXperience API (XAPI).

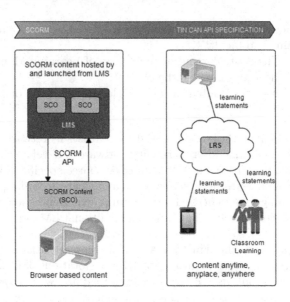

Fig. 2. Tin Can API architecture.

2.3   IMS Common Cartridge

In 2008, IMS GLC proposed the IMS Common Cartridge (IMS CC). Common Cartridge was developed primarily to support the use of digital course materials and digital books in the instructional context. It was not designed as a replacement of SCORM. The specification defines an open format for the distribution of rich web-based content. Its main goal is to organize and distribute digital learning content and to ensure the interchange of content across any Common Cartridge conformant tools. The latest revised version (1.2) was released in October 2011. The IMS CC package organizes and describes a learning object based on two levels of interoperability: content and communication as depicted Fig. 5.

At the content level, the IMS CC includes two types of resources:

- Web Content Resources (WCR) - static web resources that are supported on the Web such as HTML files, GIF/JPEG images, PDF documents, etc.
- Learning Application Objects (LAO) - special resource types that require additional processing before they can be imported and represented within the target system. Physically, a LAO consists of a directory in the content package containing a descriptor file and optionally additional files used exclusively by that LAO. Examples of Learning Application Objects include QTI assessments, Discussion Forums, Web links, Basic LTI descriptors, etc.

In the communication level the cartridge describes how the target tool of the cartridge (usually a LMS) should communicate with other remote web applications using the IMS Basic LTI specification. Both levels enhance the interoperability of the cartridge among a network of e-learning systems. In this scope

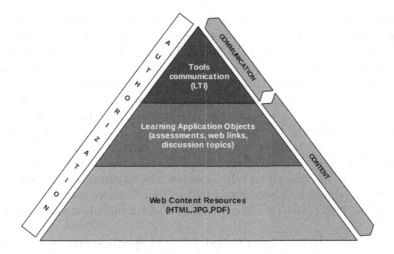

Fig. 3. Common cartridge content hierarchy.

a new IMS CC specification feature is introduced to support authorization at two levels: the whole cartridge or individual resources. The following subsections detail the most important elements of the CC content hierarchy (Fig. 3).

The Common Cartridge builds upon a profile of the CP package whose manifest is composed by four sections: metadata, organizations, resources and authorizations. The Metadata section is used to store the cartridge metadata restricted to a loose binding of LOM elements based on the DC specification. The Organization section is used to represent the Common Cartridge Folder content type as a structural approach to organize content. The Resources section is used to refer assets included in the cartridge.

An IMS CC learning object supports authorization at three levels: on cartridge import, on cartridge usage and on usage of specific resources in the cartridge. The authorization mechanism to access to particular resources is enforced by the tool and is not defined by the profile.

The Common Cartridge uses the IMS QTI specification as a data model for questions and tests. This specification is represented on the manifest through two LAO resource types: assessments and question banks. An assessment represents an ordered question set (e.g. Multiple Choice, True/False, Fill in the Blanks, Pattern Match, and Essay) and may include optional attributes (e.g. number of attempts, time limit and whether late submission is allowed) that apply to the set as a whole. A question bank can embed any of the question types supported by the CC v1.1 profile of QTI. Only one question bank can optionally be included in a cartridge.

A Basic LTI resource refers to an XML file that contains the information needed to create a link in a Tool Consumer (TC) (e.g. LMS). Upon the user's click, the execution flow passes to a Tool Provider (TP) along with contextual information about the user and Consumer. The Basic LTI link is defined in the resource section of an IMS Common Cartridge. The hypertext reference ("") attribute in the resource entry refers to a file path in the cartridge that contains an XML description of the Basic LTI link. A BLTI link contains several elements. The most important are: the title and description elements contain generic information about the link; the custom and extensions elements allow the Tool Consumer to extend the basic communication data; the launch url element contains the URL to which the LTI invocation is sent; the secure launch url element is the URL to use if secure HTTP is required. The LTI message signing is performed by a security mechanism designed to protect POST and GET requests called OAuth. OAuth 1.0 specifies how to construct a base message string and then sign that string using a secret. The signature is then sent as part of the POST request and is validated by the Tool Provider using OAuth. Upon receipt of the POST, the TP will perform the OAuth validation using the shared secret.

In a recent study [4] the CC and SCORM specifications were compared regarding interoperability from the point of view of key users: the teachers. Teachers showed special interest CC packages and in particular in their use in Moodle system. In detail, teachers enjoyed the possibility of editing a package, taking some elements and mixing them with their own teaching resources very much in the same way as they do with the non-digital resources in their classrooms.

2.4 Specifications Comparision

Based on this survey a comparative table was made and it is presented in Table 1. Four specifications are compared characterized on their strongest and weakest points.

In order to select the most suitable specification for the Ensemble framework we chose the IMS CC specification. The reason is twofold: the massive support for systems interoperability using the fresh LTI specification and the support to represent an entire course with different levels of authorization (e.g. administators, teachers, students).

3   Ensemble Framework

In this section we present the overall architecture of Ensemble as a network of e-Learning systems participating in teaching-learning process in complex domains. The architecture depicted by UML component diagram in Fig. 4 is composed by the following systems and tools:

- Learning Objects Repository - to store/retrieve exercises;
- Evaluation Engine - to evaluate students exercises;
- Learning Management System - to present exercises to students;
- Integrated Development Environment - to code the exercises.

Table 1. Aggregation Standards comparision

Standards	Strongest points	Weakest points
IMS CP	- Fairly widespread	- Often used as the base for other specifications
	- Supported by most Learning Management System	- Not flexible for specific domain contents
SCORM	- Supported by most Learning Management System	- Limited selection of types of activities (true or false, multiple choice, fill in the gap and multiple matching and a few variations of these type)
	- Support portability of self-paced computer-based training content	- Learning interactions use a lot of Internet bandwidth and server storage space
XAPI	- New approach for tracking both formal and informal learning	- Lack of adoption because it is a recent specification
IMS CC	- Can describe an education resource from a single asset to an entire course	- Lack of adoption because it is a recent specification
	- Easier to implement than SCORM	- Lack of documentation for package extension through LAO
	- Supports web links, authorization and an interoperability way of communication with third party applications (LTI)	

Petcha is the pivot component that coordinates the communication among all the components of the network, from the LMS where students receives the activity to the IDE where students solve them. In order to fulfill this goal, the integration of the pivot component with the other systems must rely on content and communication standards to abstract the use of specific systems for each type of system. For instance, we can use on this network any repository as long it supports the IMS CC specification (selected from previous section) to formalize the description of programming exercises and it implements the IMS DRI specification for communication with other services.

Another important point was the choice of the systems that comprise the current network. Since we made several efforts to address interoperability issues, the selection of the tools was straightforward. On the LMS side we choose Moodle since it is a popular and open source LMS, arguably the most popular LMS nowadays. We used the version 1.9 that supports the Basic LTI specification with the further installation of an IMS bLTI consumer. Currently, the version

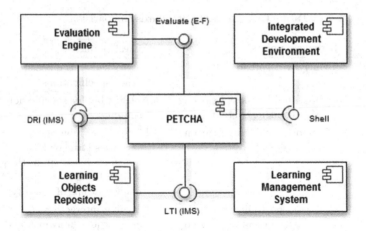

Fig. 4. Network component diagram.

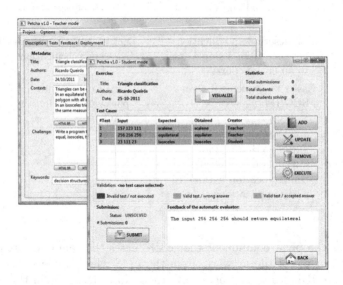

Fig. 5. The GUI of Petcha with teacher and student modes.

2.2 supports the IMS LTI 1.1 (a merge version of basic and full LTI) and import IMS CC packages. The exportation of CC packages will come in version 2.3. We successfully tested also the Sakai LMS on this network evidencing the interoperable characteristics of the proposed approach. For the LOR selection, we selected a home-made system called CrimsonHex - a repository of programming exercises described as learning objects and complying with the IMS CC specification. The repository also adheres to the IMS DRI specification to communicate with other systems. The EE system selected was Mooshak [5]. Mooshak is an open source system for managing programming contests on the Web including automatic judging of submitted programs. The current version (1.6a2) supports the Evaluate service (E-F) [6]. On the IDE side we selected Eclipse. Eclipse is a free and open source multi-language software development environment comprising an IDE and an extensible plug-in system. We tested also the Visual Studio Express IDE on this network with success for C assignments. As happens with a human TA, Petcha needs to interact both with teachers and students. Thus, these two use cases provide an overview of Petcha features.

In order to author and deploy a programming exercise in Petcha teachers must perform the following three tasks: create programming exercises; deploy programming exercises in a repository; and configure programming activity in LMS. On the other hand, in order to solve programming exercises using Petcha students performs the following two tasks: select an activity in the LMS and execute the activity using the IDE and Petcha.

4   Conclusions

This paper gathers information on e-learning content aggregation most prominent specifications (e.g., IMS CP, SCORM, XAPI and IMS CC) and their main contributions in the e-learning field.

This study is part of an effort to choose the most suitable specifications and standards for an e-learning framework called Ensemble. As conclusion of this study we highlight two issues that may hinder the proliferation of e-learning: fragmentation and complexity. The former is a typical technological issue. From the dozens of specifications found only the most prominent were presented. It is important to emphasize that standard fragmentation may reduce the amount of e-learning available content. Other issue is related with the complexity of specifications. A good example is the IMS SS that few systems support. A modular approach (based on profiles) in the design of these specifications could help in the adequacy to real scenarios and domains and could facilitate their dissemination among communities.

Despite all these issues we concluded that the most suitable specification for the Ensemble framework is IMS CC specification. The reason isbased on its massive support for systems interoperability using the fresh LTI specification and its support to represent an entire course with different levels of authorization (e.g. administators, teachers, students).

References

1. Queirós, R., Leal, J.P.: Petcha - a programming exercises teaching assistant. In: ACM SIGCSE 17th Anual Conference on Innovation and Technology in Computer Science Education, Haifa, Israel, ACM (2012)
2. Mason, R., Rehak, D.: Keeping the learning in learning objects. In: Littlejohn, A. (ed.) Reusing online resources: a sustainable approach to e-learning, Kogan Page, London, pp. 20–34 (2003). http://oro.open.ac.uk/800/

3. Queirós, R., Leal, J.P.: A survey on eLearning content standardization. In: Lytras, M.D., Ruan, D., Tennyson, R.D., Ordonez De Pablos, P., García Peñalvo, F.J., Rusu, L. (eds.) WSKS 2011. CCIS, vol. 278, pp. 433–438. Springer, Heidelberg (2013)
4. Clements, K., Gras-Velázquez, À., Pawlowski, J.M.: Educational resources packaging standards scorm and ims common cartridge the users point of view. In: Search and Exchange of e-learning Materials 2010 Proceedings (2010)
5. Leal, J.P., Silva, F.: Mooshak: A web-based multi-site programming contest system. Softw. Pract. Exper. **33**, 567–581 (2003)
6. Leal, J.P., Queirós, R., Ferreira, D.: Specifying a programming exercises evaluation service on the e-Framework. In: Luo, X., Spaniol, M., Wang, L., Li, Q., Nejdl, W., Zhang, W. (eds.) ICWL 2010. LNCS, vol. 6483, pp. 141–150. Springer, Heidelberg (2010)

2014 The Future of e-Textbooks Workshop

MatchMySound: Introducing Feedback to Online Music Education

Kristo Kão[(⊠)] and Margus Niitsoo

University of Tartu, Tartu, Estonia
{kristo80,margus.niitsoo}@ut.ee

Abstract. The quick spread of the internet has made music education, once only the domain of the rich elite, accessible to an unprecedented number of people around the world. As private tuition is still expensive, however, most people currently learning an instrument do so based purely on one-way instructional materials that provide information without any feedback. In this paper, we describe and implement a system which can be used to add interactive exercises to web-based self study materials that will provide immediate feedback on student's playing by comparing it to the example played by the teacher. To evaluate the quality of the feedback produced by the system, its scoring is compared to two conservatory level teachers on 216 guitar exercise attempts made by 108 beginner hobbyist guitarists. Results indicate that the system shows strong promise as its grades correspond quite well with the grades given by human teachers.

Keywords: Online music education · Music information retrieval · Automatic feedback · E-textbooks · Guitar

1 Introduction

Since the first printed music in the 1400s the concept of a music textbook has evolved from plain notes and text into modern packages of rich multimedia information presented through companion website with accompanying videos, sound examples and backing tracks. This has been a huge and needed improvement, as sheet music alone can be incomplete at best and even misleading at worst, but with the same material provided in audio form, the probability of false interpretations decreases markedly.

While the inclusion of multimedia can solve one problem that is caused by the lack of a human instructor - demonstrating and explaining - another important feature, feedback, is usually lost. In the middle of having all the music gadgets and information around us, most of the instructional materials in informal music education are still unidirectional, i.e. only provide information without responding or adapting to each student's individual needs.

In 2007 a guitar textbook entitled 'Guitar School - the Key to the Practical Guitar Playing' was published (English version: [12]) by one of the authors of

© Springer International Publishing Switzerland 2014
Y. Cao et al. (Eds.): ICWL 2014 Workshops, LNCS 8699, pp. 217–225, 2014.
DOI: 10.1007/978-3-319-13296-9_24

this paper. The book came bundled with a companion website with an innovative twist. Namely, it was possible for students to submit recordings of them playing the exercises and have a professional teacher give feedback based on them. Over 6 years, approximately 12,000 self-learners studied with this material, uploading a total of 2,601 audio recordings all of which were given written feedback.

Although the textbook enjoyed success on the local market and had promising educational outcomes, the model had two major shortcomings. The first was low cost efficiency and poor scalability from the teacher's side, which could, at least in theory be fixed with more manpower. The second and more fundamental problem was that of a delay in feedback, with students usually waiting at least a day before receiving it. This is a major problem, as it has been shown in numerous cases that feedback has to be fairly immediate in order for it to have maximum impact [11], especially so in learning motor skills [20] like playing an instrument.

Luckily, modern technology has come far enough to help alleviate this problem. The first tools that are capable of providing automatic feedback are on the market already and the current state-of-the-art in the field of Music Information Retrieval (MIR) suggests that music education will soon be changed fundamentally by music analysis technologies [5].

This paper reports on the authors' progress in developing a system that will match student's playing to the ideal version supplied by the teacher and that could be used in the companion web sites of textbooks alongside other multimedia to provide students with instant feedback on their playing.

2   Theoretical Background

The first commercial music rhythm game ("PaRappa the Rapper") dates back to 1996 [5]. Since then, the genre enjoyed a fair amount of popularity in the 00's with series such as Guitar Hero and Rock Band [1,18] that were based on tapping buttons on plastic toy instruments. However, in the past few years, it has become possible to play music games with actual authentic musical instruments with commercial titles like Rocksmith, BandFuse, Guitar Bots, WildChords, Songs2See and strumProfessor.

In many cases, games are a very good way of fostering learning as they generally lead to increased engagement with the material, which means more time spent working on the skills [1,15]. However, in the context of music education, the gaming approach may not be optimal for two distinct reasons.

The first of those is real-time feedback. As noted above, immediate feedback has been shown to lead to increased rates of learning. However, in music, there seems to be an important distinction between real-time (i.e. supplied during the playing) and immediate (i.e. supplied immediately after) feedback. Research on real-time visual feedback to singing and tapping exercises has shown a decrease in performance and authors have proposed that it can possibly be attributed to the increased information processing load [19,24], which is consistent with the effect of split attention in cognitive load theory [9,21]. In games, this effect may be further exacerbated by the need to make the games visually appealing and engaging by using detailed but spurious graphics.

Another potential questionable aspect with games is to what extent the skills learned in-game actually transfer to real life useful skills [7, 8, 17, 22]. For instance, in the context of music games, optimizing the game score may potentially lead to sloppy technique that might later need to be re-learned for the playing to actually sound musical.

Other products like Smart Music, Garage Band and Songs2See that also utilize sound recognition are developed directly with a clear educational purpose in mind. However, to date, these systems are often limited only to either a very specific instrument (like just guitar or monophonic instruments) or platform (like OSX or iOS for GarageBand). Also, they all have dedicated exercise banks, which indicates that adding each new exercise probably requires a fair amount of work.

Most of the technology used in both games and the educational products mentioned above is based on approaches developed by the scientific discipline of music information retrieval (MIR), which is a wide field concerned with a range of problems from automatic structural analysis of music to instrument identification and separation on harmony and pitch detection. The discipline is fairly practical in nature and holds yearly competitions for many of the most common tasks where the researchers submit their current state of the art algorithms for evaluation against large corpuses of real-life audio files [3].

3   MatchMySound System

The goal of this development project is a web application that compares two audio files - a pre-recorded etalon provided by the teacher and the one recorded by a student through the application. The algorithm finds the differences between the etalon and the user's audio input in two main dimensions: sound and timing. The former includes the differences in sound qualities such as the pitch, intonation and articulation, while the latter includes correctness of rhythm, changes of tempo and overall speed. The feedback is presented as two numerical scores along with two graphs that provide a finer level of detail. When creating an exercise, the teacher has to specify goals for both sound and timing scores. If the goals are not reached by a student then he/she is advised to try again.

Figure 1 depicts the current user interface of the system. The upper waveform represents the teacher etalon and the lower graph the user input audio. The matching spots in music are connected by grey vertical lines. The inside of the student's waveform is colored, symbolizing the differences in sound, and the line between the two waveforms indicates the differences in timing - small curves mean possible rhythm mistakes and bigger waves stand for tempo changes. The average tempo of the recording is displayed as the number of beats per minute (BPM). Both recordings can be listened to and seamlessly switched between, even while playing. As the two audio files are matched, switching the file always brings the listener to exactly the same place in music, allowing instant aural comparison.

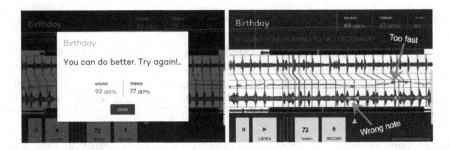

Fig. 1. Screenshots of the user interface right after playing and in feedback view.

During recording, the only thing shown to the student is the progress bar that loosely shows how far he/she is in playing the track. The main function of this is to just confirm that the computer is still in fact listening, which is akin to the teacher slightly nodding the student to go on playing. Feedback is shown only after the system determines that the student has finished playing. This feedback model is referred to as the KR or Knowledge of Results (evaluative feedback from an external source) and is common in the traditional classroom teaching practice [23]. It also emulates the classical teaching practices in music education, where the teacher usually lets the student finish her playing before he gives his comments and suggestions. We stress that not providing real-time feedback is a conscious and deliberate design choice to avoid potential problems related to real-time feedback mentioned in the background section.

One of the main design considerations was to avoid giving binary judgements of correct or incorrect in favor of a more continuous approach that stresses musicality. Music education has historically been based around apprenticeships where a student learns to imitate her teacher before setting off to develop her own style. This tool follows in that same tradition by trying to match what the student is playing to what the teacher did, going beyond mere pitches and rhythms to enter the area of expressive qualities of a musical performance. As such, it just reports the musical differences between the two recordings. The difference measure used is informed by music theory, meaning musically "logical" mistakes such as omitting one note in a chord or substituting a note with the same note one octave higher or lower are penalized less 4 than those that do not make musical sense, such as playing a dissonant note in a chord. The system is also fairly robust to tempo changes, easily dealing with a student playing even up to 30 % faster or slower than the teacher example she is being matched to.

Another design consideration for the system was that it would be easy to add new exercises. This has been achieved to a fairly large extent, as the only things needed for a new exercise are the recording of how the exercise should sound when played properly along with the average tempo of the piece as played in the etalon (in BPM) and, optionally, thresholds for the scores the student should exceed in order to "pass" the exercise.

A third consideration is that it work for as many musical instruments as possible. This has also been achieved to a large degree. We have currently tested it with recordings of guitar, piano, xylophone, violin, flute, accordion and also singing, and it has worked comparably well with all of them, both with monophonic as well as polyphonic pieces. However, tests with purely non-pitched instruments (drums, clapping) have thus far failed. Considering the range of instruments tested, we have reason to believe it to work with all pitched instruments.

The algorithm used in matching is based on the dynamic time warping approach that was developed in the '80s [14]. It has been one of the main tools in the MIR toolbox since the inception of the field as it is a convenient and adaptable way of aligning two signals to match one another. Our version of the algorithm uses a real-time implementation similar to that developed in Dixon [6] with a custom distance metric based on chroma features, along with numerous small engineering adaptations to make it both fast and robust enough for practical use. As this is a more conceptual paper, the full detailed specification of the algorithm is outside the current scope.

As the system is intended for future use in on-line teaching materials, the choice was made to implement it in languages suitable for web deployment. The real-time part of the analysis is therefore performed in JavaScript with the subsequent scoring delegated to a web server running in Python. The system is tested to work on the newest versions of Google Chrome (34) and Mozilla Firefox (29), and also on Chrome for Android (33). There are no plans to provide support for any versions of Microsoft Internet Explorer.

4   Evaluation

To compare the performance of the algorithm to human teachers, a study was conducted on a set of 216 exercises received from 108 different self-learning students who had completed the first chapter of [12] and sent in all the required exercises for submission. The first exercise was an Estonian folk tune "Vares vaga linnukene". The second was a choice between the melody of either Happy Birthday, Brother John or a famous estonian tune "Meil aiaäärne tänavas". Three recordings were removed from consideration due to audio files having become corrupt in uploading.

In the first phase of the comparison, two conservatory-level guitar teachers (Kristo Käo and Julia Kahro both from Estonian Academy of Theater and Music) separately graded all of the submissions in 3 dimensions (notes, tempo, rhythm) on a 5-point scale. The three grades of both teachers were averaged together to create the overall teacher score of the exercise.

In the second phase, the same recordings were compared to the corresponding sample audio files accompanying the textbook [12], and the timing and sound scores of the algorithm were averaged to produce the overall algorithm score. Although the system is meant to work directly with the microphone data, an extension was implemented for this analysis that allowed already recorded files to be analysed as if they had just been played into the input stream.

The algorithm failed to produce meaningful results for 19 exercises (9 % of the sample). The two most common reasons for this were either the guitar being very badly out of tune (9 cases) or the recording being too noisy (8 cases).

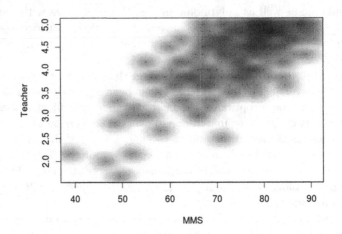

Fig. 2. Teacher grades plotted against the MMS Algorithm score.

Figure 2 shows the relationship between the two averaged scores. As can be seen, there is a strong linear correspondence between the two grades ($r = 0.68$) which is highly significant ($p < 10^{-16}$). This implies the scores of the algorithm align well with those of human teachers.

Looking separately at the dimensions and using the average of teachers rhythm and tempo scores as an equivalent to the algorithms timing score, the correlations diminish ($r = 0.39$ for sound/notes and $r = 0.65$ for timing). This is probably mediated by some errors (such as a student skipping a note) being categorized differently by the teachers and the algorithm.

MMS algorithm proved to be relatively robust to non-musical background noise and to the quality of recording hardware. The sample of audio files included recordings on four different types of guitars (steel string, classical, electric and even two on 12-string guitar). All but 3 recordings were made by the students in their home without specialist equipment and sometimes with background noises such as dogs barking or people talking. Despite this, only about 4 % of the audio files had to be excluded from the final sample due to excessive sound card hum or extremely low signal to noise ratio.

To the question 'Would you have preferred an automatic feedback to human feedback?' 84 % of the participating guitar students answered 'No' and 10 % 'Yes', which is in line with previous findings that suggest people prefer feedback from other people over that given by automations and irrespective of the quality of the actual feedback [10].

5   Discussion

While the human and algorithm feedback results were strongly correlated, there were cases where the scores diverged considerably. Some of the mismatches can be explained by (1) out of tune recordings, (2) different scorings of the repeated mistakes, (3) articulation errors (eg. staccato vs legato), and (4) resonating open strings.

If the recording departed from $A = 440$ Hz tuning by more than a quarter of tone (half a semitone), the MMS started to count some of the tones as slightly wrong. Even if the difference of tuning was audible to the human experts, they either dismissed it or counted it as a single mistake while for the algorithm, every note played on the detuned string counted as an error. However, these mistakes do not relate to playing technique of the students, and would be presumably detected and corrected given the automated feedback.

As for the differences in articulation and unwanted resonating of open strings, the human experts disregarded them as unimportant for novice guitarists. If the goal of this development project was be the best possible match between human and automatic feedback, having some of the common novice mistakes made by the teacher in the etalon files would probably have improved the match. However, this would have been wrong didactically as it would have made a wrong impression of the desired musical result and downplayed the importance of learning by imitation [2, 13].

6   Conclusions and Future Directions

In this paper we introduced a web application for the instant automatic feedback for musical exercises - MatchMySound (MMS) - that is intended to be integrated with music instruction websites and e-textbooks. We described the foundations and the process of the development project and reported the results of an initial comparison of the feedback given by the MMS algorithm and human experts. We have detected a strong and statistically significant correlation between the human and automatic scores given to 216 audio recordings of 108 self-learning guitar players and discussed some potential reasons of the mismatch between human and automatic assessment scores.

Regardless of the quality of the automated feedback, students often learn much from just the process of recording and listening to their playing. Experiments with self-analysis of recordings have showed it being a strong alternative to an instructor's feedback [4, 16], which backs up the musician folklore that "the ear is always ahead of the fingers". This implies that such a recording tool would be useful in teaching even as a placebo tool. However, the current results suggest that the feedback is quite well aligned with that of human teachers so the expected gains are hopefully even larger.

The current system is fully functional, but still in a prototype phase as it has some stability and scaling issues that prevent it from being deployed to large number of students. However, considering the promising initial results, the authors plan to work out the issues and make it available to the wider public as early as possible.

A demo for MMS can be found at http://demo.matchmysound.com.

References

1. Cassidy, G.G., Paisley, A.M.: Music-games: a case study of their impact. Res. Stud. Music Educ. **35**(1), 119–138 (2013)
2. Criss, E.: The natural learning process. Music Educators J. **95**(2), 42–46 (2008)
3. Cunningham, S.J., Bainbridge, D., Downie, J.S.: The impact of mirex on scholarly research (2005–2010). In: Proceedings of 13th International Society for Music Information Retrieval Conference (2012)
4. Deniz, J.: Video recorded feedback for self regulation of prospective music teachers in piano lessons. J. Instr. Psychol. **39**(1), 17–25 (2012)
5. Dittmar, C., Cano, E., Abeßer, J., Grollmisch, S.: Music information retrieval meets music education. Dagstuhl Follow-Ups 3 (2012)
6. Dixon, S.: Live tracking of musical performances using on-line time warping. In: Proceedings of the 8th International Conference on Digital Audio Effects, Citeseer, pp. 92–97 (2005)
7. Hill, L.: Violin Virtuoso: A game for violin education. Ph.D. thesis, Rice University (2011)
8. Jenson, J., De Castell, S.: From simulation to imitation: new controllers, new forms of play. In: Proceedings of the 2nd European Conference on Games-Based Learning, Barcelona, Spain, pp. 16–17 (2008)
9. Kalyuga, S., Chandler, P., Sweller, J.: Managing split-attention and redundancy in multimedia instruction. Appl. Cogn. Psychol. **13**(4), 351–371 (1999)
10. Karlsson, J., Liljeström, S., Juslin, P.N.: Teaching musical expression: effects of production and delivery of feedback by teacher vs. computer on rated feedback quality. Music Educ. Res. **11**(2), 175–191 (2009)
11. van der Kleij, F.M., Eggen, T.J., Timmers, C.F., Veldkamp, B.P.: Effects of feedback in a computer-based assessment for learning. Comput. Educ. **58**(1), 263–272 (2012)
12. Kão, K.: Guitar School - the Key to the Practical Guitar Playing. Kitarrikool Publishing, Tallinn (2009)
13. Kohut, D.L.: Musical Performance: Learning Theory and Pedagogy. Prentice-Hall, New Jersey (1985)
14. Kruskal, J.B., Liberman, M.: The symmetric time-warping problem: from continuous to discrete. In: Sankoff, D., Kruskal, J. (eds.) Time Warps, String Edits and Macromolecules: The Theory and Practice of Sequence Comparison, pp. 125–161. Addison Wesley, Reading (1983)
15. Muntean, C.I.: Raising engagement in e-learning through gamification. In: Proceedings of the 6th International Conference on Virtual Learning ICVL, pp. 323–329 (2011)
16. Napoles, J., Bowers, J.: Differential effects of instructor feedback vs. self-observation analysis on music education majors' increase of specific reinforcement in choral rehearsals. Bull. Counc. Res. Music Educ. **183**, 39–48 (2010)
17. Peppler, K., Downton, M., Lindsay, E., Hay, K.: The nirvana effect: Tapping video games to mediate music learning and interest. Int. J. Learn. Media (2011)

18. Richardson, P., Kim, Y.: Beyond fun and games: a framework for quantifying music skill developments from video game play. J. New Music Res. **40**(4), 277–291 (2011)
19. Sadakata, M., Hoppe, D., Brandmeyer, A., Timmers, R., Desain, P.: Real-time visual feedback for learning to perform short rhythms with expressive variations in timing and loudness. J. New Music Res. **37**(3), 207–220 (2008)
20. Shute, V.J.: Focus on formative feedback. Rev. Educ. Res. **78**(1), 153–189 (2008)
21. Sweller, J.: Cognitive load theory: recent theoretical advances. In: Briinken, R. (ed.) Cognitive Load Theory, pp. 29–47. Cambridge University Press, New York (2010)
22. Tanenbaum, J., Bizzocchi, J.: Rock band: a case study in the design of embodied interface experience. In: Proceedings of the 2009 ACM SIGGRAPH Symposium on Video Games, pp. 127–134. ACM (2009)
23. Welch, G.F., Howard, D.M., Himonides, E., Brereton, J.: Real-time feedback in the singing studio: an innovatory action-research project using new voice technology. Music Educ. Res. **7**(2), 225–249 (2005)
24. Wilson, P.H., Lee, K., Callaghan, J., Thorpe, C.W.: Learning to sing in tune: Does real-time visual feedback help. In: CIM07: 3rd Conference on Interdisciplinary Musicology, Tallinn, Estonia, vol. 2, p. 1519 (2007)

e-Textbooks: Towards the New Socio-Technical Regime

Kai Pata, Maka Eradze, and Mart Laanpere[(✉)]

Tallinn University, Center for Educational Technology, Tallinn, Estonia
{kpata,maka,mart.laanpere}@tlu.ee

Abstract. This paper discusses the niche technologies that have and possibly will contribute to the future e-textbooks as a new socio-technical regime. We propose the conceptual map of textbook functionalities aiming at opening the conceptual discussion for brainstorming and finding scenarios how the niche technologies that explored novel textbook applications in learning might be best combined into the new "artifact ecosystems" regime. Jointly with workshop participants we aim to come up with metaphors and concepts depicting learning in this regime.

1 Introduction

For a century dreams of new types of e-textbooks have existed as niche technologies within the mainstream socio-technical regime [1] of traditional classroom learning with paper textbooks. These alternatives to textbook have mimicked its core functions, complementing some of the missing but desired textbook features.

Late changes towards wide access of mobile technologies, World Wide Web and seamless access to it accompanied with new prosumer [2] and produsage [3] cultures have now opened opportunities for societies to transpose the etextbook from niche technology into the new mainstream socio-technical regime in teaching and learning.

We posit in this paper, that it is the utmost time to develop a new conceptual system for denoting what we expect from the future learning in artifact ecosystems. Deliberately, we do not use here the concept etextbook that we find constraining us into the old socio-technical regime of teaching and learning with paper-based textbook. We have coined the open concept "artifact ecosystems" to denote the yet not existing concept for the future generations of e-textbooks. With this workshop paper we aim at opening the conceptual discussion for brainstorming and finding scenarios how the niche technologies that explored novel textbook applications in learning might be best combined into the new "artifact ecosystems" regime. Jointly with workshop participants we aim to come up with metaphors and concepts depicting learning in this regime.

© Springer International Publishing Switzerland 2014
Y. Cao et al. (Eds.): ICWL 2014 Workshops, LNCS 8699, pp. 226–235, 2014.
DOI: 10.1007/978-3-319-13296-9_25

2 e-Textbooks as Niche Technologies: Realizations and Expectations

2.1 Mimicking the Traditional Functionalities of Textbooks in Pdf Textbooks

The first generation e-textbooks have followed the common socio-technical regime of teaching and learning with traditional textbooks, mimicking in large scale the functional expectations driven from traditional textbooks with some new reading cultures appearing [4]. For example, it is expected that etextbook ...*presents its contents in accordance with paper-book style* and ...*meets students' reading habits* [5].

Functions of e-textbooks that have been considered important in several studies [e.g. 5–9] blend the **functions from the digital devices** (portability/mobility, instant access to content, high-quality screens, zooming and scaling, convenience, space saving, environmental impact) with those of the **reading software** (good customer services, ease the management process with tools, variety of purchasing options (for lifetime or renting), ease of making copies, up-to-datedness, easy shifting between several user-devices, digital rights management, printing capability, ability to email text, and download to a handheld device, searching capabilities, sharing, personal and shared bookshelves, highlighting and un-highlighting, annotating, notes with labels, copying and pasting, hypertext links, glossary lookup, search and browse dictionary and in dices, cross reference functions, convenient monitoring the classroom) and the **textbook appearance and content** (presenting multiple views of the content, personalizing the look and feel, increased interactivity with multimedia objects (interactive quizzes, videos, audio clips, graphics), supportive reference materials). Reading pdf-based electronic textbooks comprises several novel reading habits, such as not reading the books cover-to-cover but rather skimming the text to find bits of information; ability for more than one student to use an e-book at the same time; ability to share notes etc. [6, 7, 10]. However, not all students find pleasure in reading e-textbooks and using its novel functionalities [4, 7, 9], reading is often accompanied with multitasking and appears to be more time-consuming than with paper-based textbooks [4].

Core textbook functions copied at etextbooks are: **Meaning-making with texts** – Finding and annotating relevant texts or its parts to reflect upon them (catalogue, index, bookmarks, underline and note-taking on the text); **Predetermining learning-paths for optimal comprehension** – sequenced chapters, texts, illustrations, figures are combined; **Guided learning from text** – giving assignments about the text (questions and tasks about the text); **Understanding concepts in text** – glossary. *Additional functions available at first generation e-textbooks are:* **Learning everywhere** – instant and anytime access, portable, mobile; **Ecologically shared and environment-friendly** – allowing different ownership modules (downloadable, rentable or purchased for lifetime)**; Providing customer services; Providing contents flexibly** – contents can be updated and optimized; materials can be combined from different modules.

2.2   Complementing the Textbooks with New Functionalities

In parallel to these traditional functionalities, several teaching and learning niches of e-textbook alternatives have been explored that have opened what roles e-textbooks could be taking in the future. Some of these expectations towards e-textbooks have long historical roots. Particular is to take notice that for introducing new approaches to using textbooks in the teaching process the new conceptual frameworks were proposed as well for each socio-technical niche.

2.2.1   Teaching Machines and Tutorials Allowing Programming Personalized Instruction for Achieving Pre-determined Learning Results

Thorndike [11] wrote of new textbooks already in 2012: *Books could be written **giving** data, directions for experiments and problems with the data, and questions about the inferences. The student could be **instructed** to read each helping piece of information, suggestive question and the like only after he had spent a certain time in trying to do for himself what he was directed to do. If, by a miracle of mechanical ingenuity, a book could be so arranged that **only to him** who had done what was directed on page one would page two become visible, and so on, much that now requires **personal instruction could be managed by print** (p. 165).*

Skinner [12] realized Thorndike's idea and proposed the Teaching Machine: *The student completes material by moving sliders bearing printed figures or letters. The student turns the crank and, if setting was correct, the machine presents the new set of materials. If his response was incorrect, it is cleared, and the same material must be completed again. In studying by machine something is happening all the time. The student continues to participate... he is achieve, and he gets something positive out of it which keeps him going. Though the teacher may not strike out a good teaching program all at once, the teacher will have the benefit of a remarkable **corrective feedback**. By analyzing the responses of perhaps fifty students to a set of, say, thirty items, one can spot every bad item. Nothing like this is possible in a textbook or instructional film.*

At later years (1950–60s), the first personal computers enabled to realize **teaching programs and tutorials** for self-paced differentiated learning – Computer Based Training (CBT) and Computer Assisted Instruction (CAI) emerged. But only recently **adaptive teaching programmes** have become technically realistic due to user-modeling and semantic technologies.

Browsing the articles of etextbooks the expectation of allowing differentiated learning is one of the repeated visions. It is expected that the textbook **adjusts** to student, adapts to student progress, provides tasks at suitable level, allows learning about mistakes, checks student's work, and provides automated personalized feedback and formative assessment through book interface [5, 9, 13]. Such programmed instruction assumes textbooks to have **learning analytics** [14] functionalities available for teachers and students for **monitoring learning** and making corrections as they learn and teach. Being defined as the measurement, collection, analysis and reporting of data about learners and their contexts, for purposes of understanding and optimizing learning and the environments in which it occurs, learning analytics is regarded as one of the crucial factors to be embedded into the teaching and learning process. Analytics should, for example, **record students' responses, track multitasking** and **reading paths, record errors**.

2.2.2   Hyperlinked and Semantically Annotated Web Pages and Wikis as Learning Resources with Partial Learners' Locus of Control Allowing to Personalize Learning Experiences Using the Wisdom of the Crowd in Learning

Bush [15] wrote in 1945: *Consider a future device for individual use, which is a sort of mechanized **private file and library**. It needs a name, and to coin one at random, memex will do. A memex is a device in which an **individual stores** all his books, records, and communications, and which is mechanized so that **it may be consulted with exceeding speed and flexibility**. Most of the memex contents are purchased on microfilm ready for insertion. Books of all sorts, pictures, current periodicals, news-papers, are thus obtained and dropped into place.*

*There is, of course, **provision for consultation** of the record by the usual scheme of **indexing**. If the user wishes to consult a certain book, he taps its code on the keyboard, and the title page of the book promptly appears before him, projected onto one of his viewing positions. A special button transfers him immediately to the first page of the index. Any given book of his library can thus be called up and consulted with far greater facility than if it were taken from a shelf. As he has several projection positions, he can leave one item in position while he calls up another... Memex affords an immediate step, however, to **associative indexing**, the basic idea of which is a provision whereby any item may be caused at will to select immediately and automatically another. This is the essential feature of the memex... The process of **tying two items together** is the important thing. Wholly **new forms of encyclopedias** will appear, ready-made with a mesh of **associative trails** running through them, **ready to be dropped into the memex and there amplified**. ...The lawyer has at his touch the associated opinions and decisions of **his whole experience, and of the experience of friends and authorities**.*

Realizing the dreams of Memex as hyperlinked and globally accessed web-pages, Berners-Lee [16] wrote the first technical proposal that later turned to World Wide Web (commonly known as the web) as we know it now. According to Berners-Lee [17] the WWW browser used hypertext "**to link and access information** of various kinds as a web of nodes in which the user could **browse at will**". The first ever web **browser was also an editor,** making the web an interactive medium, however editing was not possible externally of CERN.

Cunningham, on the other hand developed the first wiki implementation WikiWikiWeb named after the shuttle bus that runs between airport terminals in Honolulu (wiki meaning fast and quick in Hawaiian language). The welcome page of this wiki [18] highlights the following ideas: *...This **community**.... consists of many people. We always **accept newcomers** with valuable contributions...The usefulness of Wiki is in **the freedom, simplicity, and power** it offers...All Wiki **content is work in progress**...this is **a forum where people share ideas**... **It changes** as people come and go. Much of the **information here is subjective**...The wiki allows to browse... or search...to bookmark and **watch how things change...edit pages...you can also select one of the random pages**, so with some luck you start from the good point.*

The associative hyperlinks also have some negative features, that is over time, many web resources pointed to by hyperlinks disappear, relocate, or are replaced with different content that makes hyperlinks obsolete. The Semantic Web collaborative movement encourages the inclusion of semantic context in web-pages, that potentially can convert the currently unstructured web into "Web of data" – the **semantically structured network of knowledge**. Berners-Lee and Fischetti [16] envisioned: *I have a dream for the Web [in which computers] become capable of analyzing all the data on the Web – the content, links, and transactions between people and computers*. The semantic, ontology-based solutions (e.g. semantic wiki; social-semantic solutions) have started to emerge in last decade that allow getting suggestions based on the knowledge of the crowd using the community browsing, personal recommending and dynamic visualizations.

The dream of **students and teachers as prosumers** (prospective consumers who are involved in the design, manufacture, or development of a product or service) [2] and **produsers** (the users turned creators and distributors of content) [3] of **etextbooks** [5] is gradually becoming technically realistic and mature enough to be used in the future "artifact ecosystems". What does social-semantic technology allow for "artifact ecologies" for learning has yet to be explored from instructional as well as cognitive points of view. Some of the early expectations driven from e-textbook papers are: **social recommendations for learning resources** – e.g. Providing student-customized annotations as reading scaffolds; **taking and sharing perspectives** – for example viewing corresponding theories or approaches; **shared meaning-making** with texts – going beyond individual annotations, highlighting, bookmarking and note-taking practices towards shared meaning-making (sharing and making use of shared questions, resources and bookshelves, bookmarks and annotations, notes (such as learning experiences, ideas) [19].

Learning analytics may be used for **mediating peer-scaffolding**, **recommending learning patterns** (for example, alternative reading paths), and for **highlighting learning opportunities and chances** in learning [10, 19].

2.2.3 Modular Textbook Approach and Appropriate and Interactive Representation: Multimedia-Enriched Complex and Ubiquitous Learning Environments for Authentic, Situated and Augmented Learning

Solutions towards e-textbook modularization have been Learning Object Initiative [20–22] and the Open Educational Resources initiative from Hewlett Foundation [23] that should allow **open sharing, reusing and remixing** of annotated learning resources. Polsani [21] defines LOs as **independent and self-standing units** of learning content that are predisposed to being **reused in multiple instructional contexts**. Open educational resources are of **high quality, freely accessible, openly licensed online educational materials** that offer an extraordinary opportunity for people everywhere to share, use, and reuse knowledge [23].

Merrill [24] has proposed that the greatest impact on learning results from the **appropriate representation and organization of the knowledge** to be learned. Complex virtual learning environments that provide facilities for problem-based inquiry learning [25] have been considered as **integrated learning objects with high level of aggregation, interactivity, and semantic density** [26], serving as the **pedagogically constrained gateways for knowledge construction** with multiple learning objects to **enable authentic learning experiences**. In complex learning environments **co-controlling models and simulations** has become possible, sensor-based inquiry learning has made it possible to **use real data to run the experimental models** in the learning environments.

The e-textbook definitions reflect this socio-technical niche: ...digital object with textual and/or other contents, ...made available electronically (or optically) for any device (handheld or desk-bound) that includes a screen, ...with features such as search and cross reference functions, reference materials, monographs, hypertext links, bookmarks, interactive dictionaries, highlights, multimedia objects and note taking [8, 9]. Choi and associates [13] on the other hand, emphasize the e-textbook's opportunity for learning by integrating sources. The main plusses highlighted for etextbooks are **greater interactivity level**, better **possibility to link a variety of representations** such as hyperlinked texts and various types of quizzes, interactive animations, inquiry models, **using actively media contents for involving more senses** than traditional textbooks can do. For example, the etextbooks are expected to redirect students from memorizing and consuming knowledge towards using and constructing knowledge for solving problems and making decisions. Some of the future possibilities towards even greater interactivity of "artifact ecosystems" might be extending the learning experiences towards augmented reality, **allowing embodied experiences** and **opportunities for enaction. Secondly, making use of the learning crowds - swarming for collecting** evidence or opening the perspectives of knowledge, **co-creating geo-locative narratives** etc. may be the directions towards which e-textbooks might be evolving.

2.2.4   Collaborative Learning and Knowledge Building at E-Courses and MOOC-S the Collaborative Approach to Textbooks

From 1990s e-courses have investigated the **co-creation, sharing, collaborative usage and mediating role of learning resources** that opens up the **collaborative usage potential of e-textbooks**. Stahl [27] summarizes the developments in Computer Supported Collaborative Learning (CSCL) as follows: it is the phenomenon of the whole group learning as well as individual learning, and at some level organizational-societal relationships between them that are placed in the center of attention in CSCL. The theoretical point of CSCL is interacting with people to **accomplish work tasks and associated cognitive tasks (including articulation tasks and power struggles) through group interaction processes**. The cognition is conceptualized as product of group collaboration where there are no boundaries to who separate and to attribute the knowledge building. Learning of students is **mediated by situations, technological networking as well as by collaborative interaction.**

New form of massive open online courses (MOOC) has emerged that combine the ideas of CSCL as well as **extend the openness from the usage of learning resources to the open courses.** MOOCs are the units of learning with specified institutional affiliation, schedule, content and learning tasks which **engage self-directed and self-organized learners and leading practitioners** in the field by fostering open enrollment, open curriculum, open and partially learner-defined learning goals and - outcomes, **the usage of open resources and open learning environment,** and the enabled open monitoring of learning activities [28–30] with the aim of facilitating learning as a process of navigating, growing and pruning connections and interactions within distributed networks, and **generating coherence, resonance and synchronization in knowledge** [31].

In spite of elearning approaches, there is still the tendency in seeing learning with e-textbooks as part of the individual learning assignments in which **learner is creating content individually** (copying, pasting, remixing contents) [13]. Such scenarios predict that part of **learner-created contents collected in their portfolios** will **make up the personalized version of the textbook in the end of the course**. The collaborative learning functionalities similar to e-learning (such as **collaborating and co-constructing contents** (diagrams, stories, storyboards)) have rarely been associated with current e-textbooks, however several opportunities are offered by text-creation widgets [32]. Sun and associates [10] and McFall and associates [19] emphasize **etextbook's social involvement in learning**. Yet, the general understanding has been that collaborative activities are ought to be triggered by e-textbooks, but the activity itself is expected to take place in face-to-face settings. It is presumed, however, that one of the futures of "artifact ecosystems" usage may resemble MOOCs – the distributed students participate at the courses and interact across school borders, **the textbooks are formed from distributed resources with multiple origin** (such as different editors, teachers, students). The **collaborative activities around contents** may make use of what we have learned from best examples of elearning and going beyond of it. For example, combining such distributed courses and resources with social-semantic technologies allows forming **artifact-actor networks for scaffolding** learning (for example with hints and feedback, resources, strategies etc.), and may promote **new forms of co-creation for maturing knowledge etc.** Future eTextbooks as "artifact ecosystems" may represent **a kind of collective mind, which could embody many learners' shared learning experiences**, become aware of what the learners in this level of knowledge and competences collectively desire, believe and intend, and may as the shared mind **help each learner to act proactively to enhance the collaborative learning experience**.

3   Vision for the New Socio-Technical Regime

In this workshop, particularly we would like to discuss the teaching and learning as well as cognitive practices that could be incorporated to the artifact ecosystem from different socio-technical niches. From the literature review above, we have mapped the functionalities from different textbook electronic analogues to the initial concept map of "artifact ecosystems" (see Fig. 1). Some of these functions (marked with white background) are already available in the first generation e-textbooks, whilst others (marked with blue) are ought to be moved from the niches into making up the new socio-technical regime. In this workshop we aim at brainstorming for (1) finding scenarios how these potential e-textbook functionalities originating from different approaches to teaching, learning and cognitive practices could be best incorporated from niche technologies into the new e-textbook regime. Secondly, we aim at jointly with workshop participants (2) coming up with metaphors and concepts depicting this regime of "artifact ecosystems". Post-workshop we intend to incorporate the joint results of these discussions about the future of e-textbooks into the white paper about the new vision for the e-textbooks as "artifact ecosystems".

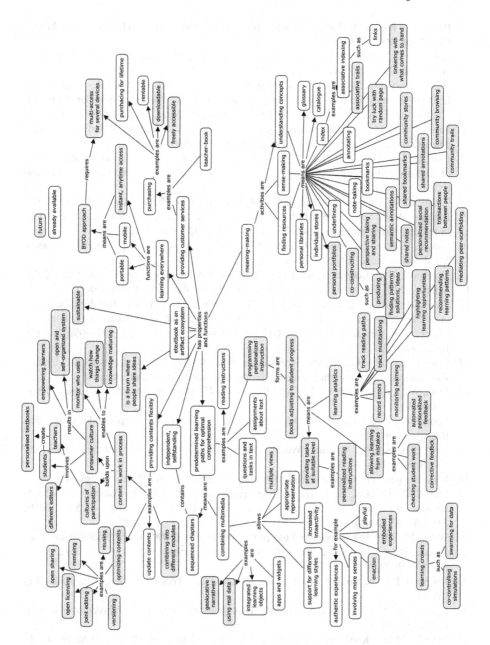

Fig. 1. Concept map of current and expected e-textbook functionalities

References

1. Geelse, F.W.: Technological transitions as evolutionary reconfiguration processes: a multi-level perspective and a case-study. Res. Policy **31**, 1257–1274 (2002)
2. Toffler, A.: The third wave: the classic study of tomorrow. Bantam, New York (1980)

3. Bruns, A.: Blogs, Wikipedia, Second Life, and Beyond. From Production to Produsage. Peter Lang, Bern (2008)
4. Daniel, D.B., Woody, W.D.: E-textbooks at what cost? Performance and use of electronic v. print texts. Comput. Educ. **62**, 18–23 (2013)
5. Huang, R., Chen, N.-S., Kang, M., McKenney, S., Churchill, D.: The roles of electronic books in the transformation of learning and instruction. In: The Proceedings of IEEE 13th International Conference on Advanced Learning Technologies, pp. 516–518 (2013)
6. Oliveira, S.M.: E-textbooks usage by students at Andrews University. A study of attitudes, perceptions, and behaviors. Libr. Manag. **33**(8/9), 536–560 (2012)
7. Elias, E.C., David, C., Phillips, D.C., Luechtefeld, M.E.: E-books in the classroom: a survey of students and faculty at a school of pharmacy. Curr. Pharm. Teach. Learn. **4**, 262–266 (2012)
8. Vassiliou, M.: Progressing the definition of "e-Book". Libr. Hi Tech **26**(3), 355–368 (2008)
9. Embong, A.M., Noor, A.M., Hashim, H.M., Ali, R.M., Shaari, Z.H.: E-Books as textbooks in the classroom. Procedia – Soc. Behav. Sci. **47**, 1802–1809 (2012)
10. Sun, J., Flores, J., Tanguma, J.: E-Textbooks and Students' Learning Experiences. Decis. Sci. J. Innov. Educ. **10**(1), 63–77 (2012)
11. Thorndike, E.L.: Education: A First Book. Macmillan, New York (1912). (published 1923)
12. Skinner, B.F.: The technology of teaching. Am. Educ. Res. J. **6**(3), 454–458 (1969)
13. Choi, J.-I., Heo, H., Lim, K.Y., Jo, I.-H.: The development of an interactive digital textbook in middle school English. In: Kim, T.-h., Adeli, H., Slezak, D., Sandnes, F.E., Song, X., Chung, K.-i., Arnett, K.P. (eds.) FGIT 2011. LNCS, vol. 7105, pp. 397–405. Springer, Heidelberg (2011)
14. Long, P., Siemens, G.: Penetrating the fog: analytics in learning and education (2011). http://www.educause.edu/ero/article/penetrating-fog-analytics-learning-and-education
15. Bush, W.: As we may think. The Atlantic, July (1945). (Reprinted in Life magazine, 10 Sept 1945)
16. Berners-Lee, T., Fischetti, M.: Weaving the Web, Chapter 12. HarperSanFrancisco, San Francisco (1999)
17. Tim Berners-Lee's original World Wide Web browser (2014). http://info.cern.ch/NextBrowser.html
18. Welcome page of WikiWikiWeb (2014). http://c2.com/cgi/wiki?WelcomeVisitors
19. McFall, R., Deshem, H., Davis, D.: Experiences using a collaborative electronic textbook: bringing the "guide on the side" home with you. In: Proceedings of SIGCSE'06, pp. 339–343 (2006)
20. Wiley, D. (ed.): The instructional use of learning objects (2000). http://reusability.org/read/
21. Polsani, P.R.: The use and abuse of reusable learning objects. J. Digit. Inf. **3**(4), Article No. 164 (2002)
22. Parrish, P.E.: The trouble with learning objects. Educ. Tech. Res. Dev. **5**(1), 1042–1629 (2004)
23. Open educational resources (2014). http://www.hewlett.org/programs/education/open-educational-resources
24. Merrill, M.D.: Knowledge objects and mental models. In: Wiley, D.A. (ed.) The Instructional Use of Learning Objects (Online) (2000). http://reusability.org/read/chapters/merrill.doc. Accessed 2014
25. van Joolingen, W.R., deJong, T., Lazonder, A.W., Savelsbergh, E.R., Manlove, S.: Co-Lab: research and development of an online learning environment for collaborative discovery learning. Comput. Hum. Behav. **21**, 671–688 (2005)
26. 1484.2.1-2002 IEEE Standard for Learning Object Metadata (2006). Accessed 2014

27. Stahl, G.: Theories of cognition in collaborative learning. In: Hmelo-Silver, C., O'Donnell, A., Chan, C., Chinn, C. (eds.) International Handbook of Collaborative Learning, pp. 74–90. Taylor & Francis, New York (2012)

28. McAuley, A., Stewart, B., Siemens, G., Cormier, D.: The MOOC model for digital practice (2011). http://www.elearnspace.org/Articles/MOOC_Final.pdf. Accessed 2014

29. Kop, R.: The challenges to connectivist learning on open online networks: learning experiences during a massive open online course. IRRODL **12**(3) (2011). http://www.irrodl. org/index.php/irrodl/article/view/882

30. Kop, R., Fournier, H.: New dimensions to self-directed learning in an open networked learning environment. Int. J. Self-Dir. Learn. **7**(2) (2011). http://selfdirectedlearning.com/ documents/Kop&Fournier2010.pdf. Accessed 2014

31. Siemens, G.: What is the theory that underpins our MOOCs? (2012). http://www. elearnspace.org/blog/2012/06/03/what-is-the-theory-that-underpins-our-moocs/. Accessed 2014

32. Encheff, D.: Creating a science e-book with fifth grade students. TechTrends **57**(6), 61–72 (2013)

Designing Interactive Scratch Content for Future E-books

Mario Mäeots[(✉)], Leo Siiman, and Margus Pedaste

Faculty of Social Sciences and Education,
Centre for Educational Technology,
Institute of Education, University of Tartu,
Salme 1a, 50103 Tartu, Estonia
{mario.maeots,leo.siiman,margus.pedaste}@ut.ee

Abstract. In the current paper we propose a framework for designing interactive content to make future e-books more dynamic. The problem with typical e-books today is that they seem to have a lack of interactivity. Considering the rapid advancement of digital technology there are many opportunities to change this situation. We focus on using the multimedia authoring tool Scratch as an option to create interactive content. The Scratch platform is valuable because content can be easily created, shared, embedded in websites and even possibly embedded in future e-books. Thus it opens up a possibility for making e-books more interactive and dynamic. Scratch by its very nature also promotes the constructivist pedagogy of learning by design. The framework we propose for designing interactive Scratch content was derived from creating a specific Scratch model to teach biology content. However, the framework is a promising start to producing interactive content that can apply potentially to any subject.

Keywords: E-books · Learning by design · Digital learning material · Interactive simulations · Visual programming environments

1 Introduction

The variety of technological tools to design and develop digital learning materials that support students in their learning has no boundaries. Digital learning materials exhibit a range of complexity, starting from simple text-only e-books to interactive computer-enhanced learning environments like PhET Interactive Simulations [1], SCY lab [2], or Young Researcher [3]. E-books provide a great convenience and are easy to access [4]; but have less interactivity since they often just present static (text, images) information [5]. Computer-enhanced learning environments have shown to be effective tools for supporting learning, in part because they provide ample interactivity and thereby allow students to control parameters in simulations, or perform experiments using remote and virtual laboratories [6].

In general, interactivity involves activities which occur between learners and their learning environment by inducing cognitive processes that foster learning [5]. In the inductive constructive learning approach students are responsible for their own knowledge construction [7]. Students who are actively involved in learning are also better supported through possibilities to learn by design [8].

© Springer International Publishing Switzerland 2014
Y. Cao et al. (Eds.): ICWL 2014 Workshops, LNCS 8699, pp. 236–242, 2014.
DOI: 10.1007/978-3-319-13296-9_26

Recent developments in educational technology have progressed so far that there are several opportunities for students to act like designers (e.g., SimSketch [9]) or even to the point where they can take the role as a programmer (e.g., Scratch [10]). López-Ortega [11] describes the technology as facilitating computer-assisted creativity, with direct interaction between the computer program and the student. Technology allows students to construct models that make their understandings of a domain visible, sharable, and executable [12].

However, all of this requires teachers' who are ready to support students' in their activities. This can only happen when a teacher has enough knowledge, skills, and experience to design and create interactive content. To support technologically enhanced learning activities, we propose a framework for designing interactive Scratch content. As a specific example we created Scratch content to teach a biology topic. This also demonstrates the flexibility of Scratch, since it is typically oriented towards teaching programming.

The organization of the paper is as follows. First we introduce the Scratch environment. Then we describe the specific example we created to teach biology content. Next we extract a framework propose it as a general paradigm. Finally we conclude with a discussion of the benefits of this framework and the value it offers to future e-books.

2 Scratch Programming Environment

Scratch (see http://scratch.mit.edu) is a visual programming environment targeted to students which allows them to create interactive models, games or animations [10, 13]. The typical use of Scratch has been to help students develop their elementary programming skills, and in this regard recent research has indeed verified its benefits [14]. Furthermore, Scratch and visual programming environments in general, have been shown to be effective in recruiting and retaining more students towards studying information and communications technology [15].

Scratch is open source software, and has been translated to several languages all over world. This is extremely valuable because it encourages the sharing Scratch projects without any language barriers – just a simple press of a button switches the language and a user can even begin making modifications in that new language. Hence one major reason to focus on Scratch software is because it contributes to cross-cultural dissemination of ideas [16].

To create a model or animation in Scratch students must snap together syntactically correct visual programming blocks [13, 16]. To avoid syntax errors, different command and data type blocks are visually shaped so that they fit together only if the syntax is correct [16]. Therefore, Scratch is designed to be user-friendly and intuitively visualized.

Although Scratch is typically oriented toward teaching programming, the benefits of the software convinced us to consider using it to teach biology. We expect that this will have a positive impact on students' understanding of biological processes since they have the opportunity to actively create for themselves visual models that illustrate abstract concepts. Moreover, due to the sharing possibilities of Scratch projects collaborative activities can easily be included into the learning process.

3   Example of an Interactive Scratch-Based Model for Teaching Biology

In the Estonian biology curriculum, one learning outcome that students are expected to achieve is "to have the capability to analyze the energy needs and energy-producing methods used by autotrophic and heterotrophic organisms" [17]. Based on supporting this specific learning goal we proceeded to design in the context of "Biodigi project" (see http://biodigi.edu.ee) a relevant Scratch learning activity.

First, we devised the general pedagogical goal of our Scratch activity. In our example it was to teach students to identify which energy containing substances are associated with which organisms and why those relations exist. For example, plants need carbon dioxide to grow. Next we made the abstract learning outcome more concrete and visual by thinking of specific examples. We decided to use a plant as representative of an autotrophic organism, an animal (lamb) as an example of a heterotrophic organism, several vital molecules (carbon dioxide, oxygen, water, glucose) as important sources of energy, and minerals as another source of energy. Finally, the model scenario was created using these components (see Fig. 1).

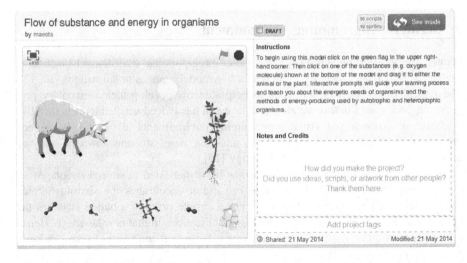

Fig. 1. Screenshot of the Scratch learning environment to teach biology content.

In the Scratch learning activity students have to link the energy substances with the correct organism. For example, carbon dioxide is a source of energy for plants but not for animals. On the other hand, glucose is a source of energy for animals but not for plants. Water is needed by both plants and animals. In the course of this activity students learn to analyze the energy needs and energy-producing methods used by autotrophic and heterotrophic organisms.

Once the pedagogical scenario was constructed we employed the services of a professional artist to create visual content. Figure 1 shows the appearance of all the essential components in our Scratch example. However, simply having visual pictures is not enough for a Scratch project. We need to animate the pictures to create an interactive story.

In Scratch this is done through a visual programming environment (see Fig. 2). To see the programming user interface view it is necessary to click on the 'See Inside' button shown at the upper right-hand corner of the project page view. In our biology scenario the task of programming involved several steps. The energy producing objects had to be programmed so that when a student clicks on an object; a prompt appears telling them the name of that substance. Furthermore, the user has to then drag the object onto the animal or plant. When the object is placed on top of one of the organisms another prompt appears revealing if and why there is a link between that source of energy and that organism.

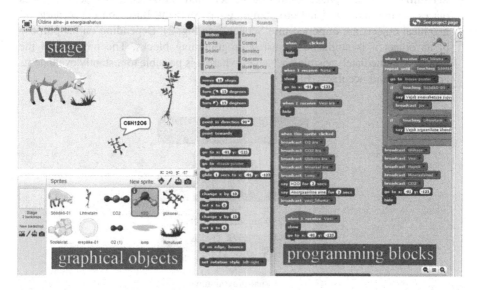

Fig. 2. Screenshot of the Scratch learning environment to teach biology content after the 'See Inside' button has been pressed. There are three separate windows: stage, graphical objects and programming blocks.

4 A Framework for Designing an Interactive Scratch Based Model

Our experience creating interactive Scratch biology content allowed us to generalize the process and create a general design framework. The framework has not yet been empirically tested, but soon will be in an actual school situation.

The design process to create a new interactive model (see Fig. 3) is implemented as a flow of three main processes:

- **Pedagogical content** – this is essentially a preparatory phase where curriculum objectives and age issues are considered and a detailed model scenario is composed. In our example we focused on the secondary school biology topic covering the general flow of substance and energy in organisms. Basically we produced a mock-up of the model with a scenario that outlined step by step the entire pedagogical content and described how it should interact with the learner. Also it was necessary to figure out what kind of visual components were needed.
- **Visual content** – based on the scenario 2-D graphical objects ("sprites") are prepared. The Scratch environment has its own drawing tool so students can use it to free-hand draw and make graphical objects. Also, Scratch has a repository of different graphical objects that can be used. In addition it is possible to use your own drawings or pictures that are in a suitable image file format (e.g. jpg, png). In our case we employed the services of a professional artist to create images files.
- **Scripting** – in this phase animating objects and introducing interactivity takes places via the Scratch visual programming environment. Based on the scenario all graphical objects are imported into Scratch (see Fig. 2). Depending on the purpose of an object it is animated by using programming blocks. The progress of the project is immediately visible on "stage" where it is possible to instantly evaluate its appearance and accuracy (Fig. 2).

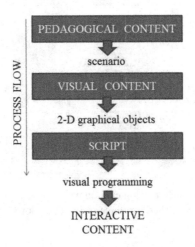

Fig. 3. A framework for designing interactive Scratch content.

5   Discussion and Conclusions

The problem with many e-books today is that they are static and do not take advantage of the full technology capabilities of digital content. Furthermore, static e-books appear to restrict learning to traditional learning techniques like rote memorization. In contrast, inductive constructive learning approaches have been shown to be more effective in fostering student-centered learning [7]. Therefore, e-books require content that is interactive and explicitly engages in active learning. One example is to use the visual programming environment Scratch to create and apply this content.

The flexibility of the Scratch software goes beyond teaching programming skills, and offers a unique opportunity to present content in e-books. The Scratch-based biology model we presented shows that interactive digital content can be a promising method for students to actively engage with content in order to learn using a constructivist learning approach. Often digitization of traditional learning materials are accompanied by adoption of traditional teaching techniques (i.e. passive transmission of knowledge from an authority to a learner). To avoid the disadvantages of traditional teaching we require new learning resources that facilitate interactivity.

The future of e-books is increasingly moving towards more interactivity. In this work we showed how teachers and students can engage with interactive Scratch web-based models, which offer exciting possibilities to embed into future e-book formats. The specific Scratch content examined in this work dealt with a biology topic. The promising potential to apply our framework for designing interactive models for any school topic needs to be empirically tested.

Acknowledgements. The Scratch models used in this research were produced in the context of a project Biodigi (http://www.biodigi.edu.ee/), financed by the European Social Fund. We would like to thank Meelis Brikker who created all drawings for the models.

References

1. Wieman, C.E., Adams, W.K., Perkins, K.K.: PhET: simulations that enhance learning. Science **322**, 682–683 (2008). doi:10.2307/20145153
2. De Jong, T., Lazonder, A., van Joolingen, W., Wasson, B., Vold, V., Hovardas, T., Giemza, A.: Using scenarios to design complex technology-enhanced learning environments. Educ. Technol. Res. Dev. **60**, 883–901 (2012). doi:10.1007/s11423-012-9258-1
3. Mäeots, M., Pedaste, M., Sarapuu, T.: Developing students' transformative and regulative inquiry skills in a computer-based simulation. In: Paper presented at the 8th IASTED International Conference on Web-Based Education, Phuket, Thailand, 16–18 March 2009
4. Huang, Y., Liang, T., Su, Y., Chen, N.: Empowering personalized learning with an interactive e-book learning system for elementary school students. Educ. Technol. Res. Dev. **60**, 703–722 (2012). doi:10.1007/s11423-012-9237-6
5. Kuhl, T., Scheiter, K., Gerjets, P., Gemballa, S.: Can differences in learning strategies explain the benefits of learning from static and dynamic visualizations? Comput. Educ. **56**, 176–187 (2011)
6. Renkl, A., Atkinson, R.K.: Interactive learning environments: contemporary issues and trends. An introduction to the special issue. Educ. Psychol. Rev. **19**, 235–238 (2007). doi:10.1007/s10648-007-9052-5
7. Prince, M.J., Felder, R.M.: Inductive teaching and learning methods: definitions, comparisons, and research bases. J. Eng. Educ. **95**, 123–138 (2006)
8. Vreman-de Olde, C., de Jong, T., Gijlers, H.: Learning by designing instruction in the context of simulation-based inquiry learning. J. Educ. Technol. Soc. **16**, 47–58 (2013)

9. Bollen, L., van Joolingen, W.: SimSketch: multiagent simulations based on learner-created sketches for early science education. IEEE Trans. Learn. Technol. **6**, 208–216 (2013). doi:10.1109/TLT.2013.9

10. Maloney, J., Resnick, M., Rusk, N., Silverman, B., Eastmond, E.: The Scratch programming language and environment. Trans. Comput. Educ. **10**, 1–15 (2010). doi:10.1145/1868358. 1868363

11. López-Ortega, O.: Computer-assisted creativity: emulation of cognitive processes on a multi-agent system. Expert Syst. Appl. **40**, 3459–3470 (2013). doi:10.1016/j.eswa.2012.12. 054

12. Bravo, C., van Joolingen, W., de Jong, T.: Modeling and simulation in inquiry learning: checking solutions and giving intelligent advice. Simulation **82**, 769–784 (2006). doi:10. 1177/0037549706074190

13. Lee, Y.: Scratch: Multimedia programming environment for young gifted learners. Gifted Child Today **34**, 26–31 (2011)

14. Scaffidi, C., Chambers, C.: Skill progression demonstrated by users in the Scratch animation environment. Int. J. Hum.-Comput. Interact. **28**, 383–398 (2012). doi:10.1080/10447318. 2011.595621

15. Siiman, L.A., Pedaste, M., Tõnisson, E., Sell, R., Jaakkola, T., Alimisis, D.: A review of interventions to recruit and retain ICT students. Int. J. Mod. Educ. Comput. Sci. **28**, 383–398 (2014). doi:10.1080/10447318.2011.595621

16. Maloney, J.J., Burd, L.L., Kafai, Y.Y., Rusk, N.N., Silverman, B.B., Resnick, M.M.: Scratch: a sneak preview [education]. In: Proceedings Second International Conference on Creating, Connecting and Collaborating Through Computing, p. 104 (2004). doi:10.1109/ C5.2004.1314376

17. Estonian National Curriculum for Upper Secondary Schools. Appendix 4: Natural Science, p. 12 (2011). http://www.hm.ee/index.php?popup=download&id=11228

Hybrid User Centered Development Methodology: An Application to Educational Software Development

António Pedro Costa[1,3]([✉]), Luis Paulo Reis[2,3],
and Maria João Loureiro[1]

[1] CIDTFF - Research Centre "Didatics and Technology in Education
of Trainers", DE/UA - Education Department,
University of Aveiro, Aveiro, Portugal
pcosta@ludomedia.pt, mjoao@ua.pt,
[2] DSI/EEUM – Information Systems Department, School of Engineering,
University of Minho, Guimarães, Portugal
lpreis@dsi.uminho.pt
[3] LIACC - Artificial Intelligence and Computer Science Laboratory,
Porto, Portugal

Abstract. This paper describes a Hybrid User Centered Development Methodology (HUCDM). This is a simple, iterative and incremental development process that has as building blocks the principles of User Centered Design (UCD), specified in the International Organization for Standardization 9241-210. In its base lies the disciplined structure of development processes as well as practices and values from agile software development methods. The process consists of four main phases: planning, design, implementation and maintenance/operation. The prototyping and evaluation are carried out across the entire process. The HUCDM was implemented in an Educational Software Small and Medium Enterprise (SME) developer. The first feature based on this methodology was Courseware Sere. The quality of this educational resource has been internationally recognized. This Courseware was finalist in the national contest of multimedia products and thus got the interest of multinational companies such as BP - British Petroleum, which financed a new phase for the product development.

Keywords: Software engineering · Educational software development methodologies · Agile methods · Hybrid user centered development methodology · User centered design

1 Introduction

Software development is a highly complex activity, and in the large majority of cases it occurs without being properly planned, supported only by short-term decisions of [1]. This approach may work for small software packages and projects, but as the system grows, so the difficulty of adding new features also grows. Additionally, Shneiderman and Plaisant [2] state that 60 % of the software development projects fail in setting goals. This particular problem arises because in most projects there is a lack of

© Springer International Publishing Switzerland 2014
Y. Cao et al. (Eds.): ICWL 2014 Workshops, LNCS 8699, pp. 243–253, 2014.
DOI: 10.1007/978-3-319-13296-9_27

communication between team members and between team members and end users. Therefore, choosing the appropriate method for developing software have obvious economic and competitive advantages, gains in terms of quality. However, if a less appropriate development method is selected, the more likely the project will exceed its time limits and problems will arise such as economic problems [3].

As regards software development methods, Sommerville [4] states that the key stages in software development, are common to most methods, comprising: (a) Software specification - software features and constraints on its operation must be completely defined; (b) Software design and implementation - the software to meet the specifications have to be produced; (c) Software validation - the software must be validated to ensure it is what customers/users want; (d) Software development - the software must evolve to meet the requirements of customers/users.

This paper includes a brief theoretical background on the evolution of software development methodologies, referring to examples of methods used in the development of educational software packages. Subsequently, a brief UCD description is made based on the exposition of its assumptions and on its importance for the development of educational software. Next, we present Courseware Sere - The Human Being and the Natural Resources and a description of the HUCDM, featuring the stages, procedures and techniques used. Finally, present some considerations about HUCDM.

2   Educational Software Development Methodologies

The first methods (referred in the literature as disciplined, traditional or classic) derived from the most common processes of software development. The method of water cascading or software development life cycle, emerged in the 70s and provided the theoretical basis for most of the subsequent methods. It is sometimes referred to as a generic method for developing software [4]. However, according to Larman and Basili [5], the iterative and incremental method already was dated back from de 50's and there were concrete examples of projects in the 70's using it. In the 80's emerged, among other methods, spiral and prototyping methods. In the 90's, agile methods and real examples of the integration of iterative and incremental approaches [4–9]. Agile methods such as Extreme Programming (XP), Scrum and Crystal Clear, by involving users in the development process, seek to provide and prioritize new requirements of software and evaluate their iterations. They give focus to the role of people, and the skills of the development team should be recognized and exploited. The team members are free to use their own methods of work without being prescribed obligatory processes [4, 9–13].

Specifically in what regards to the development of educational software, the methods described in the literature, have their genesis in premises of the above methods. Examples are the two methods used in the development of the following software packages (see Table 1): Univap Virtual [14] and Softvali [15].

Although arising with different designations, analysis, design and implementation phases that are able to identify these processes. They were introduced in early proposals for software development methods. In the phase concerning analysis a survey on software requirements, educational objectives and the target audience is performed.

Table 1. Software development main stages

Development stages [4]	Univap Virtual [14]	**Softvali** [15]
Specification	Analysis and Planning	Conception
Design and Implementation	Pre-production	Elaboration and Construction
Validation	Production Post-production	Finalization
Evolution	–	Feasibility Analysis

In the Univap Virtual, at this stage, a survey concerning scientific information on the subject of educational resource is still made.

3   The Role of User Centered Design

UCD is used to describe the processes of a project where end users have large influence and intervention on how it is conducted. Some UCD methods inquire users about the needs they have in a particular educational area, involving them in specific parts of the development process. On the other hand, there are methods in which users have greater presence integrating the team, i.e., they are involved as elements throughout the process [16].

UCD is described in ISO 9241-210 [17] - Ergonomics of Human-System Interaction (210: Human-centered design for interactive systems). This standard describes an ideal situation where there are no barriers to the use of UCD assumptions, except for the possible lack of competence on the part of the development team [18]. Authors like Facer and Williamson [19], among others, emphasize that UCD is a methodology that combines, among other things, the participation of the user and formative evaluation of prototypes. According to ISO 9241-210 [17] standard, UCD projects are governed by six principles: (i) explicit understanding of users, tasks and environments, (ii) establishment of a multidisciplinary team; (iii) interaction between the user and the system; (iv) active involvement of users; (v) user experience; and (vi) the iteration of design solutions.

The methods used to develop the Univap Virtual [14] and Softvali [15] are based on UCD assumptions, including the establishment of multidisciplinary teams, organized by education professionals (researchers from psychology and pedagogy), professionals in the field of computer science, specifically in the area of programming and software engineering, usability designers with usability knowledge and finally teachers and students.

Based on what we described in this section, we completely agree with the report "Quality Framework for UK Government Website Design: Usability issues for government websites", when it argues that UCD is a complement to software development methods and is not a substitute for them [20].

4   Courseware Ser$_e$ Development Methodology: An Approach for SMEs

Courseware Ser$_e$ - The Human Being and Natural Resources, is a resource developed through a partnership between the Education Department of the University of Aveiro that has its focus on the development of educational methodologies and processes and

Ludomedia - Educational and Ludic Contents Company that has its focus on the development of educational software.

Courseware Sere integrates various types of software (including simulations, inquiries and surveys, search, among many others) with didactic activities specified in the exploration guides, both for the teacher as well as for the students. As it can be inferred from its purpose (to promote understanding of the impact that human activity has on natural resources and raise awareness that the future of humanity will go through the adoption of attitudes and more aware and responsible behavior, particularly with regard to sources of energy used, particularly oil and forest), Sere seeks an approach to the relationship between human activity and the exploitation of natural resources, as well as environmental, social and economic consequences of exploration [21].

As an introduction to the didactic exploration of Courseware Sere, it is proposed to display an animation (left screen of Fig. 1) in which problematic situations for Human Beings are displayed related to the depletion of natural resources (focusing on forest biomass and oil). The animation serves as a starting point to a phase of questioning guiding the research work regarding, for example, the use of natural energy resources or exploitation of simulations on the impact that the increase in population and the levels and patterns of oil consumption may have on the access to natural resources.

The software is divided into two main phases: Phase 1 - Oil and Phase 2 – Forests. The phases are not necessarily sequential, i.e., the teacher or student may choose which of the phases and activities to start first on their software exploration.

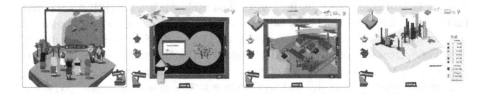

Fig. 1. *Courseware* Ser$_e$ example screens

Regarding the development methodology, the team has addressed the research questions, linked with the implementation of user centered methodologies for developing educational software [22]. Quality factors such as usability, the involvement of end users in all development stages and the creation of multidisciplinary teams, are some of the assumptions that underlie the UCD development methodology of Courseware Sere.

A multidisciplinary team was composed including elements with diverse skills in Science Teaching (ST), Educational Technology (ET), Project Management (PM), Graphical Design (GD), Software Engineering (SE), Computer Programming (CP) and Usability.

In order to reduce the time and cost of development, two of the typical disadvantages of UCD [16], the team opted to involve end-users (teachers and students) just on the resource evaluation tasks. The educational resource (including storyboard) was also subjected to evaluation by experts outside the team [22, 23]. This procedure should always be used regardless of the methodology adopted.

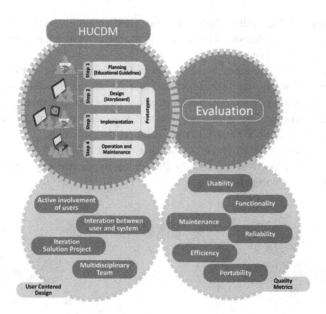

Fig. 2. Hybrid User Centered Development Methodology

Figure 2 summarizes Courseware Sere developing process which is described, in more detail, below.

- **HUCDM Development Stages**

The development stages for HUCDM are the following:

(1) Phase 1, Planning (didactic guides). This stage comprised the development of a document by three experts in Didatic of Sciences and two in Educational Technology with the definition of the resource targeted level of education/audience, the thematic and educational purposes, as well as its architecture, navigation and screen design. This phase also included the trademark and patent registration, as well as, among others, agreements on the authorship rights.

(2) Phase 2 Design (storyboard). This stage harmonized the preliminary ideas for the educational activities and disciplinary content, defined in the previous phase, with the aspects of interaction with the software, particularly navigation and interface, with the collaboration of a designer and a programmer of the company. Such as Bassani, Passerino, Pasqualotti and Ritzel [24] and Carvalho [25], we also consider that the design of scenarios resulting from this phase was essential to understand the context of resource utilization and to represent some of the interactive situations of the software.

(3) Phase 3 Implementation: This stage was divided into two sub-phases that took place simultaneously: (a) The educational part - required the specification in detail of aspects, beyond those specified in the storyboard, as the initial animation and scripts for teachers and students; (b) The technical part – was composed by the software design and programming and the development of the accompanying user manual.

During this task, the multidisciplinary team tested and adjusted the software scripts for screen content exploitation. This involved the permanent cooperation of all elements, in person or online.

Prototypes: The prototypes were developed collaboratively between all team members. Among others, the team identified that the interface aspects have implications for the software architecture, which in some cases led to changes in the educational resource scripts. The prototype software was also used in the development process, in order to explore some software solutions in particular.

During the resource development, the team used three types of prototypes, as it may be seen in Fig. 3 respectively: (a) Early Paper prototypes; (b) key screens; (c) Programmed running prototypes.

Fig. 3. (a) Paper Prototype for a scenario at Phase 2; (b) Characters Selection Screen Prototype; (c) Courseware Ser$_e$ Screen (Phase 1- Petrol)

Evaluation: Intending to evaluate both the resource as its development process. This phase is transversal to all phases described above. The first resource version released, was also the target of evaluation, by:

– Teachers – In the assessment by teachers, the questionnaire for evaluating the technical and didactic Courseware Sere, was answered in workshops (practice sessions with a maximum duration of 120 min in which teachers in groups of two or three elements, exploited two activities of one of the phases of the courseware) by a heterogeneous group of potential users of the resource [23];

– Students - For the evaluation by students a questionnaire on technical and didactic evaluation was answered, after using the resource in classroom context (in 90-minute blocks, students in groups of three to four elements, exploiting the courseware activities, properly planned by the teacher), being in this case a controlled assessment [27].

(4) Phase 4, Operation and Maintenance: This phase included technical and educational error correction, which were not detected in the early stages of the life cycle of the courseware development process. Thus, it is possible to improve the software and implement new functionalities through new requirements that are detected during this process [4, 8]. Three types of maintenance were taken into consideration: corrective, preventive and perfective.

The HUCDM also was based on some principles of agile methods, such as: (a) simplicity, only the essential was developed to answer to current requirements; (b) team (mainly developers) sought to correct and improve the software code continuously; (c) the delivery was incremental, with each screen of the software independent of the other screens. While design solutions were tested/validated/evaluated, others were developed based on the requirements.

- **HUCDM Procedures and Techniques**

To streamline the development process and assuming that the collaborative work is carried out simultaneously in two states: online and face-to-face, HUCDM incorporates the Verification and Validation Procedure (VVP), represented in Fig. 4 workflow. This procedure comes integrated in one of the UCD activities, Project Solutions Production (prototypes), preceding the assessment phase of these solutions, with the end user and/or experts. Support for these activities is conducted using collaborative software (groupware): the Learning Management System (LMS) Moodle[1] platform. Although, this platform is not oriented for software development process management, it was essential to streamline communication between multidisciplinary team elements, to store and distribute documents, discuss ideas, among many other tasks.

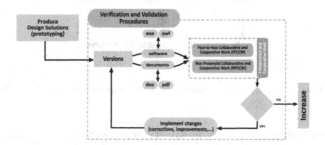

Fig. 4. Verification and Validation Procedures

At the Verification and Validation Procedures (VVP), it is up to the elements of the multidisciplinary team to perform verification and validation of software versions, and versions of documents (guidelines of the teacher and the student, user manual, etc.). Being identified changes to be made, a new version is released at Moodle, for verification and validation. These iterations only end when it is impossible to identify changes to be made.

At the Collaborative Work in Classroom (FFCCW), commonly, it is the project manager who makes a first survey of the points to be discussed at the in-person meetings. These points are ordered by importance and/or areas, being previously sent to the members of the multidisciplinary team. To facilitate this task a mailing list or forum called "News and Announcements" is used. The FFCCW is recorded through audio recording (see Fig. 5).

When identified changes to be made on NPCCW, these are made available on the platform. In this context, the tools (resources, activities and blocks modules) used

---

[1] *Moodle* is a learning support freeware software that works in a virtual environment.

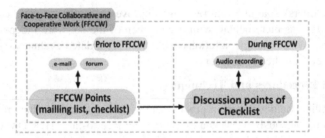

Fig. 5. Face-to-Face Collaborative and Cooperative Work (FFCCW)

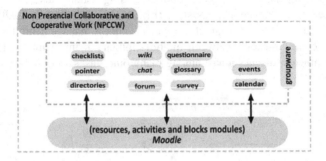

Fig. 6. Non Presencial Collaborative and Cooperative Work (NPCCW)

(see Fig. 6) on Collaborative Work in Non Traditional (NPCCW), promote and allow greater interaction between the members of the multidisciplinary team.

Moodle is a software for managing, learning and collaborative work which enables the creation of working groups and learning communities. The work environment was created consisting of three main sections: (a) Blocks, are available vertically on the left or right side, allowing you to enter, for example, the schedule or calendar of events; (b) Resources, allow the insertion of documents, images, make links to external documents through, for example, directories, glossaries; (c) Modules of activities (tasks), provide tools that allow you to promote debate and discussion, such as forums, chats, referendums.

The collaborative and cooperative work "was grown" during the development of Courseware Sere, allowing greater accuracy in the tasks. For example, tasks essentially techniques were performed cooperatively, since the manager of the project subdivided into several interdependent subtasks (thus revealing a functional hierarchy). Collaborative work (face and not face) served mainly to create new design solutions based on user requirements, by developing prototypes later evaluated [23, 26, 27]. During the development of design solutions (prototypes), designers, illustrators conceived a first prototype screen and through the tools available in Moodle, it was discussed and then improved. Only later, programmers added the prototype to the main structure of the educational software. One can show that the collaborative work functioned as the "engine" of the project, having leveraged cooperative work through the tasks' commitment. The collaborative and cooperative work, sat on iterative and incremental processes, is essential to obtain a thorough and timely feedback to the changes of coordination requirements.

5 Conclusions

Although the methods choice depends on the environment in which the project operates and of a set of variables that are sometimes difficult to define, there are methods to help on software development, minimizing uncertainty, to allow obtaining the expected result in the most efficient way possible. As Toth [3] and Sommerville [4], we consider that the adoption of the same approach for all software development projects is unlikely to be a good choice. Mostly if we take into account the diversity of users, software purpose of use and constant changes in technology.

Based on the work developed we agree with Abbas, Gravell and Wills [28], which describe software development as an unpredictable activity, that an adaptive method to control this unpredictability is required. Regarding the development of educational software, iterative and incremental processes associated with prototyping procedures, including monitoring and evaluation tools in different phases, are an efficient way for a given process to be able to adapt itself to changing requirements and technology [26]. In parallel, we reviewed and are also in accordance with Abras, Maloney-Krichmar and Preece [16], that two of the disadvantages of UCD, are concerned with the projects requiring more time to be developed and thus become more expensive. However and according Shneiderman and Plaisant [2], UCD methods allow the software to create fewer problems during development and thus reducing costs in the maintenance phase that is typically considered the most expensive on the software lifecycle [29].

Assuming that, in particular when developing educational software, all processes require practices that lead to continuous improvement, we conclude that the Hybrid Methodology for User-Centered Development is a very good solution for the development of educational software. The methodology was used to develop Courseware Sere whose quality has been recognized by end user, particularly as a finalist of a multimedia product competition and having succeeded in arousing the interest of a multinational company such as BP – British Petrol [22].

References

1. Fowler, M.: The New Methodology (2005). http://www.martinfowler.com/articles/newMethodology.html (2008)
2. Shneiderman, B., Plaisant, C.: Designing the User Interface - Strategies for Effective Human-Computer Interaction. 4th edn., 652 p. Pearson Education, Boston (2005)
3. Toth, K.: Which is the Right Software Process for Your Problem? (2005)
4. Sommerville, I.: Software Engineering, 8th edn., 840 p. Addison Wesley, Boston (2007)
5. Larman, C., Basili, V.R.: Iterative and incremental development: a brief history. IEEE Comput. Soc. 36(6), 47–56 (2003)

6. Boehm, B.: Get ready for agile methods, with care. Computer (Long. Beach. Calif) **35**(1), 64–69 (2002)

7. Boehm, B., Turner, R.: Observations on balancing discipline and agility. In: Proceedings of Agile Development Conference 2003, ADC, pp. 32–39 (2003)

8. Miguel, A.: Gestão de Projectos de Software. FCA - Editora de Informática, 498 p. (2003)

9. Paelke, V., Nebe, K.: Integrating agile methods for mixed reality design space exploration. In: Proceedings of 7th ACM Conference on Designing Interactive Systems (DIS'08), pp. 240–249 (2008)

10. Beck, K.: Extreme Programming Explained: Embrace Change. Addison-Wesley, Reading (2000)

11. Bergin, J., Caristi, J., Dubinsky, Y., Hazzan, O., Williams, L.: Teaching software development methods: the case of extreme programming. In: SIGCSE '04, Norfolk, Virginia (2004)

12. Keith, E.R.: Agile Software Development Processes - A Different Aprroach to Software Design (2002). http://www.cs.nyu.edu/courses/spring03/V22.0474-001/lectures/agile/AgileDevelopmentDifferentApproach.pdf (2009)

13. Petersen, R.R., Wiil, U.K.: ASAP : a planning tool for agile software development. In: Proceedings of the Nineteenth ACM Conference on Hypertext and Hypermedia (HT'08), pp. 27–31 (2008)

14. Bicudo, S.F., Nogueira, T., Oliveira, G.S., Machuca, V.F., Romero, J.P.F., Montenegro, E., Oliveira, C.E., Tanaka, N.F., Prado, M.S., Leon, Í.O.R. e Júnior, L.C.F.: Projecto e Desenvolvimento de Jogos Educativos em 3 Dimensões: a experiência da Univap Virtual (2007)

15. Benitti, F.B.V., Schlindwein, L.M.: Processo de Desenvolvimento de Software Educacional: proposta e experimentação. CINTED-UFRGS. Novas Tecnol. na Educ. **3**(1), 1–10 (2005)

16. Abras, C., Maloney-krichmar, D., Preece, J.: User-Centered Design, pp. 1–14 (2004)

17. ISO9241-210. Ergonomics of Human-System Interaction (210: Human-centred design for interactive systems). Geneva: International Standards Organisation (2010)

18. Svanaes, D., Gulliksen, J.: Understanding the context of design - towards tactical user centered design. In: Proceedings of the 5th Nordic Conference on Human-Computer Interaction: Building Bridges (NordiCHI2008), pp. 353–362 (2008)

19. Facer, K., Williamson, B.: Designing educational technologies with users - a handbook from Futurelab (2004). http://www.futurelab.org.uk/resources/documents/handbooks/designing_with_users.pdf (2009)

20. e-Envoy: Quality Framework for UK Government Website Design: Usability issues for government websites (2003)

21. Sá, P., Guerra, C., Martins, I.P., Loureiro, M.J., Costa, A.P., Reis, L.P.: Development of computerized educational resources in the field of education for sustainable development. Example of Courseware Sere. Journal Eureka about Enseñanza y Divulgación de las Ciencias **7**, 330–345 (2010)

22. Costa, A.P., Loureiro, M.J., Reis, L.P.: Hybrid user-centered development methodology applied to educational software. Iberian J. Inf. Syst. Technol. – RISTI **6**, 1–15 (2010)

23. Costa, A.P., Loureiro, M.J., Reis, L.P., Sá, P., Guerra, C.: Courseware sere: technical and didactic evaluation. In: V International Conference on Multimedia and ICT in Education (m-ICTE2009), Lisbon, pp. 1–5 (2009)

24. Bassani, P.S., Passerino, L.M., Pasqualotti, P.R., Ritzel, M.I.: In search of a methodology for the development of collaborative educational software. Em busca de uma proposta metodológica para o desenvolvimento de software educativo colaborativo. New Technologies in Education **4**(1), 1–10 (2006)

25. Carvalho, C.V.: Basic concepts for the multimedia courses development - Trainer Manual. 1st edn., p. 64, Portuguese Society for Innovation, Oporto (2003)
26. Costa, A.P., Loureiro, M.J., Reis, L.P. (eds.): Hybrid User Centered Development Methodology: The Practical Case of Courseware Sere. In: Iberian Association of Systems and Information Technology (ed.) 5ª Iberian Conference on Information Systems and Technologies (CISTI2010), AISTI, Santiago de Compostela, Spain, pp. 192–197 (2010)
27. Costa, A.P., Loureiro, M.J., Reis, L.P. (eds.): Courseware Sere: Technical and Didactic Evaluation made by Students. In: Iberian Association of Systems and Information Technology (ed.) 5ª Iberian Conference on Information Systems and Technologies (CISTI2010), AISTI, Santiago de Compostela, Spain, pp. 198–203 (2010)
28. Abbas, N., Gravell, A.M., Wills, G.B.: Historical Roots of Agile Methods: Where did Agile Thinking' Come from?, Limerick, Irlanda, pp. 1–10 (2008)
29. Duim, L., Andersson, J., Sinnema, M.: Good practices for educational software engineering projects. In: Proceedings of the 29th International Conference on Software Engineering, Minneapolis, USA, pp. 698–707. IEEE Computer Society (2007)

Observing the Use of e-Textbooks in the Classroom: Towards "Offline" Learning Analytics

Maka Eradze, Terje Väljataga, and Mart Laanpere[✉]

Institute of Informatics, Tallinn University, Narva mnt 25, 10120 Tallinn, Estonia
{Maka.Eradze,Terjev,Mart.Laanpere}@tlu.ee

Abstract. Learning analytics is an emerging approach that is equally popular among researchers and educators-practitioners. Although the methods and tools for LA have been developing fast, there still exist several unsolved problems: LA is too much data driven, weakly connected to theory and is able to analyse only the activities documented in an online setting - in LMS. We propose a solution for the LA unit of analysis drawing upon the research of existing practices and tools used for offline contexts: the data is coming from the physical learning interactions based on the observations in the classroom setting and captured with classroom observation application. We argue that if the unit of analysis has a particular logic and structure, it can unleash the possibilities for "offline" analytics that can be later integrated with online LA.

Keywords: LEARMIX · Learning analytics · eTextbooks · Unit of analysis · TinCan API · xAPI

1 Introduction

Textbooks have been playing an important part in teaching and learning in the formal education context for more than one century. As the textbook publishers, editors and authors are the most careful readers and implementers of curricula and subject-related news, the textbooks have gained large impact in educational development. On the other hand, widespread use of printed textbooks is hindering the advancement of modern learning analytics, as the learning activities that take place outside of digital realm leave no digital trace behind. Emerging e-textbooks might change a lot in that sense, but it depends on the approach taken in e-textbook development. Currently, the majority of e-textbooks are released either as e-books (in epub, mobi, pdf formats), apps or content packages integrated into online course (e.g. SCORM or CommonCartridge). In most of the cases, only the latter format allows acquiring rich data about learning interactions in a standardized format. LEARNMIX project in Tallinn University aims at exploring alternative forms for e-textbooks of the future that should support innovative pedagogical scenarios and advanced learning analytics. But even if most of the textbooks and other learning resources will be turned into digital format, there will remain many learning activities that will take place in the physical classroom setting without leaving any digital trace behind for learning analytics. The research problem addressed by this

Y. Cao et al. (Eds.): ICWL 2014 Workshops, LNCS 8699, pp. 254–263, 2014.
DOI: 10.1007/978-3-319-13296-9_28

exploratory study was to find out the existing approaches and tools for collecting learning analytics data in the offline settings.

2 Unit of Analysis in Education and Computer Supported Collaborative Learning

When addressing research questions, it is important to have a consistent and theory driven unit of analysis. The discussion on the different *units of analysis,* approaches and developments throughout centuries and the philosophical stances they take on is important when it comes to learning analytics and its *unit of analysis.*

Educational research concentrates on different *units of analysis*; Stahl [1] discusses the issue of *unit of analysis* in cognition that had different foci in different times: *concepts* (Plato), *mental and material objects* (Descartes) (and relationship between them), *observable physical objects* (empiricism), *mind's structuring categorization efforts* (Kant). All of the approaches dealt with the inner functions of an individual mind. Hegel entered the discussion with a larger unit of analysis – which was historically, socially and culturally determined.

Hegel's philosophy shaped three mainstream schools of thought – Marx (critical social theory), Heidegger (existential phenomenology) and Wittgenstein (linguistic analysis). To Stahl, these three main directions influence how the CSCL units of analysis are formed: For Heidegger the unit of analysis was the *man with unified experience of being-in-the-world.* Wingenstein entered the discussion with the *unit of analysis* from *mental meanings* to *interpersonal communications in the context of getting something done together.*

In some cases CSCL research takes socio-cognitive or socio-cultural approaches. But in both cases the *unit of analysis* is mostly *an individual mind.* Engestrom is the one taking the unit of analysis to the whole *activity system.* But to Stahl's understanding Engestrom's theory is not interested in group knowledge building but rather with organizational management of the group. Influenced by Marx, theory tries to see societal issues in the making. Even in distributed cognition, which deals with group-cognitive phenomena, mostly socio-technical systems and highly developed artifacts are analyzed [1].

3 Learning Analytics: The Concept, the State of the Art

One of the leading definitions of learning analytics suggests that it is *the measurement, collection, analysis and reporting of data about learners and their contexts, for purposes of understanding and optimizing learning and the environments in which it occurs.* This definition had been set out at the 1st International Conference on Learning Analytics and Knowledge [2]. The field is still emerging, rapidly developing and experiencing *a gradual shift away from technology towards an educational focus,* while the three main drivers for learning analytics have been defined as technological, pedagogical and political/economic [3].

These drivers are conceptualized by Ferguson as challenges [3]:

- Big Data - a challenge for its volume, difficulty to handle the interaction data and most importantly extracting value from the big data-sets.
- Online Learning that poses an educational challenge - how to optimize opportunities for online learning.
- Political Concerns - how to improve learning opportunities and results at different levels?

According to Ferguson the drivers draw attention to the three groups of interest - governments, educational institutions and teachers/learners. The development of learning analytics shifts the balance between the three drivers and three groups.

Greller and Draschler give a general framework of learning analytics [4] and offer considering six critical dimensions within the research lens. Each of the dimensions can have several values and it can be extended upon a need. Represented dimensions are: stakeholders, objectives, data, instruments, external constraints and internal constraints.

Greller and Draschler also give a model of information flow between the stakeholders and it is based on a common hierarchical model of the formal education. A pyramid view (with the learner as a cornerstone) is illustrating how data analysis from lower layer can inform the above layer. According to Buckingam Shum the convergence of the Macro, Meso and micro levels is the key to the successful learning analytics [5].

3.1 Units of Analysis in LA

When we are to consider what has to be analyzed and what information do we need to infer using LA, firstly, the level of learning analytics must be defined. The interest groups may overlap but different granularities are needed for different groups: *The choice of target audience affects how researchers conceptualize problems, capture data, report findings, predict what will happen, act on their findings and refine their models* [3]. Within the context of our research interest the micro-level, teacher/learner learning analytics should be directed to the activity, an event consisting of interaction between **a subject** and **an object** that are bound with **a verb.** There is a need for theory driven, event oriented unit of analysis [6, 7].

Suthers et al. with the uptake framework proposed that the event is the core for analyzing data and understanding which interactions lead to learning [9]. The *Uptake Framework* [7, 9] assumes that interaction is fundamentally relational, so the most important unit of analysis is not isolated acts, but mostly relationships between acts.

Conceptualizing the Uptake Framework hierarchies and the possibilities of learning analytics, it has also been suggested to view Learning Flow as a main unit of analysis for the learning interaction analysis [7].

3.2 Limitations of LA and Potential of xAPI

Most of the tools for gathering the learning analytics data are directed to the closed LMS systems, while the most of the learning happens outside the LMS - in distributed setting or offline part of the learning which is most of learning. Currently, LA covers only the part of the learning that happens within the LMSs. In most of the cases, LMSs data is harvested and analyzed. The problem is that it is not enough. Siemens believes, that LMSs are adopted as learning analytics tools and reflect the learner's interactions within a system. The capabilities of tracking and visualisation of interaction data has also been limited [3, 8].

The similar problem persists with the physical world i.e. offline "data" - library uses, learning support, in case of blended learning - the part of the learning that happens outside of LMS, online or offline. Long and Siemens suggest mobile devices as prospects of *"bridging the divide between the physical and digital worlds"* [8].

One way of dealing with the limitations of leveraging the data from the settings outside LMS is to explore potential of Experience API [10]. The Experience API is a service that allows for statements of experience (typically learning experiences, but could be any experience) to be delivered to and stored securely in a Learning Record Store. Learning activity is a unit of instruction, experience or performance that has to be tracked. A Statement consists of <Actor (learner)> <verb> <object>, with <result>, in <context> to track an aspect of a learning experience. Several statements can be used to track the whole experience. The statements are recorded in the LRS - Learning Record Store [10].

Another problem with learning analytics within the limits of the current development is a weak connection to theory. This limitation of data monitoring and harvesting could be overcome by having a particular theory in mind before recording the data [7].

Our paper targets the "offline" analytics dilemma and explores the potential of xAPI and Uptake Framework working together towards a new type of *unit of analysis* in the context of learning analytics.

3.3   Ethical Considerations

It should not be argued that the privacy of the data subjects must be protected. There are several factors influencing the process of protection that can work against individual freedoms (if privacy is abused) or restrict using the full potential of LA. We believe these two factors shall be balanced. According to Hilderbrandt [11], the core of privacy must be found itself in the idea of identity and this is not only because of the advancement of high-tech identification technologies but also because the process of identity building can harm the privacy of individuals.

Slade et al. [12] believe that students shall be involved in the data harvesting and analysis. According to Kruse et al. [13] there should be a "student-centric", as opposed to an "intervention-centric", approach to learning analytics. This suggests the student should be seen as stakeholders of their own data. And also as co-interpreters of own data - and perhaps even as participants in the identification and gathering of that data. Greller et al. [4] list the ethical side of the use of personal data in the external limitations of learning analytics.

Based on the literature overview, currently we may refer to some of the solutions for data privacy protection: 1. Involving students [data subjects] in the process, make it transparent and make it a student analytics. 2. Anonymization/deidentification of data. 3. Consent forms.

4   eTextbook Analytics

4.1   Studies on eTextbooks Use

According to Baek et al. [14] *in order to effectively support students' learning, it is important to comprehend students' experiences using eTextbooks.* There are several possibilities to understand the patterns of use for future inferences – 1. For the deployment of appropriate pedagogic strategies 2. For student self-reporting 3. For decision making processes – in terms of the design and etc.

Research on the use of eTextbooks mainly focus on the issues of satisfaction of use, preference of use over traditional textbooks and other factors [15–18]; The study conducted by Baek et al. [14] in the various campuses of US focuses on the understanding of students' eTextbook use experiences. This study used surveys to assess students' perceptions of the eTextbook in terms of satisfaction and ease of use. Cutshall et al. [17] also assessed perceptions on the use of etextbooks and web-based homeworks. When assessing the use of eTextbooks logs were only used to understand student reading behaviors (number of page prints) and correlated to the satisfactions of use [18].

An example of analytics in eTextbooks is a research conducted by Nicholas et al. [19] using the data from digital footprints on (a) volume, duration and timing of use; (b) where use took place; (c) individual book titles used; (d) location of use; (e) type of page viewed; (f) institutional and subject diversity; (g) scatter of use; (h) nature of use; and (i) method of searching/navigating. The log data were analysed to describe how users interacted with the system. The authors, though, conclude that *logs only provide us with a very superficial idea of who the e-book users were (their institutional affiliation was known), so for a better picture we have to turn to the questionnaires.* Khurana et al. [20] deployed text analytics to assess the coverage, readability and comprehensibility of eTextbooks. They use different units of analysis: sections, bookmarks, topics, sub-topics.

Having a goal to build an open source online eTextbook for DSA courses integrating textbook quality text with algorithm visualization and interactive exercises, Fouh et al. [21] concentrate on the development of a OpenDSA interactive eTextbook where they also incorporate a kind learning analytics – mainly for the self-reporting for students, and also inferring meaning from student-content interactions for "studying the pedagogical effectiveness for various approaches and support for gathering data about usability of system components for future improvement. So the unit of analysis is mainly student-content interaction centered. The study on the use of the eTextbook was aimed at the student perceived satisfaction evaluation and a test whether the eTextbook helped reduce the grading burden.

Studies on eTextbook use are developed around the ideas of satisfaction of use or reading behaviors. *Units of analysis* are individual student perceptions and sometimes student-content interactions to gain insight on reading behaviors, not the analysis of the design or pedagogical rationale behind it. Very often, when the study aims at uncovering the learning design principles of an eTextbook, it does not refer to the possibilities of learning analytics as for instance, in case of the study of Choi et al. [22].

4.2 Offline Learning Analytics: Observing the Use of Textbooks in the Classroom Lesson Observation Apps: Critical View

Two different approaches can be used in the eTextbook use observations: taking advantage of online data coming from clicks, resource access etc. and "offline" analytics with its wide range of possible interactions, written in different statements and formats.

Classroom observation apps are very useful tools for recording classroom learning interactions on the use of textbooks in "offline' settings. For this particular observation study we overviewed and compared 6 classroom observation apps based on particular requirements. These applications are: LessonNote, iObserve, Observation 360, iAspire, GoObserve, SCOA. Applications were chosen according to their free access to at least demo versions.

The applications were compared considering several features: 1. Interface affordances 2. The ways of input 3. Pedagogic scenario/model 4. Output of the generated data 5. Possibilities of analytics and most important part of our research scope 6. Units of analysis. The features were chosen based on the importance to the scope of the research. The table describes the proportion of certain features used in those applications (Table 1).

Table 1. Application comparison

Feature	Value					
Interface	Tapping .6	Drag&drop .1	Sliders .3			
input	Handwritting .09	Typing .36	Photo .27	Audio .09	Video .09	Other .09
Scenario/ model	Based on a spec.model .5	Based on several models .33	Flexibility of switching models 0	Neutral .17		
Output	.pdf .25	Cvs .0	Word .08	Email .42	database/ cloud .25	
Analytics	No analytics .31	No datasets .15	visualisations 0.31	datasets/ cloud .3		
Unit of analysis	individual/ teacher .43	individual/ student .14	Event/activity .07	Group .07	Class .29	individual/ teacher .43

Based on the overview LessonNote app was chosen for it represents the closest possible app to what we have envisioned for the use in observations, namely for its event-driven *unit of analysis*.

5 Empirical Study

In the remaining part of the paper we will describe our effort to use a LessonNote application for supporting the collection of offline learning analytics while observing the use of textbooks in the classroom settings. We will continue with analysing and demonstrating benefits and drawbacks of LessonNote application for recording offline learning analytics. The study mainly focuses on the *unit of analysis* and its importance in the "offline" analytics based on the classroom observation application.

5.1   Method and Sample

In the context of Learnmix project we carried out an intervention study in K-12 education. Our aim was to intervene into current teaching and learning practices with the purpose to enable learners to become actively engaged constructors of their own experience and knowledge by creating, modifying and integrating various physical, and digital artefacts. For that we designed five different scenarios (flipped- classroom, project-based learning, game-based learning, inquiry-based learning, problem-based learning) for teachers to choose from and implement it in her/his lessons. In these scenarios the role and use of textbooks changed from textbooks as an object of knowledge construction to textbooks as a source of inspiration, etc. We have to mention here that we do not treat the aforementioned list of scenarios as a definite one, but rather as a starting set of potential scenarios for enabling students to become constructors of their own experience and knowledge in the midst of the digital transformation.

We observed 12 lessons in 6 different K-12 schools. These schools were chosen because of their more advanced IT infrastructure and teachers with open-minded learning and teaching practices. For documenting the flow of a lesson and emerging interactions we made use of LessonNote application. LessonNote application allowed timing, recording photos of student work and activities, which were inserted into the notes; and creating seating charts. As an additional tool we video recorded all the observed lessons. For the research described in this paper the videos didn't play an essential role.

For understanding the use of (e-)textbooks in the aforementioned scenarios we created a framework for extracting the statements of students and teachers' experience (learning flow) in a similar way to Experience API. Our framework consists of three main items:

1. Actors - a teacher or student(s) specifying whether the activity was done in groups, peers or individually.
2. Artifacts - artifacts were divided into three groups:
   - Display artifacts are physical objects in the classroom (for instance computer, projector, screen) whose function is to display conveyor artifacts. Display artifacts themselves are not representations of knowledge, but are seen as carriers for other artifacts.
   - Conveyor artifacts are various applications, which support the mediation or creation of knowledge representations (for instance iBooks, Prezi, Weblog, etc.). The affordances of conveyor artifacts very often define potential actions.
   - Content artifacts are representations of knowledge displayed in different formats (for instance text, video, image), which are created by professional textbook authors, by teachers, by students or others.

3. Actions - actions performed by a teacher or student(s) during the learning experience.

Such a framework allowed us to focus on specific actions and every accompanying (digital) artifact used or created before and during the learning experience. Furthermore, for our intervention study it was important for us to determine the role of students and teachers in learning experiences (whether a teacher or a student is a creator of an (digital) artifact, whether a student takes control and responsibility for what he/she is doing, etc.).

5.2   Results and Discussion

We implemented our analytical framework to our data set extracted from LessonNote application and video transcript. Despite of its many useful affordances, such as allowing recording activities according to timeline, shooting photos and adding them to a particular activity, LessonNote application also has some deficiencies. With the following 2 examples we demonstrate the deficiencies of LessonNote application as a tool for supporting the collection of offline learning analytics and translating its data into a form that supports Experience API statements and Uptake framework (Table 2).

Table 2. Results

Activities	LessonNote activities	Video transcript: (Subject verb object)
Teacher activity		Teacher organizes class **Teacher gives assignment** Teacher forms groups
		Group A moves out **Group A organizes tools** Group A starts a discussion

In the table we presented examples from the LessonNote app aligned with data coming from video transcripts. Video transcripts were produced by two researchers putting in the matrix compatible with xAPI statements. The examples brought here demonstrate how the LessonNote app captured activities and what can be extracted from videos. LessonNote captures one particular activity (shown in bold) and with video and later analysis it is possible to capture *preceding* and *proceeding* activities with the LessonNote captured activity encapsulated by the two (and more). But also this is to show that it is possible to structure the data in the form of Experience API compatible statements.

5.3 Conclusion and Future Work

The intervention study showed that it is possible to transcribe the interaction data in the form of statements, but recording "offline" interactions with LessonNote app did not offer satisfactory results for several reasons:

1. It proved to have interface problems – it is not possible to handwrite data as it is happening in real time.
2. It does not capture nested activities.
3. It does not allow quick documentation of activities.
4. It has no enough affordances, for instance it is not possible to define/form groups and assign numbers for later analysis.
5. Though it more or less focuses on event as a unit of analysis, it does not give full possibilities to automatize the process.
6. It does not show the dyadic interactions - who is interacting with whom.

Based on the overview of classroom applications and the empirical study we plan to develop a classroom observation application to be used on offline observations and learning analytics. This application will cover the gaps and offer "offline" analytical features that can potentially be aligned with online data. The application will be based on the overview of the similar applications and xAPI statement and event-driven *unit of analysis.*

References

1. Stahl, G.: Theories of cognition in collaborative learning. In: Hmelo-Silver, C., O'Donnell, A., Chan, C., Chinn, C. (eds.) International Handbook of Collaborative Learning. Taylor & Francis, New York (2012)
2. Learning Analytics & Knowledge, Banff, Alberta, February 27–March 1 2011. https://tekri.athabascau.ca/analytics/
3. Ferguson, R.: The state of learning analytics in 2012: a review and future challenges. Technical report KMI-12-01, Knowledge Media Institute, The Open University, UK (2012)
4. Greller, W., Drachsler, H.: Translating learning into numbers: a generic framework for learning analytics. Educ. Technol Soc. **15**(3), 42–57 (2012)
5. Buckingam, S.S.: Learning Analytics. UNESCO Policy Brief, Enhancing Teaching and Learning Through Educational Data Mining and Learning Analytics: An Issue Brief U.S. Department of Education Office of Educational Technology (2012)
6. Barab, S.A., Evans, M.A., Baek, E.O.: Activity theory as a lens for characterizing the participatory unit. In: Jonassen, D.H. (ed.) Handbook of research on educational communications and technology, pp. 199–214. Lawrence Erlbaum Associates, Mahwah (2004)

7. Eradze, M., Pata, K., Laanpere, M.: Analyzing learning flows in digital learning ecosystems. In: Huang, Y.-M., Li, F., Jin, Q. (Toim.) Knowledge Management and E-learning. LNCS, pp. 1–10. Springer, Heidelberg (in press)

8. Long, P., Siemens, G.: http://www.educause.edu/ero/article/penetrating-fog-analytics-learning-and-education (2011). Accessed 20 June 2014

9. Suthers, D. D., Rosen, D.: A unified framework for multi-level analysis of distributed learning. In: Proceedings of the First International Conference on Learning Analytics and Knowledge, pp. 64–74. ACM, Banff, New York (2010)

10. Experience API Specification. http://tincanapi.wikispaces.com/file/view/Experience+API +Release+v0.95.pdf. Accessed 20 June 2014

11. Hildebrandt, M.: Privacy and identity. In: Claes, E., Duff, A., Gutwirth, S. (eds.) Privacy and the Criminal Law, pp. 61–104. Intersentia, Antwerp/Oxford (2006)

12. Slade, S., Prinsloo, P.: Learning analytics: ethical issues and dilemmas. Am. Behav. Sci. **57** (10), 1509–1528 (2013)

13. Kruse, A., Pongsajapan, R.: Student-Centered Learning Analytics. https://cndls.georgetown.edu/m/documents/thoughtpaper-krusepongsajapan.pdf (2012). Accessed 20 June 2014

14. Baek, E., Monagham, J.: Journey to textbook affordability: an investigation of students' use of eTextbooks at multiple campuses. Int. Rev. Res Open Distance Learn. [S.l.] **14**(3), 1–26 (2013). ISSN 1492-3831. http://www.irrodl.org/index.php/irrodl/article/view/1237. Accessed 6 June 2014

15. Weisberg, S.: Student attitudes and behaviors towards digital textbooks. Publishing Res. Q. **27**, 188–196 (2011). Springer

16. Dennis, A.: e-Textbooks at Indiana University: A Summary of Two Years of Research. http://etexts.iu.edu/files/eText%20Pilot%20Data%202010-2011.pdf. Accessed 6 June 2014

17. Cutshall, R.C., Mollick J.S., M. Bland E.M.: Use of an e-Textbook and web-based homework for an undergraduate business course: students' perceptions. J. Acad. Bus. Educ. **10** (2009)

18. Falc, E.O.: Assessment of college students' attitudes towards using an online e-textbook. Interdisc. J. E-learn. Learn. Objects **9**, 1–12 (2013)

19. Nicholas, D.: E-textbook use, information seeking behaviour and its impact: case study business and management. J. Inf. Sci. **36**(2), 263–280 (2010)

20. Khurana S., Relan, M. Singh, V.K.A.: Text analytics-based approach to compute coverage, readability and comprehensibility of eBooks. In: 2013 Sixth International Conference on Contemporary Computing (IC3) (2013)

21. Fouh, E., Karavirta, V., Breakiron, D.A., Sally Hamouda, S., Hall, S., Naps, T.L., Shaffer, C. A.: Design and architecture of an interactive eTextbook – the OpenDSA system. Sci. Comput. Program. **88**, 22–40 (2014)

22. Choi, J.-I., Heo, H., Lim, K.Y., Jo, I.-H.: The development of an interactive digital textbook in middle school English. In: Kim, T.-h, Adeli, H., Slezak, D., Sandnes, F.E., Song, X., Chung, K.-i, Arnett, K.P. (eds.) FGIT 2011. LNCS, vol. 7105, pp. 397–405. Springer, Heidelberg (2011)

Re-conceptualising E-textbooks:
In Search for a Descriptive Framework

Terje Väljataga[✉] and Sebastian H.D. Fiedler

Centre for Educational Technology, Tallinn University, Tallinn, Estonia
{terje.valjataga, fiedler}@tlu.ee

Abstract. The goal of this workshop paper is to present our first steps towards reconceptualising e-textbooks in the context of a research and development project called Learnmix. We propose an initial descriptive framework that helps us to gain a comprehensive understanding of students as active constructors of their knowledge while operating with numerous (digital) content items and mediating artefacts.

Keywords: E-textbooks · Digitisation · K-12 education · Descriptive framework

1 Introduction

Whenever a new tool or technology comes along there is the potential for disruption to the existing order of activity and practice. According to Smith et al. [11] in the field of e-textbooks disruption comes mainly in two forms: "e-[text]books can enable us to do the same things but in different ways, but they can also enable us to do different things – things that we were not able to easily do before they arrived or even do at all" (p. 50).

So far the evolution of the textbook is predominantly driven by economic considerations - from the printing press to digital production, and from digital production to digital distribution [12] - thus, creating a situation, where we continue doing the same things but in slightly different ways. This simple content digitisation that currently forms the basis for many contemporary e-textbook initiatives serves as yet another example for the rather restricted and uninspired ways in which ICT is used in today's classrooms and schools, basically recreating traditional teaching and studying approaches with some digital means [5]. However, it is quite obvious that the ongoing digital transformation enables us to do much more with content than just merely digitising it.

That means the evolution of the textbook has left many issues of educational practice untouched, although the socio-technological landscape of our societies is increasingly dominated by digitisation and networking. Apparently, the development rather follows what Fischer and Scharff [4] had so aptly called the "gift wrapping approach" in which digital technology is merely wrapped around old frameworks for education.

To overcome this state of affairs we need more analytically driven efforts that follow a research rationale that is based on a notion of systemic intervention into

© Springer International Publishing Switzerland 2014
Y. Cao et al. (Eds.): ICWL 2014 Workshops, LNCS 8699, pp. 264–273, 2014.
DOI: 10.1007/978-3-319-13296-9_29

current educational practice [12], taking into account affordances of technology and its potential to fundamentally change learning and teaching experiences.

2   Breaking Down the Textbooks

In the midst of the unfolding digital transformation the textbook will most likely go through thorough changes over time. An ever-widening range of digital artefacts is constantly transforming our daily lives as we communicate, play, learn, and work with and through them. Digitising any kind of material allows us to compartmentalise content into smaller pieces, which can be easily reused, modified and adapted according to one's specific needs. At the same time constantly changing configuration of technologies and applications are creating more options and triggers for users (thus also for learners) to take control and initiative to manipulate with various artefacts.

Our literature review on attempts to re-conceptualise the notion of e-textbooks demonstrated the trend, in which e-textbooks were mainly seen as digital versions of paper-based textbooks (see [12]). However, we found a few promising position papers that argued for a more ambitious kind of change. For instance, Salpeter [9] in her paper refers to Matt Federoff, director of technology for the Vail School District (Arizona), who has claimed that "the textbook delivery model is out of gas. No job in the world says read the chapter and answer the questions at the end of the book... Why should we take pre-packaged bulky content and try to shoehorn it into what we need to teach?" The proposed closest possible alternative is "the iTunes model" which allows for buying individual songs rather than the whole album. Similarly, instead of acquiring the whole textbook, a teacher might want to use only some parts of it. Since such a system of provision is already available for video and music content, some think it could easily be transferred to the field of learning and teaching [8].

Davy [3] takes a similar stance in suggesting that professionally authored content items should be clustered around a specific learning objective, rather than providing a complete textbook. In this model the textbook becomes a resource, which is broken down into its components that can be accessed in a number of different ways. Butler [1] envisions a practice in which teachers can customise e-textbooks as aggregations of various materials, not just what a single publisher has already aggregated in a particular package. However, the report delivered by MindCET [7] warns us that we are running "the risk of taking the digital textbook to become a collection of digital items, missing the main educational message of offering a meaningful educational learning environment" (p. 2).

These authors want to do away with textbooks and the "all done by the textbook"-approach entirely - no matter if its realised on print or via digital material. They claim that textbooks are becoming less and less useful, both to students and instructors [6]. They see it as increasingly problematic that both textbooks and e-textbooks are designed to be worked through in a linear fashion - from beginning to end [1] - by learners and teachers alike.

Furthermore, if teachers have an opportunity to customise digital content, rearrange and modify digital artefacts, or combine them with physical ones, then why should learners not be enabled to do the same? This idea was already pondered by Warlick [13], for example, he wrote:

"Think for a minute about learning environments where one of the jobs of the student is to research, select, collect, organise, and adapt content from various re-sources and assemble that information into a growing and evolving digital textbook, supervised both directly and digitally by the teacher. The student's textbook would be crafted for his or her learning style, special interests, and personal sense of visual preference. Teachers would monitor their students' textbooks by suggesting additional resources, questioning others, and supporting the ongoing assembly" (p. 29).

In this vision students become producers of their learning resources rather than just mere consumers. They become contributors of knowledge by offering their own interpretations, explanations and examples [8]. These deliberations are well aligned with the work of Scardamalia and Bereiter [10] who - over 20 years ago – conceived of students as a resource that had been largely wasted in formal education and that could be brought into play through pervasive technology. With appropriate procedural and technical support, students can construct their own knowledge by incorporating and elaborating on content items that are professionally developed by instructional designers, teachers, and so forth. Students as creators are expected to gain more profound knowledge and become part of the collective intelligence [8].

It seems somewhat obvious that developing the notion of "student as creator" in the light of the unfolding digital transformation requires a careful analysis and re-conceptualisation of how we work with (micro-)content and content collections in our pedagogical practice throughout the educational system. In the following paragraphs we are going to present snapshots from an ongoing research and development project at Tallinn University that tries to address core issues of how to work with digital (micro)-content and content collections within the Estonian School System.

3   Intervening into Current Learning and Teaching Practices

Our research and development efforts are carried out as part of the research and development project "Learnmix". The overall goal of Learnmix is the re-conceptualisation of the notion of "e-textbooks". The project aims to advance interaction design and evaluation approaches and to better understand how various actors interact with and through ecologies of artefacts when pursuing their teaching and learning activities. In addition to human-computer interaction (HCI) related challenges, the project attempts to address the re-design of learning and teaching practices so that students can become actively engaged in their knowledge building processes while operating within various configurations of digital instruments and content.

The starting point of the project was to understand through rapid ethnography the current situation in K-12 education in terms of teaching strategies and the use of material and digital artefacts. Our goal was to capture patterns of use of digital artefacts in current teaching and learning practices in the classroom in order to inform the re-conceptualisation of "e-textbooks" and the ideation of new approaches and instruments for working with content within the Estonian School System. The ethnographic study largely confirmed the outcome of the literature review on e-textbooks that we had conducted before [12]. It appeared that the digitisation of content has had little influence on the learning and teaching strategies currently dominating the system. The transmission view of learning seems to be very much alive, focusing almost exclusively on deficits in particular domains of knowledge and practice. Traditional, classroom-based learning and teaching practices are replicated and digital technology is mainly used just as another medium for replacing paper, pencil and blackboard. Systematic experimentation with the affordances of digital technology in relation to a pedagogical vision of student-as-creator was hard to find throughout our field observations.

Therefore, our next step in the Learnmix project was to propose to teachers in Estonian K-12 a range of pedagogical strategies and lesson designs that try to enable learners to become actively engaged constructors of their own experience and knowledge by creating, modifying and integrating various physical, and digital arte-facts. We were interested if and how such a relatively moderate type of interventions would effect the use patterns of digital content within the classroom.

As our main instrument of intervention we designed five different scenarios (flip-ped-classroom, project-based learning, game-based learning, inquiry-based learning, problem-based learning) for teachers to choose from and implement it in their lessons. The main idea of the scenarios, potential content types and technology were discussed with teachers before they started to design their lessons. It has to be noted here that we do not treat the aforementioned list of scenarios as a definite one, but rather as a starting set of potential scenarios for enabling students to become constructors of their own experience and knowledge in the midst of the digital transformation.

We observed 12 lessons in 6 different K-12 schools, in which teachers implemented the chosen scenario in their lessons. For documenting the flow of a lesson, emerging interactions and used (digital) content and content collections we made use of a soft-ware application called "LessonNote". The LessonNote application allows for docu-menting activities along the timeline, shooting photos of student work and activities, adding these to observational notes, and creating seating charts. As an additional data gathering instrument we video recorded all observed lessons.

4   In Search for a Descriptive and Analytical Framework

The previously introduced scenarios assume changing the locus of control within the learning experience in various significant ways. Students are expected to become active participants, who take initiative and control for what and how they are doing. In these scenarios a "textbook" – or rather a "content collection" - doesn't function anymore as the main reference tool and primary means of delivering course content as a coherent and predefined whole that learners and teachers need to work through in a linear fashion. Instead, the scenarios emphasise making use of various micro content and content collections from a wide range of authors (from professional content designers to students and other people in the Internet). To capture and convey the particularities of these scenarios, the various (inter-)actions within them, the different configurations of digital instruments, and participants engagement with content and content collec-tions, an appropriate descriptive and analytical framework is needed.

Our initial attempt to find a framework that could suit our particular purpose didn't produce any considerable results. Apparently no coherent descriptive framework has been brought forward so far that would emphasise the active role of students, the role of mediating (digital) artefacts, and the use of configurations of content and content collections from various sources and authors. The artefact taxonomy proposed by Ching, Levin and Parisi [2] was the closest to our needs. These authors had elements important for our case, however, their work was done in the context of higher education and from a classroom design perspective. Through the successive analysis of 3 lessons from our intervention study, a descriptive framework was created which encompasses 7 elements:

1. Actors - a teacher, a student, or students. Here it is also necessary to specify whether the activity was done in groups, with a peer, or individually.
2. Actions - any kind of action performed by a teacher or student(s) as part of the observed teaching-learning activity. Teaching approaches that follow a "transmission" model treat students mostly as passive receivers. In the scenarios mentioned earlier, students take a more active role, thus, extending the list and range of actions performed by them. To fully grasp what students are doing while constructing their own knowledge through artefact manipulation, it is necessary to specify what kind of actions are carried out, by whom, and how they are mediated.
3. Displays – physical objects in, or outside of, the classroom (for instance computer, projector, screen) that function as a "display" for content and that provide an interface for "conveyors" (see below) that support the manipulation of content. Displays are seen as carriers for other (digital) artefacts. The affordances of a display define the general range of purpose of it, but do not determine classroom activity. Their affordances impact participants' expectations and afford greater ease of use for some functions over others. For example, overhead projectors allow for presenting something to a wider audience, but they don't determine what this "something" is.
4. Conveyors - applications that explicitly support the mediation or creation of content items (for instance, iBooks, Prezi, Wordpress, etc.) as knowledge representations in a wider sense. The perceived affordances and the level of individual and collective appropriation of *conveyors* limit the range of potential actions and interactions. In our specific observational context *displays* are generally hardware used in and outside of the classroom and *conveyors* are various software applications that run on tablets, computers or smartphones.
5. Micro-content collections – to steer away from pre-conceived ideas of content being generally packaged and delivered as "textbooks" within School environments, we treat all elaborate, compound content items as *micro-content collections*. While in traditional textbook use micro-content (see below) tends to come from the same source and authors, in the midst of the digital transformation teachers and students can now more easily integrate micro-contents from a wide range of sources or self-author items.
6. Micro-contents - digitisation enables content compartmentalisation. Micro-content are items that can meaningfully stand on their own, such as images, paragraphs, photos, tables, and so forth. They are generally mediated and produced by configurations of *displays* and *conveyors*.

7. Authors – the aforementioned scenarios emphasise the importance and growing complexity of using various micro-contents and micro-content collections developed and designed by a (potentially wide) range of authors (professional textbook authors, teachers, students, other content producers outside of the formal educational system).

It is important to note here that in our scenarios the choice of display and conveyor configurations, together with the use and production of micro-content and micro-content collections by various authors, play an essential role in our attempt to foster a vision of "student as creator" within Estonian K-12.

The outlined elements in our descriptive analytical framework allow us to focus on specific actions, mediating artefacts, and micro-content used or created before and during the learning experience. Furthermore, to better understand how students work with micro-content and content collections, it is important to determine who is making choices over all the elements that within an instructional setting that we are trying to map in our descriptive framework. Who decides, for example, which digital instruments (hard- and software) and micro-contents (or micro-content collections) are made use of?

5   Applying the Descriptive Framework

With the following example we want to demonstrate how we apply the descriptive framework outlined above for re-constructing and mapping particular teaching scenarios on the basis of our observational data. The action sequence that is shown below in Fig. 1 depicts an inquiry-based, teaching scenario that we observed in a 1st grade natural science lesson. The visualisation tries to capture actions and interactions the teacher and students carried out during this particular lesson. This visualisation captures the active role of students as creators and authors working with and creating micro-content and micro-content collections using a range of mediating instruments. This particular example shows that the inquiry was done in student groups. Very often working in groups means also division of roles and tasks, discussions and negotiations about the sequences of tasks and mediating artefacts for supporting the necessary procedures within the group and the actual content work.

In current K-12 practices these issues are very often predefined and decided by a teacher. How exactly all the individuals in our observed lessons worked together in groups wasn't in the focus of our intervention, mainly due to our limited resources to observe and document all the groups' activities at the same time. Furthermore, at this point in time that level of detail in our intervention study was not considered relevant. In our intervention study we were concentrating on mapping activities, interactions and content items of the whole group together. Nevertheless, our descriptive framework allows mapping specific group members and their actions and use of mediating instruments.

One can see in Fig. 1 that the actual actions in the inquiry-learning scenario that were carried out by students groups are very often referring to creation of something. By mainly operating with iPads as a display and with a rather diverse set of conveyors,

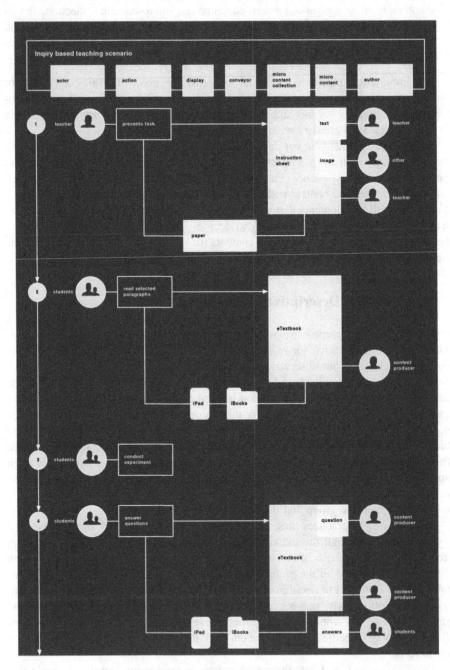

Fig. 1. Inquiry-based learning scenario.

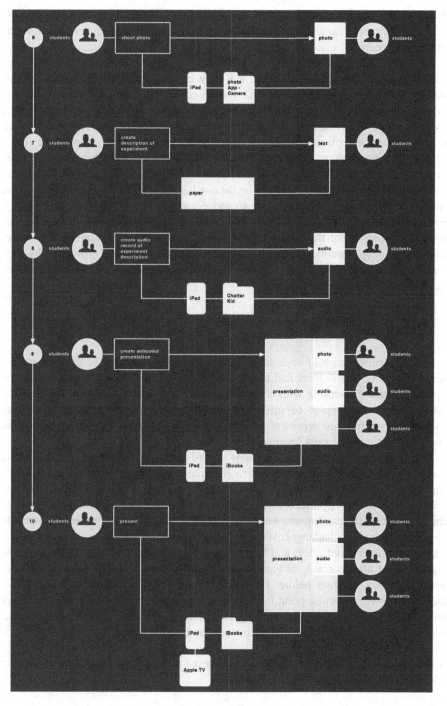

Fig. 1. (continued)

students could produce and design micro-content items exploiting at the same time the results of their own experiment within the particular inquiry and micro-content items produced by others.

In some cases teachers have dropped already their traditional textbooks and exclusively use their digital materials that they curate or design themselves or supplement their lessons with informational resources and micro content items found and customised from the Internet. Our exemplary scenario provides subtle indications that a textbook as the main reference tool and primary means of delivering course content in K-12 education is replaced by teacher's own selection of content items drawn into a learning experience from numerous sources. Of course one of the biggest challenges we have to deal with in the context of Learnmix project is the level of granularity accepted and appropriated by teachers on the one hand and by content publishers on the other. For clarification, we don't aim to move away entirely from any kind of professionally produced content and content collections. Regardless, it is crucial for our re-conceptualisation of the notion of e-textbook that teachers or students can reuse, modify and adapt innumerable micro content items designed and produced by professionals, teacher or students, but also re-cluster and reconfigure their collections according one's needs and purposes.

6 Conclusion

An ever-widening range of accessible artefacts and configurations of technology creates a myriad of possibilities and temptations for teachers and students to disrupt the current practice of working with content in an educational setting. Both, teachers and students with the support of mediating artefacts can interpret, process, transform content into various new representational states according to their purposes and needs, thus constructing their own learning experiences and knowledge.

We have demonstrated our first steps towards reconceptualising e-textbooks in a way that enables somewhat richer and more variable opportunities for interaction with content and content collections drawn in to a learning experience from multiple sources. These new opportunities together with new types of mediating instruments change the overall learning and teaching practices, thus throwing in front of us also new methodological challenges. With the proposed descriptive framework we can ask various questions about actors and their roles in a learning process, mediating artefacts, granularity of used content, its types and collection, authorship of content items, etc. which were not relevant before. However, our proposed taxonomy and descriptive framework is yet a starting point for developing a more comprehensive analytical tool for understanding learning and teaching experiences and working with content items while transcending the boundaries of material and digital world.

Acknowledgement. This research has been produced in the context of LEARNMIX project (No RU/3013) funded by Archimedes Foundation.

References

1. Butler, D.: The textbook of the future. Nature **458**(2), 568–570 (2009)
2. Ching, C.C., Levin, J.A., Parisi, J.: Artifacts of knowledge and practice in university teaching and learning. In: Symposium: Perspectives on Artefacts in Physical and Virtual Learning Environments. American Educational Research Association, Chicago (2003)
3. Davy, T.: E-textbooks: opportunities, innovations, distractions and dilemmas. Serials **20**(2), 98–102 (2007)
4. Fischer, G., Scharff, E.: Learning technologies in support of self-directed learning. J. Interact. Media Educ. **98**(4), 1–32 (1998)
5. Hedberg, J.G., Chang, C.H.: G-Portal: supporting argumentation and multimodality in student solutions to geographical problems. In: Kommers, P., Richards, G. (eds.) Proceedings of ED-MEDIA 2005 World Conference on Educational Multimedia, Hypermedia and Telecommunications, pp. 4242–4247. Association for the Advancement of Computing in Education, Norfolk (2005)
6. McFall, R.: Electronic textbooks that transform how textbooks are used. Electron. Libr. **23** (1), 72–81 (2005)
7. MindCET: The future of digital textbooks (2012). http://www.mindcet.org/wp-content/uploads/2012/10/Digital-Textbooks.-A-literature-review1.pdf
8. Moorefield-Lang, H.: An exploration of e-textbooks. Libr. Media Connect. **31**(6), 18–19 (2013)
9. Salpeter, J.: Textbook deathwatch. Technol. Learn. **30**(1), 26–30 (2009)
10. Scardamalia, M., Bereiter, C.: Higher levels of agency for children in knowledge building: a challenge for the design of new knowledge media. J. Learn. Sci. **1**(1), 37–68 (1991)
11. Smith, M., Kukulska-Hulme, A., Page, A.: Educational use cases from a shared exploration of e-books and iPads. In: Goh, T.-T. (ed.) E-Books and E-Readers for E-Learning, pp. 25–53. Victoria Business School, Victoria University of Wellington, Wellington (2012)
12. Väljataga, T., Fiedler, S.H.: Going digital: literature review on E-textbooks. In: Zaphiris, P., Ioannou, A. (eds.) LCT 2014, Part I. LNCS, vol. 8523, pp. 138–148. Springer, Heidelberg (2014)
13. Warlick, D.: Textbooks of the future: it's time the textbook industry redefined what they do and how they do it. Technol. Learn. **24**, 28–29 (2004)

Incorporating Values into the Design Process: The Case of E-Textbook Development for Estonia

Arman Arakelyan, Ilya Shmorgun[✉], and Sonia Sousa

Institute of Informatics, Tallinn University, Narva Rd. 29, 10120 Tallinn, Estonia
{arman.arakelyan,ilja.smorgun,sonia.sousa}@tlu.ee

Abstract. The purpose of this paper is to illustrate how interaction designers can reflect on values in interactive artifacts through an adapted method of design space analysis. We claim that value inclusion can be analyzed and incorporated into the design through design spaces. The method we are in the process of developing and present in this paper allows us to critically evaluate existing artifacts. It also allows us to evaluate our design work on a formative basis. The formative evaluation approach enables us to reflect on whether the intended values are reflected in the design. In this paper we establish the role of values in design criticism and critical design and illustrate how values can be incorporated into both activities through the development and application of design spaces. We propose that the method developed and tested by us could be used by others for identifying, evaluating, documenting, and sharing design rationale.

Keywords: Value-based design · Critical design · Design criticism · Design spaces · Design rationale

1 Introduction

As the field of Human Computer Interaction (HCI) has evolved over the years, a need has arisen for highlighting the value proposition of the designed system, instead of only focusing on functionality and usability, and thus moving away from artifact-centered design to an intentional creation of value [4]. In this paper we maintain a value-centric interaction design approach and illustrate how values can be evaluated or incorporated into interaction design by making design rationale explicit through design spaces. This approach is based on design space analysis, which aims to help interaction designers better understand the potential design options and reasons for choosing them, as well as find appropriate solutions for their particular design challenges within the design space [7].

We begin by briefly presenting our view of value-centered design and linking it to the context of design critique and critical design. Examples are provided to illustrate how the proposed design method can be applied. This paper ends by discussing and reflecting on our experiences during the application of the

© Springer International Publishing Switzerland 2014
Y. Cao et al. (Eds.): ICWL 2014 Workshops, LNCS 8699, pp. 274–281, 2014.
DOI: 10.1007/978-3-319-13296-9_30

proposed method in a specific design case called LearnMix [6], which is a project aiming to re-conceptualize the e-textbook as an aggregation of professional and user-contributed content available on a wide range of devices.

1.1 Value-Centered Design

Arguably design can be defined as the intent of the designer to create some type of value through artifacts [4]. In an abstract sense, the overall meaning of "value" of an artifact can be referred to a reason or the purpose for its creation. A more specific understanding would place "value" as something cared for or having desirable qualities by the designers or the users. In this paper we are focusing on the values of the designers and on how the perceived inclusion or absence of values can be reflected upon to evaluate existing systems and work in practice.

For us value-centered design implies identifying and acting on opportunities where the intended values for digital products are specified. This approach also allows us to incorporate the values into the design outcomes in alignment with other important design characteristics, like goals of the stakeholders, require-ments of the context where the newly designed artifact is going to be used, and the opportunities that are expected to become available in the future.

1.2 Design Critique

Blevis [3] defines design critique as "a process of discourse on many levels of the nature and effects of an ultimate particular design". This approach implies identification of different lenses on how we see the artifact, for example from the perspective of an individual interacting with the artifact, the artifact mediating communication between individuals, or how the artifact creates advantages for some individuals or groups, while "preserving or adding to disadvantages of others".

Design critique enables designers to understand particular designs in specific terms. Design critique is a means of creating design knowledge as well as a means of facilitating the practice of design. Design critique focuses on considering the specific details of a particular artifact and the overall context from a holistic perspective in terms of the role and value of the artifact in the environment. Finally, design critique helps consider the artifact by comparing it to alternative designs and historical examples and reflect on the identified differences, achieving an outcome, which is both historically informed and predictive [3].

Design critique is important for analyzing the existing artifacts and under-standing their limitations. However, when designing artifacts all considerations need to be explained together in a holistic way, which cannot be reduced to individual properties, but instead needs to be considered in terms of how all aspects are combined into a single whole. Design critique enables assessment of the design as a whole [3]. Design critique aims to promote the understanding and interpretation of current ways of doing things and is strategic [2].

1.3   Critical Design

When design critique is formative, then designers can be said to engage in a form of critical design, where critical design is the design based on a critical lens. In this case the design becomes a starting point for inviting design critique, which helps uncover opportunities for improvements [5]. We can also do critical design by ensuring that design actions lead to the inclusion of a value in "future ways of being" [2]. Critical design facilitates either reflection-in-action or reflection-post-action [5].

In our understanding one form of critical design can start with identifying the values and measures upon which the design actions should be critically reflected. Once you identify what you are critical about, then you can apply your lens to the act of design and further evaluate if your propositions have been reflected in the design outcome. According to Bardzell [1] critical design is a design approach that implies provocation and challenging the current ways of design trends based on values. Critical design aims to ensure that the undertaken actions lead to a desired outcome and is tactical [2].

2   Contextualization

To show how value-based design can be practiced through design criticism and critical design with our method, we will briefly introduce the LearnMix project and discuss our values for its implementation. The LearnMix project aims to re-conceptualize the e-textbook as an aggregation of professionally developed and user-contributed content. The project deals with a complex set of phenomena ranging from the definition of the envisioned e-textbook to the specific interactions that should be enabled by it [6].

To give a background of the project in its entirety Fig. 1 shows the values, marked with blue, used to guide the design of the artifact. These values are also connected to the project stakeholders through their expectations. The stakeholders, marked with yellow, are those, whose expectations are addressed in the project, while the expectations of stakeholders marked with white are not being addressed.

The concepts in Fig. 1 are used as values informing the actual design process and they are used to identify the aims that need to be achieved in the design of the artifact. During the design process the values need to be viewed as lenses used for formative and summative critical design. For each of these lenses we develop what is referred to as attributes, which enable a more nuanced understanding of how the artifact in question corresponds to the values selected by the designers.

2.1   Developing Design Rationale for Critical Design

Critical design allows us to reflect on design values. We propose that the reflection on design values should be documented as design rationale for communication purposes. This also allows others to understand the design choices and extend them to their own artifacts.

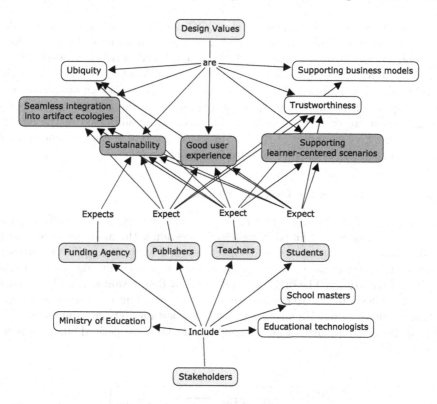

Fig. 1. Design values and their connection to the expectations of stakeholders

Thus, for both critical design and design criticism design rationale is an important communication tool. But how to communicate design rationale? Narrative accounts can be informative, but also time-consuming and too detailed. Our approach to developing and documenting design rationale is through design spaces. They justify the need for producing a particular design and explain why the alternatives would not be adequate or sufficient to reach the design goals or values.

2.2 Developing Design Rationale through Design Spaces

We used design spaces to document and explicate design rationale. They were used for making our design decisions among an array of alternative propositions. Our attempt to rationalize the design space was supported by what MacLean et al. [7] proposed as elements of design space analysis. The basic building blocks of the Design Space Analysis (DSA) are Questions, Options, and Criteria (the QOC notation). Questions identify the design issue, Options provide possible answers to the questions, and Criteria are the means for assessing and comparing the Options.

Although we tried to adhere to the QOC notation where possible, we also used a different vocabulary where needed. Thus, we have used "Sub-question" to stand for design issues instead of "Questions". We also used "Feature" to stand for different "Options" and "Attributes" to denote "Criteria" from the QOC model. The main characteristic of our approach is that an analytical lens is developed, where the design space serves for establishing the dimensions for design, which are the critical aspects that need to be addressed in the design. We will now give examples of the design spaces for design critique and critical deign and then reflect on their application in our practice.

2.3   Design Spaces for Design Critique

The creation of the design space for design critique begins by identifying the driving design question. The driving design question is the main question, which needs answering from an overall perspective when analyzing artifacts. Further, the generic questions are broken down into sub-questions inquiring about specific aspects of an artifact. The division is informed by design values. Finally, for each of the sub-questions the attributes are identified. Attributes in this case are providing possible alternative answers to the sub-questions. The attributes are used to evaluate if the features of an existing artifact have the desired characteristics (see Fig. 2).

Main question			
	Sub question 1		Count
	Attribute 1.1	Attribute 1.2	
Feature 1	1	0	1
Feature 2	0	-1	-1
Feature 3	1	1	2

Fig. 2. Template for design critique through design spaces

To illustrate how this technique could be applied for design criticism, we provide an example of design space analysis of Human-Computer Trust, conducted in the context of our project [8] (see Fig. 3).

What influences the user's predisposition to trust a particular system?							
	What supports users' belief that the systems' features will benefit them?		What features support users' confidence in someone or something to perform a particular desired action?		What features support users' belief in the integrity of the system and its users?		
	Motivation	Willingness	Predictability	Competency	Reciprocity	Honesty	Benevolence	Count
Feature 1	1	1	1	1	1	1	1	7
Feature 2	0	1	1	-1	1	1	1	4

Fig. 3. Example of design critique through design spaces

This technique allows us to identify those features of existing artifacts that better answer the main questions identified in the design critique. Starting from an established analytical lens, this technique allows us to methodically and systematically analyze artifacts to identify if the intended values are present or missing. In the example above the ratings stand for specific grades, of which 1 is chosen for "contributes to the intended value", −1 for "diminishes the intended value" and 0 for "not applicable" (Fig. 5).

2.4 Design Spaces for Critical Design

A similar approach can be applied when designing artifacts. Here the dimensions of the design space are the questions and sub-questions, which have multiple alternative attributes that answer them. In this case, we identify design values as criteria and rate each attribute as to how well it meets the design values (see Fig. 4).

Sub question 1	Design Value 1	Design Value 2	Design Value 3	Count
Attribute 1	0	1	1	2
Attribute 2	1	-1	0	0
Attribute 3	0	1	0	1

Fig. 4. Template for critical design analysis through design spaces

To illustrate how critical design analysis can be applied through design spaces, we provide the example of the Sustainable Software Appropriation analysis, conducted for our project (see Fig. 3).

How can we ensure that designers learn from appropriation?	D: Integration into existing artifact ecology	D: Sustainability	D: Providing a good user experience	D: Supporting learner-centered scenarios	Count
Incrementality	0	0	1	1	2
Usage visibility	1	1	0	1	3
Community creation	1	1	1	1	4

Fig. 5. Example of critical design analysis through design spaces

3 Discussion

As noted before, the design spaces presented here have been applied in the framework of the LearnMix project. From the perspective of the usefulness of the design spaces, they have proved to be informative in discussing perceived or intended design rationale. The benefits of such an approach is that it ensures the establishment and communication of design rationale among all stakeholders. From our experience, the design spaces have proven much more successful and useful for design criticism than for critical design. The reason for this is that an existing artifact can be analyzed against a set of criteria and evaluated as

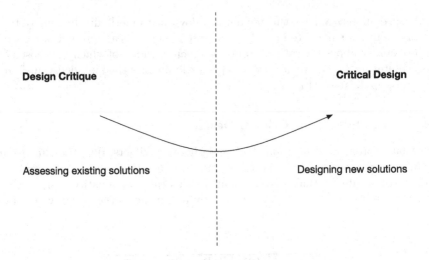

Fig. 6. Design critique to critical design curve

to how well it meets the criteria, if at all. This will facilitate reflecting on the characteristics of existing artifacts and designing better solutions as shown in Fig. 6.

Using design spaces for critical design has proven to be more challenging due to their time-consuming nature and the need to consider multiple interconnected attributes against a set of criteria. If both of these lists are kept to the minimum, the design space, as suggested by us, could serve as an important value-sensitive design rationale visualization tool. However, if the process is followed in meticulous detail, formalizing the design space can have the negative effect of impeding creativity or hindering progress within the project. Thus, our suggestion for using design spaces would be to consider them as additional inputs for value incorporation and reflection, rather than final recommendations showing exactly what attributes to design for. This is especially important as some of the initial attributes might be too general and specifying them can introduce even more complexity to this procedure.

4   Conclusion

In this paper we present an adapted method of design space analysis used to evaluate existing artifacts and design new ones based on values. Our initial work has shown that design spaces are better for analyzing existing solutions rather than creating new ones. However, the method described here holds value for showcasing, communicating, and reflecting on design rationale as long as it is used as a decision support tool.

References

1. Bardzell, S., Bardzell, J., Forlizzi, J., Zimmerman, J., Antanitis, J.: Critical design and critical theory. In: Proceedings of the Designing Interactive Systems Conference on - DIS '12, p. 288. ACM Press, New York (2012). http://dl.acm.org/citation.cfm?doid=2317956.2318001
2. Blevis, E.: Advancing Sustainable Interaction Design Two Perspectives on Material Effects. Design philosophy papers, pp. 1–19 (2006)
3. Blevis, E., Lim, Y.k., Roedl, D., Stolterman, E.: Using Design Critique as Research to Link Sustainability and Interactive Technologies, pp. 22–31 (2007)
4. Cockton, G.: A development framework for value-centred design. In: CHI '05 Extended Abstracts on Human Factors in Computing Systems - CHI '05, p. 1292. ACM Press, New York (2005). http://dl.acm.org/citation.cfm?id=1056899
5. Kolko, J.: Endless nights–learning from design studio critique. Interactions 18(2), 80–81 (2011). http://portal.acm.org/citation.cfm?doid=1925820.1925838
6. Lamas, D., Väljataga, T., Laanpere, M., Rogalevits, V., Arakelyan, A., Sousa, S., Shmorgun, I.: Foundations for the reconceptualization of the e-Textbook. In: Proceedings of the International Conference on e-Learning ICEL 2013, p. 510 (2013). http://connection.ebscohost.com/c/articles/88431552/foundations-reconceptualization-e-textbook
7. MacLean, A., Young, R.M., Bellotti, V., Moran, T.P.: Design space analysis: bridging from theory to practice via design rationale. In: Proceedings of Esprit '91, pp. 720–730 (1991)
8. Sousa, S., Lamas, D., Shmorgun, I., Arakelyan, A.: A design space for trust enabling interaction design. In: Proceedings of the International Conference on Multimedia, Interaction, Design and Innovation MIDI 2014. ACM (2014)

Slovenian "E-school Bag"

Andrej Flogie[1]([⊠]), Vladimir Milekšič[2], Andreja Čuk[2],
and Sonja Jelen[2]

[1] The Institution of Anton Martin Slomšek, Maribor, Slovenia
andrej.flogie@z-ams.si
[2] The National Education Institute of the Republic of Slovenia,
Ljubljana, Slovenia
{vladimir.mileksic,andreja.cuk,sonja.jelen}@zrss.si

Abstract. Article presents a summary of current activities in the field of development of modern e-contents in Slovenia. It is based on the current development of e-learning materials and later on the development of interactive textbooks for science. All of the findings, acquired in previous Slovenian national projects in the area of e-content development, are upgraded with vision and concrete work, which will be done in the part of "e-school bag" project (development and use of e-contents). The key emphasis is in the area of the vision itself and in an integrated approach of development and use of advanced e-contents and evaluation of them in practice.

Keywords: E-school bag · i-textbooks · Educational platform · 1:1 pedagogy · Education

1 Introduction

All of the international research, in particular the research on literacy, which we also performed in Slovenia (PISA, PIRLS), indicate, that the biggest part of student achievements depends on factors found at home, especially educational attainment of parents and the amount of books at home. Both of these factors have a direct and an indirect affect; educational attainment of parents has an indirect effect on the life-style and provides an opportunity for a child to receive a sufficient amount of reading stimuli, as parents and school will probably expect high academic achievements, which a child will most likely meet (this is not the case for each individual). The percentage of difference in literacy provided by the school is, according to the most recent data by PIRLS in 2011, only 8 %. This does not mean that the school is not able to do anything about it, on the contrary, the school does so little, that the effect of domestic environment is (too) great. If we compare reading literacy of children in families with differently educated parents, we can see that there is a 100 points difference in reading literacy among a group of children, who have university educated parents, and children whose parents only completed primary school, and we know that a difference of 40 points means a difference of a year (1 year older and one grade higher students would achieve this amount of reading literacy), which means, that at the age when differences begin to vary steeply, various groups of children have a difference of two and a half years [2].

© Springer International Publishing Switzerland 2014
Y. Cao et al. (Eds.): ICWL 2014 Workshops, LNCS 8699, pp. 282–294, 2014.
DOI: 10.1007/978-3-319-13296-9_31

In this context a question arises, whether modern information technology may have an effect on schools, which would help increase achievements of students, as well as development of literacy as one of the fundamental conditions for successful learning. Information technology may have a direct or an indirect impact on literacy; directly with an exposure to reading stimuli, especially if the computer is connected to the Internet and indirectly with exposure to a large quantity of information, which can be processed with knowledge of information technology use. This process is circular: the more we read, the better we read and the better we read, the more we like it. Anyone who reads more (if difficulty increases over time) reads better [3].

On the basis of these fundamental reasons, general and specific competences of the 21st century, required innovative approaches to teaching and learning supported by advanced e-services, quality e-content [1] and future technologies (mobile devices, tablets, etc.), we want, in the framework of the "E-school bag" project, to develop mechanisms, examples of good practices and modern e-services and e-content (i-textbooks), which will be a foundation for further infrastructure and systemic measures in the Slovenian educational environment.

The "E-school bag" project is a development project with the aim of i-textbook evaluation at selected public educational institutions. In order to successfully carry out pilot projects we will establish appropriate infrastructure, develop e-services and e-content (i-textbooks). Developed e-services and e-content will be, after successfully completed pilot projects, accessible to all schools [7] (and not just those involved in pilot projects).

2 The Purpose and Objectives of the Project

The purpose of this project is to establish an appropriate infrastructure for the use and development of modern e-services and e-content in Slovenian language, providing support for application of these materials (didactic, technical) and organizational/management process of each educational institution in increasing the level of e-competences and knowledge of our teachers/professors, and indirectly an improvement of *competitiveness of knowledge of* our students in the European Union [2]. Developed e-services and e-content will be supported by consultants and experts and tested in practice in the educational institutions' pilot network. In the future, an application of developed e-services and e-content will also be made available to other educational institutions in the Slovenian educational environment.

The objectives and associated priority areas of this project are:

- development of modern e-services for the Slovenian educational environment,
- development of e-content (i-textbooks) for social sciences (8th, 9th grade of primary school and 1st year of gymnasium),
- ensuring accessibility and support of newly developed e-services and e-content,
- development of a single authorial user interface for "online" preparation of e-content,
- development of a single platform for access to e-content – "EduStore" (i-textbooks, e-books, etc.),

– development of e-services for the use of developed e-content with different clients,
– establishment and development of infrastructure (transition to Internet Protocol version 6 (IPv6), the Slovene educational network II (SIO II) and pilot projects),
– implementation of pilot projects of "E-school bag" use (which will cover both pedagogic-educational and organizational-management part of every educational institution).
– evaluation of effects.

The project contributes to a better quality and efficiency of the educational process for social sciences subjects in 8th and 9th grade of primary school and 1st year of gymnasium by creating conditions for the use of ICT in school work (teaching and management) through teacher training (both in school and individual work at home), implementing project results into the educational process and development of digital competencies of teachers and students [8].

The pilot project "E-school bag" is an upgrade and a continuation of some already established activities in the field of computerisation of education. Public institution Arnes has established a foundation for SIO - Slovenian educational network (developed certain e-services, established a necessary part of ICT infrastructure) and the public institution ZRSŠ has already started with the construction of modern e-content (i-textbooks) in the field of natural sciences (12 are already confirmed, others are in the process of certification by the Council of Experts for General Education). Good practice, knowledge and experience gained from these projects will be transferred to the "E-school bag" project, upgraded and expanded. Arnes already established some basic e-services (e.g. Vox - videoconferencing systems, voting system, etc.), e-content for natural science areas is being developed and a network of consultants for the use of e-services and e-content has already been developed for Slovenia, etc. A tool for development of modern e-content already exists, but it is still available on a "desktop" level with limited use and not online as a web application. Knowledge, approaches and experience gained at this level will serve as a basis for building web platforms to develop e-content. For development of other platforms and interfaces, however, a HTML5 standard will form a basis for future work, so that all e-services will be developed in accordance with the recommendations of this standard (in the framework of the EU interoperability environment).

Pilot projects on modern e-services and e-content use on tablets in educational institutions will be based on the experience and help of consultants from The National Education Institute of The Republic of Slovenia, experts from Arnes, Innovative schools programme titled "Partners in Learning", which runs in more than 65 countries around the world [6], project »Inovativna pedagogika v luči kompetenc 21. stoletja [5]« (Innovative pedagogy in the light of 21st century competences) and on the basis of the »e-kompetentni učitelj« (e-competent teacher), which was developed in the framework of the »E-šolstvo« (E-educational system) project.

3   The Role of i-textbooks in the "E-school Bag" Project

Development of i-textbooks [4] in the Slovenian education environment is based on the findings and conclusions of e-materials development, production of which is financed through a public call for tenders by the Ministry of Education, Culture and Sport. The next step was developing a concept, methodology, and in the last phase, prototype i-textbooks in the field of natural sciences, which were held under the auspices of The National Education Institute of The Republic of Slovenia, and a project financially supported by MIZS titled "Razvoj i-učbenikov za naravoslovje" (Development of i-textbooks for science) under the leadership of dr. Igor Pesek. All the methodology of developing i-textbooks, including their didactic and educational role in the education process was developed in the framework of this project. Many innovative teachers from all over Slovenia (both primary school and secondary school teachers) as well as other experts in specific fields were involved in this project. From a technological point of view, we developed an editorial web portal and an upgraded/modified editor for development of i-textbooks (eXeCute). The e-school project represents the next logical step in development of i-textbooks. All already developed methodology, knowledge, steps, etc., are used and upgraded in areas where they are required.

An upgrade is especially needed in the area of technology, licensing model and use in a classroom, while the didactic-methodological concepts and approaches of already developed i-textbooks in the field of natural sciences are also relevant for development of i-textbooks in the field of social sciences. Within the "E-school bag" project, in the field of development of i-textbooks, we adopted all substantive work methodology in development of each textbook [8, 9].

4 Platform Development

4.1 Online E-content Editor

A general assessment of the existing i-textbook editor (eXeCute), which has been developed and refined in the framework of the "Razvoj naravoslovnih i-učbenikov" (Development of science i-textbooks) project, is very high. The key issue is, of course, that this application functions only locally and is limited to a local computer's operating system. This means that it has to be installed on a local computer with a suitable operating system Windows and is not compatible with other operating systems. It also does not provide team work or direct storage in a cloud. However, it is much more advanced than most of the other existing applications/tools for development of e-content, as its functionality is actually tailored to the needs of modern e-content as well as i-textbooks. This is why we decided, already in planning of the "E-school bag" project, to develop an identical application (e-service), which will include all the functionality of the eXeCute tool and will be upgraded in the sense of:

- working online (local installation is not required)
- runs in Arnes' cloud
- provides online data storage (Arnes' cloud, etc.)
- provides a free online registration for each publisher (a teacher can also be a publisher) and assigning corresponding rights to manufacturers of content (every textbook may have one or more authors)
- provides direct communication via APP with EduStore (a developed i-textbook can be directly exported to EduStore)

– provides joint editing of documents (multiple authors can edit the same textbook - each a specific part)
– provides direct communication with an existing administrative web portal (reviewer, editorial policy, etc.)
– provides different types of export of developed i-textbooks (export directly to EduStore, ePub, html5, SCORM packages, etc.)
– all records are compatible with an attached XML scheme
– enables different CSS-styles (prepared form of content)
– etc.

An installation of the online e-content (i-textbooks) editor in an integrated platform is shown in (Fig. 1).

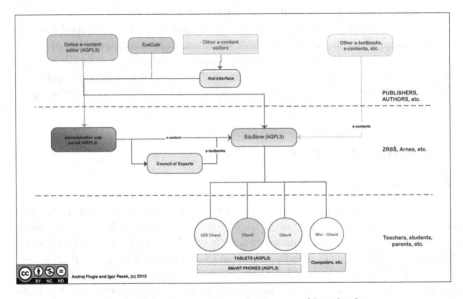

Fig. 1. Ecosystem - platform for the use of i-textbooks

4.2   XML-Interface (A Conversion System for i-textbooks from XML to HTML5 Format)

The overall vision of the platform is to enable free access and open source features and functions. From a substantive view of e-content development, this means that we do not want a closed and restricted environment. We want authors to also use other tools for development, publish their final product in the EduStore and thus apply another already developed and established infrastructure for distribution. In the long-term, this means that a publishing house can also use the established infrastructure as a distribution channel for use of their i-textbooks and e-content on a tablet, smart phone, online, etc. This is why we developed an XML-interface system for conversion of e-content from XML to HTML5. The basic purpose of the XML-interface is to enable conversion of i-textbooks into a uniform format regardless of the type of software used in its development. We want to enable a conversion from a standardized XML to a HTML format and maintain the flexibility of using templates and CSS-styles to define the final form of an i-textbook, which will be uniform regardless of the type of software used in its development.

Authors and publishers have a choice to use the free access online e-content editor or any other commercially available product. In any case, they have a possibility to use any other established infrastructure, which is of key importance to us (i.e. an open environment and a wide range of creative and innovative approaches to development of e-content).

4.3   Administrative Web Portal

The administrative web portal functions as a tool for organising the entire process of i-textbook development. The portal enables formation of a concept layout of an i-textbook, assignment of content sets to authors, supporting authors in creating individual units, unit reviews (simultaneous reviews), proofreading, final technical processing and development of an i-textbook (Fig. 2).

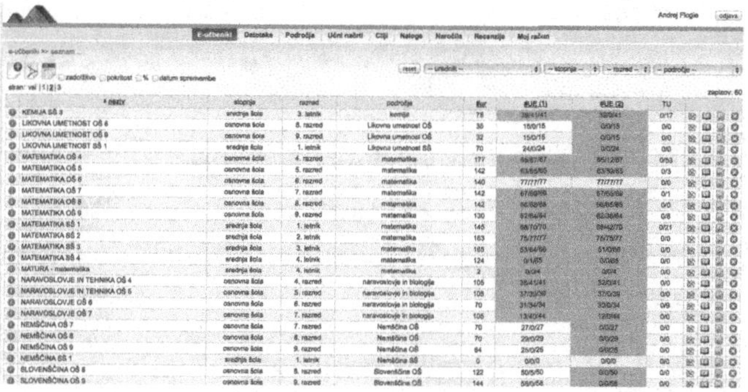

Fig. 2. Screenshot of an administrative web portal

The portal was fully developed in the framework of the project of developing textbooks for natural sciences. In the framework of the "E-school bag" project, the portal will be upgraded in certain segments, which have become just as important due to an integrated approach. It will be upgraded in the field associated with the online e-content editor, because it is necessary to ensure connectivity via APP or via appropriate technological solutions. Reviewing cycles will also have to be upgraded, since they will be implemented in different ways, depending on the approach of an individual or a single publishing house to development of e-content. All of these adjustments and upgrades will contribute to the corporate platform image. Administrative management of the portal will continue to remain in the domain of The National Education Institute of The Republic of Slovenia, which is also closely involved in the process of validation of textbooks and professional assessment of their suitability.

4.4   EduStore

When development of content is complete, it is simply exported to the EduStore. It is a uniform e-content storage for a large part of the Slovenian educational environment. We can say that it is, from a logical and technological point of view, an upgrade to the current catalogue of e-materials Trubar (which is located on the portal SIO). The Trubar catalogue has 8500 active e-materials. These are stored in a form of external links, SCORM files, pdf and ppt files, etc. The whole system is composed of two components: the Alfresco document system, in which all e-materials are stored, and a Typo3 user interface, which allows users to search and browse e-materials. Because of a specific record of documents in the Alfresco system, classification was made using a tree structure (level → class → subject).

For easier search and subsequent integration with the e-materials database, we introduced a fourth level: thematic sets. All the elements of classification operate on a user interface level as search engine filters. Because it turned out that a tree structure is not the most suitable record structure in the long-term (e.g., it is impossible to find all materials for physics at all levels of education), we decided to use independent metadata. In doing so, we will improve the quality of the search engine as well as its speed (Fig. 3).

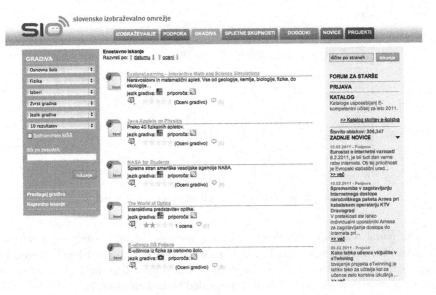

Fig. 3. The current catalogue of e-materials on SIO portal

Materials that have been submitted in the catalogue as SCORM files are currently displayed in a dedicated online Moodle classroom, which can be substituted with a special SCORM viewer. A user will be able to preview specific e-material and upload it to an online classroom. Another problem is external links that, due to the nature of the Internet, do not always provide a valid link. A long-term goal that we have set for ourselves a long time ago was that all materials would be stored locally in a catalogue. A catalogue and collections of material are a good basis for new generations of e-materials, i-books and other e-content.

EduStore presents a logical upgrade to the existing Trubar catalogue both from a substantive and from a technical point of view. EduStore is composed of two components i.e. web applications:

- administration part
- user part.

The administration part is intended for publishers and system administrators as a tool for various functionalities such as summary statistics, content management, publishing of content, user administration, etc. The user part provides another set of functionalities, such as access to e-content, purchase of e-content, editing and reading e-content, etc. The user part also serves as an API through which mobile device users communicate with the EduStore system.

Both parts of the application are separated and access data trough a single uniform database, but each part has its own access rights. Users can access the administration part of the application only via a PKI infrastructure, while the user part of the applications has multiple authentication methods. Both parts of the application use SSL.

4.5 Clients

Prepared content (i-textbooks, e-content, etc.) will be stored in EduStore. Due to various providers of mobile phone hardware and software, tablet computers, etc., a problem occurs on how to ensure access to the same content with different devices with different operating systems. Our vision is, of course, that authors prepare their content only once. The technology then provides a function to generate content in appropriate technological formats, which will allow access regardless of device type used. This is why we developed an application which enables access for three different operating systems: Windows, Android and IOS (Fig. 4).

Fig. 4. Application download - Google play

This mobile application will provide users with an access to e-content from various devices, but the user will have to download the "E-torba" ("E-school bag") application from official stores (AppStore, Google Play, Windows Store). Development of native applications for each operating system is needed to ensure a good user experience, which also demands a tailored look/appearance/external image and functionality of the mobile application. We have contracted a design of information architecture, which will provide an intuitive use of the application and a unique graphical interface, which will follow trends of other mobile applications and best user experience.

The purpose of this mobile applications is for the users (students, teachers, parents, etc.) to use the "E-bag" application to download i-textbooks to their device and use them in all forms (browsing, interactive solving of exercises, etc.). The exercise solutions will, if the user chooses to, be saved within the application or in his/her device.

The introduction page of the application shows i-textbooks and other e-content that has already been transferred to the device. We also want to offer other i-textbooks (e-contents) according to user preferences, past searches and already downloaded content and suggest new ones (if there are any and if the administrator added them to the EduStore). All suggestions are presented with a preview image of the i-textbook (e-content), title and a brief description of the content. A button for simple and quick transfer of content is also available.

5 Testing i-school Textbooks and First Findings

In the framework of the "E-school bag" project we are developing i-textbooks for social sciences subjects for the 8th and 9th grade of primary school and the first year of gymnasium. The developers of i-textbooks, which were selected based on the conditions set out in the public call for tenders, will prepare i-textbooks for Slovene, English and German as a second foreign language (primary school), fine arts, musical arts, geography and history. Textbooks will be ready by the end of 2014.

We plan to continue making i-textbooks for homeland and civic culture and ethics, German language (for secondary school), sports (for primary school) and science (for secondary school), which will be ready by the end of this project (April 2015).

I-textbooks, prepared in the framework of the "E-school bag" project, cover the full curriculum for each subject for a specific class or grade. They must correspond to the required substantive-didactic, technical-organizational and design requirements. With interactive and dynamic elements we will provide a better presentation of facts and achieve deeper understanding of content and active participation of students. Textbooks will be confirmed by the Council of Experts for General Education of the Republic of Slovenia and will be able to replace confirmed printed textbooks. Textbooks will also be available free of charge on stationary, portable or tablet computers and other mobile devices. They will function on all operating systems (IOS, Android, Windows).

Textbooks will be tested in schools, which are included in the pilot project "Uvajanje in uporaba e-vsebin in e-storitev" (Implementation and use of e-content and e-services) for projects "E-šolska torba" ("E-school bag") and "I-učbeniki s poudarkom naravoslovnih predmetov v OŠ" ("E-textbooks for science classes in primary schools") and the pilot project "Preizkušanje e-vsebin in e-storitev" (Testing of e-content and e-service) included in the projects "E-šolska torba" ("E-school bag") and "I-učbeniki s poudarkom naravoslovnih predmetov v OŠ" ("E-textbooks for science classes in primary schools").

The pilot projects "E-šolska torba" ("E-school bag") and "I-učbeniki s poudarkom naravoslovnih predmetov v OŠ" ("E-textbooks for science classes in primary schools") include 92 teachers from 14 schools, and the projects "Preizkušanje e-vsebin in e-storitev" (Testing of e-content and e-service) and "I-učbeniki s poudarkom naravoslovnih predmetov v OŠ" ("E-textbooks for science classes in primary schools") include 147 teachers from 44 schools.

With these pilot projects we want to determine whether i-textbooks contribute to better knowledge of students in comparison to traditional textbooks. For this purpose we will perform qualitative and quantitative evaluation. The evaluations will include quality of i-textbooks (advantages over the classic), the impact of i-textbooks on learning and the impact of i-textbooks on teaching.

The National Education Institute of The Republic of Slovenia provides live or distance support. This includes joint education of teachers, counselling and regular communication. Members of school project teams are being trained to use e-content and e-services in professional meetings under the leadership of ZRSŠ consultants to develop good practice of use. They are accompanied and evaluated on learning, teaching and findings of use, monitoring and evaluation of e-content and e-services.

5.1 School Project Teams Members

- work on development: planning, implementing, monitoring, evaluating lessons and knowledge and skills of students in the use of e-services and e-content;
- develop new or update/upgrade existing models of teaching and learning, supported by the information technology and empower teachers and students in digital literacy;
- explore theoretical framework on the contemporary forms of teaching and learning, as well as various examples of quality practice of e-content and e-services use, which encourages development of diverse types of knowledge and skills (e.g. digital literacy, learning to learn, co-operation and communication, creativity, self reflection, working with e-resources, problem solving, critical thinking);
- learn about practice of e-content and e-services use, mobile applications and web services on devices (tablets, phones, laptops, etc.).

In the first year of pilot projects implementation (2013/14) teachers plan their lessons with the use of e-services and e-content at the level of individual learning sets. In the second year (2014/15) the use of e-services and e-content will be planned on a school year basis. The entire duration of pilot projects is divided into 6 testing periods. In each period a planned thematic curriculum unit and monitoring of classes is carried out by the ZRSŠ, followed by an evaluation at the end of each period.

6 Management of Copyright, Findings and Recommendations

Taking into account the contract with the Ministry of Education, Science and Sport and The National Education Institute of The Republic of Slovenia, all developers of i-textbooks must, in accordance with the Law on Copyright and Related Rights (hereinafter referred to as LCRR)[1] transfer all material copyright exclusively, time and territorial unlimited. The Institute must then make all i-textbooks in relation to third persons (users) available under the Creative Commons license (hereinafter referred to as CC).[2] The use of CC licence lets the users know in a clear and unambiguous way, in advance, how an i-textbook can be used. A Slovenian license version 2.5 is used for existing i-textbooks, which stipulates "recognition of authorship" + "non-commercial" + "share alike". This means that the user can reproduce, distribute, rent, make publicly available or modify i-textbooks, but the author must be named, they cannot be made for commercial use and the original work or modified version have to be shared alike. It is an approach, which has gained acclaim during the first Ministry projects, relating to the development of e-materials.

This raised some questions from the manufacturers of i-textbooks as well as The National Educational Institute. We wondered if such a volume of material copyright transfer is necessary, if it would be prudent to use a license, which would allow commercial use of i-textbooks or limit the possibility of i-textbook modification due to difficulties in clarifying copyright, because some copyright holders, in some cases, markedly averse any further adaptations of copyright work, etc.

The need of transferring all material copyright to the National Education Institute has proven to be justified due to already known changes and adaptations of i-textbooks. Either due to change of curricula, needs for other substantive changes or due to adjustments for learners with special needs and students of ethnic minorities. A choice of a license, which allows modifications of i-textbooks is crucial for the fulfilment of one of the essential attributes of i-textbooks, since it enables teachers to legally use and adapt the content of i-textbooks for the needs of lessons, examination, etc. In the future, it would perhaps be wise to consider free license, which would allow commercial use of i-textbooks, since it would most likely further stimulate interest in upgrades of i-textbooks.

Dilemmas in management, especially in clarifying copyright, have also occurred due to low awareness and knowledge of copyright of all actors involved in a rather new area (e-educational content) and modest jurisprudence. The lack of Slovenian legislation makes clarifying copyright even more difficult since the LCRR does not follow the needs of different copyright arrangements in the case of education (i-textbooks, use of e-content in class, etc.). For printed textbooks this is quite straightforward, since the law[3] explicitly provides a legal license. In this way, it is possible, without a transfer of copyright, but with a payment of remuneration, to reproduce parts of copyright works as well as individual work in the areas of photography, fine art, architecture, applied arts, industrial design and cartography, in the case of already published work of multiple authors. In the case of printed textbook rights are therefore clarified by a

---

[1] Uradni list RS, št. 21/1995, 9/2001, 30/2001 - ZCUKPIL, 43/2004, 17/2006, 114/2006 - ZUE, 139/2006, 68/2008, 110/2013.

[2] More information on CC licenses is available at: http://creativecommons.si/licence.

[3] 47th article of LCRR (lessons, periodicals).

collective organization, the Association of Slovenian authors (ZAMP).[4] The needs in the educational sphere should certainly be taken into account with the changes of LCRR in the future.

In the management of copyright for software, we followed the need for a free access and long sustainability (in terms of upgrades and maintenance) regardless of the time limit on the project (as a result, a time-limited funding). The most appropriate license for open source software has proven to be the AGPL 3.0 license, which is applied to all software produced in the framework of the project. This license allows commercial use and any further adaptations, which should allow upgrades of the software outside of project frameworks, which are, as we have said, time and financially limited.

7 Conclusion

Due to rapid development of digital technology we require different options in technical, cognitive and social field to perform tasks and solve problems in a digital environment of our everyday and working lives.

The "E-school bag" pilot project is based on three areas:

- establishment of an e-learning environment (appropriate infrastructure and e-services),
- development of appropriate e-content (i-textbooks),
- teacher training and pilot projects.

Establishment of a complete platform and development of an example of an interactive textbook, which are in accordance with the renovation of the pedagogical paradigm (the didactic-pedagogical work) and with the current guidelines of information systems (technological and licensing), brings a new freshness in the Slovenian educational environment. The implementation of the project, in a wider European context, is seen as a gap reduction in the level of development of various regions, since the Slovenian environment is, in comparison with some other areas in the EU (mainly North and West), unfortunately, unable to produce the same or similar solutions. The establishment of planned e-services, e-content, pilot projects and equipment will strengthen the competitiveness as well as innovation of the Slovenian educational environment. To ensure sustainable development of the entire platform, as well as content, all planning is done on the basis of a licensing model, because it allows implementation of new business models for both publishing houses and our country. If we titled the activities of informatisation in the Slovene educational institutions as "Slovenian e-education 1.0", we can title further activities, which are beginning to use contemporary global ICT trends (cloud computing, GRID computing, interoperability based on HTML5, use of mass devices for accessing e-content, such as tablets, smart phones, mini laptops, etc.) as "Slovenian e-education 2.0" or with an appropriate metaphor as project "E-school bag".

---

[4] ZAMP is a collective organization, which in accordance with LCRR collectively protects and manages rights of authors and works of literature, science and publishing and their translations.

References

1. Evropska komisija: Sporočilo evropskemu parlamentu, svetu, evropskemu ekonomsko-socialnemu odboru in odboru regij (COM 2013, 654 final) (2013)
2. Evropska komisija: Official Journal of the European Union. ISSN 1977-091X (2012)
3. Doupona, M.: Bralna pismenost in uporaba računalnikov, delovno gradivo, Ljubljana (2012)
4. Pesek, I., Zmazek B., Mohorčič G.: Od e-gradiv do i-učbenikov, Slovenski i-učbeniki, Ljubljana (2014)
5. Šverc, A., Flogie, A.: Učenje 1 na 1 na Škofijski gimnaziji v okviru Zavoda Antona Martina Slomška. Didakta. ISSN 0354-0421, letn. 23, no. 163, pp. 21–24 (2013)
6. Evropska komisija: Compendium of Good Practice Cases of e-learning, i2010 (2010). http://ec.europa.eu/education/lifelong-learning-programme/doc/elearningcomp_en.pdf
7. Vlada RS: Strategija razvoja informacijske družbe v RS – si2010 (2009). http://www.mvzt.gov.si/fileadmin/mvzt.gov.si/pageuploads/pdf/informacijska_druzba/si2010.pdf
8. Ministrstvo za izobraževanje, znanost in šport: Rezultati CRP-projekta DIDIKTA - analiza in razvoj didaktike uporabe IKT pri poučevanju in učenju, Ljubljana (2009)
9. Ministrstvo za izobraževanje, znanost in šport: Rezultati CRP-projekta Stanje in trendi uporabe IKT v izobraževanju v Sloveniji, Ljubljana (2010)

Author Index

Printed in the United States
By Bookmasters